Abnormal Behavior and the Criminal Justice System

Abnormal Behavior and the Criminal Justice System

Robert G. Meyer, Ph.D.

LEXINGTON BOOKS
An Imprint of Macmillan, Inc.
NEW YORK

Maxwell Macmillan Canada
TORONTO

Maxwell Macmillan International
NEW YORK   OXFORD   SINGAPORE   SYDNEY

Library of Congress Cataloging-in-Publication Data

Meyer, Robert G.
    Abnormal behavior and the criminal justice system / Robert G.
Meyer.
        p.   cm.
    Includes index.
    ISBN 0-669-24450-3.–ISBN 0-669-24449-X (pbk.)
    1. Criminal behavior.   2. Insane, Criminal and dangerous.
3. Criminal justice, Administration of.   I. Title.
HV6133.M53   1992
364.2'4—dc20   91-3702
                                                            CIP

Lexington Books
An Imprint of Macmillan, Inc.
866 Third Avenue, New York, N. Y. 10022

Maxwell Macmillan Canada, Inc.
1200 Eglinton Avenue East
Suite 200
Don Mills, Ontario M3C 3N1

Macmillan, Inc. is part of the Maxwell Communication
Group of Companies.

Printed in the United States of America

printing number
1   2   3   4   5   6   7   8   9   10

Contents

9. The Childhood Disorders and Mental Retardation 175

10. Violence   203

11. Deception Detection   229

12. Competency, Criminal Responsibility, Civil Commitment, and the Prediction of Dangerousness   247

Preface

This book is written for the practitioner and the student in the criminal justice field—that is, law-enforcement officers and related personnel; attorneys and judges; probation, parole and corrections personnel; and the like. It covers issues of abnormal behavior and their psychology, in terms of their interaction with the criminal justice system. All of us periodically encounter patterns of abnormal behavior in our everyday lives—even, God forbid, occasionally in ourselves. For those who work in the criminal justice field, this is a common if not a daily experience, often consumed at high dosages; certainly imparted by the "customers" and occasionally by our colleagues.

There are numerous texts that to some degree explain abnormal behavior; I myself have written one such text. There are no books, however, that thoroughly cover all the standard patterns of abnormal behavior (or psychopathology) and, in turn, consistently relate these to issues relevant to the criminal justice system. In addition to providing the most up-to-date factual information on these disorders, related legal and social issues and also guidelines for responding to these disorders are included in this book.

I start with an overview and introduction. Many books that deal with abnormal behavior patterns spend an inordinate amount of time on introductory material, often from three to five chapters. From my experience in conducting seminars for law-enforcement and corrections personnel, and from teaching related courses primarily to criminal justice and prelaw students, I have condensed the essential introductory material into one chapter. Then I move into chapters 2 through 9, which cover the standard categories of psychopathology. Contrasted to many books on psychopathology, there is much greater emphasis here on the criminal personality and psychopath (chapter 2), the personality disorders (chapter 3), and the alcohol- and drug-use disorders (chapter 4), since they are so often an issue in criminal justice.

Chapters 10 to 14 deal with topics that are of direct application and practical consequence to the criminal justice student and practitioner: violence; the detection of deception; incompetency, criminal responsibility, civil commitment and the prediction of dangerousness; psychopharmacology in the criminal justice system; and specific criminal justice personnel issues.

Consequently, this book is useful for all practitioners and students within the criminal justice system. It is easily adaptable to seminars and workshops for such personnel. It is also adaptable as an adjunct text for numerous criminal justice, prelaw, and sociology courses, and as a primary text in any course wherein the two primary foci are abnormal behavior—mental health and some component of, or the overall scope of, criminal justice. Most people find the focus of study to be very interesting in both fields, abnormal behavior and criminal justice. By combining good scholarship with efficient organizational summaries of concepts, interesting case anecdotes, and some humorous quotes, I believe I have come up with a book that is both highly informative and interesting to read.

It is appropriate to comment here on the issue of sexist language. It is difficult to avoid the use of the generic *he,* and I have decided not to use that awkward *he-she* compromise term. Where possible, I have avoided sexist implications by the use of rephrasing and plurals.

While I was writing the book, I obtained helpful information and critiques from a number of colleagues in various disciplines. A list of their names follows. I thank all of them, and I hope you find the book to be useful and interesting.

These contributors are: Steven R. Smith, dean of the Cleveland Marshall School of Law, Cleveland, Ohio; Price Foster, dean of the College of Urban and Public Affairs, University of Louisville; Theodore Feldmann, Department of Psychiatry, University of Louisville; Leonard Miller, Kentucky Correctional Psychiatric Center, LaGrange, Kentucky; Phillip Johnson, Kentucky State Reformatory, LaGrange, Kentucky; Sarah Deitsch, Psychology Department, Notre Dame University; David Connell, Department of Psychology, University of Louisville; Curtis Barrett, Department of Psychiatry, University of Louisville; Carleton Gass, private practice, Miami, Florida; Joseph Gutmann, Commonwealth Attorney's Office, Louisville, Kentucky; Al Parke, warden, Kentucky State Reformatory, LaGrange, Kentucky; Wilfred Van Gorp, Veterans Administration Hospital, West Hollywood, California; Will Bickart, federal prison, Milan, Michigan; E. Rhett Landis, federal prison, Butner, North Carolina; and Deborah Wilson, School of Justice Administration, University of Louisville.

Abnormal Behavior and the Criminal Justice System

1

Mental Health Issues for Criminal Justice Personnel

> "It's all in your head, Buster, but don't get the idea it's any of that psychological crap."
> — Major Frank Burns
> from the TV show *M A S H*

The judicial and criminal justice systems face an enormous task in modern American society, which is not surprising since American society has the world's highest per-capita imprisonment rate. The nation's prison population jumped 8.2% in 1990, to a record total of 771,243 inmates, a 134% increase since 1980. On an average day in this country (factoring in the continuing population increase), approximately 100,000 crimes are committed (including at least 50 murders, 250 cases of arson, and 12,000 home burglaries), and well over 35,000 people are arrested (Heymann 1990).

The task of these systems is complicated by the fact that a substantial proportion of these individuals suffer from some form of mental disorder (Toch and Adams 1989). The best consensus estimates are that approximately 20 percent of the general population suffers from some form of mental disorder during any given six-month period (see the section in this chapter on rates of mental disorder). No exact data are available, but it is reasonable to assume that a somewhat higher proportion (at least 35 percent) of those being served by the criminal justice system suffer from a significant mental disorder.

Police and correctional officers often report that interacting with these individuals is an undesirable part of their work for several reasons. There is a lack of information about what defines the various behavior patterns and what kinds of behaviors can be expected; they lack the training necessary for dealing with this population; there is uncertainty over where the role of criminal justice personnel changes to that of therapeutic personnel; and there is often a lack of control and a sense of frustration in dealing with this population. This chapter, and the book as a whole, addresses these issues.

Dr. Joel Dvoskin, the associate commissioner for forensic services in the New York State Office of Mental Health, has said that "the most prolific mental health worker in the United States is the police officer, and there's

1

not even a close second" (1990). This statement is certainly amplified if one adds correctional, probation, and parole workers. Yet the criminal justice and mental health systems often do not communicate well with each other, when they even talk to one another. It is hoped that this book will stimulate more of what Saleem Shah (1991) refers to as "boundary spanners," especially more informed people who can increase the needed communication and sharing of services in both systems.

In this chapter we examine concepts of abnormality, the types of mental health professionals, a brief history of society's response to mental disorder, various myths about mental disorder, rates of mental disorder, classification and assessment approaches, and a listing of the consensus themes about abnormal behavior that are used throughout this book.

Concepts of Abnormality

Abnormal is a common term in everyday life, and quite simply it means "away from the norm." More specific criteria are typically used to define the term *abnormal* in the study of human behavior. People can be "away from the norm" in several different ways or dimensions.

A commonly used criterion is *subjective discomfort,* the individual's own judgment as to whether the individual is content with his or her own functioning and feelings. Although people often used this criterion, the subjective discomfort criterion by itself is not a good basis for judgments of abnormality. Few alcoholics, paranoids, or criminals see themselves as having psychological problems. Persons are labeled abnormal by the *statistical rarity* criterion if they differ significantly from the average, or from what people agree is normal behavior. But statistical rarity, too, can be a problematic criterion, since it would not distinguish people who are geniuses, highly creative, or only eccentric from people who are mentally disordered or retarded.

The criterion of *maladaptive functioning* judges people to be abnormal if their thinking, feelings, or behavior interferes with their ability to function in their own lives and within society. This is probably the best criterion of all, as it incorporates the best aspects of both the statistical rarity and subjective discomfort criteria.

Using these criteria, several general guidelines have evolved that are consistently relevant to the issue of abnormality throughout history and across most cultures. These guidelines, amplified in subsequent chapters, can be summarized as follows:

1. Some recurring behaviors that seem indicative of potential, developing, or existent mental disorder are (*a*) an inability to inhibit self-destructive behaviors; (*b*) seeing or hearing things that others in the culture agree are not there; (*c*) sporadic and/or random outbursts of violence; (*d*) a consistent inability to deal interpersonally in an effective manner; (*e*)

persistent academic and/or vocational failure; (f) anxiety and/or depression; and (g) an inability to conform to codes of behavior whether or not one verbalizes a desire to do so.

2. Based on the above behavioral factors, the most consistent criteria for deciding whether a specific individual is abnormal are (a) the deviance (or bizarreness) of behavior from the norms of that society; (b) the continuity and/or persistence of the disordered behavior over time; and (c) the resulting degree of disruption in intrapersonal and/or interpersonal functioning.

The meanings of *mental disorder, mental illness,* and *emotional disorder* are so similar that they are virtually interchangeable. In this book we typically employ the term *mental disorder. Mental illness* is sometimes used to designate such disorders, especially those that are thought to have a significant biological component as a cause.

Although the term *neurosis* no longer has a formal role in diagnosis according to the American Psychiatric Association's *Diagnostic and Statistical Manual of Mental Disorders,* or DSM (1987), it is still used when paired with *psychosis.* Disorders in which reality is greatly distorted or personality is severely disorganized are considered psychotic disorders. Disorders in which self-defeating behavior, guilt, or anxiety render a person unhappy and ineffective are considered neurotic disorders.

Mental Health Professionals

Persons in the judicial and criminal justice systems commonly encounter people referred to in general as mental health professionals, a label applied to members of a number of specific professional groups. Most have been trained in some form of psychotherapeutic intervention. The duration of that training is relatively short for psychiatric nurses and social workers; psychiatrists receive additional medical training, including instruction in the administration of medications. Clinical psychologists receive additional training in psychodiagnostic tests and in the design and evaluation of research studies. Forensic psychologists and psychiatrists specialize in matters that significantly overlap both mental health and the judicial-criminal justice system, including many of the topic areas of this book.

Types of Mental Health Professionals

Mental health professionals may be classified as follows:

- *Clinical psychologists* have a master's degree and a Ph.D. in psychology (or in some cases a Psy.D., which requires less research training), with specialized training in assessment techniques (including psychodiagnostic tests) and research skills.

- *Counseling psychologists* have a Ph.D. or Psy.D. in psychology. They typically work with adjustment problems (such as in student health or counseling centers) that do not involve severe emotional disorders.
- *Psychiatric social workers* have a master's degree in social work, sometimes a B.A., and very occasionally a Ph.D., with a specialized interest in mental health settings.
- *Psychiatrists* have a M.D. with a specialization in emotional disorders, just as other physicians might specialize in pediatrics or family medicine.
- *Psychoanalysts* usually have either an M.D. or a Ph.D., with a training emphasis on some form of psychoanalytic therapy.
- *Psychiatric nurses* have an R.N., and sometimes with an M.A., with specialized training for work with psychiatric patients.

Adjunct Mental Health Personnel

Persons in the following categories do not usually deliver the full range of primary services that the mentally disturbed require, yet they play important roles in care and treatment programs.

- *Occupational therapists* have B.S. training in occupational therapy, with extra training in helping the emotionally handicapped become more self-sufficient and effective.
- *Art or expressive therapists* have B.S. training, sometimes at the masters' level. They are trained to help the emotionally disturbed express feelings and conflicts and develop more life satisfaction through painting, sculpting, and other expressive modalities.
- *Pastoral counselors* have a ministerial degree, with some additional training in counseling techniques, to help those clients whose emotional difficulties center on a religious or spiritual conflict.
- *Alcohol- or drug-abuse counselors* often have nothing higher than a bachelor's degree, and sometimes less than that, but they have specific training to assist in the treatment of alcohol- or drug-abuse problems.
- *Community mental health workers* have limited training, but they assist in a variety of roles, usually in community mental health centers.

Licensure and Certification

Mental health professionals may be licensed, or certified, or both. *Licensure* is granted by a state. In essence, a license is a permit to practice, and it establishes that the professional has met at least minimal standards (and in many instances, *minimal* is certainly the correct term).

Certification is typically granted by an independent board. The quality of board certification is only as good as a board's qualification and examination procedures, and the truth is that you yourself could get a group of your friends together and decide to certify people as "Really Good Therapists" and not do much worse, since in most states none of the terms used are controlled by licensure. You could make up fancy diplomas and charge people outrageous fees to become certified, and frankly that appears to be the quality level you will find in some very impressive-sounding boards that certify in the mental health field.

Medicine has the best system of board certification, as it has somehow managed to eliminate "outlaw" boards. In psychology, I would respect only those boards that are controlled by the American Board of Professional Psychology (ABPP). The truth is that, in many instances, board certification may dupe the public as much as it facilitates good practice in other situations.

Major Historical Developments Related to Mental Disorder

I. Western Society in general
   A. Early Greeks—Hippocrates (460–377 B.C.)—focus on brain; emphasis on life stressors
   B. Romans—Galen (A.D. 2nd century)—hospital as a treatment center; thorough classification of disorders
   C. Middle Ages—physicians as a higher-status social class; rediscovery of Greek and Roman texts; contact with Near Eastern and Oriental cultures
   D. Renaissance (1500–1650)—beginning of the rejection of witchcraft; naturalistic explanations of emotional disorder; building of asylums
   E. Enlightenment (1700–1800)—more humane care; keeping of case histories and rudimentary statistics

II. United States
   A. Early colonial period—regression to witchcraft and demonology; first hospital specifically for mental patients, in Williamsburg, Virginia, in 1773
   B. Late 1700s—"moral therapy" becomes popular
   C. Approximately 1850–hospital reform movement
   D. Late 1800s—medical model increases in influence
   E. Early 1900s—Freudian model increases in influence
   F. Early to mid-1900s—behavioral model increases in influence

G. 1950s and 1960s—humanistic and cognitive models increase in influence

H. Early 1960s—community mental health care centers change care-delivery structure

I. 1980s—"corporatization" of mental health care delivery. Those who pay for services (or their administrators, as in the Preferred Provider Organizations) begin to capture the system from those who deliver the services

Myths about Abnormal Behavior

Many myths focus not only on abnormal behavior but on how abnormal behavior intersects with the criminal justice system. The following list of common myths, most of them negative, is adapted from a publication of the U.S. Department of Health and Human Services (DHHS Pub# [ADM] 88-1391, revised 1988). Myth does not necessarily connote "inaccurate," though this is the position of this DHHS document and is also what many people believe. Myths are simply commonly accepted beliefs, and they have varying degrees of truth value.

Most of these myths are built on the stigma of "mental illness." If the victim of a disorder or those around him have inaccurate beliefs about the disorder—such as that a mental patient can never recover—they can actually bring that belief into reality in this individual case; when these myths have significant truth value, they are too simplistic to apply to any one person. So it's important that such myths be challenged. You may find it useful to consider your own response to them.

Persons who have been mentally ill will never be normal. Many mental-health-movement advocates argue that this is a totally inaccurate belief. It's true that the majority of significantly mentally disordered individuals eventually return to the normal range. It's equally true, however, that some recover only minimally, that many show periodic reoccurrences, and that many bear lifelong psychological scars and impairments as a result of their trauma.

Mentally ill people are more dangerous than the non–mentally ill. Most studies find this to be untrue, *except* for certain diagnoses (such as paranoid schizophrenics and certain personality disorders) and except for those who showed a history of aggressive behavior prior to their disorder. In the latter individuals, the mental disorder can accentuate the propensity toward violence.

The mentally ill are unpredictable, both during and after their illness. A more accurate concept would be that they are "predictably unpredictable"

when they are directly under the influence of their disorder. Otherwise, they are very similar to the non–mentally ill.

In a classic study, approximately twenty thousand former mental patients were monitored for eighteen months after being released from the hospital. Only thirty-three were subsequently arrested for crimes involving violence. Though it's true that this is a bit higher, percentagewise, than one would expect in the average population, it's clearly very low in absolute numbers. Moreover, the majority of these patients who were aggressive had a prior history of aggression.

The concept of predictable unpredictability is a lesson that was taught early in my career. I was completing an internship at the Pyschiatric Clinic of the State Prison of Southern Michigan at Jackson, which at that time was the largest walled prison in the world. One of my clients, John, was typically lucid and affable. He was a big man, and he spent most of his free time working with weights. He was an imposing figure.

On occasion, John would withdraw over a period of several days, then lash out aggressively toward someone. His last victim was Mel, the intern who preceded me. Mel had isolated John during one period of withdrawal. Unfortunately, when he tried to get John to talk, John just kept mumbling. Mel moved closer to the bars, showing empathy but not wisdom. The next thing he saw was the ceiling as John shot a punch through the bars and put him down for the count.

One day, I was told that John was out front and wanted to talk to me. I knew John had been withdrawn the day before, but nonetheless I blithely walked up to him and asked him how he felt. He said, "I know I must punch you." Some nurses' aides—who looked like they played on the prison football team (and some did)—were nearby, and I figured I was going to receive one really good shot despite their presence. Not knowing what to say, I asked John why he felt he had to hit me. He said, "Because I'm in front of the red panel," the wall panels having been individually painted as a legacy of a prison artist. On a fortuitous impulse, I said, "Could you take one step forward?" He did, and he was now in front of a blue panel. With a hoarse voice, I asked him if he noticed that. He said, "Yes, I guess I don't have to hit you now." I agreed, then escorted John over to the nurses's aides, whereupon I hyperventilated.

Like many mental patients, John was predictably unpredictably. If you know the history of a patient, do a thorough evaluation, and generate adequate monitoring, much of the unpredictability (and isn't uncertainty the source of our greatest anxieties?) becomes more predictable.

The mentally disordered are unproductive while they are actively disturbed. Certainly this is so in most cases. But some patients remain productive in various dimensions even when they are actively disturbed. It's been documented that many great poets (see chapter 6) and other creative artists seem to have been more productive when they were actively suffering the mood swings of manic-depression. Moreover, many personality disorders and most of the anxiety-related disorders (when they are not severe) don't really impede productivity, though they are likely to disrupt other parts of the person's life.

A person who has recovered from a mental disorder is likely to be a less competent employee than the average employee. This is not so. Most studies show that recovered mental patients make fine employees. Indeed, some outperform other employees in areas such as punctuality and attendance, probably because having a particular job may mean more to them than it does to the average worker. Studies show that both groups of employees are about equal in quality of work, duration on the job, and motivation to excel.

There are two qualifications to this. First, the above results hold only where recovered mental patients continue to cooperate in a prescribed follow-up treatment or in rehabilitation. This is especially true of mentally disordered individuals who leave the criminal justice system, whether by way of probation, parole, or time served.

The second qualification is that even when cooperating in a prescribed follow-up, a few may have relapses that cause them to lose time on the job. This possibility should be anticipated, and such individuals should be employed in flexible situations that can accommodate such interruptions.

Since people who have recovered from a disabling physical illness can usually cope on their own, recovered mental patients should be able to do so too. The fact is that people who have recovered from a chronic or disabling disorder, whether physical or psychological, often need a period of *rehabilitation,* whether or not there was a *cure* for their specific disorder. For example, most individuals who have suffered from a psychotic disorder (see chapter 6), especially schizophrenia, need social rehabilitation. Studies consistently show that persons suffering from any type of severe disorder recover better and more quickly if they are returned to a consistently available network of family and/or friends. It is true that mental patients often have to overcome the added burden of the stigma of mental illness, which is the basis for most of these myths.

It's hard to talk to former mental patients, and they will probably act weird. It's not true that former mental patients cannot communicate effectively. They may occasionally talk about their disorder, as you probably would if you had recovered from a physical disorder. The greater sense of anxiety they may generate in you likely comes from your own fears of vulnerability in this area.

Former mental patients will probably seem weird on occasion, but I am certain that both you and I seem weird to others on numerous occasions.

Even if our weirdness occurs with some regularity, we label it with such benign phrases as "colorful personality," "she has character," "eccentric," and the like. When a former mental patient shows any weirdness, however, we quickly resort to a label like "ex–mental patient" or "psycho." It's the same ironic pattern wherein we sometimes require people on parole from a correctional institution to adhere to social behaviors that are more conformist than we ask of ourselves.

Too many people who deserve to go to prison get off or serve less time than they should because of alleged mental problems. This is very untrue. Though it receives a lot of media attention, the insanity defense is rarely used by attorneys. And when they do, it is often as a last resort, since as attorneys know, it is seldom effective. Any warden will testify that he deals with many inmates who would be better served if they were placed in the mental health system (and it would save him a lot of hassle).

Our correctional systems are too concerned with rehabilitation and not concerned enough with punishment. This is not true. The philosophy underlying most correctional efforts today is that of "just desserts," most clearly articulated by Wilson and Herrnstein (1985). This philosophy avoids the vindictiveness of a true punishment or retribution model, but it does say, "If you do the crime, you have to do the time." It has resulted in efforts, particularly at the federal level, to set uniform guidelines as to what amount of "time" each crime earns.

There is no evidence that the rehabilitation model is effective, but the critical issue is that it's never been truly employed. One true attempt to employ such a model was Michigan's "sexual psychopath" law, which I personally experienced in the 1960s when working in the Michigan prison system as a psychologist. The law sentenced a convicted sexual psychopath for a term that lasted anywhere from one day to life (and they literally meant "life"). The decision to release, and under what conditions, was left strictly up to the therapists. The advantage of this was that therapists had much greater leverage to generate a treatment milieu. Nonetheless, the law was quickly found to be unconstitutional.

It's interesting that aside from being held unconstitutional, nobody was overwhelmingly positive about the system. I can personally testify that my colleagues and I felt a lot more apprehension when we had to put our signature on the actual decision rather than forward our "recommendations" to the parole board. And not suprisingly, correctional officials were not at all happy having such ultimate decision power handed to the "shrinks."

Mental disorder of any significance is rare. This is not so, as the next section, on the incidence of mental disorder, points out. It's interesting that even those of us who don't believe mental illness is rare are quick to entertain the quaint axiom, sometimes attributed to old Quakers, that "All the world is insane, except for me and thee—and I'm not sure about thee." It's a comfortable but inaccurate myth.

We now know most of the important facts about mental disorder. The ancient Greek physician-philosopher Hippocrates might have bought this one, and so would some mental health professionals in every culture and during most periods of history since Hippocrates. This is one myth the professional is more likely to accept than the lay person.

Incidence of Mental Disorders

There is a great deal of misunderstanding about how common mental disorder actually is in our society and in people's lives. Over the last several decades many efforts have been made to effectively assess the overall incidence of mental disorder. Previous endeavors in this area provide some useful data, but these efforts pale in comparison with the landmark 1984 study developed by the National Institute of Mental Health (NIMH). This study was initially reported on in a series of six articles in the October 1984 issue of *Archives of General Psychiatry,* then summarized by Robins and Regier (1990).

The sheer scope of the NIMH study is unprecedented. A sample of more than seventeen thousand representative community residents (virtually a fivefold increase over the sample studied in the most exhaustive previous studies) were studied at five locations (Baltimore, New Haven, rural North Carolina, St. Louis, and Los Angeles). These individuals were given a thorough and standardized structured interview, which was followed up a year later with a reinterview. Unlike many previous studies, this study was not restricted to reporting only on hospitalized mentally disordered persons, or only on prevalence of treatment, or only on current symptoms or level of impairment. Rather, all thirteen of the major disorder categories in the third edition of the *Diagnostic and Statistical Manual* (DSM-III), the generally accepted handbook of diagnostic categories at that time, were considered.

The researchers first measured these groups from the perspective of six-month prevalence rates—that is, how many people showed a particular disorder at some time in the six months during which the population was assessed (Robins and Regier 1990). They found that about 19 percent of adults over age eighteen suffered from at least one mental disorder during a given six-month period.

The types of problems they reported include:

- Anxiety disorders, such as phobias, panic disorders, and obsessive-compulsive disorders (see chapter 7). Afflicting about 8 percent of those surveyed, anxiety disorders appear to be the most common group of psychological problems—not depressive illnesses, as previously thought. Anxiety disorders include specific intense fears, such as fear of heights or animals, as well as agoraphobia, or fear of leaving the familiar setting of home.

- Abuse or dependence on drugs (see chapter 4). This afflicts an estimated 6 to 7 percent of the population, and about four-fifths of the cases are linked to alcohol.

- Affective or mood disorders, such a major depression and manic-depression (see chapter 6). These affected about 6 percent of the adults studied.

- Schizophrenia, probably the most severely disabling of mental illnesses (see chapter 6). This was found in about 1 percent of the population studied. Another 1 percent were affected by an antisocial personality disorder.

Somewhat different results were obtained by taking the perspective of lifetime prevalence rates—that is, how often a disorder occurs percentagewise in the population. To find this out, the researchers assessed how often disorder(s) occurred in the lifetime of the persons who were sampled. From this perspective, it appears that the most common disorder pattern was substance abuse (see chapter 4), at close to 20 percent. There was also a high incidence for the anxiety disorders (12 to 20 percent) and for the affective disorders (8 to 9 percent). The range of estimated incidence for anxiety disorders reflects the fact that there was a much higher assessed rate of anxiety disorders in Baltimore than in the other sites. (This could be because the study was conducted around the year the Colts football team left Baltimore for Indianapolis. And the Baltimore Orioles didn't do all that well in baseball that year, either.) For schizophrenia, the overall rate in these studies was 1.0 to 1.5 percent, and for the antisocial personality disorder, it was 2.5 percent.

The NIMH study also looked at differences in incidence of mental disorders among those who lived in urban central city areas, in suburbs, and in small towns and rural areas. For schizophrenia, organic brain disorder, alcoholism, drug abuse, and the antisocial personality, the rates were highest in the central city, at a middle level for suburban areas, and lowest in the rural and small town populations. Incidence was relatively even throughout these three areas for major depressions and phobias, though somatization disorders, panic disorders, and some affective disorders were a bit higher in rural and small town areas than in the other groups. The only disorder that was found to be higher in the suburbs was the obsessive-compulsive disorder.

Table 1–1
DSM Diagnostic Categories

1. Disorders usually first evident in infancy, childhood, or adolescence	10. Dissociative disorders
	11. Psychosexual disorders
2. Organic mental disorders	12. Factitious disorders
3. Substance use disorders	13. Disorders of impulse control not elsewhere classified
4. Schizophrenic disorders	
5. Paranoid disorders	14. Adjustment disorders
6. Psychotic disorders not elsewhere classified	15. Psychological factors affecting physical condition
7. Affective disorders	16. Personality disorders
8. Anxiety disorders	17. Conditions not attributable to a mental disorder that are focus of attention or treatment
9. Somatoform disorders	
	18. Additional codes

Source: American Psychiatric Association, *Diagnostic and Statistical Manual of Mental Disorders*, 3rd ed., rev. Washington, D.C.: American Psychiatric Association, 1987.

The Diagnostic and Statistical Manual of Mental Disorders

The DSM-III-R (American Psychiatric Association 1987) is the revised form of the third edition of the *Diagnostic and Statistical Manual of Mental Disorders* that was published in 1980. The predecessors of DSM-III were DSM-II in 1968 and DSM-I in 1952. A new edition, DSM-IV, is expected in 1993, timed to coincide with the anticipated publication of the tenth edition of the *International Classification of Diseases* (ICD-10) in that same year. Even though the DSMs have occasionally been criticized, they have received wide acceptance not only nationally but internationally as well. Moreover, there is simply no alternative system that has reached even a minimal level of usage of acceptability. See table 1–1 for a listing of the DSM-III-R's diagnostic categories. For each mental disorder, the DSM lists the characteristics that are necessary before a mental health professional can state that a person is suffering from that disorder.

Common Mental Health Assessment Techniques

Interview data are best obtained in a controlled format, such as the Mental Status Examination, which includes assessment of (1) physical appearance; (2) motor activities; (3) speech activity and patterns; (4) mood and affect; (5) alertness and attention; (6) content and organization of thoughts; (7) perception; (8) the general areas of memory, abstract thinking, and the client's fund of knowledge; and (9) the client's attitude toward the examination and toward his or her condition (Melton et al. 1987).

Some of the questions commonly asked in the Mental Status Examination are: What is this place? Who am I? What date is it? Who are you? Who is the president of the United States? Who was president before he was president? What does "Don't cry over spilled milk" mean? Would you count backward from 100 by 7's?

Even though the interview in the Mental Status Examination provides structure, the examination contains a weakness common to all data obtained from interviews: There are few or no statistical or normative standards for the obtained responses on which to base a communicable inference and eventual diagnosis. Examiners are too often left to develop their own idiosyncratic notions of what a certain response means. While this procedure may be helpful in developing beginning inferences, these inferences are strengthened significantly (or called into question) when the more objective data of psychological testing are considered as well.

I saw the potential for idiosyncratic error in the first case conference examination of a patient that I ever witnessed. The senior clinician who was examining the client proceeded with the questions of the Mental Status Examination. The client did generally well on most of the questions, except that he did not remember what date it was, he had some trouble counting backward from 100 by 7's after he got to 86, and he gave a rather concrete interpretation of the "spilled milk" proverb. After the client left the room, the examining clinician suggested the diagnosis of schizophrenia, pointing out that the client's lack of awareness of what date it was suggested a global disorientation, that the problem in counting backward from 100 by 7's suggested general confusion, and that the difficulties with the proverb suggested concreteness.

By this time, I was uncomfortable since I also had missed the date by a full seven days. In actuality, a more parsimonious, simpler, and better explanation for the client's behavior was available. A lack of knowledge of the exact date, even being off by a number of days, is common. In addition, people who have been in an institution for any period of time easily become confused about, if not indifferent to, the date. The problems with the other two pieces of data were explainable by the fact that this client was not very bright.

Psychological test data provide control for most of the errors of interview data, if the psychological test is well designed. The Minnesota Multiphasic Personality Inventory (MMPI) and the Wechsler Adult Intelligence Scale—Revised (WAIS-R) are the most commonly used and researched objective psychological tests (Shapiro 1991; Greene 1991; Graham 1990). Virtually every clinician, regardless of theoretical orientation or type of training, has some familiarity with the MMPI and the WAIS-R. Such an extensive amount of normative data have been gathered on the MMPI that it is by far the most useful standard objective test among the clinician's diagnostic options. An improved and updated revised version of the MMPI, called MMPI-2, was developed and published in 1989, with alternative forms for adolescents and adults (Graham 1990; Greene 1991).

Consensus Themes about Abnormal Behavior

In addition to the themes about abnormal behavior already noted in this chapter, the following themes reflect the consensus of experts in the field and underlie much of the material in the rest of this book:

- The continuum of human behavior ranges from clearly normal adjustment to definitely abnormal adjustment. Much behavior belongs in that middle area, where making decisions regarding abnormality is difficult.
- A specific abnormal behavior pattern is seldom inherited genetically, but genetic factors may play a part in predisposing a person to an abnormality of one sort or another.
- The causes of any one abnormal behavior pattern are usually multiple.
- Indicators of abnormality are not necessarily obvious or flagrant. In many cases, the signs are uncommon and/or subtle.
- Both long-term and transient social value systems affect judgments as to whether a person is abnormal.
- Though there may be differences in how certain mental disorders are manifested within different cultures, most disorders are found in some form in most cultural groups. The differences are usually related to cultural traditions, expectancies, and ethics.
- A psychological handicap often has a more negative effect on social and vocational effectiveness than does a physical handicap.
- The label "psychological abnormality" is a stigma that often remains with a person even after the disorder no longer exists. Such a label, resulting from the expectations and responses of others, may prolong the psychological disorder.
- While a small percentage of mentally disordered individuals are dangerous to other people, this percentage is not much different from the percentage of normal persons who are dangerous to others.
- In most societies there is a substantial overlap between judgments of mental abnormality and criminal behavior; that is, the same specific behavior may receive either label, depending on who is doing the labeling.

Another perspective on abnormality is provided by examining the elements of positive mental health. These are listed at the end of chapter 14, and the reader is referred there for further clarification.

Notes

American Psychiatric Association. 1987. *Diagnostic and Statistical Manual of Mental Disorders (DSM-III-R)*. 3rd ed., rev. Washington, D.C.: American Psychiatric Association.

Dvoskin, J. 1990. Personal communication.

Graham, J. 1990. *MMPI-2: Assessing Personality and Psychopathology*. New York: Oxford University Press.

Greene, R. 1991. *The MMPI-2/MMPI: An Interpretive Manual*. 2nd ed. Needham Heights, Mass.: Allyn and Bacon.

Grob, C. 1983. *Mental Illness and American Society (1875–1940)*. Princeton, N.J.: Princeton University Press.

Heymann, T. 1990. *On an Average Day* . . . New York: Fawcett. Melton, G., J. Petrila, N. Poythress, and C. Slobogin. 1987. *Psychological Evaluations for the Courts*. New York: Guilford.

Melton, G., Petrila, J., Poythress, N., and Slobogin, C. (1987). *Psychological Evaluations for the Courts*. New York: Guilford.

Millon, T. 1985. "The MCMI Provides a Good Assessment of DSM-III Disorders: The MCMI-II Will Prove Even Better." *Journal of Personality Assessment* 49:379–91.

Patrick, J. 1988. "Concordance of the MCMI and MMPI in the Diagnosis of Three DSM-III Axis I Disorders." *Journal of Clinical Psychology* 44:186–90.

Robins, L., and D. Regier. 1990. *Psychiatric Disorders in America*. New York: The Free Press.

Selling, L. 1940. *Men against Madness*. New York: Greenberg.

Shah, S. 1991. Personal communication.

Shapiro, D. 1991. *Forensic Psychological Assessment*. Needham Heights, Mass.: Allyn and Bacon.

Toch, H., and K. Adams. 1989. *The Disturbed Violent Offender*. New Haven, Conn.: Yale University Press.

Van Gorp, W., and R. Meyer. 1986. "The Detection of Faking on the Millon Clinical Multiaxial Inventory (MCMI)." *Journal of Clinical Psychology* 42; 742–48.

Wilson, J., and R. Herrnstein. 1985. *Crime and Human Nature*. New York: Simon and Schuster.

Zwelling, S. 1985. *Quest for a Cure: The Public Hospital in Williamsburg, Virginia, 1773–1885*. Williamsburg, Va.: Colonial Williamsburg Foundation.

Background and Current Status

The term *antisocial personality* is the result of an evolution through a number of terms, the most widely known of which is undoubtedly *psychopath*. In about 1800, Philippe Pinel coined the term *manie sans délire* to reflect the fact that these individuals manifest extremely deviant behavior but show no evidence of delusions, hallucinations, or other cognitive disorders (Cleckley 1964). Late in the nineteenth century, the label *psychopathic inferiority*, introduced by Johann Koch, became the accepted term. Expositions by a number of individuals, particularly by Cleckley (1964), brought the term into common usage.

Despite this history of the term, early editions of the DSM used the term *sociopathic personality* to emphasize the environmental factors that allegedly generated the disorder. Nevertheless, both concepts remained in lay and professional usages. The DSM-II substituted the label *antisocial personality disorder*, with an emphasis on patterns of observable, definable behavior that conflict chronically with agreed-upon societal norms. The trend toward objective criteria continues in the *DSM-III-R*, and the term *antisocial personality disorder* is also retained. (Incidentally, if the individual is younger than eighteen, the appropriate diagnosis is conduct disorder [Quay 1987].)

Confusion of Terms

As we see, there is considerable overlap among the terms *antisocial personality disorder* (the present official DSM term), *psychopath*, and *sociopath*. Throughout this chapter, we will use the overall term *antisocial personality*, recognizing that the psychopath (or sociopath) is typically seen as a subgroup of this category.

Many experts feel that there is reasonable evidence to further subdivide the antisocial personality category, such as into "primary" and "secondary" psychopaths. They would reserve the term *primary psychopath* for those antisocial personalities who show very little anxiety or avoidance learning and who are particularly unlikely to learn under standard social controls. Further, a special type of primary psychopath is the individual who shows a consistent and high level of aggression. Numerous brain-wave disorders have been noted in such individuals (Doren 1987). *Secondary psychopaths* are generally considered antisocial personalities, but compared with primary psychopaths, they show higher potentials for learning, to profit from experience, for response to standard social controls, such as guilt, and for higher levels of anxiety. Also, secondary psychopaths tend toward introversion, whereas primary psychopaths are usually extroverted.

Both primary and secondary psychopaths are quite different from individuals who are antisocial because they grew up in and adapted to a delinquent subculture (Loeber 1990). These delinquent individuals are normal in relation to the subculture in which they were reared; they follow (often totally) the rules and mores of this group. They are often as conformist as the middle-class, middle-management person.

Characteristics of the Pattern

To receive a diagnosis of antisocial personality disorder, the DSM now requires that the individual be eighteen years of age, but there has to be evidence of onset of the disorder before age fifteen. Also, there should be evidence that the behavior has been relatively persistent. Onset before the age of fifteen should be supported by evidence of three or more separate types of acting-out behavior. In addition, at least four of the following must have occurred since the age of fifteen: (1) problematic occupational performance; (2) repetitive, easily elicited fighting; (3) repetitive avoidance of financial responsibility; (4) failure to plan ahead, as indicated by transient traveling without a goal or by a lack of fixed address for a month or more; (5) recklessness; (6) failure to accept social norms; (7) lack of regard for the truth, as indicated in repetitive deception of others; (8) indication of inability to function as a responsible parent; (9) inability to sustain a monogamous relationship for a year; and (10) lack of remorse.

From an overall perspective, the antisocial personality (AP) often glibly voices a willingness toward a variety of interpersonal commitments, but carrying these to fruition is another matter. Like the passive-aggressive personality disorder (see chapter 3), the AP often used aggression or the threat thereof for interpersonal manipulation, but unlike the passive-aggressive person, the AP is likely to actually be aggressive. Behavior patterns are marked by impulsivity, narcissism, egocentrism, socially deviance, poor judgment, and seeming failure to profit from interpersonal experiences.

Cleckley (1964), a particularly influential early theorist, asserted that psychopaths are often intellectually superior, and this concept has unduly influenced attitudes toward the antisocial personality. But Cleckley was clearly in error here; such a characterization fits only the unique subsample with which he was dealing in his private clinical practice. As a whole, antisocial personalities show lower-than-average scores on intelligence tests. This is logical considering their inability to adjust to school, and it is especially so if genetic and/or brain dysfunction is involved (Eysenck and Gudjonsson 1989).

Difficulties in Studying the Psychopath

There is a reasonable concern that some of the research data available on APs are based on inadequate sampling techniques. Two populations are a favorite target of researchers: persons (often college students) who score high on the Psychopathic Deviate, or Pd (4), scale of the MMPI, and incarcerated criminals. Neither group is composed of a majority of APs.

Causes of Antisocial Personality

Like many psychopathological disorders, there are varied ideas about the genesis of this disorder. Heredity, brain dysfunction, individual developmental experiences, and subcultural conformity are all promoted as generic to the antisocial personality and are often seen as *the critical* factor by their individual proponents.

Physical Causes. Cesare Lombroso's very early theory that one can tell a criminal by certain physical features—such as a low forehead—has been discarded. But modern researchers (Eysenck and Gudjonsson 1989; Athens 1989) have shown that criminal behavior is affected by heredity—thus providing strong, though indirect, support for the belief that the antisocial personality also is affected by heredity.

One of the first twin studies studied a sample of Bavarian prisoners with twins and found that 77 percent of the identical pairs were concordant for criminality, but only 12 percent of the same-sex fraternal pairs were concordant. A number of other similar studies have had varying results, but the general trend has been to support the notion of a genetic component (Smith and Meyer 1987; Eysenck and Gudjonsson 1989).

As yet, it is unclear how a genetic component actually comes into play in eventual behavior. Genetically based low general intellectual ability or specific learning deficits are possibilities. Brain dysfunction is a second potentially mediating factor between heredity and behavior, and differences in learning by conditioning are a third. At present, however, data that would indicate a clear link of hereditary factors to eventual behaviors are not available.

Because of its ease and accessibility, the electroencephalogram (EEG) is often used to study this issue. But most EEG studies have produced very mixed results. The problem with EEG analysis is illustrated by Ostrow and Ostrow's study of criminality and psychopathy (cited in Smith and Meyer 1987). They obtained EEGs on 440 convicts, then designated a subgroup of 69 psychopaths using the criteria of lack of empathy, impulsivity, and inability to accept social limitations. (This designation of a subgroup is a desirable methodological step that is often missing in studies.) Half of this psychopathic subgroup had abnormal EEGs, which would seem to offer strong support for a brain-disorder hypothesis. Yet 80 percent of the schizophrenics and 56 percent of the homosexuals also had abnormal EEGs. More surprisingly, 65 percent of the conscientious objectors in the sample had abnormal EEGs. The problem in using any sign of EEG abnormality to indicate disorder is that there are significant percentages—usually from 15 to 20 percent—of EEG abnormalities or disorders among normals.

In spite of the problems in EEG measurement, one interesting EEG phenomenon has shown some replication. Abnormal temporal-lobe slow-wave activity is found in a greater proportion of antisocial personalities than in other subgroups of the criminal population. A related pattern of EEG abnormality, the positive-spike phenomenon, has been shown to occur in a small subgroup of extremely impulsive and aggressive antisocial personalities in rates as high as 45 percent, while the incidence in the normal population is only approximately one percent.

On the basis of this and similar research, a consensus theory is that the dysfunction is in the temporal lobes and limbic system. This is a reasonable view since these are considered to be central regulators for emotional and motivational behavior. The limbic system is particularly involved in the regulation of fear-motivated behaviors, and lesions in analogous areas in animals significantly lessen their ability to inhibit aggression and other impulsive behaviors.

At this point, it is reasonable to say that indisputable evidence of significant brain dysfunction is found in only a small proportion of antisocial personalities. Even when brain dysfunction is detected, one is left with the vexing problem of establishing a causal sequence between the specific dysfunction and real-world behavior—an issue that has definite legal ramifications.

There is evidence that aggressive antisocial personalities are more likely to be mesomorphic (that is, to have the build of the powerful athlete) than would be expected statistically (Doren 1987). This makes sense in that individuals who are slight in stature are less likely to be successful in using aggression to deal with the environment. Hence, aggression tends to drop out of their behavioral repertoire, even if they had an initial push of heredity or modeling.

Psychological Causes. Two areas of research that have been consistently linked with the psychopathic pattern are stimulation-seeking behavior and conditionability. Quay (1987, 1965) theorizes that antisocial personalities almost constantly search for environmental stimulation and have only a minimal tolerance for bland environments and routine behavior patterns.

Lykken (1957) originated an interesting line of research, suggesting that at least a subgroup of antisocial personalities may be different in their conditioning to punishment stimuli. He divided criminal subjects into primary psychopaths, secondary psychopaths (two different types of antisocial personality), and "normal" criminals and presented them with a "mental maze" consisting of a sequence of twenty choice points. At each point, the subject had a choice of four levers; one of the levers was the correct choice and was denoted as such by a green light. If the green light flashed, the subject moved on to the next array of four. But if the subject pulled a lever other than the correct one, he received a strong electric shock. Learning the sequence of correct levers was the overt task; avoidance of the punishment levers was the latent task. The three groups did not differ on the overt task. But the primary psychopaths were noticeably poorer at learning to avoid the punishing shock than were either the secondary (or neurotic) psychopaths or the normal criminals. A variation by Schachter and Latane, with a replication of the Lykken study, is of interest (cited in Smith and Meyer 1987). When the investigators injected adrenaline into the primary psychopaths, they performed at least as well or better than normals on the avoidance task.

Lykken's general findings were also replicated by Schmauk (1970). His variation found that primary psychopaths *do* respond like normals when a tangible reinforcer, such as money, is used; but they do not learn the required response if the reinforcer is either electric shock or directions combined with social reprimand. Thus, if one presents a punishment to primary psychopaths that is within their value system, they can learn the response. Thus, ability to learn is not the issue; rather, it is a reduced original tendency to respond at all to certain types of standard punishment stimuli that makes it difficult for antisocial personalities to develop socially appropriate patterns of behavior.

Factors in early childhood development, particularly relationships with parents, have also been studied as causes. Three styles of parenting have often been noted in the background of antisocial personalities. One is the cold and distant parent, whose offspring are similarly unable to empathize with others or to understand the complexities of human relationships. The second is the parent who is neglectful in providing adequate love and supervision.

The third parental style involves parents who administer rewards and punishments with such inconsistency that it is impossible for the child to develop a clear set of expectancies about how to behave. More important, the child learns to respond only to rather concrete and immediate parental directives. In this pattern, punishment is often inconsistent, sporadic, and ill timed; further, there is often a significant difference between the rules as verbalized and the rules as actually operationalized in the family—that is, "Do as I say, not as I do." Unfortunately, such parents (or surrogates)—and they are most often the male—additionally provide a clear and direct model for such behaviors as aggression, alcoholism, sexual promiscuity, and interpersonal manipulation.

All three parenting styles produce individuals almost devoid of basic trust, the necessary foundation for committed interpersonal relationships. Such children learn to respond only to quite concrete reinforcements. One prisoner who was incarcerated for theft typifies this. As an adolescent he had stolen a TV, which his parents found in his room. They proceeded to give him a lengthy lecture on how wrong stealing was. But that evening after dinner, the family gathered in the living room around the new TV set he had provided, where it remained to be enjoyed by all.

From an overall perspective the sequence then goes something like this. (1) Persons subjected to such parental patterns do not learn to respond to standard interpersonal stimuli. They may be starved for meaningful stimuli. (2) Basic trust, the foundation for committed interpersonal involvement, is absent or suppressed. (3) The psychopathy is likely directed toward violence if there is a parental model for such behavior, especially if violent or antisocial behavior is then rewarded. (4) The psychopath responds to stimuli that do not have the same value for normals, hence are labeled "impulsive." Psychopaths, and more generally APs, are then directed into one of the three major antisocial "paths" seen in table 2–1.

Related Issues

The DSM argues against applying the term *antisocial personality* to any individual under the age of eighteen. This is reasonable on several counts. First and foremost, it is difficult to get rid of such a stigmatizing label once it has been applied. Since adjustment is in a high state of flux at this age, such caution is important. Second, the individual may be what has been termed a subcultural socialized delinquent—that is, one whose behaviors are almost totally generated by the need for peer or gang acceptance. Such behavior can change radically if the individual's peer contacts change. It does seem reasonable to reserve the *antisocial* term for individuals who have shown a clear pattern through several developmental stages. But even when a formal label cannot yet be applied, it is evident that psychopathic or antisocial characteristics can be manifest rather early. Many experts would argue that the antisocial pattern, especially in a primary psychopath, is set almost irrevocably early in childhood.

The DSM states that the antisocial personality is significantly more common in males than in females and that it tends to occur later in females. Signs are often obvious in the male in early childhood, while in the female they more commonly appear first during puberty. For the most part, these differences reflect social roles and expectations rather than any inherent propensities, although from the moment of birth on, males, on the average, tend to show higher levels of activity and aggression. Concomitant with the rise of women's liberation, there has been a rise in incidence of the antisocial personality in females, just as there has been a lowering of the incidence of disorders centering on passivity. But while crime rates involving women have risen, the incidence of violent crimes has risen only slightly. Any racial differences as regards incidence can be explained more parsimoniously in terms of socioeconomic level and/or societal response and restriction than in terms of race.

Basic intelligence is also an important issue. Those with lower IQ scores are more inclined to criminality. While there is fierce debate here, most agree

Table 2–1
Paths to Various Antisocial Patterns and Their Characteristics

The Aggressive/Versatile Path, Leading to "Cafeteria Style" Offending, Including Violent, Property, and/or Drug Offense/Abuse	The Nonaggressive Antisocial Path, Leading to More Specialized Offending, Including Property, and Drug Offenses/Abuse	The Exclusive Substance-Abuse Path Leading to Drug Offenses/Abuse
• Higher rate of genetic prenatal and birth disorders	• Lower rate of genetic, pre-natal, and birth disorders	Standard and Progression in Substance Abuse
• Onset of conduct problems in preschool years	• Onset in late childhood or early to middle adolescence	Beer or Wine → Cigarettes and/or Hard Liquor → Marijuana → Other Illicit Drugs
• Aggressive and concealing problem behaviors	• Mostly nonaggressive conduct problems	Onset of illicit drug use in middle to late adolescence
• More hyperactive/impulsive/attention problems	• No appreciable hyperactive/impulsive/attention problems	No appreciable prior conduct problems
• Poor social skills	• Capable of social skills	
• Poor peer relationships	• Association with deviant peers	
• Academic problems	• Sporadic or minimal academic problems	
• High rate of instigation of offenses	• Low rate of instigation of offenses	
• Low remission rate	• Higher remission rate, at least for delinquency	
• More boys than girls	• Higher proportion of girls than in aggressive/versatile path	
• Higher rate of drug abuse	• Lower rate of drug abuse	
• Higher rate of stimulation-seeking	• Lower rate of stimulation-seeking	

Source: Adapted in part from R. Loeber, "Development and Risk Factors of Juvenile Antisocial Behavior and Delinquency," *Clinical Psychology Review* 10 (1990): 1–42.

that numerous factors that contribute to IQ are inherited, and many experts would argue that the majority of them are.

Treating the Antisocial Personality

The treatment problem common to all the personality disorders (see chapter 3)—getting the client into therapy and meaningfully involved—is acute with the antisocial personality. Most effective are controlled settings, in which the antisocial resides for a significant period of time with personnel who are firm and caring and sophisticated in controlling interpersonal manipulations, or "conning" behaviors.

All plans for treatment of the psychopath encounter difficulty with control (Doren 1987). It is axiomatic that the greater level of control, the greater the initial impact. But is also true that the greater the level of control, the more other cognitive variables—such as degree of resentment—must be considered a problem. These are all confounded by the psychopath's inherent negativism toward being treated. A therapist's control of tangible positive reinforcers may permit some control. But when the treatment is consequently "successfully terminated," control is returned to the psychopath, and this may just reinforce a pattern of manipulation.

Various medications can be of help with certain components of the antisocial personality (Gorton and Akhtar 1990). For example, antipsychotics can be helpful with various paranoid components, especially when there are additional indications of seizures. Antipsychotics, lithium, carbamazepine, or beta blockers can be helpful for various dimensions of lack of control or violent tendencies, though benzodiazepines (such as Valium or Xanex) may be counterproductive.

One important component in rehabilitating the psychopath, and possibly in preventing psychopathic tendencies from evolving into criminal acting-out, is to provide an outlet for the high need for the stimulation-seeking component (Quay 1965). It is reasonable to believe that there are numerous individuals whose high need for stimulation and high potential for criminal behavior is kept within socially acceptable limits by their work or lifestyle: as ski instructors (or ski bums), as stock and commodity traders, even as politicians. Directing persons with psychopathic tendencies into high-energy, high-risk activities such as mountain climbing, certain forms of racing, and physically aggressive-competitive sports (such as football) can help.

Sometimes a change of life circumstances engineers such an outlet, as in the case of movie and television star Don Johnson. Johnson had a problematic early childhood, showed a consistent pattern of delinquency while he was growing up in the Missouri Ozarks, had a long string of tumultuous and broken relationships with women, and was heavily into alcohol, drugs, and a fast-lane lifestyle before attaining fame in his role of Sonny Crockett on

Miami Vice (*Newsweek*, November 7, 1985, pp. 96–100). Even after that he still enjoyed any activity filled with "excitement," smoked incessantly, and was rather hyper in his behavior. But his fame and image provided enough outlets for behaviors (and enough "slack" from the system when there were some violations) that in the average person might cause a drift into a clearly antisocial pattern.

Various therapists (Doren 1987; Hare 1986) who have worked extensively with psychopaths both in and out of prisons come to the conclusion that at least some therapeutic change is possible for psychopaths, though not all are optimistic that significant, permanent changes can be made. They suggest that when working with psychopaths it is important to remember that they are not a homogeneous group and that each individual may therefore require a different treatment. In general they are more likely to be motivated by tangible rewards than by physical punishment; they are likely to respond to positive reinforcement if the reinforcement closely follows the behavior; they may respond well to immediate verbal feedback; and they often seek constant and very high levels of stimulation.

Any inpatient treatment program should include four major components: (1) supervision, manipulation of the environment, and provision of education by the staff to facilitate change; (2) a token economic system that requires successful participation for one to receive *anything* beyond the basic necessities; (3) medical-psychiatric treatments to deal with ancillary psychopathology, such as neurological disorders and depression; and (4) the requirement that the patient live in a system of necessary social cooperation to maximize conformity and encourage development of the group ethic. This last component is seldom a consideration in inpatient programs. But a system of necessary social cooperation, every task that can be found that can reasonably be performed by another, and that is not essential to health, is *required* to be performed only by one inmate *for* another. No inmate is allowed to go to the Coke machine for himself, for instance; he must get someone else to go. Again, this encourages cooperation and reciprocation and may help inmates to internalize some mores. When some inmates are left out by others, it sometimes becomes necessary to assign "partners" to fulfill these functions for each other.

Currently, subjecting psychopaths to the criminal justice system may be the only practical way to limit or control their antisocial activity. Treatment of psychopaths is inherently difficult because they often are not interested in treatment, may feign a "cure" to obtain release, and often revert to old behaviors after release. Also, unfortunately, most clinicians of all professional types have had little contact with the antisocial personality in their training or, for that matter, with many of the groups engaged in criminal behavior. Hence, the long-term prospects for successful treatment of many psychopaths appear to be rather bleak.

Psychopaths and Corrections

Within the corrections system the psychopath presents special issues of treatment and release. The rehabilitative efforts of the penal system are seldom effective with psychopaths. Therefore, decisions to release psychopaths on probation or parole may be complicated by the difficulty of determining whether any long-term change has been achieved. Similarly, questions arise about the treatment of juveniles with psychopathic tendencies. Can the juvenile system, which is based on an ideal of guidance and treatment, have any realistic meaning or application for psychopathic juveniles? Experience suggests that the juvenile system may be as likely to facilitate such behavior as it is to curb it.

Because people with the antisocial personality disorder are able to appreciate the wrongfulness of their acts and because the insanity defense is in general so difficult to use successfully (see chapter 12), it is unlikely that such offenders would resort to an insanity defense, except when there is no other evident option, such as when there is a "smoking gun" and even a "smoky hand." The antisocial or criminal personality just does not seem to be "sick" enough to qualify for the insanity defense. Furthermore, the labels *antisocial* and *criminal personality* make these defendants appear to juries to have a particular need for criminal sanction.

Conclusions about Psychopathy

From a societal perspective, there is a tremendous ethical problem in dealing with the psychopath. For example, the legal system depends heavily on the presentation of honest testimony. Do psychopaths possess characteristics that should limit or preclude their presenting sworn testimony? Are psychopaths "fit" parents, and should the disorder be a factor in child-custody cases? Most experts would answer yes to these questions.

Even as early as 1800, Pinel captured this issue in his concept *manie sans délire*. Antisocial personalities show irrational behavior in that they are particularly unlikely to learn from experience, but they are neither retarded nor overtly "crazy" nor bizarre in thought or action. The question is: Do we hold these individuals legally responsible for their behaviors, or are they "sick"? This question becomes even more difficult to answer when research reveals high correlations of a particular brain dysfunction pattern with a particular disorder, or a high correlation between genetic deviation and a behavior pattern. The difficulty is in figuring out whether there is a causal link, and then whether a probable causal link should be allowed as an exculpatory factor, such as in an "insanity defense" or even just as a mitigating factor in placement or sentencing.

In summary, the antisocial personality presents a murky conflux of observations and issues: (1) an apparent rationality and social appropriateness; (2) an apparent inability to process experience effectively under standard social controls and punishments; (3) some evidence of behavior-determining variables, such as genetic defect and/or brain dysfunction; and (4) an absence of evidence of variables that connect these possible causes with eventual antisocial behavior. For good measure, consideration should be given to the free will–determinism issue and a varying level of political opinion in the populace relative to the "coddling of criminals."

In actual practice, the legal system has usually acted under the assumption that the antisocial personality is responsible for all his actions. An "irresistible impulse" defense has been employed successfully in rare instances, although it is most often reserved for crimes of impulse or passion committed by otherwise respectable citizens. But the dilemma will persist and will likely worsen as more sophisticated techniques of assessment of genetic disorders and brain disorder further isolate subsets of this diagnostic category with clear indicators of brain or genetic dysfunction.

Classification in Corrections

Within the corrections system, classification is a constant and critical challenge. Several systems of classification are in use in corrections (National Institute of Corrections 1981; Megargee and Bohn 1979; Quay 1984). Various commentators have mentioned that a good system is one that is clear, complete, internally consistent, economical, as simple as is feasible, valid, reliable, and dynamic and that it inherently points to treatment and custody recommendations. The concept underlying virtually all of these systems is that "identification + separation = reduced problems."

Many of these systems are a variation of the system used by the Federal Bureau of Prisons, which classifies inmates into four custody levels: "close," "in," "out," and "community." *Close custody* indicates that the inmate requires virtually continuous supervision. This custody is for individuals who by their behavior have identified themselves as assaultive, predatory, riotous, or serious escape risks, thereby demonstrating their inability to associate with the general prisoner population without becoming dangerous to the well-being of others or disruptive to the orderly running of the facility. When they are not in their secure cells, these individuals are restricted to more secure areas within the prison and kept under close staff surveillance. Given these constraints, they can participate in available institutional programs and work assignments.

In custody assigns the prisoner to regular housing quarters, such as a single cell/room, possibly double bunked (a multiple cell or squad rooms might also be appropriate). These inmates are eligible for all program activities inside the institution's secure perimeter and under normal levels of supervision, but *not* for work or program assignments outside.

Out custody means that the inmate can be assigned to less secure housing quarters within the institution, such as open dorms, cubicles, or rooms. With intermittent supervision, these individuals are eligible for work details and program assignments outside the facility's secure perimeter.

Community custody designates the offenders who are eligible for the least secure living quarters, including housing outside the facility's perimeter. These inmates may work on outside work details or program assignments with minimal supervision. They are eligible to participate in community-based program activities (National Institute of Corrections 1981; Quay 1984).

My perspective is that two of the best systems are those devised by Edwin Megargee and Herbert Quay. Megargee's system, which classifies inmates primarily on their MMPI patterns, was discussed at length earlier in this chapter (Megargee and Bohn 1979).

The system developed by Quay (1984) is the Adult Internal Management System, or AIMS system. The AIMS system sorts inmates via observational and life-history data into five groups, which are then typically further combined into three groups; table 2–2. The primary purpose of the AIMS classification is to sort inmates into three homogeneous living groups.

- *Alphas:* Typically aggressive, manipulative, victimizers, multiple disciplinary problems, hostile, little concern for others.
- *Gammas:* Typically reliable, cooperative, industrious, avoid fights, even-tempered.
- *Betas:* Typically dependent, unreliable, passive, clinging, self-absorbed, easily victimized, anxious, easily upset.

Housing may be further subdivided based on the original five categories, but most important, Alphas and Betas must *never* be housed together. Gammas may be housed with *either* Alphas or Betas. Though differential housing is the primary purpose of the AIMS system, the system also allows differential programming in other areas. (See table 2–3).

The AIMS approach fits the earlier definition of a good system. Like any system that comes close to fitting that definition, it has proven to be useful; specifically, it has been shown to significantly reduce the levels of inmate-to-staff violence, inmate-to-inmate violence, and inmate misconduct.

No matter which correctional philosophy dictates institutional policy—whether it is "just desserts," rehabilitation, deterrence, punishment, or incapacitation—it works most efficiently if each inmate is individually sorted. This sorting should provide a security designation, based on an assessment of the level of security the new arrival needs in order to

Table 2–2
AIMS Groups and Their Characteristic Behaviors

I	Alphas (II)	III — Gammas	IV	Betas (V)
• Aggressive	• Sly	• Not excessively aggressive or dependent	• Dependent	• Constantly afraid
• Stimulation-seeking	• Stimulation-seeking	• Adequate cooperation	• Unreliable	• Anxious
• Confrontational	• Not directly confrontational	• Industrious	• Passive	• Easily upset
• Easily bored	• Untrustworthy	• Do not see selves as criminals	• "Clinging"	• Seek protection
• Hostile to authority	• Hostile to authority	• Low rate of disciplinary infractions	• Low-to-moderate rate of disciplinary infractions	• Moderate rate of disciplinary infractions
• High rate of disciplinary infractions	• Moderate to high rate of disciplinary infractions	• Some concern for others	• Self-absorbed	• Explosive under stress
• Little concern for others	• "Con artists," manipulative	• Avoid fights	• Easily victimized	• Easily victimized
• Victimizers	• Victimizers			

Source: Adapted from H. Quay, *Managing Adult Inmates: Classification for Housing and Housing Assignments.* College Park, Md.: American Correctional Association, 1984.

Table 2–3
Differential Programming by AIMS Group

	Education	Work	Counseling	Staff Approach
Alphas (Groups I & II)	• Individualized • Programmed learning	• Non-repetitive • Vigorous • Short-term goals • Individual goals	• Clear, matter-of-fact, but individualized (behavioral contracts)	• By the book • Straightforward • No-nonsense
Gammas (Group III)	• Classroom lecture plus research assignments	• High level of supervised responsibility	• Group and individual (problem orientation)	• "Hands off" • Direct only as needed
Betas (Groups IV & V)	• Classroom lecture plus individual tutoring	• Repetitive • Team-oriented goals	• Group and individual (personal orientation)	• Highly verbal • Supportive

Source: Adapted from H. Quay, *Managing Adult Inmates: Classification for Housing and Housing Assignments.* College Park, Md.: American Correctional Association, 1984.

adequately protect society; it should provide a custody-level assignment, based on the level of supervision the offender requires in order to maintain an appropriate level of control; it should assign the inmate to a housing area in a such a manner as will reduce internal management problems and interprisoner conflicts—that is, provide an internal management classification; and it should develop an individualized schedule of program activities that will keep an inmate productively occupied during incarceration and better prepare the offender to succeed upon his or her return to the community.

Notes

Athens, L. 1989. *The Creation of Dangerous Violent Criminals*. London: Routledge.

Cleckley, H. 1964. *The Mask of Sanity*. 4th ed. St. Louis: Mosby.

Doren, D. 1987. *Understanding and Treating the Psychopath*. New York: John Wiley.

Edinger, J. 1979. "Cross-Validation of the Megargee MMPI Typology for Prisoners." *Journal of Consulting and Clinical Psychology* 47: 234–42.

Eysenck, H., and G. Gudjonsson. 1989. *The Causes and Cures of Criminality*. New York: Plenum.

Gorton, G., and S. Akhtar. 1990. "The Literature on Personality Disorders, 1985–88: Trends, Issues, and Controversies." *Hospital and Community Psychiatry* 41: 39–51.

Hare, R. 1986. "Twenty Years of Experience with the Cleckley Psychopath." In W. Reid, D. Dorr, J. Walker, and J. Bonner, eds. *Unmasking the Psychopath*. New York: Norton.

Hare, R. D. 1970. *Psychopathy: Theory and Research*. New York: John Wiley.

Loeber, R. 1990. "Development and Risk Factors of Juvenile Antisocial Behavior and Delinquency." *Clinical Psychology Review* 10: 1–42.

Lykken D. 1957. "A Study of Anxiety in the Sociopathic Personality." *Journal of Abnormal and Social Psychology* 55: 6–10.

Megargee, E., and M. Bohn. 1979. *Classifying Criminal Offenders*. Beverly Hills, Calif.: Sage.

Megargee, E., and M. Bohn. 1979. *Classifying Criminal Offenders: A New System Based on the MMPI*. Beverly Hills, Calif.: Sage.

National Institute of Corrections. 1981. *Prison Classification: A Model Systems Approach*. National Institute of Corrections: U.S. Department of Justice.

Quay, H., ed. 1987. *Handbook of Juvenile Delinquency*. New York: John Wiley.

Quay, H. 1984. *Managing Adult Inmates: Classification for Housing and Housing Assignments*. College Park, Md.: American Correctional Association.

Quay, H. C. 1965. "Psychopathic Personality as Pathological Stimulation Seeking." *American Journal of Psychiatry* 122: 180–83.

Schmauk, F. J. 1970. "Punishment, Arousal, and Avoidance Learning in Sociopaths." *Journal of Abnormal and Social Psychology* 76: 325–35.

Shapiro, D. 1991. *Forensic Psychological Assessment.* Needham Heights, Mass.: Allyn and Bacon.

Smith, S., and R. Meyer. 1987. *Law, Behavior and Mental Health.* New York: New York University Press.

Walters, G., and T. White. 1989. "Lifestyle Criminality from a Developmental Standpoint." *American Journal of Criminal Justice* 13:257–78.

Yochelson, S., and S. Samenow. 1976. *The Criminal Mind.* New York: Aronson.

3
The Personality and Impulse Disorders

> The cold fact is that today's players know that the fundamentals of baseball include not only hitting, fielding and running but also corking, spitting, scuffing, tarring, popping greenies, throwing shineballs, slimeballs, sleazeballs and some tricks you probably never even dreamed of.
> — Dan Gutman
> *It Ain't Cheatin If You Don't Get Caught*

The Case of Ted Bundy

Theodore Robert Bundy is often thought of as the classic psychopath. And there are indeed clear psychopathic components in his characterological makeup. But he also has clear narcissistic-disorder personality components, and in that sense he illustrates the fact that many persons with strong personality disorder features (common in the criminal population) have characteristics of more than one disorder pattern.

Since Bundy never fully confessed (and delighted in tantilizing the public with possible new victims), it remains unclear how many young women he killed. It was at least twenty and possibly as many as forty. He murdered his first victim, a twenty-one-year-old psychology major at the University of Washington, on January 31, 1974. He committed eight other confirmed murders in Washington, then moved to Salt Lake City and entered the University of Utah Law School. He eventually moved on to Colorado. He was eventually imprisoned on a kidnapping charge but escaped and moved to Tallahassee and posed as a graduate student at Florida State. He killed at least three other women and attacked several others. Usually, he raped them, and became more vicious and bizarre over time.

The existence of psychopathy is obvious, but Bundy revealed his narcissism in such comments as "I wouldn't trade the person I am, or what I've done . . . for anything." "College people [his usual victims] are beautiful people. Good looking people." "I'm a psychologist [he did earn an undergraduate degree in psychology] and it really gives me insight." "Personalized stationery is one of the small but truly necessary luxuries of life." "I want to master life and death."

The previous chapter focused on the antisocial personality disorder and various associated criminal patterns and types. This chapter looks at the other personality disorders, as well as at another, often related, category that is commonly encountered in the judicial and criminal justice systems: the impulse disorders.

The Personality Disorders

The *personality disorders* are chronic, pervasive, and inflexible patterns of thinking and behaving that are sufficiently maladaptive to cause disruption in functioning and consequently in environmentally generated subjective distress. Personality disorders do not reach the psychotic or dramatic proportions that many other disorders often reach. Yet they are more common in the general population than those other forms of psychopathology and are especially common in populations served by the criminal justice system.

While personality disorders are not as bizarre as other disorders, they are severely maladaptive, because (1) the psychopathology is thoroughly and significantly integrated in the personality; (2) the patterns are chronic; (3) parents with personality disorders tend to create significant psychopathology in their children; and (4) personality disorders are very difficult to treat. Although these patterns are commonly modeled and learned in childhood, the family usually reaches a state of mutual detente. But the pattern causes severe problems later when it is transferred into any new intimate, consistent contact relationship such as marriage, and/or when it must confront group living situations such as incarceration or other demanding life arenas.

Most individuals in need of a personality disorder diagnosis see little reason for changing themselves, at least originally (Turkat 1990). Distress, and an occasional realization that this stems from their deficit, comes only when they move into situations that require higher levels of intimacy or more flexible behavior. The fact that they cannot meet these requirements results in coercion from the environment (such as a spouse or legal authorities), or at least feedback that they cannot ignore, resulting in a referral for intervention and/or legal control.

It is important to understand that personality disorders are logical extensions of normal personality development. A normal or mildly dysfunctional personality pattern may become dysfunctional when the person moves out of the original family that nurtured such a pattern, or moves into a situation of demanding or intimate interpersonal relationships, as in a bad "match." In other people, normal or mildly dysfunctional personality patterns may become exaggerated by stress or a change of reinforcements in their immediate world. Finally, abnormal patterns may begin to dominate a personality by other means. In all these cases, a personality disorder may be diagnosable. Table 3–1 shows the correlates of the ten most common normal personality

Table 3–1
Personality Types and Correlated Traits and Disorders

Personality Types

Correlates	Controlling	Aggressive	Confident	Sociable	Cooperative
Typical Behaviors	Manipulative	Bold Initiating	Poised	Animated Engaging	Docile
Interpersonal Patterns	Authoritarian	Intimidating	Unempathic	Demonstrative	Compliant
Thinking Styles	Calculating	Dogmatic	Imaginative	Superficial	Open
Mood-Affect Expression	Disappointment	Anger	Calm	Dramatic	Tender
View of Self	Unappreciated	Assertive	Self-assured	Charming	Weak
Probable Personality Disorders	Paranoid Antisocial Sadistic	Passive-Aggressive Anti-social Sadistic	Narcissistic Paranoid Antisocial	Histrionic Boderline Narcissistic	Dependent Compulsive Avoidant

Personality Types

Correlates	Sensitive	Respectful	Inhibited	Introverted	Emotional
Typical Behaviors	Erratic	Organized	Watchful	Passive	Energetic
Interpersonal Patterns	Unpredictable	Polite	Shy	Withdrawn	Flamboyant
Thinking Styles	Divergent	Respectful	Preoccupied	Vague	Distracted
Mood-Affect Expression	Pessimistic	Restrained	Uneasy	Bland	Intense
View of Self	Misunderstood	Reliable	Lonely	Placid	Interesting
Probably Personality Disorders	Passive-Aggressive Bor-derline Avoidant	Compulsive Paranoid Passive-Aggressive	Avoidant Schizotypal Self-defeating	Schizoid Schizotypal Compulsive	Borderline Schizotypal Histrionic

Source: Adapted in part from T. Millon and G. Everly, Personality and Its Disorders (New York: John Wiley, 1985).

types (not disorders) and points to the probable personality disorders that are likely to emerge if conditions do exaggerate or stress that particular personality type.

For example, people with the controlling personality type can live effectively in the social and vocational arenas if their personality traits do not become exaggerated, and if they find people and positions compatible with their traits. A strongly controlling female could develop a relationship with a strongly confident or a sociable male. But if she went into a marriage with him, it would very likely fail, and that stress could exaggerate the traits of each person into a personality disorder. She would be much more likely to succeed with a cooperative or a respectful type of male, or even with an inhibited or introverted type. Similarly, in order to stay a personality type and not become a personality disorder, she probably needs to find a job where she can feel she exerts control.

Personality Disorder Subgroups

The overall descriptions of the personality *disorders* are best listed in order of decreasing severity. The classification system first proposed by Millon (1981) has three basic groupings. In the first, and at the lowest level of personality integration, are the borderline, paranoid, and schizotypal disorders. These are the personality disorders most likely to be confused with the psychoses. Profound difficulties with interpersonal relationships are common to people with these disorders, and their characteristic behavior patterns include overt hostility and/or confusion. Next come the obsessive-compulsive, passive-aggressive, schizoid, and avoidant disorders. Persons with these personality disorders are either ambivalent about interpersonal relationships (obsessive-compulsive and passive-aggressive) or are virtually isolated from external support. The last grouping comprises the dependent, histrionic, narcissistic, self-defeating, sadistic, and antisocial personalities. This grouping is characterized by relatively coherent, nonconflicted behavior patterns. Whether oriented toward or against other people, these individuals tend to function in comparatively effective ways and, at least initially, to function effectively interpersonally (Millon and Everly 1985; Millon 1981).

Borderline Personality Disorder

Borderline personalities are quite moody and emotionally unstable, and they appear to be very liable to further personality deterioration. They are irritable, anxious, and occasionally spontaneously aggressive, yet they have difficulty being alone. An excellent example of this disorder is the character portrayed by Glenn Close in the movie *Fatal Attraction*. An additional feature of this disorder is *pseudologia fantastica*, a form of extreme pathological lying that may reflect an attempt to control or to enhance self-esteem. Some borderline individuals may be aware of their lying, while others may only be peripherally aware of it.

To diagnose a borderline personality disorder according to the DSM, there should be a pervasive pattern of mood, self-image, and interpersonal instability, beginning by early adulthood. At least five of the following traits are required: (1) physically self-damaging behaviors; (2) uncontrolled, inappropriate anger responses; (3) unstable and intense interpersonal relationships; (4) unstable mood; (5) unstable identity; (6) persistent boredom experiences; (7) avoidance of being or feeling alone or abandoned; and (8) unpredictable impulsivity in two areas, such as sex, drugs, or alcohol use.

Persons in the borderline personality disorder category show obvious and significant emotional instability. There is some evidence that as these individuals improve, they show more predictable behavior patterns, but ironically, improvement is often combined with increasingly evident narcissism. Disorder in both parents (i.e., they are both less caring and more controlling) is common in the background of borderline personalities (Frank and Paris, 1991). This category is truly a variable syndrome, so it will therefore require equally variable treatment responses. It is difficult to treat, and the success rate is not high (Turkat 1990).

Paranoid Personality Disorder

Paranoid personalities are suspicious, envious, rigid in emotions and attitudes, authoritarian, and hyperalert for intrusions into their psychological world. But since there are no thought disorders, or even well-formed minor delusional systems, in the paranoid personality disorder, it is not listed under the DSM paranoid disorders and is not a psychotic condition. Since paranoid personalities manifest hyperalertness toward the environment and have a chronic mistrust of most people, their information base is consistently distorted and their effect is constricted. Consequently, they find it difficult to adapt adequately to new situations and relationships, which is paradoxical because of their hyperalertness to their environment. They may often be right in assuming that other people are against them, but their paranoia is usually a disabling overreaction to a low initial level of scrutiny by the others.

The DSM requires evidence of chronic, pervasive, unreasonable mistrust of others for a diagnosis, beginning by early adulthood. This mistrust is indicated when the person manifests at least four of the following behaviors: (1) expects harm or exploitation; (2) reads hidden threatening or demeaning messages where they are unwarranted; (3) is unforgiving and bears grudges; (4) fears confiding in others, thinking the information will be used against him or her; (5) is easily slighted or angered; (6) engages in unwarranted questioning of the sexual fidelity of his or her partner; (7) engages in unwarranted questioning of the loyalty of others.

Unless these individuals have an almost absolute trust in another person, they cannot develop intimacy and are continually seeking various ways to be self-sufficient. They avoid the emotional complexities of working out a meaningful relationship, and they tend to be litigious. They may write negative letters to public figures, for example, or may bring lawsuits on minimal grounds. It is rare for them to come into treatment without significant coercion from others. (See chapter 6 for comparisons between this nonpsychotic paranoid personality disorder and psychotic paranoid patterns.)

Schizotypal Personality Disorder

Schizotypal personalities show minor variations in their behavior and thinking similar to that manifested by schizophrenics (see chapter 6). They are isolated interpersonally, somewhat suspicious, and illogical. Whereas the *schizoid*'s behavior remains rather constant, the *schizotypal* person may decompensate into actual schizophrenia under stress (such as under segregation in a correctional institution). The essential difference between the schizotypal and schizoid personality disorders is that in addition to the disturbances in social functioning, the schizotypal personality disorder manifests peculiarities in communicating. Schizotypal individuals are much more likely than the schizoid to show depression and anxiety, and because of their odd thinking patterns, they are more likely to develop eccentric belief systems and become involved in fringe religious groups.

A diagnosis of schizotypal personality disorder can be supported by establishing at least four of the following: (1) evidence of magical thinking of odd beliefs; (2) ideas of reference; (3) high social anxiety; (4) presence of occasional illusions (rather than delusions) or odd perceptual experiences; (5) peculiar communications (metaphorical, vague, digressive); (6) inappropriate or constricted emotional responses; (7) suspiciousness; (8) no close friends or confidants (other than first-degree relatives); and (9) odd or eccentric behavior or appearance. It is not uncommon to find some evidence of schizophrenia in family members.

Schizoid Personality Disorder

Schizoid personalities are asocial, shy, introverted, and significantly defective in their ability to form social relationships. They are usually described as loners. Though schizoids have few if any friends, they show no communication disturbances. The essential feature of this disorder is an impairment in the ability to form adequate social relationships.

The disorder is specifically noted in a pervasive pattern of indifference to emotions and social relationships as indicated when the person does at least four of the following: (1) typically, chooses solitary activities; (2) neither appears to have, nor claims to have, strong emotions; (3) neither enjoys nor desires close friendships; (4) shows little interest in sexual experience with another; (5) is indifferent to criticism or praise; (6) has no close friends or confidants other than first-degree relatives; and (7) shows constricted affect.

Schizoid personalities gravitate into jobs that require solitude, such as work as a night watchman. As they age or become vocationally dysfunctional, they are likely to move into a hermit or skid-row situation. But even though they fantasize excessively and communicate in peculiar ways, they show no consistent loss of contact with reality.

Passive-Aggressive Personality Disorder

Passive-aggressive personalities live life as a double message: they engage others in dependency-oriented relationships, then express much resistance and hostility in the relationship. They are stubborn and inefficient, often procrastinate on deadlines, and resort to threats or pouting if they are confronted with their inconsistent behavior. The actual behavior they express may be either passive or aggressive, but physical aggression seldom occurs. An example of the extremes to which such people may go in passively expressing hostility is the California surgeon who allowed his flourishing practice to deteriorate, then lost his license, became a drifter, and eventually accepted a six-year prison term rather than pay a cent of child support, perceiving it as money his ex-wife really didn't need. As he was led from the courtroom after being sentenced, he commented to the prosecutor, "Prison will seem like a picnic compared to life with that bitch."

To warrant a DSM diagnosis, there has to be evidence of dysfunction in social or vocational areas of functioning that result from indirect resistance to performance demands. At least five of the following behaviors are required to substantiate this indirect resistance: (1) dawdling; (2) sulking, irritability, or argumentativeness when asked to do something he or she does not want to do; (3) procrastination; (4) purposeful inefficiency; (5) convenient forgetfulness; (6) unjustified protests that others are unreasonably demanding; (7) resentment of productive suggestions from others; (8) unreasonably criticism of or scorn for authority figures; and (9) a belief that he or she is doing a much better job than others think he or she is doing.

Most parents have had the experience of a child pushing them to the limits of their control and then backing off. Like that child, the passive-aggressive becomes acutely sensitive to such limits and is consistently able to go that far but not farther. Additionally, the passive-aggressive personality disorder takes the standards and the belief systems of significant others and turns them around to effectively immobilize others. The strategy (which is not thought to be a conscious behavior) is to present the "enemy" (often a person depended on) with a choice that forces the enemy either to capitulate or to violate individual belief systems. That person is thus immobilized, yet does not usually become aware of an adequate reason to justify retaliation.

Obsessive-Compulsive Personality Disorder

Traditionally termed *compulsive,* these "workaholics without warmth," are overly controlled emotionally and find it hard to express warmth or caring. According to Sigmund Freud, their essential characteristics are that they are "exceptionally orderly, parsimonious and obstinate." Obsessive-compulsive personalities are formal and perfectionistic, and they place inordinate value on work and productivity.

This disorder is occasionally confused with the obsessive-compulsive disorder (which is an anxiety disorder—see chapter 7), but there are significant differences between the two syndromes. First, the obsessive-compulsive personality seldom becomes obsessed about issues. Second, for the obsessive-compulsive personality the term *compulsive* refers to a lifestyle in which compulsive features are pervasive and chronic, but it does *not* refer to a specific behavior such as persistent hand-washing. Third, the person with an obsessive-compulsive personality disorder is not upset, anxious, or distressed about his or her lifestyle, whereas anxiety is generic and often obvious at times in the functioning of the obsessive-compulsive disorder.

To diagnose an obsessive-compulsive personality disorder, the DSM requires a clear pattern of rigidity and perfectionism as indicated by the presence at least five of the following: (1) an overemphasis on details and lists, to the exclusion of an overall perspective (seeing the trees rather than the forest, and usually not even all of the trees); (2) perfectionism that interferes with performing tasks; (3) constriction of affection and emotionality; (4) excessive devotion to vocation and productivity; (5) a need for dominance in personal relationships; (6) indecisiveness; (7) hoarding behavior, even where the objects have no sentimental value; (8) a lack of personal generosity where no personal gain accrues; and (9) overconscientiousness or inflexibility in matters of ethics or morality.

It is true that having a degree of compulsivity is effective, particularly in our society. It becomes a problem when it overwhelms the rest of the personality. Paradoxically, obsessive-compulsives are often indecisive and poor planners of their time because of their narrow focus and concern with precision; their precision often has an irrelevant focus. They are inclined to be excessively moralistic, litigious, and hyperalert to criticism and perceived slights from others (Kernberg 1984). One psychologist who worked with a number of obsessive-compulsive personality disorder cases exclaimed in a moment of frustration, "This is a person who can get a complete physical from a proctologist."

Avoidant Personality Disorder

Avoidant personalities are shy and inhibited interpersonally, yet at the same time they do desire to have interpersonal relationships, which distinguishes them from those with the schizotypal or schizoid personality disorders. They do not show the degree of irritability or emotional instability that is seen in the borderline personality disorder.

To earn a DSM diagnosis of avoidant personality disorder, at least four of the following should be manifest: (1) an unwillingness to be involved with people unless sure of acceptance; (2) no confidants or close friends, except first-degree relatives; (3) avoidance of occupational or social activities high in social contact; (4) reticence in social situations; (5) embarrassment easily shown by blushing or anxiety; (6) exaggeration of the dangers from risks and a strong need for routine; and (7) excessive fear and sensitivity to rejection or criticism.

A major feature of this chronic disorder is an unwillingness to tolerate risks in deepening interpersonal relationships. Avoidant personalities are extremely sensitive to rejection and seem to need an advance guarantee that a relationship will work out—a relationship with an attached warranty. They resonate negatively to the refrain from W. B. Yeats: "Only God, my dear / Can love you for yourself alone / and not for your yellow hair." Naturally, such guarantees are seldom available in healthy relationships. Thus, the friends avoidant personalities do manage to make often show a degree of instability or are quite passive.

Dependent Personality Disorder

Dependent personalities have a great need to cling to stronger personalities who will make a wide range of decisions for them. Dependent personalities are naïve and docile, and they show little initiative. There is some suspiciousness of possible rejection, but not to the degree found in the avoidant personality. In one way, dependent personality disorders can be seen as successful avoidant personality disorders. They have achieved a style that elicits the desired relationships, if at the cost of any consistent self-expression of their personality.

To earn a DSM diagnosis of dependent personality disorder, the person must exhibit five of the following with some consistency: (1) be unable to make everyday decisions alone; (2) allow others to make most decisions; (3) be overly agreeable; (4) lack initiative; (5) volunteer in order to gain approval; (6) feel uncomfortable or helpless when alone; (7) be overly disrupted by minor losses; (8) be preoccupied with abandonment; and (9) be easily hurt by criticism.

Narcissistic Personality Disorder

Narcissistic personalities display a pervasive pattern of grandiosity, hypersensitivity, and lack of empathy, beginning in early adulthood. They have an inflated sense of self-worth and care little for the welfare of others, despite occasionally making a pretense of caring. They accept the flippant saying, "Beauty is only skin deep—but then, that's the only part you can see." They are usually asocial rather than antisocial, though Ted Bundy is an obvious exception. The pattern is usually evident in adolescence, and the disorder is chronic. The narcissistic personality may be even more difficult to engage in therapy than the antisocial personality, in large part because the therapist seldom has as much coercive control with the narcissist.

They are "flattery-operated"; that is, they manifest an unrealistic sense of self-importance; exhibitionistic attention-seeking; an inability to take criticism; interpersonal manipulation; and a lack of empathy, with substantial consequent problems in interpersonal relationships. They may become chronic customers of plastic surgeons, abetted by such surgeons as the one quoted in *W* (May 14–21, 1990) who replied, when asked how much surgery is too much, "Just as long as there is a space between their hairline and eyebrows, I think it's terrific."

A DSM diagnosis of narcissistic personality disorder must include five of the following: (1) grandiose self-evaluation with related fantasies; (2) a consistent need for attention; (3) emotional lability after cricitism or defeat; (4) little ability to empathize; (5) an assumption that they will receive special treatment from others without any need for reciprocal behavior—that is, a sense of "entitlement"; (6) exploitative interpersonal behaviors; (7) a belief that their own problems are unique; (8) a preoccupation with fantasies of unlimited success and power, beauty, brilliance, or love; and (9) a preoccupation with feelings of envy.

In 1984, Kernberg introduced the subdiagnosis of *malignant narcissist*. It was first applied to people like Adolf Hitler and Joseph Stalin, and more recently it has been suggested as fitting Saddam Hussein. The four characteristics of this pattern are (1) a strong suspiciousness, occasionally to the point of paranoia; (2) an extremely inflated sense of self, often grandiose; (3) sadistic cruelty (which in some individuals is turned inward as self-mutilation—"for a higher goal"); and (4) an utter lack of remorse.

There are numerous *productive narcissists* in society. One night while we were on a recent fishing trip, my friend and I had dinner at a fine Chinese restaurant. The restaurant was named after the owner, an aging but still attractive Chinese woman. The walls were totally covered with formal photographs of her, there was a bulletin board filled with candid shots from throughout her life, the restaurant's cards had a photo of her as a young woman, and you could even purchase postcards with various pictures from her life. A short conversation with her quickly revealed her narcissism, but it should have been evident to any customer. She was not especially offensive (it was a short conversation), however, narcissistically including her restaurant as a part of her "self," and turning it into an excellent operation that she groomed as carefully as her hair. Certain media-created stars, "personalities," and politicians are also examples of extreme but productive narcissism.

Narcissists are a natural product of our modern social value system. No doubt narcissistic personality disorders have always existed, but this pattern appears to have become more common recently. It is not surprising to come across advertisements about "the arrogance of excellence" and self-help seminars urging people to live out the axiom "I'm Number One" (with little evidence that there is much room for a number two or three close behind).

Histrionic Personality Disorder

Traditionally referred to as hysterical, histrionic personalities have problematic interpersonal relationships that others perceive as superficial and shallow, as well as problematic marital and sexual adjustments. These persons seek attention and are fickle and overreactive, and their responses are expressed more dramatically and intensely than is appropriate—hence the term *histrionic*. There has been a traditional controversy as to whether this disorder occurs with any frequency among males. It is clear that this disorder is found among males, but because the symptoms are a caricature of the traditional social role expectations for women, it is more common among women.

The DSM diagnosis of this disorder requires dramatic and intensely manifested behavior, beginning by early adulthood, as evidenced when the person does at least four of the following with regularity: (1) constantly seeks or demands reassurances; (2) is inappropriately sexually seductive; (3) is overly concerned with physical attractiveness; (4) expresses emotion with inappropriate exaggeration; (5) is uncomfortable when not the center of attention; (6) has rapidly shifting and shallow emotions; (7) is self-centered and has no tolerance for frustration; and (8) has a style of speech that is excessively impressionistic and lacking in detail. Television characters like Stephanie on *The Bob Newhart Show,* or Suzanne on *Designing Women,* are excellent portrayals of the histrionic personality.

Histrionic personalities may elicit new relationships with relative ease because they appear to be empathic and socially able. But they turn out to be emotionally insensitive and have little depth of insight into their own responsibilities in a relationship. They quickly avoid blame for any difficulties of interpersonal relationship, and in that sense, they show a degree of the projection that is characteristic of the paranoid disorders. Even though they may be flirtatious and seductive sexually, there is little mature response or true sensuality. If one accepts the apparent sexual overture in the behavior, the histrionic individual may act as if insulted or even attacked. While most cases of date rape are the result of a coercive assault, some are the result of a histrionic's upset over an overture she had a large part in generating.

Self-defeating Personality Disorder

Self-defeating behaviors are integral to many forms of abnormal behavior, such as alcoholism, phobias, paranoid patterns, and the like. However, the specific category of the self-defeating personality refers to individuals in whom such patterns are consistent and repetitive, especially in interpersonal relationships. Hence, people with self-defeating personality disorders are often "victims," as of spouse abuse (Montgomery and Greif 1989) (see chapter 10). But the diagnosis is made only if there are also self-defeating behaviors unrelated to abuse or depression.

In order to diagnose a self-defeating personality disorder, the DSM requires a pervasive pattern of self-defeating behaviors, starting at least by early adulthood and manifested in a variety of contexts and indicated when the person exhibits at least five of the following: (1) chooses situations and/ or people that lead to disappointment, failure, or mistreatment, even when better options are evident and available; (2) rejects or subverts the efforts of others to help him or her; (3) responds with guilt, depression, and/or pain-producing behavior (such as accident-proneness) to positive personal events; (4) incites rejecting or anger responses from others, then feels devastated; (5) rejects opportunities for pleasure, or has difficulty acknowledging that he or she is enjoying himself or herself; (6) subverts or fails to accomplish tasks critical to his or her own personal objectives; (7) engages in excessive self-sacrifice that is unsolicited by the intended recipient; and (8) rejects, or is uninterested in, people who consistently treat him or her well. It is required that these behaviors do not occur only when the person is depressed and do not occur exclusively in response to, or anticipation of, some form of abuse.

This is a controversial category, as a number of mental health profession-als believe that it tends to shift the blame from the abuser to the victim, by labeling the victim as abnormal. This is especially so when the traditional and less accurate term *masochistic* is applied to people with this pattern.

Sadistic Personality Disorder

Though this is an optional rather than an official DSM-III-R diagnosis, the concept has a long history. The sadistic personality might also be thought of as an antisocial pattern, with more prominent qualities of cruelty and revenge.

To make this diagnosis, the DSM requires that a pervasive pattern of cruel, aggressive, and demeaning behavior, starting at least by early childhood, be established when the person repeatedly engages in at least four of the following: (1) uses violence or cruelty to establish a dominance relationship; (2) demeans or humiliates people in the presence of others; (3) takes pleasure in physical or psychological suffering of other humans or animals; (4) has disciplined someone under his or her control with unusual harshness; (5) has lied with the goal of inflicting pain or harm; (6) uses intimidation, or even terror, to get others to do what he or she wants; (7) restricts the autonomy of someone with whom he or she has a close relationship; and (8) is fascinated by weapons, martial arts, injury, torture, or violence in general.

The dominant trend is a love of cruelty and an absence of remorse (Kernberg 1984; Weinberg 1984). Extreme cases described in the literature on those in which the torture and murder of innocent victims with knives and through garroting and flagellation are performed (Athens 1989). The motive for these actions is described as an irresistable urge, the fulfillment of which produces strong satisfaction for the sadist. The sadist is most often male, and his behavior is described as being both coercive and seductive, frequently promising children amusement, candy, or gifts and attracting women by posing in some fashion, such as a scout for a modeling agency.

There is a noteworthy distinction between sadism, which is a paraphilia (sexual deviation; see chapter 5) and the sadistic personality disorder. While sadistic sexual patterns are common in people with the sadistic personality disorder, they are not a necessary part of the pattern. In essence, the sadistic personality disorder is marked by a very assertive lifestyle based on power motives, commonly accompanied by gender dominance, the inflicting of pain for pleasure, and extreme aggression with or without sexual motivation. Yet the sadistic behavior is well rationalized, and the individual may even present a self-righteous air.

Kernberg (1984) offers some intervention suggestions: eliminate possibilities of harm to the client or counselor; establish an honesty promise or contract; confront the inability of the client to depend on the counselor; confront the client's desire to destroy the counselor because he or she represents an autonomous nurturing person and generates resentment. Any confrontations should be calculated to cause the sadistic personality to project dishonesty and attempts at sadistic control onto the counselor—a process Kernberg calls "paranoid regression in transference." Yet his approach consistently emphasizes maintaining a consistent affirmation of reality. While these suggestions are helpful, they are not easy to implement, and the success rate with this disorder is low.

The Impulse Disorders

Two impulse disorders that receive a fair amount of attention in the media are pyromania and kleptomania. Pyromania, or compulsive fire-setting, is rare; kleptomania, or compulsive stealing, is more common. Another fairly widespread impulse disorder that is receiving increasing media attention is pathological gambling.

Pyromania

Like thievery, deliberate fire-setting behavior appears to have increased substantially in modern society. Of course, most cases of arson are not really indicative of pyromania. The following traditional categories of arson, as listed by Boudreau and colleagues (1977), still provide a good overall schema:

1. *Revenge, spite, or jealousy.* Revenge is still the primary cause of arson, and arsonists in this category include jilted lovers, feuding neighbors, disenchanted employees, and people who want to get back at someone they believe cheated or abused them. Drug or alcohol abuse is often associated with this motive. Revenge accounts for approximately 50 percent of the fires set by adults, compared with only 5 percent of those set by juveniles.
2. *Vandalism or malicious michief.* Fires set to challenge authority or to relieve boredom are by far the most common of those set by juveniles. About 80 percent of the fires set by juveniles stem from this motive.
3. *Crime concealment or diversionary tactics.* About 7 to 10 percent of convicted arsonists are believed to be trying to obliterate evidence of burglaries, larcenies, and murders. The offender in this category expects that the fire will destroy any evidence that a crime was committed. Arson has also been used to divert attention while the offender burglarizes another building or residence.
4. *Profit or insurance fraud.* This is the category most likely to attract professional arsonists, who generally escape detection. Consequently, there is little hard data and few statistics to support this motive. But since the profits gained from arson of this type are so large and the probability of detection so small, the actual incidence is believed to be much higher than reported statistically.
5. *Intimidation, extortion, or sabotage.* This category refers to fires set for the purpose of frightening or deterring. Examples are fires set by striking workers or employees to intimidate management or by extortionists to show that they mean business. By most accounts, arson with this motive is extremely rare.
6. *Pyromania or other psychological motives.* Pyromania, the focus of this section, is the term for an irresistible urge or passion to set fires, along with an intense fascination with flames.

It is now estimated that as many as 80 percent of business-property fires are caused by arson. In these cases, the perpetrator's motive is far more likely to be in a category other than pyromania. Cases of arson in which there is no clear reward for the individual who started the fire could indicate pyromania, but mental retardation should also be considered. Pyromanics may show an inordinate interest in firefighting paraphernalia, and they usually like to watch the results of their efforts, making detection easier than might be expected.

Pyromanics, like kleptomaniacs, experience a buildup of tension prior to the behavior, as well as a sense of release upon performing the fire-setting. The behavior is often first seen in childhood or adolescence, is more common in males, and is seldom the only antisocial behavior displayed. Hyperactivity, problems in school, poor peer relationships, a lack of self-esteem, and stealing are commonly associated behaviors. It has been found that fire-setting in childhood, when combined with either enuresis and/or cruelty to animals, is predictive of assaultive crimes in adulthood, but these crimes may or may not include fire-setting.

Two specific behavioral techniques can be used in counseling to help reduce fire-setting behaviors. Overcorrection requires the individual to make a new and positive response in the area of specific disorder. Public confession and a restitution of damages through working for the individual who has been offended would be one example of overcorrection for pyromania. Negative practice has also been used; it requires the pyromaniac to perform a behavior ad nauseum until it takes on aversive qualities—for example, being required to strike thousands of matches in sequence over several sessions.

Explosive Disorder

The distinguishing feature of the explosive disorder is a sudden eruption of aggressive impulses and the loss of control of those impulses in an individual who normally inhibits or does not experience them (Goldstein and Keller 1987). Regret and guilt are common, and the behavior is disproportionate to any environmental stressors. This disorder is discussed at length in chapter 10.

Kleptomania

Police were stunned when they entered the home of Ka Kin Chan and stumbled onto a cache of 28,000 items, stolen over a seven-year period. Chan's shoplifting career had come to an end when he was nailed by a store detective in early 1990 in Mold, Wales. Chan's loot included 989 pairs of socks, 1,200 ties, 45 salt shakers, stacks of wallets and purses, bottles of after-shave, toys, and games. All were precisely catalogued—and many still bore their original price tags. Room after room was packed to the ceiling with more than $40,000 worth of items that had been stolen one at a time over the previous seven years.

Fortunately, Chan is not your typical shoplifter. Shoplifting (referred to in the retail trade as "inventory shrinkage") is a common crime in American society; statistics compiled by the U.S. Department of Commerce indicate that about one of every twelve shoppers is a shoplifter, although only one in thirty-five is apprehended. Many people shoplift for a thrill, to be "one of the gang," or to get something for nothing. But a substantial number, like Chan, are kleptomaniacs who have no real need or use for the stolen object; their solitary act is a response to an "irresistible impulse," followed by a sense of release or even pleasure. They are less likely than the "normal" shoplifter to be deterred by an increased probability of being punished. Kleptomaniacs frequently stole with friends during adolescence, and the reinforcement they gained at that time established their later solitary behavior. As adults, they usually prefer to steal while alone, and there is an "irresistible impulse" quality to their behavior.

Kleptomania often begins in childhood, primarily through stealing small items or sums of money from parents or friends. Stealing behavior as a means of being accepted into an adolescent peer group is common in the background of kleptomaniacs. There is usually evidence of depressive features, reflecting an inability to control the behavior, as well as some problems in interpersonal relationships. For example, many older women who show a kleptomaniac pattern are widowed or emotionally neglected by their husbands; the behavior gives them a thrill, sometimes sexually tinged, though they often pay for it with remorse. In fact, many show a clear sense of relief when they are apprehended. Kleptomaniacs are not necessarily significantly disturbed psychologically in areas other than the lack of this specific behavioral control. Yet the condition is often chronic.

Kellam (1969) employed a particularly ingenious aversive procedure to control shoplifting in a chronic kleptomaniac. Kellam required this person to simulate his entire shoplifting sequence, which was filmed. As the film was played back, the client was asked to participate in what was going on, with parallel internal imagery, and a painful shock was administered at crucial points. Such a technique could be amplified by having a person take a portable shock unit and self-administer a shock whenever the impulse arose. If the shock unit is clumsy, such persons could be instructed to hold their breath until discomfort ensues, since this acts as an aversive cue.

An alternative aversive technique is to have such clients go into a store, and if the impulse becomes so severe that they feel they will not be able to resist, they are to take an expensive and fragile object and drop it on the floor. Embarrassment, the need for a coping response with store employees, and the need for restitution all act to create a very aversive moment.

Pathological Gambling

> Everybody does, don't they? If you don't bet on the Super Bowl how
> could you watch?
> — Pete Rose
> > Former All-Star baseball player and Cincinnati Reds manager, later
> > imprisoned for tax evasion and banned from baseball for gambling

The characteristics of the pathological gambler are a progressive and chronic preoccupation with the need to gamble and consequent disruption in some area of the individual's world. Many compulsive gamblers report that they only feel alive when they are gambling, and they may refer to the rest of their life experience as boring. They are generally nonconformists and tend to be narcissistic and aggressive (Walker 1985). Most gamblers are extroverted and competitive individuals and are brighter than average; they tend to show a combination of depression and moderate psychopathy, and surprisingly many experienced learning difficulties as they were growing up.

A number of compulsive gamblers work only in order to make enough money to gamble heavily when they get to a spot like Las Vegas. Others have a more normal outward appearance, especially those who gamble in more legitimate outlets such as the stock market.

With the rapid expansion of state lotteries, virtually all of the general population has now participated in gambling of some form. Approximately five million Americans at some time in their lives show at least some characteristics of compulsive gambling, and conservative estimates are that there are more than one million gamblers in the United States who meet the DSM criteris for pathological gambling. Compulsive gamblers, like antisocial personalities, are stimulation-seeking, and both specifically show "disinhibition" or the inability to control impulse (Zuckerman et al. 1980; Wildman, 1992). The initial streak of compulsive gambling is usually set off by a first big win.

As with the stimulation-seeking component of the antisocial personality, some disorder or dysregulation of the brain may predispose a person to pathological gambling. Blaszczynski and his associates (1986) found that pathological gamblers who bet on horses have lower baseline levels of D-endorphin than do those addicted to poker machines. As betting on horses is a more demanding and exciting activity than repetitious machine-playing, it was speculated that horse-race addicts are engaging in a stimulating endeavor that has the reinforcing effect of triggering the release of this natural pain-killer and mood-elevator.

Jacobs (1987) postulated two predisposing factors to pathological gambling:

1. A physiological resting state that is chronically either underaroused or overaroused.
2. A psychological problem or problems, such as low self-esteem, rejection, or feelings of insecurity, that create significant amounts of psychic pain. Often, there has been a significant physical or psychological "loss."

From this theoretical perspective, the pathological gambler is either underaroused—that is to say, "bored"—or overaroused—"harried" or "anxious"—and has some psychological problem from which she or he seeks relief by entering into a form of hypnotic or fantasy state associated with the gambling.

It appears that several other factors can predispose a person to pathological gambling. These include family values that emphasize material symbols rather than saving and financial planning; an absent parent before age sixteen; an extroverted and competitive personality; a gambling model in the family; and a narcissistic component that allows one to assume that one's own "specialness" will help one overcome the laws of probability with which mere mortals have to live. In most cases, the habit continues throughout life.

Treatment. In many cases, high levels of anxiety or a specific disorder like manic-depression is the initial treatment focus, and family or couples therapy is often necessary (Wildman 1990). In addition, the following phases of intervention, similar to those used in the treatment of other addictions, are useful here (Walker 1985):

1. Elimination of any immediate opportunity to gamble by means of inpatient hospitalization.
2. Immediate initiation of an educational process about pathological gambling and the insidious role it takes in every individual's life.
3. Individual and group psychotherapy to help the individual explore attitudes and beliefs that have supported his or her gambling behavior over a period of years.
4. Economic counseling for living within a set income.
5. The option of periodic inpatient hospitalization as a preventive measure once every six to eighteen months.
6. Regular attendance at Gambler's Anonymous.

For the overaroused gambler, the anxious and harried type, the following additional treatment procedures appear to be indicated (Wildman 1990; Jacobs 1987):

1. Relaxation training. The use of this procedure is particularly important as a self-control device to combat symptoms of nervousness and related discomforts.

2. Various forms of meditation and stretching techniques for achieving relaxing, and mind-altering states.

3. Regular exercise. Walking, jogging and swimming appear to be particularly helpful in this regard.

4. The short-term use of tranquilizing medications to help the client through a particularly stressful period, such as dealing with the legal and finanacial consequences of previous excessive gambling. Great care has to be exercised here because of the potential for addiction-dependency.

5. Employing the old truism to "take a vacation" should not be dismissed out of hand. Time away does allow a person a temporary escape from impending stressors, which in turn short-circuits a buildup of stress to an unbearable level.

Managing a case involving hypo- or underarousal is more problematic. In general, the strategy is to help the client find some source of stimulation and challenge that does not involve gambling. Some possibilities to consider are:

1. Hobbies or sports that would seem to give the gambler the needed amount of excitement. Gamblers, like alcoholics, tend to be deficient in recreational skills, and the counselor may find referral to the university PE department or a YMCA helpful.

2. A challenging activity like taking a course or undertaking a project such as building a boat.

3. Vocational assessment and guidance should be considered in an effort to help the pathological gambler find a job in which more of his or her needs are met. An assembly-line worker, for example, might find gambling no longer necessary after switching to work as a private investigator.

The Criminal Justice System and the Impulse and Personality Disorders

Several of the personality disorders and many of the impulse disorders result in activities that will come to the attention of the criminal justice system.

The paranoid, antisocial, and sadistic personalities, for example, may engage in aggressive behavior that can result in violence against others. Some of the impulse disorders will directly result in criminal conduct, such as pyromania in arson, the explosive disorder in violence, and kleptomania in theft offenses. Other personality disorders, such as compulsive gambling, may indirectly result in criminal conduct, as where someone engages in embezzlement to obtain money for gambling purposes.

Some defendants with personality or impulse disorders may successfully use the insanity defense, though as noted in chapter 12, this defense is extremely difficult to use successfully. Where there has been very limited violence, the police or prosecutors may be willing to divert offenders with some of these disorders out of the criminal justice system if they are going to receive treatment. The best example is kleptomania. Shoplifters, upon making restitution and seeking therapy, are not infrequently permitted to avoid prosecution.

The insanity defense may be available to those with explosive, apparently uncontrollable outbursts. The explosive disorder is perhaps the best example. The key here is that these offenders cannot control their explosive tendencies. At the same time, jurors may feel that they are too dangerous to be left walking around in public. Juries seldom permit repeatedly dangerous defendants to successfully use the insanity defense. Many states recognize an "irresistible impulse" form of the insanity defense, and it is included in the Model Penal Code's provision of inability to "conform conduct to the requirements of the law." The trend, however, has been away from recognition of this "volitional" arm of the insanity defense.

People with other impulse disorders, such as pyromania, and the more severe forms of paranoid and sadistic personality disorders may in rare cases be subject to the insanity defense. Because such disorders are characterized primarily by antisocial or criminal behavior, some scholars suggest that by definition they should be excluded from the insanity defense. Regardless of the legal technicalities of the issue, the insanity defense is successfully used infrequently in these areas.

Offenders suffering from these disorders present special corrections problems when they are convicted and incarcerated. It may be difficult to control them in the institutions, and their need for treatment is apparent and significant. Without treatment, the possibility of recidivism after release is high. Unfortunately, present systems are often not oriented to providing such treatment in intensive form within prisons.

Notes

Athens, L. 1989. *The Creation of Dangerous Violent Criminals*. London: Routledge.
Blaszczynski, A., S. Winter, and N. McConaghy. 1986. "Plasma Endorphin Levels in Pathological Gambling." *Journal of Gambling Behavior* 2: 3–14.

Boudreau, J., Q. Kwan, W. Faragher, and G. Denault. 1977. *Arson and Arson Investigation*. Washington, D.C.: U.S. Government Printing Office.

Frank, H., and J. Paris. 1991. *Parents' Emotional Neglect and Overprotection According to the Recollections of Patients with BPD. American Journal of Psychiatry* 148:648–65.

Gardner, D., P. Lucas, and R. Cowdry. 1987. "Soft Sign Neurological Abnormalities in Borderline Personality and Normal Control Subjects." *The Journal of Nervous and Mental Disease* 175: 177–80.

Goldstein, A., and H. Keller. 1987. *Aggressive Behavior*. New York: Pergamon.

Gorton, G., and S. Akhtar. 1990. "The Literature on Personality Disorder, 1985–88." *Hospital and Community Psychiatry* 41: 39–51.

Jacobs, D. 1987. "A General Theory of Addictions." In T. Galski, ed. *Handbook of Pathological Gambling*. Springfield, Ill.: Charles Thomas.

Kellam, A. 1969. "Shoplifting Treated by Aversion to a Film." *Behavior Research and Therapy* 7: 125–27.

Kernberg, O. 1984. *Severe Personality Disorders*. New Haven: Yale University Press.

Millon, T. 1981. *Disorders of Personality, DSM-III: Axis II*. New York: John Wiley.

Millon, T., and G. Everly. 1985. *Personality and Its Disorders*. New York: John Wiley.

Montgomery, J., and A. Greif. 1989. *Masochism*. Madison, Conn.: International Universities Press.

Turkat, D. 1990. *The Personality Disorders*. New York: Pergamon.

Walker, G. 1985. "The Brief Therapy of a Compulsive Gambler." *Journal of Family Therapy* 7: 1–8.

Weinberg, M. 1984. "The Sub-culture of Sado-masochism." *Social Problems* 31: 379–89.

Wildman, R. 1990. "Gambling." in L. L'Abate, Ferrar. J., and D. Serritella (Eds.), *Handbook of Differential Treatments for Addictions*. Needham Hghts. MA: Allyn & Bacon.

Zuckerman, M., M. Buchsbaum, and D. Murphy. 1980. "Sensation Seeking and Its Biological Correlates." *Psychological Bulletin* 88: 187–214.

4

The Alcohol- and Drug-Abuse Disorders

> There were few more dangerous positions, he had distilled from experi-
> ence, than to be the best friend of or to be married to a drunk.
> — Martin Cruz Smith
> *Gorky Park*

The Case of the Charles Manson Clan

On August 9, 1969, four followers of Charles Manson invaded the home of Sharon Tate. On the command of Manson, they savagely murdered Tate and four of her friends. The following night they were joined by another young woman in another brutal (but manifestly enjoyable to the perpetrators) murder of Leno LaBianca, the owner of a chain of grocery stores, and his wife. They were later made famous by Vincent Bugliosi's book *Helter Skelter*. Manson certainly had a number of grandiose fantasies along with his substantial psychopathic component, and his followers showed a wide range of psychopathology.

Besides their obvious psychic interdependency, a strong link (and causal factor in the violence) among all of Manson's followers was a pattern of chronic substance abuse. While it is clear that Manson at least occasionally abused drugs and alcohol, it is even clearer that his followers were major abusers. Indeed, prosecutors commented that various followers were useless as witnesses for numerous events in these incidents because they were so "stoned" at the time. Coming at the end of the 1960s, the drug-fueled barbarism of Manson's followers came to symbolize the excess permissiveness regarding drugs that characterized that era.

It is clear that drug abuse in all forms has risen dramatically over the last several decades, though the estimated percentages seem to depend upon what group is doing the estimating (Weisheit 1990). But the news is not all negative. For example, the National Institute of Drug Abuse's continuing National Household Surveys on Drug Abuse report a modest drop in the levels of illicit drug use by high school students over the last several years. Some of this change, however, reflects decreases in the age cohorts most likely to use drugs, so without a true change in social attitudes, renewed increases are probable.

61

Before proceeding further, let us clarify several terms that are common in the substance-abuse literature.

- *Physiological dependence.* This state occurs when a drug that has been used for some time alters the user's body functions in such a way as to necessitate continued use of the drug in order to prevent withdrawal, such as happens with heroin, nicotine, and even caffeine.

- *Habituation.* Dependence on a drug because of a strong desire to replicate the psychological state produced by the drug, and/or from indirect reinforcement of psychological needs, such as oral needs and relief of depression.

- *Tolerance.* The need to ingest increasing amounts of a drug to gain its effect and/or the capacity to absorb large or continuous doses of it without adverse effects.

- *Withdrawal.* The production of a characteristic pattern of physical symptoms upon reduction or cessation of use.

- *True addiction.* The status of being physiologically addicted to a drug that generates *both* tolerance and withdrawal.

- *Synergy.* A compounded effect resulting from using a drug combination. The effect is *antagonistic* if the effects of one or more of the drugs are reduced or canceled out; *addictive* when the effect is a sum of the effects of the separate drugs; or *supra-addictive* when the effect of the combination is greater than a sum of the separate drugs. A good example of supra-addictive synergy is the lethal potential that results when relatively small amounts of alcohol and barbiturates are taken together.

General Causes of Substance Abuse

American culture is addicted to drugs and alcohol for several reasons. First, we are a very free and generally permissive society. Second, we are inundated by advertising that implies that taking a pill or a drink can be a quick solution to any problem (Weisheit 1990). Additionally, we expect some kind of individual response from our physicians, and that quick response is all too often a prescription for pills. Writing a prescription is a clear signal to the patient that his or her time with the doctor is up, and it is financially efficient—and therefore reinforcing—for the physician. Last but not least, drugs often generate their effects rapidly and intensively, so that the reinforcement effect is immediate and strong. And, the more refined the substance, the more powerful and addicting is the effect. While chewing coca leaves causes a mild habituation, cocaine, refined from coca leaves, generates stronger effects, and "crack," a refined cocaine product, causes an even stronger addiction.

Why a potential abuser chooses one substance over another depends on such factors as media exposure, parental modeling, and peer subculture influences. Moreover, specific reinforcement properties in the drugs themselves may lead certain individuals to choose them over others. Alcohol, tranquilizers, and depressants primarily dull anxiety and release inhibitions. Opiates and other narcotics reduce aggression, pain, sexual desire, and negative ruminative fantasy. Amphetamines and other stimulants reduce hunger, fatigue, and depression and increase motor activity. Hallucinogens intensify fantasy activity (Segal 1988).

Intervention in Substance Abuse

Confrontation of a substance-abuse pattern is often required of the "consumers" in the criminal justice and judicial situation, as well as of staff. Intervention programs in prisons have had only modest success at best (Rouse, 1991), but at least they are relatively inexpensive to operate. Steps common to most intervention situations with substance abuse are (1) breaking through the denial, often massive denial, that there is a problem; (2) bolstering the person's often-wavering motivation; and (3) avoiding manipulations and rationalizations (Milkman and Sederer 1990; L'Abate 1992). Such confrontation is critical with any substance-abuse pattern. Several guildelines make such a confrontation more likely to succeed.

1. The facts relevant to the abuse behavior that are presented should be very specific, with descriptions of concrete events or conditions.

2. These facts should be presented in detail.

3. These facts should be directly related to abuse behaviors, and any inferences should be clearly tied to these facts.

4. Arguments over facts or inferences should be avoided. But it should be made clear that denials or excuses (such as "I'm not an alcoholic because ———;" fill in the blank with almost any statement—they have all been tried) are not accepted.

5. The facts should be presented by persons who are meaningful to the abuser.

6. The confrontation should be made in a firm and clear style, but with love and support. A judgmental tone should be avoided.

7. The goal that intervention is directed toward helping the abuser first accept the reality of his or her pattern to obtain an open acknowledgment that help in changing is needed, should be maintained.

8. Once such an acknowledgment is made, available intervention options are presented, and a commitment is made to some menu of treatment options.

Alcohol Abuse

The good news is that as of 1990, alcohol consumption was at its lowest level in two decades. But alcohol is, still used more widely than any other drug. In 1990, per capita consumption was about 2.5 gallons of pure alcohol, the lowest level since 1970. The steady decline in drinking since 1981 may be the result of increased public awareness about the risks of alcohol use, as well as the aging of the population. Consumption is typically lower among people over age sixty.

The bad news is that today more than 100 million Americans drink alcohol at least occasionally; that the deaths of more than 100,000 Americans per year are directly attributable to alcohol use and abuse; that alcohol costs American society (in health care, police, lost productivity, and other factors) more than $12 billion yearly; and that one in eight people is on the way to having a significant alcohol problem—that is, *alcoholism*. Chronic alcoholics live almost twenty years fewer than average. Long-term alcohol abuse is likely to result in central nervous system dysfunction, or in organicity, especially in older alcoholics. Alcohol is a factor in almost half of all suicides, homicides, and other violent crimes. Alcohol-related accidents are a leading cause of death among fifteen-to-twenty-five-year-olds, taking almost ten thousand lives in that age range yearly. Drivers with severe drinking problems are responsible for at least half of all traffic fatalities.

Additionally, consider that there are between 25 and 30 million people in the United States who are children of alcoholics, more than six million of them under the age of eighteen. Children of alcoholics are at four times greater risk of eventually become alcoholics than are children of nonalcoholics. Almost 100,000 children between ten and eleven years of age reported getting drunk at least once a week in a 1985 survey; and the strongest predictors of alcohol use and abuse in adulthood is its use and abuse in high school, and having an alcoholic role model.

Alcohol is not digested. It is absorbed through the stomach and intestinal walls, then broken down by oxidation, primarily in the liver. In oxidation, alcohol is converted into acetaldehyde, then to acetic acid (vinegar), and finally to carbon dioxide and water, which are passed out of the body. The liver can break down only about one ounce of 100-proof whiskey or its equivalent per hour, so any excess remains in the bloodstream and affects the brain, causing intoxication.

Pharmacologically, alcohol acts as a depressant that first inhibits the higher brain centers, then later depresses the lower brain centers. As a result, there is a loss of inhibition in overt behavior since the normal censoring faculties of the higher brain centers are inhibited. This has led to the mistaken belief that alcohol is a stimulant. Continued alcohol intake leads to a loss of the more complex cognitive and perceptual abilities and eventually to a loss of simple memory and motor coordination.

Most states in the United States define *intoxication* as a blood alcohol level of 0.10 percent. Blood alcohol levels and behavior are correlated as follows:

- At less than 0.03 percent, the individual is dull and dignified.
- At 0.05 percent, he is dashing and debonair.
- At 0.01 percent, he becomes dangerous and devilish.
- At 0.20 percent, he is dizzy, disturbed, and very dangerous.
- At 0.25 percent, he is disgusting and disheveled.

0.10 [handwritten annotation in margin next to third bullet]

It is interesting that the strength of the effect partly depends on whether people are getting drunk or sobering up. Those who are sobering up perform better on short-term memory and perception tasks than do those who have the same blood level of alcohol but who are getting high. Researchers such as Alan Marlatt and his colleagues (1988) have found that the *belief* that one has ingested alcohol is often more critical than whether one has actually done so or not. Both aggression and sexual behavior are highly dependent on the belief system of the individuals who use alcohol. Believing that alcohol has been consumed causes a loss of inhibitions, and many times the alcohol is a learned excuse for acting-out behavior in these areas (Blane and Leonard 1987).

Gender Differences and Alcohol

It has long been speculated that women may have a differential response to alcohol than men. A landmark study by Frezza and colleagues (1990) supports this. The study found that women typically get drunk more quickly than men, even when their smaller size is taken into account, and they are more likely to suffer liver damage from alcohol abuse.

These researchers found that men make far higher amounts of a protective stomach enzyme that breaks down alcohol before it hits the bloodstream. The result is that men don't get as tipsy as women on the same number of drinks. Thus, women should be more careful than men relative to a given amount of alcohol.

Among the Frezza study's other findings:

- Women absorb almost one-third more alcohol into their blood than men do, even when they are the same size and drink the same amount.
- The protective enzyme, called alcohol dehydrogenase, works better when people have a full stomach.
- Alcoholics make less of the protective enzyme than social drinkers do.

The study found that nonalcoholic women make about 30 percent less of the enzyme than nonalcoholic men do. While alcoholic men produce less of the enzyme than social drinkers, the difference was most dramatic in alcoholic women, who make virtually none of the enzyme.

It is worth noting that female alcoholics usually have a better response to treatment than do male alcoholics (Anderson 1992).

Stages of Dependence on Alcohol

Dependence on alcohol typically develops in stages (Blane and Leonard 1987). The development of the behaviors and symptoms listed in sequence below is not necessarily inevitable. For example, many so-called social drinkers never move into the second stage and become alcoholics. Nonetheless, this progression is fairly common.

1. *Prealcoholism.* Social drinking and an occasional weekend drink are the major symptoms. Both tolerance and frequency of drinking increase, usually slowly. Alcohol use serves primarily as an escape from anxiety, mild depression, and boredom.

2. *Initial alcoholism.* Tolerance, frequency, solitary use, and abuse increase. More is drunk per swallow; often there is a shift to more potent drinks. Depression increases, along with loss of self-esteem over drinking patterns. Occasional blackouts occur.

3. *Chronic stage.* True loss-of-control patterns (such as drinking throughout the day and using any source of alcohol) predominate. Inadequate nutrition affects functioning and physical health. Signs of impaired thinking, hallucinations, paranoid thoughts, and tremors emerge.

Genetic Issues and Responsibility

Alcoholics' irresponsible behavior while they are "under the influence" often lands them in court. Some experts argue that alcoholics should not be held responsible for either their alcoholism or for any criminal offenses that ensue from their alcoholic problems; there are clear individual differences, moreover, in how people respond to drink of alcohol. And there is evidence that some individuals will drive "drunkenly" when they have received a placebo they thought was alcohol. But most experts do agree that there is significant evidence that a predisposition to alcoholism can be inherited (Finn et al. 1990; Milkman and Sederer 1990). Indeed, there is evidence that like people, certain genetic strains of rats prefer alcohol virtually undiluted, some prefer it diluted, some prefer either to water, and some totally avoid alcohol. Some people can ingest a drink or two without noticeable effect but quickly "feel drunk" if they take in more, while others can take in huge amounts and appear relatively normal. Unfortunately, in this latter group motor and perceptual processes are markedly disrupted, and since they may perceive themselves as "normal," they can put themselves and others at great risk, such as by driving. Nevertheless, any evidence related to such individual differences may be critical to testimony in a particular case.

There are marked individual differences to alcohol use among people within any cultural group, based on genetic factors. It is not surprising, for example, that there are differences across cultural and racial groups. Psychological expectancies can influence such differences, but there are still primary differences in how the alcohol is metabolized. For example, a high proportion of people of Oriental extraction show sensitivity reactions (such as flushing) to small amounts of alcohol. This innate aversive response may act as a block to developing alcoholism. Only three to six percent of Caucasians show this response. It is clear that genetic differences do affect an individual's response to alcohol. Such racial differences may be the basis for differential legal strategies at trial, as well as for differential treatment plans proposed to courts.

Treatment Approaches

In recent years, the primary treatment mode for alcoholism has been Alcoholics Anonymous (AA), which was founded in 1935 by two recovered alcoholics, Bill Wilson and a man known only as Dr. B.

Four elements of AA seem particularly useful in helping people overcome alcoholism. First, the requirement that they clearly and publicly self-label themselves as alcoholic by admitting to themselves and to others that they need help; second, the quasi–group therapy structure of AA meetings; third, the availability of consistent rituals to respond to crises in their lives; and fourth, the chance for a broad new spectrum social contact and network with nondrinkers (Blane and Leonard 1987). AA's self-collected data claims high rates of success; although these are flawed methodologically, AA is especially helpful for persons who have trouble with impulse drinking, who need a new social network, and who are able to work within the somewhat fundamentalistic and rigid demands of the AA belief system (Marlatt et al. 1988).

For the problems shared by most alcoholics who come into contact with the judicial and criminal justice systems, several techniques may be employed in various combinations, depending on the individual client (Peele 1984; L'Abate 1992; Milkman and Sederer 1990).

1. *Detoxification.* Many alcoholics who have been chronically imbibing need an initial period of detoxification to "dry out." This period of hospitalization or other controlled living situations also keeps them from giving in to compelling habits that would return them to drinking.

2. *Antabuse.* Antabuse can be helpful in controlling the immediate impulse to drink, although the effects of the Antabuse can be bypassed in short order by simply not taking it (Barrett 1986). Antabuse is of help to alcoholics who want to change, but it is generally accepted that the drug is of little use as the sole or predominant intervention technique.

3. *Aversion therapy.* Aversion therapy can be helpful in controlling specific problem behaviors unique to the client.

4. *Alcoholics Anonymous.* Involvement with AA or a similar group provides the advantages noted eariler, especially the opportunity for consistent associations with nondrinkers (Barrett 1986).

5. *Family and/or marital therapy.* Because alcoholism is extremely disruptive to family life, family and/or marital therapy to repair the damaged relationships is necessary, as well as in helping to maintain abstinence.

6. *Psychotherapy.* Alcoholics commonly experience conflicts, anxiety, and self-esteem problems. For these problems, a variety of psychotherapy techniques (such as rational-emotive therapy or traditional insight therapy) can be of help.

Treatment Follow-up. The treatment of alcoholism has made progress. Still, only a few of all alcoholics in treatment remain abstinent for as long as a year. Most resume drinking and are rehospitalized. Gorski and Miller (1986) and Barrett (1986), agreeing that the one-year period following a client's entering treatment is critical, focus much of their effort on this period. Virtually all experts advise support groups such as AA during the first year of abstinence. Gorski and Miller systematically teach clients about the "relapse process" and emphasize that resumption of drinking does not occur suddenly. This counters the myth that alcoholics are "suddenly taken by drink."

Barrett argues that it is necessary to "use a chemical to fight a chemical." Since the therapist's task is to have the client abstinent long enough for biological functions to return to normal, clients are required to come to the hospital for disulfiram (Antabuse) daily for one year. Unfortunately, alcoholics act above all else to protect their opportunity to drink alcohol again if they choose to do so. Alcoholics assume that they will *need* alcohol at some future time. In response to this, Barrett has devised a number of strategies to influence alcoholics to comply with the disulfiram-based program, such as having employees contract with employers that the latter are to be notified if the client-employee does not show up daily for medication and therapy. Most of these who do make it past the one-year mark are well on their way to recovery.

Implanted time-release drugs whose action is similar to Antabase to help maintain abstinence from alcohol is a recently developed option, although there are potential legal liabilities, since it is possible for the client to fatally overdose with alcohol and the drug.

Predictors of Treatment Success. Several factors increase the probability of success in treating alcoholics. Older alcoholics and alcoholics who have a reasonably stable marriage have much higher success rates. Being female and/or being Caucasian increases the probability of success, the latter probably because members of ethnic minorities are more likely to drop out of therapy (Anderson 1992). Not surprisingly, persons higher in motivation, self-respect, and self-esteem do better.

Prevention

The difficulty of successfully treating alcoholism once the pattern has been established suggests the immense value of prevention. The following steps are recommended in any prevention effort:

1. Recognize that alcohol abuse patterns start to consolidate in the eleven-to-fifteen-year age range, much earlier than most people imagine. Recognize that genetic and modeling factors are both important.
2. If children are to be allowed to drink alcohol at all in later life, introduce it to them relatively early and in moderation.
3. Associate the use of alcohol with food and initially allow its use only on special occasions; de-emphasize its value in controlling feeling states.
4. Provide a consistent model of low-to-moderate drinking; use beverages such as beer and wine that have a low alcohol content, rather than hard liquor.
5. Make sure there is a thorough understanding of and agreement on the family rules for what is and is not allowed about drinking.
6. Never associate drinking behavior with evidence of attainment of adulthood or other identity accomplishments.
7. Label excess drinking behaviors as stupid and in bad taste rather than as stylish or "cool."
8. Label help-seeking behaviors in people who have an alcohol problem as evidence of strength rather than weakness.
9. Encourage alcoholism education programs in the community and public health measures, such as a restriction on the use of alcohol in certain settings and age groups.

Polydrug Abuse

Mr. P.

When Mr. P. died August 1977, it was at first assumed to have been the result of a simple heart attack; he had been quite overweight and lived a frenetic lifestyle. But an autopsy confirmed that he had a pattern of long-term polydrug abuse, which had no doubt contributed significantly to the heart attack that was the final cause of death. Most of the drugs had been obtained by prescription. Mr. P.'s blood and tissues were found to contain toxic levels of the sedative methaqualone (Quaaludes), ten times more codeine than would be needed for any therapeutic purpose, and residual amounts of at least ten other drugs, including Valium, barbiturates, and various stimulants and opiates.

Mr. P.—Elvis Presley—exemplifies a pattern that is increasingly evident in our society, polydrug abuse. It typically involves alcohol abuse, combined with one—or usually, several—of the various prescription or nonprescription drugs.

Characteristics

Polysubstance abusers could be described as psychotics who have not lost reality contact. That is, they show deterioration of behavior in a wide variety of arenas, such as work, school performance, interpersonal relationships, and motivation, especially if they have been abusing for a substantial length of time. Their affect is generally flat, or when emotion is manifest, it is quite labile. Like the alcoholic, polysubstance abusers make many protestations of future positive change, and like the alcoholic's their promises are seldom fulfilled. This does not appear to be a manipulative deception, as polysubstance abusers seem intellectually committed to changing, yet the motivation and behaviors necessary to actuate that change cannot be generated.

Prescription Drug Abuse

Our culture has a long history of intensive use of legally available drugs, many of which are available only by prescription. Before 1914, a significant proportion of the U.S. population was pharmacologically and psychologically dependent on legally obtainable patent medicines (often marketed in combination with alcohol) whose other main ingredients were opium compounds, morphine (a derivative of opium), heroin (a semisynthetic opiate), or barbiturates. The Harrison Drug Act of 1914 made the great majority of these compounds illegal and unavailable, except by prescription. The 1970 Controlled Substances Act updated all previously existing federal drug laws and categorized all dangerous drugs into one of the five schedules that are still used today. These schedules rate drugs from the most dangerous (Schedule I) to the least dangerous (Schedule V) (see table 13–1).

Factors in Prescription Drug Abuse

Several factors have contributed to prescription drug abuse in the United States. We have some cultural traditions that suggest that any pain should be avoided, and they allow large-scale use of drugs. Drugs are intensively promoted to physicians by drug companies. Many mood-altering drugs are available only by prescription; and there is strong cultural acceptance of the idea most disorders can be remedied by a quick cure, such as a pill. Another factor intensifying prescription drug abuse is the shift in physicians' behavior from a personal approach to a production-line approach, accompanied by use of the prescription as cure, placebo, pacifier, and end-of-session cue.

The Minor Tranquilizers

The benzodiazepines, like diazepam (Valium), are still among the most commonly prescribed classes of drugs in the United States today. They cause muscle relaxation and reduce anxiety. Typical side effects are skin rash, nausea, and impairment of sexual functioning. Meprobamate, developed in 1954, is functionally similar to the benzodiazepines, but it differs chemically and usually produces a more severe withdrawal after prolonged use. The traditional assumption has been that many of the minor tranquilizers have little addiction potential, but it is now clear that they can be addictive, and all of them easily generate psychological dependence (Segal 1988). Physicians who do not specialize in psychological problems—that is, who are not psychiatrists—may underestimate this potential. Unfortunately, these physicians issue the great majority of prescriptions for mood-altering drugs.

Barbiturates

Barbiturates are another class of drugs that have consistently been abused. Though traditionally thought of as tranquilizers, barbiturates actually function as sedatives or hypnotics. The first commercially marketed barbiturate, Verinol, was first discovered in 1894 and was introduced in 1903. Since then, barbiturates have been commonly used to induce sleep and to calm very agitated (not hyperactive) children.

Like the minor tranquilizers, barbiturates quickly produce dependency (Segal 1988). They also produce a withdrawal syndrome similar to that of alcohol, but often more intense. They are commonly implicated in drug overdose; a lethal dose is usually only ten times the dose to which the user has developed tolerance. Physicians have become more aware of the dangers of barbiturates, and drug companies are promoting other (newer and more expensive) compounds. Consequently, the legal use of barbiturates has declined in the last ten years.

Amphetamines

Another commonly used group of prescribed medications is the amphetamines. Though first synthesized in 1887, amphetamines did not come into wide use until Benzedrine inhalers for nasal congestion were marketed in 1931. During World War II, amphetamines were used to combat fatigue in American servicemen, and the Japanese used them to help kamikaze pilots complete their suicide missions.

Amphetamines and the methamphetamines—more potent versions of amphetamines—produce euphoria in some people, irritability and anxiety in others. Because tolerance to and psychological dependence on amphetamines increase rather rapidly, persons abusing them quickly increase their intake. Continuation of this pattern may lead to a binge, followed by a crash, when fatigue catches up and the person needs to sleep for the better part of several days. Continuation of this "speeding" causes paranoid and psychotic symptoms that may continue for some time after the drug is discontinued.

Anabolic Steroids

The anabolic steroids are androgenic hormones that include, or are derivatives of, the male sex hormone testosterone (Segal 1988). Both the federal Anti-Drug Abuse Act of 1988 and recent legislation in numerous states establish criminal penalties for the distribution or possession of anabolic-androgenic steroids, except for legitimate treatment of disease. Because of the addition of section 303(e), "Prohibited Distribution of Anabolic Steroids," distribution is now linked to the seizure and forfeiture penalties of the Comprehensive Drug Abuse Prevention and Control Act of 1970. The new legislation makes it unlikely that a physician can defend prescribing anabolic-androgenic steroids to enhance performance of a healthy athlete. Ironically, data on use by athletes are inconclusive and do not clarify whether these drugs substantially enhance athletic performance. Yet stringent control of steroid abuse is hampered by the conviction in the sports world that these drugs markedly enhance performance.

High serum levels of anabolic steroids can produce euphoria, increased libido, and a sense of well-being. Steroid-induced grandiose ideas may explain claims of increased strength, less fatigue during workouts, faster healing, and better overall health. Intoxication may be accompanied by severe mood swings, including excitement with paranoid delusions. The psychoactive effects, withdrawal symptoms, and underlying biological mechanisms of steroid hormone dependence are similar to those of alcohol, cocaine, and opioid abuse. Other symptoms of intoxication include overly aggressive and violent behavior; loss of inhibitions; increased irritability; and impulsivity with impaired judgment; psychomotor agitation; insomnia; anxiety; panic;

and paranoid delusions. Intoxication can lead to compulsive and uncontrollable use. Abusers may continue use despite severe deterioration in personal life, the committing of criminal acts, or the occurrence of psychiatric disturbances that they believe are induced by the drugs.

Erythropoietin (EPO)

Enhancing performance by "blood doping" was often practiced by endurance athletes (Weisheit 1990). They stored their own frozen blood for months before a competition, then injected it back into their veins the day before their event, providing a huge concentration of new red blood cells to carry oxygen. Blood doping was so common before it was banned by the International Olympic Committee and other groups that as many as half the American cyclists on the 1984 Olympic team admitted doing it.

Synthetically produced erythropoietin (EPO) presents a new potential for abuse, as it produces effects similar to blood doping. EPO is usually produced in minute amounts within the human kidney. It stimulates the bone marrow to produce oxygen-carrying red blood cells. Now, however, EPO can be produced in the laboratory by bacteria implanted with the human gene that direct cells to make the substance.

The ability to ferry oxygen around the body is especially important for endurance athletes. That's the job of hemoglobin molecules found in red blood cells. The more of them athletes have to carry oxygen, the more aerobic power athletes have at their disposal.

It is unclear what side-effects occur at high doses, though several experts suggest that the blood, now thickened with red blood cells, could generate strokes or heart attacks. In fact, EOP is suspected in the deaths of seven bicycle racers from the Netherlands during the 1988–90 period. Because it is a natural hormone manufactured by the body, EOP poses a difficult challenge to detection.

Nonprescription Drug Abuse

Fewer nonprescription drugs than prescriptions drugs are subject to abuse, but the degree and intensity of abuse is typicaly greater for nonprescription drugs. Table 4–1 shows the physical signs of many nonprescription drugs.

Cocaine

Cocaine has risen markedly in popularity in recent years and is now second only to marijuana in popularity (Lyman 1989). Its abuse by many sports and entertainment idols has received much media attention. Nevertheless, cocaine has been used for centuries. It is an alkaloid derivative of coca leaves,

Table 4–1
Physical Effects of the Commonly Abused Nonprescription Drugs

Drug	Physical Effects
Marijuana	Red eyes Dry mouth Delayed reactions to questions
Cocaine[a]	Moving faster than normal Runny nose Red or watery eyes White powder molecules in nose hairs Dilated pupils Irritable
PCP[b]	Illogical or slurred speech Difficulty standing up Unruliness and aggression Paranoid reactions
Heroin	Delayed reactions to questions Slow walking ("floating") Slow speech Sweating or scratching Dry mouth Nodding Caked white powder around corners of mouth Constricted pupils (pinhole)
LSD	Overstimulated perceptions of reality Objects appear brighter to the user Overexaggerated reactions to ordinary objects Unusual descriptions of the ordinary Users may be sad and depressed over something minor in nature Bad trips—users feel their body is actually changing or they are dying.

Source: Adapted from M. Lyman, *Practical Drug Enforcement*. New York: Elsevier, 1989.

[a] When attempting to identify the cocaine user, look for horizontal nystagmus (bouncing eyes); if you move a pen slowly toward the suspect, the eyes will bounce back to look straight ahead (this differs from alcohol use, where the eyes will most likely cross).

[b] The user can be identified by horizontal nystagmus (the eyes will bounce back and forth). Vertical nystagmus may also occur, which is not common with those under the influence of alcohol. Persons dealing with them should be prepared for physical confrontations. Remember that PCP is an anesthetic, which minimizes pain in the user.

which were chewed by the Aztecs and are still used by at least four million Indians in South American countries such as Peru and Bolivia. Such diverse personages as Arthur Conan Doyle's character Sherlock Holmes, John Phillip Sousa, and even Sigmund Freud have sung the praises of cocaine.

Cocaine first attained importance in 1860 when Gaedecke and Niemian discovered its effectiveness in alleviating pain. Cocaine is a stimulant, and in most people it provides a sense of euphoria (Washton 1987). In the late 1800s, John Pemberton, an Atlanta druggist, combined cocaine, sugar, and kola nut extract to produce Coca-Cola, so the shortened trademark Coke is not inaccurate, and indeed it was at one time "the real thing." When the Pure Food and Drug Law of 1906 outlawed the use of cocaine, caffeine was substituted as "the real thing."

Most of what passes for cocaine is not pure ("free base") cocaine but cocaine hydrochloride, a salt that is approximately 85 percent cocaine by weight. Pure cocaine is sometimes smoked, a far more dangerous psycho-physiological process than sniffing.

Crack cocaine, which is usually anywhere from 60 percent to 90 percent pure, is highly addictive and is much cheaper to use. It is typically produced by the following fragile process: cocaine hydrochloride is mixed with an equal part of ammonia or baking soda; this mixture is dissolved in water, then heated, then cooled, then allowed to dry; and the result, crack, is cut into small "rocks."

In an acute reaction to cocaine, the standard stabilization sequence may require the use of (1) oxygen to stabilize respiration; (2) Inderal for any cardiac arrhythmias; (3) a barbiturate to reduce central nervous stimulation or (4) benzodiazepines to control convulsive reactions (Washton 1987). This response must be short-term and very carefully monitored in order to avoid secondary abuse patterns. Putting it in perspective, comedian Richard Pryor comments, "Cocaine is God's way of telling you that you make too much money." He might have added, "Crack is God's way of telling you that you don't make enough."

It is agreed that the "crack" or "rock" form of cocaine is highly addicting. Indeed, cocaine in any form is highly habituating in that it creates a tenacious dependence, marked by compulsive use, loss of control over its use, and continued use despite its destructive consequences. When persons withdraw from cocaine, levels of dopamine in the brain plummet, causing an intense craving for more cocaine.

The powerful draw of cocaine was noted in a study by Bozarth and Wise (1985). They implanted tubes in the necks of twenty-three rats so that each rat could press a lever in its cage to self-administer a set dose of either heroin or cocaine into its bloodstream. The rats were divided into two groups, one for each drug. After thirty days, eleven of the twelve cocaine-using rats were dead, compared with only four of the eleven heroin-using rats. In humans, long-term use can result in numerous debilitating physical side effects, including cardiac problems and even death (Washton 1987). When cocaine is mixed with alcohol, a new substance called cocaethylene forms in the liver, which amplifies the effects the cocaine and increases the risk of heart attack by almost twenty times.

Marijuana and Derivatives

The Chinese emperor Shen Nung wrote the first pharmacological text, called *Psen Tsao,* or *The Great Herbalist,* in 2737 B.C. In it, he described an extract of hemp as the "delight giver." The plant it was extracted from, Cannabis sativa, is more commonly known as marijuana and has been an important part of American culture since the 1960s. Three types are grown domestically: Indian hemp, which grows wild in many areas; sinsemilla, which has the highest potency but is the most difficult to grow, as male plants have to be culled out or they will change the more productive female plants to male plants; and commercial strains.

Marijuana is usually smoked, during which only 50 percent of the active component, delta-9-tetrahydrocannabinol (THC), is inhaled (Gold 1989). in high dosages, THC mimics the hallucinogenic properties of LSD. Hashish, a concentrated derivative of marijuana, is produced by compacting the crude resin of the cannabis plant into a brick. The dried "flower tops" of the female plant are most desired because of their high concentration of THC. Marijuana deteriorates rapidly in potency and must be refrigerated to retard this process. Recently there has been a steep rise in the potency of the marijuana available to the American public.

Marijuana derivatives in the blood are metabolized in the liver in much the same way as alcohol. There is a specific receptor site in brain cells that immediately responds to the active ingredient in marijuana. The main physiological effects are lowered blood pressure, reddened flesh around the eye, and dry mouth. Standard dosages produce minor change in brain physiology, and there is less impairment of muscle control than is experienced with alcohol in comparable dosages. The psychological effects in experienced users are sleepiness and mild euphoria, usually lasting one to three hours, and an increase in suggestibility (Gold 1989).

Opiates

According to archaeologists and historians, the first users of the opium poppy were primitive Neolithic farmers in the mountainous areas of western Asia Minor. Clay tablets from the Sumerian civilization, more than six thousand years old, refer to opium as the "plant of joy." The Roman physician Galen prescribed it for epilepsy, snake bite, melancholia, and virtually any other disorder he could think of. The opiates mimic the body's natural reaction to pain. When severe physical trauma occurs, cells in the hypothalamus and pituitary gland release peptide hormones called endorphins, which attach themselves to the surfaces of the cells responsible for the pain and, like opium, suppress the perception of pain (Gold 1989).

Three events spurred the use of opiates in western European culture. The first was the isolation of morphine early in the nineteenth century, followed about fifty years later by Alexander Wood's perfection of a more efficient method of administering drugs—the hypodermic needle. The third event, in 1847, was Wright's discovery of heroin. Heroin was once widely used to cure morphone addiction, just as another addicting drug, methadone, is now used to treat heroin addiction.

Morphine, a derivative of opium, was discovered in 1802 and was named after Morpheus, the god of dreams. Ten times stronger than opium, it quickly became popular as a pain-killer and was included in many patent medicines. Heroin, a semisynthetic opiate, is also a narcotic. It induces a warm, almost sensual euphoria, usually followed by lethargy and sleepiness. The user rapidly develops tolerance and needs increasingly higher doses. Some seven to twelve hours after the injection, however, minor withdrawal symptoms begin. Once addicted, a person must keep a minimal level in the system, or withdrawal symptoms will quickly ensue. Cessation after prolonged or heavy use often results in opioid withdrawal, which is diagnosed according to the DSM when at least three of the following are experienced: nausea, muscle aches, craving for an opioid, lacrimation or rhinorhea, pupillary dilation or sweating, diarrhea, yawning, fever, and insomnia. The severity of these symptoms increase in proportion to the amount of heroin used, but they are rarely as severe as the mad ravings portrayed in the media. Most addicts describe withdrawal as similar to severe flu symptoms. The pain of withdrawal can be lessened by prescribing such drugs as acetorphan or clonidine.

Heroin abuse appeared to decline in the 1970s, but two factors have caused a resurgence: the increasing use of heroin by people of middle and upper socioeconomic status, and the greater availability of extraordinarily pure heroin (which can be smoked—a more acceptable process to middle- and upper-class users than injection). Also, the prescription drugs Demerol (a synthetic narcotic) and Dilaudid (a synthetic form of morphine) are popular among illicit drug users.

As for the psychological reinforcement provided by opiates, perhaps the French humanist and poet Jean Cocteau expressed it most graphically: "Everything we do in life, including love, is done in an express train traveling towards death. To smoke opium is to leave the train while in motion; it is to be interested in something other than life and death" (quoted in Jarvik 1967, p. 52).

Methadone. Methadone, also an addicting drug, appears to be effective in treating certain cases of heroin addiction, though attending personnel must be aware of possible secondary abuse of the drug, particularly in addicts who are psychopathic. Methadone can be useful at least in the initial stages of treatment (Milkman and Sederer 1990). Since it does not cause the distinct euphoria of heroin, it can be taken orally and less often than heroin, though usually once a day; also, its lower cost may allow the addict to move out of the criminal system.

Three criticisms of methadone are fully justified. Its chronic use does produce substantial negative side effects; it is often traded on the black market to other addicts; and methadone treatments are simply substitutions of one addiction for another. Nevertheless, methadone does help wean a significant proportion of addicts off drugs altogether, and few treatments now used for drug addiction can make a substantially better claim.

Hallucinogens

LSD (lysergic acid diethylamide), mescaline, and psilocybin are popular hallucinogens; that is, they cause hallucinations and delusions of varying intensity. Mescaline, the active alkaloid of the peyote cactus, has long been used by southwestern and Mexican Indians in ceremonial rites. Psilocybin comes in a crystalline powder and is isolated from various mushrooms that grow in the United States. LSD was synthesized by two Swiss chemists in 1938, and one of the discoverers, Albert Hoffman, experienced hallucinations when he ingested it five years later. It was first used in the United States in the early 1950s and was soon popularized by cultural "gurus" such as ex-Harvard psychologist Timothy Leary. As Leary wrote in his 1983 autobiography, *Flashbacks,* I was conceived on a military reservation, West Point, New York, on the night of January 17, 1920. On the preceding day alcohol had become an illegal drug.

Many people taking these and other drugs have had "bad trips" and later, when they are no longer on the drug, "flashbacks." The bad trips are not surprising, given the odd assortment of ingredients found in purportedly pure street drugs and the marginal adjustment of many individuals when taking the drug. Although flashbacks are usually attributed to the drug itself, they are more accurately conceptualized and effectively treated as severe anxiety responses (see chapter 7). The anxiety comes from the loss of control experienced under the drug and is then cognitively conditioned to thoughts and external cues that surrounded that initial frightening drug experience.

Phencyclidine (PCP)

A psychotomimetic drug that is a hallucinogen and that also has some stimulant qualities similar to the amphetamines is phencyclidine hydrochloride, known by the street names PCP and "angel dust." PCP was first compounded and used legally as an animal tranquilizer and then, in the 1950s, as a surgical anesthetic for humans. It produced such bizarre side effects (violent and unpredictable hallucinations) that its prescribed use with humans was stopped immediately. Rather than the visual hallucinations common to LSD or the paranoid and schizophrenic symptoms common to amphetamine abuse, PCP often produces violence, commonly accompanied by either a psychotic manic pattern or psychotic behavior that resembles standard schizophrenic symptoms. Unfortunately, it is easily compounded in large quantities in relatively unsophisticated laboratories.

Various other herbs and weeds can also cause hallucinations, but many of these, such as juniper berries (a major ingredient in gin), are quite toxic. Even high dosages of nutmeg can cause hallucinations, but it is also toxic.

For centuries the common weed Datura stramonium, also known as jimsonweed or thorn apple, has been chewed for its hallucinogenic properties. In the 1970s, Don Juan (the Mexican Indian guru of writer Carlos Castaneda, not the lover) made the drug famous. Adolescents occasionally chew the seeds of the plant, a practice that is sometimes fatal.

Inhalants

Inhalants are often abused by adolescents because of their wide availability and because few adolescents are aware of the dangerous effects. The abused inhalants include anesthetics such as nitrous oxide (laughing gas), chloroform, and ether; aerosol propellants (which are less commonly available now); and volatile solvents such a glue, gasoline, and paint remover. The ready accessibility of glue and paint remover makes them particularly likely to be abused. The "high" produced by inhalants is of short duration, and chronic use carries a real risk of organic brain dysfunction.

Nicotine

The Case of Dr. S. As a result of a severe flu attack at age thirty-eight, Dr. S. experienced an irregular heartbeat. His personal physician and colleague, Dr. F., told him that his habit of smoking cigars had caused it and advised him to stop smoking. When Dr. S. tried to do so, he became depressed and occasionally suffered an even worse pulse rate. After several attempts at stopping, he returned to smoking about twenty cigars a day and developed cancer of the jaw at age sixty-seven. Despite thirty-three operations and the removal of his entire jaw because of cancerous and precancerous conditions, Dr. S. continued to smoke. At age seventy-three he developed angina pectoris (chest pains from heart disease), which was relieved whenever he stopped smoking. Yet although he continued to try to stop smoking, he could not. He died from cancer at age eighty-three after many years of severe suffering from operations, cancer, and heart disorder (Rodale 1979). Dr. S.'s case is a powerful example of the psychological and physical habituating power of nicotine, especially considering who Dr. S. is: Sigmund Freud.

As his case demonstrates, nicotine is powerfully habituating, and those who do quit are extremely prone to relapse. Statistically, two-pack-a-day smokers can expect to live about six years fewer than others, and males who smoke at this level throughout their lives will die more than fifteen years earlier than men who never start. Smokers in general are about 50 percent more likely than nonsmokers to require health care each year, and the smoke they disperse is harmful to those around them.

Nicotine, the principal active component of tobacco leaves, acts as a stimulant on persons who use it rarely. In chronic users, it functions as either a stimulant or a depressant, depending on the physiological state of the user. It is thus doubly powerful in its reinforcement effect. It raises the heart rate and increases the blood pressure by simultaneously inducing greater cardiac activity and constricting peripheral arteries. It reduces the appetite, especially for carbohydrates, such as sugar and simple starches, a fact that must be considered if gaining weight upon stopping smoking is to be avoided. Nicotine is also an effective pesticide (Segal 1988).

Six major factors are usually considered to be crucial in initiating and maintaining tobacco addiction: (1) peer pressure, especially for early adolescents; (2) physiological addiction; (3) habit and ritual; (4) the paradoxical tranquilizing effect of nicotine on the chronic smoker (pharmacologically, it is a stimulant); (5) modeling and ease of access to tobacco, promoted by significant peers, authority figures, and media idols; and (6) fulfillment of personality needs (such as oral eroticism).

Numerous methods have been examined to help individuals control their smoking (Milkman and Sederer 1990). In the seventeenth century, the Turkish sultan Murad IV tortured and executed those addicted in tobacco. A 1683 Chinese law authorized beheading simply for possessing tobacco. Neither effort was markedly successful, similar to most stop-smoking treatment programs today. Most of these programs have had some limited success, but none has shown complete success. In many cases, individuals are able to control their smoking significantly during the treatment phase, only to gradually relapse afterward. The relapse rate is very high. Quitting all at once is the best strategy for most smokers. Continued success requires that the significant persons around the smoker be supportive of a change to nonsmoking.

Legal Issues and Substance Abuse

> If you drink very much from a bottle marked "poison" it is almost certain to disagree with you sooner or later.
> — Lewis Carroll
> *Alice in Wonderland*

Drugs, especially alcohol, have been a central issue in innumerable cases in both the civil and criminal law. Two cases—*Robinson v. California* (1962) and *Powell v. Texas* (1968)—are critical to the development of legal thinking concerning alcoholism and drug addiction. The landmark *Robinson v. California* case concerned a heroin addict who had been convicted of violating a federal statute following a jury trial in the Municipal Court of Los Angeles. Two police officers testified to having examined his arms one evening and at that time noting scar tissue and needle marks. They also testified that he had admitted to using heroin. The judge in that trial instructed the jury that the accused could be convicted if they found him to have committed the act or to have been the status in violation of the statute under which the offense was being considered.

The Supreme Court's decision on the case, delivered by Justice Potter Stewart, held that Robinson could not be convicted on the basis of his *status* as an addict. The Court noted that he would still retain the status of "addict" even if he were "cured," in which case the indictment, if upheld, would allow for his repeated arrest. In addition, it was held that to punish an individual because of such a status would be cruel and unusual punishment, in violation of the Eighth Amendment.

The Supreme Court clarified other critical components of this issue in *Powell v. Texas*. Powell, who had been arrested for being intoxicated in a public place, was found guilty and fined twenty dollars in Austin, Texas. Throughout subsequent appeals, his attorney argued that he was a chronic alcoholic (a fact that was not really disputed) and that his appearance in public had not been of his own free will. The attorney thus sought to bring this matter under the cruel and unusual punishment aspects of the Eighth Amendment, following *Robinson*. But Justice Thurgood Marshall, who delivered the majority opinion, stated that this would not come under the *Robinson* holding since Powell had not been convicted for the *status* of being a chronic alcoholic, but rather for the *behavior* of being in public while drunk on a specific occasion. As such, it was asserted that there was no attempt to punish a status or even a condition but simply to regulate behavior. Thus, while it is unconstitutional to make a status (such as alcoholism) a crime, a state may punish activities or behavior that is related to the status (such as public intoxication or stealing to obtain drugs). This may seem like splitting hairs, but there has to be some sympathy with the Court's belief that to find Powell innocent would have been open the floodgates for other types of criminal defendants going free on the basis of other "compulsions," such as to steal, set fires, and the like.

The majority of reformists' thinking in *Robinson* and in the testimonry provided in *Powell* reflects the disease model of substance abuse, particularly the theories of Jellinek (1960), a source the Court often cited. This disease model assumes that substance-abuse disorders, particularly alcoholism, reflect a physiological disorder, possibly genetically determined; that abusers have virtually no control over their intake of the substance because of this dysfunction; and that with some substances, especially alcohol, they permanently retain their status, even when they are able to abstain.

Assumptions in the disease model of substance abuse have been shown to be not entirely true in these implications (Peele 1984). For example, some alcoholics are able to return to a pattern of social drinking even after many years of chronic alcohol abuse (Peele 1984). There is also clear evidence that many alcoholics, even while in the status of chronic alcoholism, can refrain from the first drink (contradicting a bedrock assumption in Alcoholics Anonymous).

As a general matter, the law does not excuse from criminal or civil liability offenses a person commits while under the influence of alcohol or drugs. An intoxicated person who becomes boisterous and hits another person and breaks several windows can be charged for assault and criminal destruction of property, even though he may not have clearly known (nor now remember) what he was doing. The voluntary act of becoming intoxicated serves as the basis for this liability. The reasons for this legal rule are that it discourages intoxication, it avoids the near impossibility of applying any other rule, and it places legal responsibility on those who drink.

There are two exceptions to the "intoxication does not excuse criminal conduct" rule. One exception is where a person has not voluntarily become intoxicated—that is, where drink has been forced on him or her, or where a drug has been unwittingly administered to him or her. The second exception is that intoxication may make it impossible for a defendant to form the *specific* intent required for some crimes. A completely drunk person may not be able to premeditate a murder for example, and thus may not be able to commit first-degree murder when killing someone. Despite the absence of first-degree intent, he still may be convicted of a lesser homicide that does not require this specific intent.

A few cases have focused on persons who have ingested substances inadvertently. For example, certain individuals who unknowingly ingested substances like LSD (such as "spiked punch" cases) have committed acts destructive to themselves or to others. It has been consistently held by the courts that the person who was responsible for the ingestion of the substance (that is, the spiker, not the spikee) is the one legally responsible for any resulting destructive acts. So if LSD, for example, is given to someone by a prankster at a party, and a subsequent destructive act occurs, the prankster would bear the legal responsibility for the act in civil cases and to a degree even in criminal cases.

Drug Testing

Another legal issue is how much leeway employers may have in requiring random drug testing. The Supreme Court has been inclined to allow drug testing where there is a plausible rationale, such as public security. For example, in 1990, the Court held that the government may force Transportation Department employees to take random drug tests. The Court rejected without comment arguments that such tests violate privacy rights.

Greater control over those driving drunk has been provided by two 1990 Supreme court decisions. One decision accepted as legal roadblock-checkpoints to assess all drivers in this regard; the second allowed police to ask a suspected drunken driver routine questions and to videotape his responses without warning him of his constitutional rights. In the latter case, Inocencio Muniz, a Pennsylvania man, had been arrested in 1986 on suspicion of driving under the influence of alcohol. The Court compared videotaping—a procedure increasingly used in many areas of law enforcement—to obtaining a sample of blood or handwriting. In a videotape made at a booking center, Muniz's speech was slurred, and when asked his age, he stumbled, initially giving the wrong age, and his address, for which he needed to look at his driver's license. Muniz was also unable to tell police the date of his birthday. During sobriety tests, which were also videotaped, Muniz offered several incriminating statements explaining his inability to perform the test. The Court said that Muniz's incriminating statements could also be used against him because they were voluntary and "not prompted by an interrogation." The Court, however, by a five-to-four margin, did say that the question to Muniz about the date of his sixth birthday would have to be suppressed as it required a "testimonial response."

Legalizing Drugs

There has long been controversy over whether illegal drugs of abuse should be legalized. Obviously, some of the drugs described in this chapter are now available legally, even though they can be quite dangerous. For example, most of the prescription drugs discussed here are addicting or have serious side effects. They are available to the general public, although only upon the advice and supervision of a physician. In practice, that supervision is often negligible, and these drugs are subject to considerable abuse.

Some dangerous compounds that have little or no medical value are generally available to adults, alcohol and tobacco being the most prominent examples. This is partly a historical accident; if tobacco were first discovered today, there is little doubt that it would be banned, but (like individuals who smoke it) to some degree American society is economically and politically addicted to it. This is one poison that we would be hard pressed to do without.

The availability of tobacco raises nicely the question of autonomy and freedom of choice that is inherent in the legalization debate. Almost all tobacco smokers would be better off if the weed were banned tomorrow. But such a proposal would produce very strong objections that it would "violate the right" of smokers to decide for themselves whether or not to smoke. This is an issue to which we will return.

An interesting study by Joan McCord (cited in Adler 1990) has further fueled the legalization controversy. McCord managed to obtain data on pairs of men who had lived through the years of Prohibition (of alcohol) as fathers and adolescent sons. She collected the data up to the point where the sons reached the age of forty-five to fifty-two years. She found that while both groups of men, fathers and sons, were equally likely to have committed at least one nontraffic crime, the sons group committed, on an average, more than twice as many crimes as the fathers group (5.24, as opposed to 2.15 crimes for the fathers group). The difference was greater in very serious crimes, where the fathers group committed an average of only 0.28 crimes and the sons group showed an average of 0.73 crimes. Those who were adolescents during Prohibition also showed higher rates of alcohol abuse as adults.

Most people in the Boston area, where the subjects in this study lived, did not support Prohibition, and McCord feels that this attitude is what contributed to the increase in crime. That is, having laws that prohibit what most people think is all right undermines people's respect for the law in general. People who argued in favor of Prohibition said that it would make adolescents more controlled in their drinking, while opponents of Prohibition thought they would show more disrespect for the law. McCord asserts that her data indicate that the pessimists were more nearly correct than the optimists.

As for the current issue of legalizing drugs: on the one hand, some believe that legalizing drugs will reduce criminal behavior and increase respect for the law, as well as decrease the lure of the tremendous amount of money now associated with drugs and the thrill of engaging in illegal, risky behavior. Advocates of this position usually admit that the nation may have to accept living with some of the harm of drugs.

Opponents of this position argue that it is narrow-minded and simplistic. They say that legalizing drugs will increase the availability of drugs, the number of people who experiment with drugs, and therefore, the number of people who become addicted. They also argue that increasing the general availability of drugs increases the chances of minors getting hold of them. Finally, legalizing drugs will not mean that people aren't going to fight over selling the stuff to adolescents and even younger children.

While many practical issues are involved in the decriminalization debate, it also involves a virtual philosophical question involving personal freedom of choice (autonomy) and paternalism (the state protecting people from their own bad choices). While people who use drugs affect those who do not use drugs through higher health-care bills, some social instability, and the like, these are indirect effects. (Virtually all activities, from eating butter to ignoring high blood pressure to driving small cars, have some such indirect effects.) Or they are risks that come not from drugs but from engaging in a dangerous activity (such as driving) while under the influence of drugs, which might be more directly prohibited, as it is with alcohol.

The philosophical issue looks at whether people ought to be able to make choices that will directly and primarily hurt themselves. In a free society, we start with the proposition that individuals should be given considerable latitude in making their own choices, even when the choices are not very sensible. (Indeed, we even let people freely root for the Chicago Cubs and the Cleveland Indians, year after year.) At the same time, at some point we draw the line and do not let people do some things that are too dangerous without offsetting benefits. During most of this century, drug use has fallen into the latter category. Just where the line between autonomy and paternalism should be drawn is extremely difficult and is at the heart of the legalization debate.

Conclusions

One rationale offered for legalizing drugs is that it would undermine the massive, illicit profit system now existent (Weisheit 1990). No doubt legalizing drugs would be a helpful factor. Any successful program must be multifaceted—that is, include reduction of drugs at the source, interdiction, law enforcement, education, punishment of drug dealers, and punishment and/or treatment of drug users. The difficulty with most current antidrug proposals is that they typically focus on only one or two factors, and usually these are factors that experience has already taught us are not the key ones.

The majority of the financial effort has been directed toward reduction of drugs at the source, interdiction, and law enforcement. The last of these three factors is probably the most likely to generate a long-term impact, but only if it is combined with effective efforts toward punishing the various levels of drug dealers and providing punishment and treatment to the drug user.

The few modern societies that have controlled large-scale drug problems have done so by putting the major focus on the drug user. But this has to be buttressed by social attitudes that truly reject illicit drug use. The most stark example was China's abolition of its massive heroin addiction problem. China had 70 million heroin addicts in 1949. When the Communists took over, all users had to register themselves. The ones who turned themselves in were put on permanent rehabilitation. They were detoxified and constantly checked. If they went back on drugs, they were put into mental institutions. Within three years, the government had eliminated the problem. Japan attained similar success with a similar program.

Many experts agree that no program will be markedly successful unless there is first a greater change in overall societal attitudes toward a clear rejection of any form of drug abuse as acceptable. This is especially true for the black community, where almost one out of four adolescent and young-adult black males has had some contact with the criminal justice system, much of it generated one way or another by the drug-abuse problem. The response of ambivalence and delay—and the at best mildly negative comments made by black leaders and the black community in response to the blatant drug abuse by former Washington mayor Marion Barry—showcases the attitude problem.

Second, there has to be more emphasis on "required rehabilitation." As in the approach that some states have taken with sex offenders, drug offenders should be given substantial sentences that can be changed to parole only with successful completion of a drug-treatment program, combined with active involvement in a *long-term*—in some cases, lifelong—maintenance treatment program.

Notes

Adler, T. 1992. "Prohibition Spurred Abuse." *American Psychological Association Monitor* 21:7.

Anderson, L. 1992. "Differential Treatment Effects." In L. L'Abate, J. Farrar, and D. Serritella, eds. *Handbook of Differential Treatments for Addictions.* Needham Heights, Mass.: Allyn and Bacon.

Barrett, C. 1986. "Use of Disulfiram in the Psychological Treatment of Alcoholism." *Bulletin of the Society of Psychologists in the Addictive Behaviors* 4:197–205.

Blane, H., and K. Leonard. 1987. *Psychological Theories of Drinking and Alcoholism.* New York: Guilford.

Blum, K., and J. Payne. 1991 *Alcohol and the Addictive Brain.* New York: The Free Press.

Bozarth, M., and R. Wise. 1985. "Toxicity Associated with Long-term Intravenous Heroin and Cocaine Self-administration in the Rat." *Journal of the American Medical Association* 284: 81–83.

Farrar, J., L. L'Abate, and D. Serritella. 1992. "The Prevention of Addictive Behaviors." In L. L'Abate, J. Farrar, and D. Serritella, eds. *Handbook of Differential Treatments for Addictions.* Needham Heights, Mass.: Allyn and Bacon.

Finn, P., N. Zeitouni, and R. Pihl. 1990. "Effects of Alcohol on Psychophysiological Hyperactivity to Nonaversive and Aversive Stimuli in Men at High Risk for Alcoholism." *Journal of Abnormal Psychology* 99:79–85.

Frezza, M., C. diPadova, G. Pozzato, M. Terpin, E. Baraona, and C. Lieber. 1990. "High Blood Alcohol Levels in Women." *New England Journal of Medicine.* 322:95–99.

Gold, M. 1989. *Marijuana.* New York: Plenum Medical.

Gorski, T., and M. Miller. 1986. *Staying Sober.* Independence, Mo.: Independence Press.

Jarvik, M. 1967. "The Psychopharmacological Revolution." *Psychology Today* 1:51–59.

Jellinek, E. 1960. *The Disease Concept of Alcoholism.* New York: Hill House.

L'Abate, L. 1992. "Treating Addictions Differentially." In L. L'Abate, J. Farrar, and

D. Serritella, eds. *Handbook of Differential Treatments for Addictions*. Needham Heights, Mass.: Allyn and Bacon.

Lyman, M. 1989. *Practical Drug Enforcement*. New York: Elsevier.

Marlatt, A., J. Baer, D. Donovan, and D. Kiviahan. 1988. "Addictive Behaviors: Etiology and Treatment." In M. Rosenzweig and L. Porter, eds. *Annual Review of Psychology* 39. Palo Alto, Calif.: Annual Reviews.

Milkman, H., and L. Sederer. eds 1990. *Treatment Choices for Alcoholism and Substance Abuse*. Lexington, Mass.: Lexington.

Peele, S. 1984. "The Cultural Context of Psychological Approaches to Alcoholism." *American Psychologist* 39:1337–51.

Powell v. Texas. 1968. (392 U.S. 514).

Ranew, L., and D. Serritella. 1992. "Substance Abuse and Addiction." In L. L'Abate, J. Farrar, and D. Serritella, eds. *Handbook of Differential Treatments for Addictions*. Needham Heights, Mass.: Allyn and Bacon.

Robinson v. California. 1962. (370 U.S. 660, 8L Ed. 2d 758, 82 S.Ct. 1417).

Rodale, J. 1979. *If You Must Smoke*. Emmaus, Pa.: Rodale Books.

Rouse, J. 1991. "Evaluation Research on Prison-based Drug Treatment Programs." *The International Journal of the Addictions*. 26:29–44.

Segal, B. 1988. *Drugs and Behavior*. New York: Gardner.

Washton, A. 1987. *Cocaine*. New York: W. W. Norton.

Weisheit, R., ed. 1990. *Drugs, Crime and the Criminal Justice System*. Cincinnati, Oh.: Anderson.

5
The Sexual Disorders

An acquired taste
But hell, aren't they all.
— Anton Myrer
The Last Convertible

The Case of Ed Kemper

Various experts attribute Edmund Emil Kemper III's crimes to antisocial personality disorder, passive-aggressive personality disorder, paranoia, paranoid schizophrenia, chromosomal disorder, and others. Yet virtually anyone who considered his case would agree that the labels *sexual deviation* and *sexual sadism* clearly apply.

Kemper was a huge man, quite intelligent (with an IQ score of 136), and he retained a mordant sense of humor. When asked by a reporter, "What do you think now when you see a pretty girl walking down the street?" he replied, "One side of me says 'Wow, what an attractive chick, I'd like to talk to her.' . . . The other side says, 'I wonder how her head would look on a stick.' "

His early forays involved mutilations of animals, possibly accompanied by sexual behaviors. He then moved to following and staring at women, fantasizing about sexual and romantic themes. He graduated to such a fantasy about one of his teachers. Eventually he stood outside her house holding his stepfather's bayonet while fantasizing about having sex with her and killing her.

At age fourteen, he impulsively shot and stabbed to death his paternal grandmother and grandfather. Eventually paroled at age twenty-one, he stood six feet nine inches tall and weighed three hundred pounds. For two years, he "trained" by picking up pretty young hitchhikers, and he would fantasize performing various sexual and sadistic acts with them.

At age twenty-three, Kemper picked up two young women and eventually stabbed them to death in a frenzied attack. He brought their bodies home, where he decapitated and dismembered them and took Polaroid pictures of and sexually assaulted various body parts.

Four months later, he picked up another girl, raped her, then killed and decapitated her. He kept her head in the trunk of his car while he went into

89

an interview with two psychiatrists, who subsequently found him "safe" and recommended that his juvenile records be sealed in order to allow him to lead "a normal adult life." Four months later, he picked up a Cabrillo College (in California) coed, shot her, took her home, put her body in a closet overnight, then made love to her corpse the next day. Later he dissected her and kept the head in a box in a closet. About one month later, he picked up two other girls, shot them both, and later performed various sexual acts with the decapitated torso of one. His last victim was his own mother; he hit her with a hammer while she slept, decapitated her, and sexually assaulted the torso. He called his mother's best friend and invited her to dinner with his mother; then he killed her as well. He later admitted to eating parts of two of his victims in a macaroni casserole and keeping teeth and pieces of hair of several of the victims he especially enjoyed sexually, likely as fetishes for masturbation.

Sexuality: Baseline Trends and Myths

Type and amount of sexual behavior commonly varies not only among individuals but across cultures. While these variations can be quite bizarre, fortunately they are seldom as violent as Kemper's. We'll return to the issue of deviant sexuality, but first let's look at some baseline trends of normal sexual behavior as well as myths and distorted beliefs about sexuality.

The General Social Survey is an in-depth study of one thousand five hundred households that has been conducted annually since 1972, directed by Tom Smith of the University of Chicago. Data published in 1990 reveal the following about modern sexual behavior.

On the average, adults have sex fifty-seven times a year. Sexual frequency drops with age, from about seventy-eight times a year for those under forty to eight times for those over seventy. Overall, married people have sex sixty-seven times a year, separated people sixty-six times, divorced and never-married people fifty-five times, and widowed people six times. But 22 percent—including 9 percent of married people—said they had no sex partners at all during the previous year. Adults also said that they had had an average of seven sex partners since age eighteen. Divorced people had thirteen, the most of any group. Married people who said they were the happiest also had the most sex.

Western culture has been undergoing a transition from sexual conservatism to sexual liberalism (Laquer 1991). The myths in table 5–1 reflect these changing attitudes. Myths are crystallizations of the beliefs of a society. Although they may have functional value to the persons who hold them, they do not often reflect the facts.

Table 5–1
Myths about Sexuality

Traditional Myth	Modern Myth
Exhibitionists, voyeurs, and "degenerates" are out to entice innocent women and children into a life of sexual perversion.	Exhibitionists and voyeurs are passive individuals who never seduce children or become aggressive toward anyone.
Women who are raped usually have stimulated the rapist by acting seductively.	Rape is solely a crime of aggression.
An active and satisfactory sex life is not related to the development of a happy marriage.	Developing an active and innovative sex life is crucial in creating a happy marriage.
Female orgasm rarely occurs and indicates perversity when it does.	The female orgasm is a cataclysmic event that affects a women's entire outlook on life.
Clitoral orgasms are less fulfilling than vaginal orgasms.	There is no difference at all between clitoral orgasms and vaginal orgasms.
Sexual disorders are difficult to cure and require long and in-depth therapies.	All sexual disorders can now be cured by simple techniques in a short time.
Love is required for a satisfying sexual experience.	Love is irrelevant to satisfying sex. Technical skill and a willingness to experiment are the essential factors.
Women have little interest in sex.	Women are so sexually aggressive and needful that men will never satisfy them.
Elderly people have little interest in sex.	There is no loss of sexual ability or interest with age.
The psychologically healthy young person is chaste.	All adolescents are promiscuous.
Masturbation is harmful psychologically and physically.	Masturbation is always a more satisfying experience than intercourse.
Homosexuals are inherently unhappy people.	Homosexuals are more sexually fulfilled than heterosexuals.
Homosexuality is seldom "cured."	Homosexuals should never to try to change their sexual orientation; they should work to change the repressive society around them.
The sexual organs may shrink in size or become distorted, causing a change in sexual identity (a popular belief in Southeast Asia).	Sexual identity is directly related to size of the breasts or penis.
Incest is rare and reflects a deep sexual aggression.	Incest is common and may even help in developing healthy adult sexual patterns.
Pornography is the first step to a life of perversion and sexual aggression.	Pornography is totally harmless.
Sexual fantasies are sinful and indicate a weak will.	Sexual fantasies are harmless and do not lead to changes in behavior.
Masochism is healthier than sadism.	Sadism is healthier than masochism.
We now know most of the essential facts about human sexuality.	We now know most of the essential facts about human sexuality.

The Paraphilias (Sexual Deviations)

Paraphilia is the DSM term for sexual deviation; the two terms are used interchangeably in this section. Sexual deviations are usually marked by one or more of the following features: (1) a violation of a legal, public health, or accepted morality standard; (2) a gross impairment in the person's capacity for affectionate sexual responses with adult human partners; and (3) acknowledged subjective emotional distress regarding the source of sexual arousal.

The essential sexual disorder is in the lack of capacity for mature and participating affectionate sexual behavior with adult partners. Common characteristics are high dependency, low self-esteem, and at best mild anxiety and/or depression (Hayes, Evans and Barnett 1991). Traditionally, sexual disorders have been far more common among males, but this discrepancy has decreased in recent years. Occasionally engaging in fantasy or behavior does not qualify one as a paraphiliac. Exclusivity, persistency (even compulsivity), and pervasiveness are the hallmarks of the disorder.

Out of all criminal sexual offenses, probably no more than five percent are committed by persons because of psychosis, central nervous system impairment, or alcoholic delirium (Ellis 1989). Many in this five percent can argue a defense of incompetency or insanity or at least diminished capacity when confronted by the judicial and criminal justice system (see chapter 12). The remaining individuals, who supposedly are operating from "free choice," can at best primarily argue a defense of irrestible impulse.

Let's now consider the specific paraphilias.

Transvestism

Transvestism, sometimes referred to as transvestic fetishism, involves cross-sex dressing and engaging in behavior typical of the opposite sex. Transvestites may seek arousal by wearing clothing of the opposite sex, often next to the genitals. Although this paraphilia includes some components of gender identity disorder, transvestism is in most respects a paraphilia, as it does not involve any strong personal identification with the opposite sex.

A DSM diagnosis requires that the person dress in clothes of the opposite sex for a period of at least six months, accompanied by intense sexual urges and fantasies that result in acting-out and/or distress. Beyond simple cross-dressing, the behavior must be sexually arousing to the person. In most transvestites the cross-dressing behavior was initiated in childhood and in some manner was significantly reinforced by parents—as by "petticoat punishment," the humiliation of a boy by dressing him in girl's clothes. It typically becomes paired with masturbation and eventuates in the classic transvestite pattern. Transvestism is considered to be a rare disorder; an even smaller subgroup eventually passes from transvestism into transsexualism. In these cases the diagnosis of transsexualism takes precedence over transvestism.

Fetishism

Fetishism is a condition wherein a person uses nonliving objects as the exclusive or consistently preferred method of stimulating sexual arousal. To a degree, mild fetishism is socially condoned, as evidenced by the widespread acceptance of objects such as perfumes, seductive clothes, and mementos with strong sexual connotations. Usually the fetishist obtains sexual excitation by kissing, tasting, fondling, or smelling the object. Shoes, bras, and panties are the most common objects in fetishism. Odors are often important in the development of fetishes, just as they can be important in normal sexual stimulation. This may explain, for example, Emperor Napoleon Bonaparte's letter to Josephine upon returning from battle: "*Ne te lave pas, Je reviens,*" meaning, "Don't wash, I'm coming home." Most fetishists are male, and most use the object while masturbating alone, but in some cases it is used as a necessary preliminary to intercourse. In normal foreplay, attention is given to sexually arousing objects or parts of the body, with consequent arousal and eventual progression to coitus. In fetishism, however, the fetish takes primacy over intercourse as a means to obtain orgasm, very often as a result of an earlier coincidental association of the object with orgasm.

Occasionally a fetishist commits an act of breaking and entering in search of women's used bras or panties. Frequently, the excitement of the illegal behavior itself increases the fetishist's sexual arousal. In other instances, the problem becomes defined as a clinical disorder only when the fetishist requests treatment.

Zoophilia

Unlike bestiality, which specifically refers only to sexual intercourse with animals, zoophilia includes all forms of sexual experience with animals. Zoophilia is a very rare condition in which a person uses animals as the exclusive or preferred method of sexual stimulation. It becomes clinically significant when the person prefers the animal even when other forms of sexual outlet become available. The incidence of zoophilia is related to access; thus, it is most common in rural areas. Zoophilia is practiced primarily by preadolescent males. Persistence of the behavior beyond this age is usually an indication of severe disorder.

Pedophilia

> "Little Red Riding Hood was my first love. I felt that if I could have married Little Red Riding Hood, I should have known perfect bliss."
> — Charles Dickens

Pedophilia (literally, "love of children") is a preference for sexual experience with sexually immature persons. It may involve either overt force or subtle coercion (Ellis 1989).

There are significant differences between homosexually and heterosexually oriented pedophiliac males. Homosexual pedophiles are less likely to be married, and they prefer a slightly older person, age twelve to fourteen; heterosexual pedophiles prefer seven- to ten-year-olds. Heterosexual pedophiles are more likely to know their victims, are more inclined to look and touch rather than proceed to orgasm, and show a better prognosis for cure. Many heterosexual male pedophiles are impotent. When ejaculation does occur, it is usually achieved through exhibitionistic-voyeuristic masturbation. Attempted intercourse with the child is likely to be traumatic and painful for the victim and increases the probability that the incident will be reported to the police.

In the largest study of pedophiles ever undertaken, an analysis of 571 cases (Becker 1987), several interesting facts emerged. One is that boys are far more likely to be victims of sex abuse than was previously believed—two out of every three victims molested outside the home are boys. Boys are also more likely to be victims of "hands-on" abuse incidents, often involving physical abuse, whereas girls are more likely to be victims of "hands-off" incidents, such as voyeurism and exhibitionism. Offenders who admitted to one to four incidents to probation officers admitted to an average of seventy-five crimes each when guaranteed anonymity—those who molested young boys admitted to an average of 281 offenses, those who violated young girls admitted to an average of twenty-three incidents, whereas adult rapists admit to seven incidents each. Molesters typically engage in a wide variety of sexually deviant behaviors, and typically start molesting by at least age fifteen, and often younger.

Incest

Incest, though not traditionally a formal DSM category, refers to socially prohibited sexual interactions between close family members. There is evidence that the breakdown of traditional institutions and the "future shock" of change and mobility have decreased the sense of family bonding, thus diminishing the taboo against incest and increasing its incidence.

Incest is extremely rare between mother and child but not at all uncommon between brother and sister. Father-daughter incest is the usual target of legal and public health authorities. The strength of this last taboo is evident even in a prison subculture, where inmates are likely to socially isolate and physically abuse those incarcerated for incest.

Several situational factors increase the probability of incest. These include geographic isolation of the family, long periods of separation between father and daughter, a family pattern of going nude or seminude in the house, the mother's consistent absence from the house, and alcohol abuse. Male children who have been the target of father-son incest or who have had a long period of brother-sister incest are more likely to repeat the pattern in their own families (Gomes-Schwartz et al. 1990).

There are three basic subpatterns in father-daughter incest (Horton et al. 1990):

1. *Pedophilic incest.* A psychosexually immature and inadequate father who is functionally a pedophile has incestuous contacts with his sons, his daughters, and other children.

2. *Psychopathic incest.* A psychopatic father relates to most people as objects, shows little or no guilt about his behavior, and is usually promiscuous with adults and children, both in and out of the home (see chapter 2).

3. *Family-generated incest.* The father is passive and the mother has a personality disorder (see chapter 3). The marriage is shaky, and the child who is the target of the incest, most commonly the eldest daughter, takes on more than just a sexual function. She becomes a mistress in all meanings of that word. The mother is likely to be aware of the incest but helps keep it a family secret, believing that the family will fully disintegrate if the incest ceases (Horton et al. 1990).

Exhibitionism

> We are filled with terror. All those afternoons we went skinny-dipping, the curiosity about what each other looked like—is something terrible going on? . . . Once, at the river, Jim made his pecker talk, moving its tiny lips as he said, "Hi, my name's Pete. I live in my pants." Now it doesn't seem funny at all. If it's not wrong, why were we worried somebody would come along and see?
> — Garrison Keillor
> *Lake Wobegon Days*

Exhibitionism is the exposure of one's genitals to a stranger in order to become sexually aroused. The exposure is unexpected by the victim, arousal in the exhibitionist occurs immediately or shortly afterward, and the act of exposure is usually the only sexual encounter sought. Onset is usually in adolescence, with peak incidence in the middle to late twenties (Cox 1980). Exhibitionists are almost always male (though there are exceptions), perhaps because there are a number of acceptable outlets for exhibitionism available to women, such as exotic dancing. Even if true female exhibitionism occurs, males seldom react negatively and are unlikely to report it to authorities (O'Connell et al. 1990).

Exhibitionists constitute about one-third of all sex offenders and show the highest rate of recidivism—at least 25 percent. A wide range of personality types with a diversity of motivations may engage in exhibitionistic behavior (Levin & Stava 1987):

1. *Impulsive.* Obsessional, tense, and sexually confused individuals whose exhibitionism is an impulsive response to intrapsychic distress.

2. *Inadequate.* For people who are not only obsessional but also shy, introverted, and lacking in adequate social relationships, exhibitionism is an ambivalent combination of an anger response and an attempt at both ego affirmation and socialization.

3. *Unaware.* For some, exhibitionism is a secondary result of mental retardation, organic brain disorder, psychosis, or extreme alcohol intoxication.

4. *Assaultive.* For people influenced by a strong element of anger and hostility, exhibitionism achieves sexual arousal, but the shock response of the victim is the primary reinforcement, and there is little guilt over the behavior.

Exhibitionists are not usually dangerous, particularly those in the first three categories. However, the impulsive exhibitionist occasionally loses control and moves into aggressive pedophiliac behavior.

Wickramasekera (1976) developed a unique treatment. Wickramasekera originally required the patient to undress and dress several times before a mixed-sex audience of other counselors who first have the subject explore associated affect, bodily sensations, and fantasy during exposure. The patient is asked by the audience such questions as "What do you think we see (feel/think) as we look at you right now?" in an objective, non-critical yet non-empathic manner (Wickramasekra, 1976, p. 433). During the second component of the session, the patient is required to again undress and dress several times (at his therapist's direction) and asked questions to facilitate comparison of present feelings with antecedents, moods prior to and during exposure, and consequent moods and events. Videotaping (to be reviewed later by patient and therapist) and having the patient observe himself in a mirror are also part of this procedure. The treatment induces a high degree of anxiety in patients for whom it is appropriate (those who are nonpsychotic, non-psychopathic, and somewhat anxious), which appears critical to the success of the treatment.

In persons who do not experience the required level of anxiety, it could be increased by bringing into the audience either victims or people close to the exhibitionist (wife, mother, daughter, etc.) or even by chemically increasing anxiety, such as by injections of sodium lactate prior to the sessions.

Legal elements required for a conviction of indecent exposure typically include: (1) the person's exposure of the genitals or other private anatomical parts; (2) exposure in a public place; (3) intentional exposure; and (4) exposure in the presence of, or being seen by, others. While exhibitionists are usually indicted under indecent exposure statutes, they may also be arrested in some jurisdictions under statutes that govern "public lewdness" or "public indecency." While the elements are rather clear, the interpretation of what they actually mean may vary from jurisdiction to jurisdiction. They can vary depending on: (1) the definition of private parts or public place; (2) whether or not a witness or witnesses to the exposure are necessary; (3) whether issues of intent are considered in the actual court process; and (4) whether or not consent modifies or eliminates the criminality (Cox 1980).

Voyeurism

> Everything that is stripped has always impressed me.
> — Joan Miro
>   Painter and sculptor

A voyeur repeatedly seeks opportunities to look at unsuspecting individuals who are naked, taking off their clothes, or engaging in sexual activity. In voyeurism, the act of looking serves as the chief stimulus for arousal and orgasm. In our society, voyeurs are almost always males, approximately one-third are married, and there has usually been a significant history of sexual and other offenses throughout adolescence. As with exhibitionists, there is a long history of broken homes and marital distress. Voyeurs seldom maintained close relationships with sisters or other girls when they were young.

Most voyeurs are not markedly disturbed, and the simple act of obtaining arousal from looking is of course a normal part of many sexual experiences. Voyeurs are seldom dangerous to the victim. Those who are dangerous (1) are more likely to enter a building to do their peeping and (2) intentionally draw attention to themselves while in the act. Like pedophiles and exhibitionists, voyeurs show a high recidivism rate (Levin and Stava 1987).

Sexual Sadism and Sexual Masochism

"I used to be an obstetrician," Dr. William Masters said, "which is boring 90 percent of the time. So every time I delivered a boy I used to engage in a little contest to see if I could cut the cord before he had an erection. I won about 50 percent of the time."
— William Masters, *International Herald Tribune*

Sexual sadism and masochism are obviously interdependent patterns. People engaging in these deviations often pair up to satisfy each other, and in some persons both patterns coexist. Sexual masochism is the intentional acceptance of pain or humiliation in order to produce sexual excitement (Montgomery and Greif 1989). The term itself, coined by Kraft-Ebbing in 1886, is derived from Leopold von Sacher-Masoch (1836–1895), whose novels focused on masochistic men subjected to sadistic women. Sacher-Masoch himself lived out the concept, obtaining excitement from the fantasy that his wife was flagrantly unfaithful. Masochism, though relatively rare, nevertheless occurs a bit more frequently than sadism.

Sexual masochism predominantly occurs in males and has beginnings in childhood experience where the infliction of pain in some way becomes tied to sexual arousal (Montgomery and Greif 1989). Crystallized behavior patterns are usually evident by late adolescence. In some cases, there is an increased need for pain over a period of time (Abel and Rouleau 1990). Masochists seldom come to the attention of legal authorities, or even therapists, unless they have been a victim of extreme sadism that requires medical treatment, and this is uncommon.

In a rare pattern that was thought to be a form of sexual masochism, known as "terminal sex," or "scarfing," a man (usually) hangs himself by the neck with a noose to increase his sexual pleasure while masturbating. Releasing the noose just before unconsciousness allegedly increases the pleasure, probably by developing an oxygen debt that facilitates the orgasm, although others believe if there is any belief in an increase in pleasure from this practice, it is the result of a placebo effect. This practice of eroticized hanging is more likely to occur among adolescents and young adults.

The term *sadism* derives from the Marquis de Sade, whose writings focused on sexual pleasure gained through inflicting pain and even death on others. Most sadists show evidence of this pattern by early adolescence. The condition is chronic and is seen far more frequently in males than females. Sadism overlaps the concept of rape, though not all rapists are sadists, nor is the contrary true (Ellis 1989).

Clinical diagnosis requires the real or simulated infliction of pain or humiliation in order to produce sexual excitement. The rhinoceros is one animal that displays this behavior, the female is often observed to ram the bull viciously before mating with him, but he seems to enjoy it.

Frotteurism

Frotteurism has received increasing official recognition as a separate pattern of sexual deviation, that is, one that is not always associated in an actual case with another sexual deviation such as exhibitionism. Frotteurism is generally defined as touching and rubbing up against the body of a stranger in order to attain sexual arousal and even orgasm. *Partialism* is differentiated from frotteurism in that the partialist is attracted to and can only achieve arousal from a specific part of the body, whereas the arousal for frotteurs is generated in a more generalized manner and is not tied to a specific body part.

The great majority of frotteurs are males, and the most common sexual target is the buttocks. Not unlike many voyeurs and exhibitionists, the frotteur usually has evolved a series of coverup plans to avoid the embarrassment of being caught and publicly humiliated. The act is usually done in a crowded public place like a bus or subway or crowded dance floor. The violation of the taboo of sexual behavior in a public place is arousing, but the humiliation one could experience if caught is aversive enough to generate these coverup behaviors.

Other Variations

The DSM does not cover all known sexual deviations, merely those for which people most often seek or are sent to treatment. We mention two somewhat rare but related deviations, simply to indicate the existence of a much wider sample of deviations. In coprolalia, arousal is obtained by using crude and vulgar language descriptive of excrement. It is a kind of verbal exhibitionism and is a common factor in obscene phone calls. Coprolalia should be discriminated from Ganser's syndrome, in which the obscene language appears to be uncontrollable. Another deviation is saliromania, which is the desire to damage or soil the body of another person, often with excrement.

Pornography and the Sexual Deviations

Many people are concerned that easy access to pornography may spur the acting-out of some of the more aggressive sexual deviations, particularly toward children. Early studies on this topic found that pornography actually reduced anxiety in some people and/or stimulated a renewed interest in sexual contact within marriages. Adults who show "deviant sexual behavior" have had, on the average, much less exposure to pornography in adolescence than have normal individuals, but they then resort to increasing levels of use of pornography as they get older.

On the other hand, some studies have found that use of pornography by individuals may in some instances increase sexual acting-out and/or more unusual forms of sexual expression (Osanka and Johann 1990; Abel and Rouleau 1990). For example, White (1979) found that pornography that a person sees as positive may lessen aggression, whereas erotica that focuses on aggression or bizarre or sadistic sexual behavior increases the potential for acting-out. Since sexually explicit films account for at least 10 percent of the videocassette market, and at least twenty million Americans buy sex-related or "adult" magazines every month, it is clear that pornography does not stimulate criminal or grossly deviant sexual behavior in the great majority of users. At the same time, users of pornography do seem to become desensitized to the implications of the themes of the particular pornography they are viewing, such as demeaning and subjugating women and directly violent themes (Osanka and Johann 1990). And there is a small subgroup of people for whom pornography acts as a catalyst for various antisocial behaviors (Levin and Stava 1987).

Society's concern is evident in the 1990 Supreme Court case of Clyde Osborne, a sixty-one-year-old resident of Columbus, Ohio, who was sentenced to six months and fined one hundred dollars for possession of four photos of nude boys in sexually explicit poses. The Supreme Court upheld the conviction, saying that the law was reasonable since these were not just nude photos but had "a graphic focus" on sex organs and are kept for reasons "not morally innocent." This could certainly open a Pandora's Box since it is hard to think of any pornography kept for what many would perceive as morally innocent reasons. The continuing difficulty for society is balancing the rights of free speech and privacy against pornography's antisocial effects in certain individuals.

Pornography has been the subject of considerable legal controversy. The social control of pornography is difficult because of the practical difficulty of defining it (Justice Potter Stewart's "I know it when I see it" perhaps being the most honest definition), and because there is a considerable public demand for this material. So an underground or black market quickly develops when open sale is restricted. Furthermore, the freedoms of speech and press guaranteed by the first amendment limit efforts to control sexually explicit materials. Only if the material violates community standards, appeals to puriant or morbidly unhealthy interests, and is without serious scholarly or artistic content can it be regulated as pornographic. Furthermore, the Supreme Court has held that citizens cannot be prosecuted for having pornographic materials (kiddie-porn excepted) in their own homes for their own private use. As a practical matter, the development of home video players has probably made any realistic ban of pornographic materials all but impossible.

Overlapping of Paraphilias

The bulk of the traditional clinical and research literature leads one to believe that people who show a paraphiliac pattern stay within that same pattern consistently. But in more in-depth and recent research by Abel and his colleagues (1986) at least 50 percent of the paraphiliac clients they evaluated had multiple diagnoses that overlapped a wide variety of paraphilias. Table 5–2 shows the paraphiliac arousal pattern that developed initially for all of their clients who were diagnosed as either rapists or pedophiles as adults. These findings, taken together, suggest that people who have one category of paraphilia should be questioned extensively about other categories of deviant sexual arousal.

An interesting method of corroborating reports of sexual deviance among male persons accused of criminal sexual offenses and/or referred for counseling is the psychophysiological assessment of sexual arousal (Abel and Rouleau 1990; Abel, Rouleau, and Cunningham-Rathner 1986). The client wears a circumferential penile transducer that accurately measures not only the existence of an erection but its rigidity and persistence. While wearing the transducer, the client is presented (by audiotape, and/or by 35-millimeter slides or videotape) a variety of sexual scenes representing various normal and sexually deviant patterns. Abel and colleagues (1986) used this technique with ninety consecutive cases where there was some sexually deviant interest. In 45 percent of those cases, the client's self-reported devi-

Table 5–2
Initial Deviant Behavior Patterns of Rapists and/or Child Molesters

First Paraphilia	Rapists (percent)	Pedophiles (percent)
Pedophilia	25.8	75.0
Rape	43.8	3.4
Exhibitionism	7.9	12.9
Transvestism	1.1	1.3
Fetishism	2.2	1.3
Voyeurism	9.0	3.0
Sadism and masochism	2.2	1.3
Obscene telephone calls	0	0.4
Frottage	5.6	1.3
Bestiality	1.1	0
Arousal to odors	1.1	0

Source: Adapted from G. Abel, J. Rouleau, and J. Cunningham-Rathner, "Sexually Aggressive Behavior," in W. Curran, A.L. McGarry, and S. Shah, eds. *Forensic Psychiatry and Psychology* (Philadelphia: F.A. Davis, 1986).

ant interests were consistent with indications from physiological measurement. The remaining 55 percent were confronted with the discrepancy between their self-reported and physiologically indicated preferences. In 62.2 percent of these cases, the clients subsequently admitted that they had been deceptive, and it is very probable that some of the others were also being deceptive or were not consciously aware of an unconscious or emerging deviant behavior.

Components of a Typical Sex Offender Treatment Program

A typical sex offender treatment program has several components. The first is an *assessment of the offender*. This includes assessing the nature of the specific offense, the victim characteristics, antecedents of the offender's crime, previous offenses, level of psychopathology, developmental history, educational history, social history, sexual history-knowledge-experience, religious beliefs, occupational history, level of anger, level of ability to empathize, awareness of emotions, cognitive distortions about men, women, and children, and sexual arousal. Techniques to assess and to evaluate the offender for these characteristics include clinical interviews, self-reporting, psychological tests, questionnaires, rating scales, and physiological measures.

The second component is *group and individual therapy*. This is necessary to clarify the individual's range of deviance, level of disorder, level of commitment to change, and ability to tolerate confrontation. It provides a context for retraining the offender into more prosocial sexual patterns.

The third component is to operate and interpret *penile plethysmography*. Self-reports of offenders are usually faulty due to their tendency to minimize their involvement and their wish to conceal information. Some suffer from disorders that affect their thought processes to such an extent that self-reported information is simply invalid. Plethysmography is the use of a penile transducer to determine and register variations in the size of an organ or limb. The electronic device is attached to the penis. It detects changes in the size of the penis when the offender is presented with sexual stimuli of both deviant and nondeviant content. The associated degrees of erection provide an indication of the offender's sexual interests, preferences, and inhibitions. Therapists are trained to utilize the plethysmograph to condition the offender to appropriate sexual stimuli as well as to countercondition him from inappropriate stimuli.

In the next component, *covert sensitization* is used. This is an imagery-based counterconditioning procedure in which clients are instructed to imagine the relevant deviant sexual act of stimulus, then to imagine some negative reaction—usually severe anxiety, terror, or nausea. In *assisted covert sensitization,* a strongly noxious odor is used to aid in the development of a nausea response. Another component is *olfactory conditioning,* in which inappropriate sexual stimuli are presented to clients via slides, audiotapes, or videotapes, followed by the presentation of the noxious odor.

Satiation therapy involves having the offender masturbate to an appropriate sexual fantasy while verbalizing it aloud. Following this, the offender is required to continue to masturbate for a period ranging from fifty minutes to two hours (or try, in some cases) while verbalizing deviant sexual fantasies.

Aversive behavioral rehearsal is a powerful technique whose goal is to decrease sexually deviant behaviors and arousal by making the behavior publicly observable. The offender describes in detail the types of offense he committed, and then, by use of mannequins, clothing, or other apparatus, he reenacts the offense. The tape is narrated by the offender while he is discussing his plans, actions, feelings, and thoughts. Having victims, friends, and/or family members watch the tape heightens the aversive effect on the offender.

Relapse prevention emphasizes that sex offenses are not impulsive criminal acts, but are more commonly planned. The common chainlike sequence of factors that culminate in sexual violence are known as offense precursors. The offense precursors are emotion, fantasy, cognitive distortion, plan, and act.

There are two models of relapse. One is the internal, self-management model, and the other is external, supervisory model. The first model increases the client's awareness and range of choices concerning his behavior, develops specific coping skills and self-control capacities, and creates a general sense of mastery over life. The second model imposes external controls on the offender through teamwork that involves the parole officer, the therapist, the parole board, the family, and friends.

First, and foremost, before the offender can be accepted into sex offender programming, he has to admit guilt. He has to participate in the assessment process by taking tests, by relating his life's history, and by cooperating to the fullest extent. Most sex offender programs require the offender to sign a contract outlining his responsibilities and the results that may occur if he does not meet these responsibilities. The goals and responsibilities agreed to are developed by the treatment team. Appropriate goals of treatment include, but are not limited to:

- actively participating in and following all treatment requirements;
- learning to control deviant arousal patterns;
- placing obstacles in the path of converting nonsexual problems into sexual behavior;
- learning to solve nonsexual problems in nonsexual ways, for both offenders and their families;
- taking responsibility for his behavior without minimizing, externalizing, or projecting blame onto others; and
- making some form of restitution to the victim.

As in most disorders that require both a legal procedure and a significant course of treatment, deception on the part of the offender regarding progress is very possible. I am familiar with at least one such case, that of a voyeur whose treatment was apparently successful at the two-year mark. While the client stated that he was doing well at that time, his wife reported to the therapist that he had long ago resumed peeping. Thus, corroborative statements from significant others are needed, as well as other methods for detecting deception, when a report of the treatment progress will be used in legal procedures.

Transsexualism

Transsexualism is not considered a paraphilia—that is, a sexual deviation; rather, it is a gender disorder. Transsexuals are individuals who persistently and strongly identify with the opposite sex. This is manifested in cross-sex dressing *without* the goal of sexual excitement, and a desire for a change of sexual apparatus through hormone therapy and surgery. This strong identity with the opposite sex and desire for a gender change are what primarily differentiate transsexualism from transvestism (cross-sex dressing for arousal, discussed elsewhere in this chapter).

The first sex-change operation was performed in Europe in 1930. Most sex changes are made from male to female, in large part because there is a greater initial demand for this type of change, but just as important, because the surgery for the reverse procedure, female to male, is much more difficult and has higher likelihood of failure.

Thorough psychological screening, possibly combined with psychotherapy, is an essential first step in determining whether a person is a true transsexual. In the rare cases resulting from a hormone deficiency, hormone therapy should precede other treatment measures. Otherwise, the therapist can attempt to return the client to a nontranssexual orientation through a combination of psychosocial conditioning and sexual reorientation training (LoPiccolo and Stock 1986).

The weight of evidence indicates that sex-change surgery is generally effective for many transsexuals (Gilman 1990). But in some cases, surgery is an unnecessary intervention, as psychotherapy and the passage of time can deal effectively with these identity concerns. The well-known attorney Melvin Belli (1979) argues persuasively that clinicians can come under tort liability for taking a person through transsexual surgery, and it can possibly be considered under "criminal mayhem" statutes if there is any lack of clarity about the person's consent or ability to consent. Belli argues that adequate consent is problematical in most cases because the "compulsive" quality of the need to change sex is contradictory to the law's requirement that consent be "an affirmative act of an unconstrained and undeceived will" (p. 498). But could not this concept of being compelled into treatment be applied to almost any disorder?

Gynemimesis

There is a subgroup of people who, like classical transsexuals, cross-dress, show a high level of identification with the opposite sex, and sometimes even take hormones to change their body structure. But they are content to live with their original genitalia and never get to the point of seeking transsexual surgery. This phenomenon, which is far more common in males, is termed "gynemimesis," or "woman-miming" (Money 1987). Gynemimetic individuals thus fall between transsexualism and transvestism. They often make a living as erotic dancers and prostitutes (either catering to very specialized tastes—to gynemimetophilics—or providing a true surprise to their clients).

Sexual Addiction

In recent years, various therapists have proposed the existence of a syndrome they term *sexual addiction*. They hypothesize that sexual addiction is similar to biological addiction and that is is reinforced biologically by rising levels of phenylethylamine in the brain. Some cite a history of abuse or modeling from a sexually addicted parent as critical. The symptoms usually cited are:

- being preoccupied with sexuality to the extent that it interferes with one's functioning in several life arenas, such as work
- using sex to escape, cope, or relieve one's anxiety
- feeling guilt, remorse, or depression after sex
- turning to a lower environment when pursuing sex
- carelessness about one's own welfare or the welfare of the family when pursuing sexual encounters
- leaving the sex partner as quickly as possible after the act
- undergoing an arrest for a sex-related offense
- feeling that one's sexual behavior is out of control, that one should quit "giving in," and/or stop or limit some aspect(s) of sexual behavior.

There is little doubt that some individuals show such patterns. The problem in using a term like *addiction* for this behavior is the implication that the behavior is compelled and the related implication of lessened culpability for violating various laws by the behavior. These implications are certainly not warranted here.

Homosexuality

Homosexuality has long been a topic of controversy, both with lay persons and within professional groups; it has been especially controversial in recent years. In the present DSM, there is no clinical listing for homosexuality. Homosexuality is found in almost all societies and is considered acceptable in many. Many people in American society have had homosexual experiences themselves (Kinsey et al. 1948, 1953; Masters et al. 1991). Not even Freud himself took the uniformly negative view of homosexuals often ascribed to him. The following excerpt is from a letter he sent to a woman who had asked him for advice about her homosexual son.

> I gather from your letter that your son is a homosexual. I am most impressed by the fact that you do not mention this term yourself in your information about him. May I question you, why you avoid it? Homosexuality is assuredly no advantage, but it is nothing to be ashamed of, no vice, no degradation. It cannot be classified as an illness. . . . Many highly respectable individuals of ancient and modern times have been homosexuals, several of the greatest men among them (Plato, Michelangelo, Leonardo da Vinci, etc.). It is a great injustice to persecute homosexuality as a crime, and it is cruelty too (quoted in Friedman and Rosenman 1974)

Male and Female Homosexuality

From the perspective of behavior, there are differences between male and female homosexuals. Male homosexuals tend to be more promiscuous and to have more one-night encounters, though many also form stable, monogamous relationships (Masters et al. 1991). They are also likely to have masturbated earlier and more frequently, to have engaged in more oral-genital sex, and to have engaged in homosexual experiences earlier than female homosexuals.

Societey's Response

The tendency during the last couple of decades has been toward "decriminalization" of homosexuality in most jurisdictions, at least in practice if not statute. This trend, however, was dealt a severe blow in the Supreme Court case of *Doe v. Commonwealth's Attorney for City of Richmond* (1975). This decision did not find any inherent criminality in homosexual acts (it would be unconstitutional to make the "status" of being a homosexual a crime); nor did it support the reasoning of the relevant state statute that argued that it is criminal behavior. But the decision did clearly allow that a right-to-privacy concept would not prohibit criminal sanctions, and it affirmed the rights of states to legislate against such behaviors. So although this didn't actually

criminalize homosexuality, it did take away the excuse that many state legisla-
tors had used to argue for decriminalization prior to this decision, which was
that the courts were decriminalizing homosexuality anyway.

The criminalization of homosexual acts under certain conditions is apparently consitutionally permissible, but there have been many ironic
changes in rights for homosexuals in other areas, particularly in child-
custody decisions and vocational status. Certainly, the general trend has
been to accept that homosexuality is not a sufficient cause alone to sustain
the removal of a child. The same trend has occurred in the teaching of
children. At the same time, the recent trend has been toward increasing
acceptance of admitted homosexuality in government jobs, as well as in
many areas of the private sector. A major step was taken when the National
Security Agency decided to allow an avowed homosexual employee to keep
his job and security clearances.

One of the thorny legal and psychological issues here is how a person is
to be defined as a homosexual, whether for restrictions or rights. Courts
have labeled as homosexual married persons who admitted to having engaged in same-sex activities in their late teens; persons who have mostly
bisexual friends; persons with one conviction for a same-sex "crime";
women who wear "mannish" attire; and even a man who admitted to being
a homosexual in preference but who had not admitted or even been proven
to have committed any overt homosexual act (*Gaylord v. Tacoma School
District of Washington* 1975). The problem for society will continue, especially in light of the 1990 Supreme Court decisions upholding the U.S.
military's ban on homosexuals in certain circumstances.

Psychosexual Dysfunction

Figure 5–1 shows typical causes of sexual dysfunction.

Patterns in Males

There are three major subcategories to the category of male psychosexual
dysfunction. The first subcategory, *hypoactive sexual desire,* refers to a
psychologically generated condition in which a man consistently experiences
few fantasies or has little interest in proceeding into a sexual act. This occurs
rarely as a separate disorder, and organic dysfunction should always be
ruled out (Mohr and Beutler 1990). It is often a reflection of disorder in a
marital relationship rather than evidence of significant individual pathology.
A more extreme variation is *sexual aversion disorder,* an extreme aversion
to, and avoidance of, virtually all genital sexual contact with a partner.

The second subcategory is *premature ejaculation.* This disorder is an
inability to exert voluntary control over ejaculation accompanied by persis-

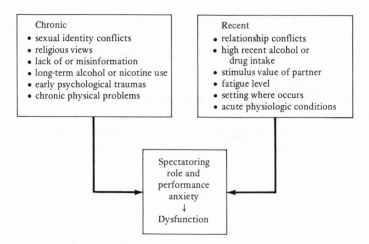

Figure 5–1. Typical Causes of Sexual Dysfunction

tent or recurrent ejaculation with minimal stimulation and before the person wishes it; it occurs in the absence of other significant pathology and is not an organic condition. It is difficult to define exactly what an absence of voluntary control means. Masters and colleagues (1991) define premature ejaculation as a clinical problem if the orgasm occurs involuntarily before the partner's orgasm more than half the time.

The third subcategory in this area is *male erectile disorder* and *inhibited male orgasm,* which refer to a disruption (at different points) of attempts to attain orgasm.

The research literature refers to male erectile disorder as "erectile dysfunction"; most people simply term it *impotence.* The latter term is undesirable for several reasons, primarily since it connotes a general personality inadequacy and weakness of character. It is interesting to note that weakness in the male and coldness in the female, as connoted by the terms *impotence* and *frigidity* respectively, are opposites of the characteristics most thoroughly prescribed by sexual roles in our society—power and competence for males and sensitivity and warmth for females. Most erectile dysfunction is partial, at least initially; that is, the male can attain erection but either cannot reach orgasm or does not maintain the erection for very long. Total erectile dysfunction over a significant period of time is relatively rare and suggests a biological cause. But biological factors play at least a part in approximately 50 percent of all cases of erectile dysfunction (Mohr and Beutler 1990).

Diagnostic Considerations. From an overall perspective, the following cues are suggestive of erectile dysfunction in which organic factors play a major part (Mohr and Beutler 1990; Masters et al. 1991):

- gradual onset;
- sequentially deteriorating erections;
- normal libido;
- can initiate but not maintain erection; and
- loss of nocturnal and masturbatory erection.

The following are generally indicative of erectile dysfunction that is psychogenic in nature:

- episodic occurrence
- sudden onset
- acute—brought on by life stress
- normal morning and nocturnal erections
- loss of libido

Patterns in Females

The subcategories entitled hypoactive sexual desire and sexual aversion disorder mean exactly the same for women that they do for men. There is no subcategory for women that is exactly comparable to premature ejaculation, since women do not have a comparable problem. Other female categories include dyspareunia or vaginismus. *Dyspareunia* refers to significant pain during intercourse. It is most common in females, but it can be diagnosed in males as well. *Vaginismus* refers to a correlated muscular spasm that either prevents intercourse or makes it extremely painful. No significant personality pathology has been found to be consistently correlated with these patterns, although depression and immediate anxiety are likely to be suggested, just as they are in premature ejaculation and erectile dysfunction.

The category of *inhibited female orgasm* is similar to that for males. *Female sexual arousal disorder* specifically refers to a woman's inability to attain or maintain the swelling and lubrication responses of sexual excitement for a period of time long enough to allow the completion of sexual intercourse, even though the person engages in sexual activity of sufficient preparation and duration; it accompanied by a persistent lack of a subjective sense of sexual excitement.

Treatment

Drugs, surgery, and a little counseling are the traditional techniques for dealing with the sexual dysfunction. Drugs and surgery are still used today, but the role of counseling has been expanded. Most of the counseling techniques used today have evolved from the pioneering work of Masters and Johnson (Masters et al. 1991). They emphasize redirecting the person's attention away from sources of anxiety or even a focus on "success of orgasm," and a return to an emphasis on just enjoying the process of sexuality.

Modern surgery has developed a variety of prosthetic devices that are useful as a last resort. Note that the idea of a prosthesis is not necessarily modern, as has been documented in R. O'Hanlon's book *Into the Heart of Borneo* (1984) in this true account of the author's discussion with the tribesman Leon:

> "But Leon, when do you have it done? When do you have the hole bored through your dick?"
>
> "When you twenty-five. When you no good any more. When you too old. When your wife she feds up with you. Then you go down to the river very early in the mornings and you sit in it until your spear is smalls. The tatoo man he comes and pushes a nail through your spear, round and round. And then you put a pin there, a pin from the outboard motor. Sometimes you get a big spots, very painfuls, a boil. And then you die."
>
> "Jesus!"
>
> "My best friend—you must be very careful. You must go down to the river and sit in it once a month until your spear so cold you can't feel it; and then you loosen the pin and push it in and out; or it will stick in your spear and you never move it and it makes a pebble with your water and you die."
>
> "But Leon," I said, holding my knees together and holding my shock with my right hand, "do you have one?"
>
> "I far too young!" said Leon, much annoyed; and then, grinning his broad Iban grin as a thought discharged itself: "But you need one Redmon! And Jams—he so old and serious, he need two!" (p. 82–83).

Notes

Abel, G., and J. Rouleau. 1990. "Male Sex Offenders." In M. Thase, B. Edelstein, and M. Hersen, eds. *Handbook of Outpatient Treatment of Adults*. New York: Plenum.

Abel, G., J. Rouleau, and J. Cunningham-Rathner. 1986. "Sexually Aggressive Behavior." In W. Curran, A. L. McGarry, and S. Shah, eds. *Forensic Psychiatry and Psychology*. Philadelphia: F. A. Davis.

Becker, J. 1987. Personal communication.

Belli, M. 1979. "Transsexual Surgery: A New Tort." *Journal of Family Law* 17: 487–504.

Cox, D. 1980. "Exhibitionism: An Overview." In D. Cox and R. Daitzman, eds. *Exhibitionism*. New York: Garland.

Doe v. Commonwealth's Attorney for the City of Richmond. 1975. (400 U.S. Dist. Ct. EVA).

Ellis, L. 1989. *Theories of Rape*. New York: Hemisphere.

Friedman, M., and R. Rosenman 1974. *Type A Behavior and Your Heart*. New York: Knopf.

Gaylord v. Tacoma School District of Washington. 1975. (559 P.2d. 1340).

Gilman, S. 1990. *Sexuality*. New York: John Wiley.

Gomes-Schwartz, B., J. Horowitz, and A. Cardarelli. 1990. *Child Sexual Abuse*. Newbury Park, Calif.: Sage.

Hayes, K., R. Evans, and R. Barnett. 1991. "Characteristics of Sex Offenders" *Corrective and Social Psychiatry and Journal of Behavior Technology, Methods and Therapy* 38: 13–16.

Horton, A., B. Johnson, R. Roundy, and D. Williams. 1989. *The Incest Perpetrator*. Newbury Park, Calif.: Sage.

Kinsey, A., W. Pomeroy, and C. Martin. 1948. *Sexual Behavior in the Human Male*. Philadelphia: Saunders.

———. 1953. *Sexual Behavior in the Human Female*. Philadelphia: Saunders.

Laquer, T. 1991. *Making Sex: Body and Gender from the Greeks to Freud*. Cambridge, Mass.: Harvard University Press.

Levin, S., and L. Stava. 1987. "Personality Characteristics of Sex Offenders." *Archives of Sexual Behavior* 16; 57–79.

LoPiccolo, J., and W. Stock. 1986. "Treatment of Sexual Dysfunction." *Journal of Consulting and Clinical Psychology* 54: 158–67.

Luria, Z., S. Friedman, and M. Rose. 1986. *Human Sexuality*. New York: John Wiley.

Masters, W., V. Johnson, and R. Kolodny. 1991. *Human Sexuality*. 4th ed. Glenville, Ill.: Scott, Foresman, Little Brown.

Mohr, D., and L. Beutler. 1990. "Erectile Dysfunction: A Review of Diagnostic and Treatment Procedures." *Clinical Psychology Review* 10: 123–50.

Money, J. 1987. "Sin, Sickness, or Status: Homosexual Gender Identity and Psychoneuroendocrinology." *American Psychologist* 42: 384–99.

Montgomery, J., and A. Greif. 1989. *Masochism*. Madison, Conn.: International Universities Press.

O'Connell, M., E. Leberg, and C. Donaldson. 1990. *Working with Sex Offenders*. Newbury Park, Calif.: Sage.

Osanka, F., and S. Johann. 1990. *Sourcebook on Pornography*. Lexington, Mass.: Lexington.

White, L. 1979. "Erotica and Aggression." *Journal of Personality and Social Psychology* 37:591–601.

Wickramasekera, I. 1976. "Aversive Behavior Rehearsal for Sexual Exhibitionism." In I. Wickramasekera, ed. *Biofeedback, Behavior Therapy, and Hypnosis*. Chicago: Nelson-Hall.

6

The Psychoses and the Organic Brain Damage Disorders

> My father's problem was this: he was in possession of information concerning the Chicago Cubs, our home town of Onamata, Iowa, and a baseball league known as the Iowa Baseball Confederacy, information that he *knew* to be true and accurate but that no one else in the world would acknowledge. He *knew* history books were untrue, that baseball records were falsified, that people of otherwise unblemished character told him bold-faced lies when he inquired about their knowledge of, an involvement with, the Iowa Baseball Confederacy.
> — W. P. Kinsella
> *The Iowa Baseball Confederacy*

The Case of Joseph Westbecker

Joseph Westbecker, whose case demonstrates much of the symptomatology that is discussed in this chapter, was treated by numerous psychiatrists. One psychiatrist diagnosed him as having a "major affective illness, depressed recurrent type" and a "schizoidal personality with paranoid trends." Another said he had an "atypical bipolar disorder," while another diagnosed him as a "schizo-affective disorder."

Westbecker often reported having symptoms such as headaches, dizziness, memory loss, fatigue, impaired concentration, "illusionary incidents" (in which walls and ceilings moved), and blackouts. He believed this was because he had worked near toxic chemicals, such as toluene. But there was never any medical support for that explanation for this plethora of symptoms, and at autopsy his brain showed no abnormalities.

Most important, he gradually developed and deepened the delusion that officials at his plant had conspired to "harass" him. He had mentioned his desire to get back at them to co-workers and family, but nobody really took him seriously enough to do anything about it.

Three days before his death, he reported to his treating psychiatrist that he had an apparent delusion that he had to commit oral sex in order to avoid working on a particular machine at the plant where he was employed. The psychiatrist believed that his personality functioning was worsening. He told Westbecker to stop taking the antidepressant Prozac, one of the medications he was receiving, since the Prozac might be increasing his agitation. He also

113

advised Westbecker to voluntarily check into a mental hospital, but Westbecker declined.

Three days later, on September 14, 1989, Joseph Westbecker carried five guns, one bayonet, and twelve hundred rounds of ammunition into the Standard Gravure plant in Louisville, Kentucky. Primarily using a Poly Tech Legend—a top-of-the-line semiautomatic AK-47 assault rifle—he fired about forty rounds during his twenty-minute walk through the plant, eventually killing eight and wounding twelve others. None of them were the officials he believed were conspiring against him. He ended his walk by pulling out a nine-millimeter pistol and shooting himself in the head. The autopsy found a concentration of Prozac in his blood at the high end of the normal therapeutic range, suggesting he had not stopped taking it. A therapeutic level of lithium, traces of three other antidepressants, and a sleep medication were also found in his blood.

Westbecker's case shows the gamut of issues covered in this chapter. It is not clear, though it is very possible, that he had occasional hallucinations—the illusionary incidents; he did show both persecutory and somatic delusions, occasional mania, much depression, and many suicidal impulses, then homicide and suicide itself.

This chapter covers those disorders that most severely interrupt an individual's ability to function psychologically—that is, the psychoses and the organic brain disorders. As such, they are often at issue when a person's culpability or competency are called into question (see chapter 13), and they can present a serious challenge to people at all levels of the judicial and criminal justice systems.

The Psychoses

The hallmark of *psychosis* is a lack of reality contact. This means that the disorder significantly, persistently, and consistently interferes with a person's reality testing. *Reality testing* is one's ability to get a clear and accurate picture of the world by effectively interacting with that world, by accurately observing how other people interact with the world, and then by processing that information without significantly distorting the information. The persons most consistently considered psychotic are those suffering from schizophrenia, the severe paranoid disorders (primarily the delusional disorder), the bipolar (manic-depressive) disorder, and the severe depressions (see figure 6–1).

Schizophrenia

Schizophrenia is the most severe of the psychoses in terms of overall disturbance, prognosis, speed of recovery, emotional and physical cost to the

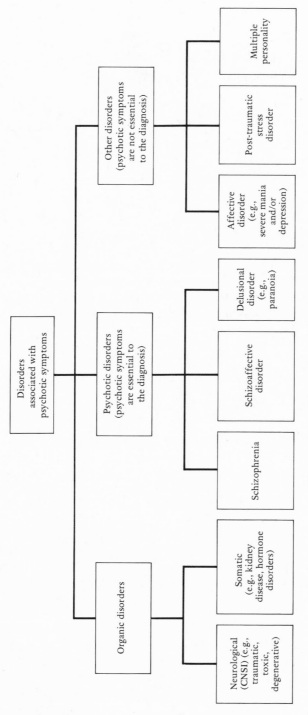

Figure 6–1. Categories of Psychotic Behavior

person, and emotional and financial cost to family and society. The odds are that one out of every hundred people in the United States will be diagnosed as schizophrenic at least once; this one percent rate has been consistent across cultures and over the years within American culture (Myers et al. 1984). A schizophrenic released after a first hospitalization has only about a 50 percent chance of staying out of the hospital for two years. Males are afflicted slightly more commonly than females.

Thought disorder, hallucinations, and/or delusions are the essential features of schizophrenia, though each may occasionally be noted in other disorders. *Thought disorder* includes delusional thinking, gaps in logic, and loose associations. *Hallucinations* are sensory experiences in the absence of appropriate stimuli—for example, seeing something that is not there. One client states that his mother constantly spoke to him, telling him to do various things. The fact that he believed she really was speaking to him, and that it was not just his imagination or a dream, made it a hallucination. It is possible to hallucinate in any of the senses, but auditory hallucinations (hearing things that are not there) are most common in schizophrenia. *Delusions* are inaccurate beliefs about the world that persist despite information to the contrary. They are most characteristic of paranoid schizophrenia and the paranoid disorder. A person who believes he is Jesus Christ, for example, is delusional. A person who believes he is being followed may be delusional, though some investigation might be necessary to clarify if he is actually being followed or not.

Auditory hallucinations are the most common in schizophrenia. But one should be suspicious of a report of auditory hallucinations if (Rogers 1988; Resnick 1990)

- they are vague, or if the person reports that it is hard to hear them or to understand them;
- the are reported as continuous rather than sporadic or intermittent;
- the hallucination is reported as not being associated with a delusion;
- stilted language is reported as the content of the hallucination;
- the content specifically exonerates the individual from some blame or responsibility;
- the person reporting the voices can give no strategy to diminish the voices; or
- the person says that he or she obeyed all command hallucinations.

Although indications of hallucinations, delusions, or thought disorder are considered essential to the diagnosis of schizophrenia, other features may be found as well. These include delirium, a sense of depersonalization, or disturbed or inappropriate affect. In inappropriate affect, for example, there is a disparity between what the person says and the corresponding emotion that is conveyed. For example, one schizophrenic individual continuously giggled while describing her mother's long and painful death from a blood disorder. Flatness (or absence) of affect would have been noted if during her description the patient had expressed no emotion at all.

Subcategories of Schizophrenia. Symptoms of two DSM subclassifications of schizophrenia may coexist in one person at the same time; the symptoms may wax and wane; some (together with specific subdiagnoses) may disappear altogether, while others emerge. Remember to consider the following as phenomenological (that is, as descriptive rather than explanatory) subtypes.

Paranoid Schizophrenic Disorder. This category is discussed in detail later in this chapter, in the section on the paranoid disorders.

Disorganized (Hebephrenic) Schizophrenic Disorder. The disorganized schizophrenic (termed *hebephrenic* in earlier DSM classifications) displays disrupted or incoherent speech and markedly inappropriate affect, often in the form of random giggling. "Silly" is an apt way of describing this behavior.

Catatonic Schizophrenic Disorder. There are two subcategories of catatonic schizophrenia; stuporous and agitated. The severe degree of disturbance associated with stuporous catatonia is observable primarily in extreme lethargy and psychomotor slowing.

Agitated catatonia, by contrast, is marked by uncontrollable motor and verbal behavior. Patients in this state are difficult to manage, and consequently can be quite dangerous to themselves or to others. This is due less to any personally directed hostility than to a tendency to see other people simply as objects to be thrown about or destroyed. Prior to the use of potent drugs that can suppress virtually all activity, agitated catatonics were sometimes put in padded cells, where they occasionally exhausted themselves to the point of stupor and even death.

Schizoaffective Disorder. This category occupies a functional midpoint between schizophrenia and the affective disorders. Individuals with this disorder show both severe affective symptoms (usually depressive) and schizophrenic symptoms (usually thought disorder and withdrawal). Compared with schizophrenics, schizoaffectives tend to have a shorter occurrence, leave the hospital sooner, and have less chance of remission. They are less likely to have other family members with a true schizophrenic disorder.

Undifferentiated Schizophrenic Disorder. This catchall category is used when the schizophrenic shows prominent signs of schizophrenia (such as thought disorder or disorganized behavior) without the clear, dominant signs of any one of the syndromes described above.

Residual Schizophrenic Disorder. Residual schizophrenic disorder is diagnosed when the person has already manifested a clear schizophrenic episode fitting one of the subtypes described above, but the symptoms have subsequently lessened. It is often applied to formerly hospitalized schizophrenics.

Problems in Diagnosis. Confused thoughts, especially confused thoughts that are not persistent or reoccurring, take place in other disorders besides schizophrenia, occasionally making it difficult to distinguish among them. Because many organic conditions (such as brain tumors and toxins) can cause hallucinations, delusions, or thought disorders, neurological screening is important in confirming a diagnosis of schizophrenia. The use of certain drugs can also result in symptoms resembling those of schizophrenia, such as high, toxic doses of amphetamines or phencyclidine (see chapter 4).

Pathological hallucinations or delusions may sometimes be difficult to distinguish from culturally sanctioned experiences that are not particularly pathological in nature. These latter experiences are usually characterized by socially appropriate, productive, and adequate coping behavior before and after the experience; a time limitation of a few hours to a few days; a reasonable degree of family and/or subgroup support; a resultant gain in social prestige or self-esteem; culturally congruent experiences in the delusions or hallucinations; and a relative absence of psychopathological indicators (Westermeyer 1987).

Causes of Schizophrenia. At this writing, most theorists agree that schizophrenia is a biologically generated disorder. Further, they agree that there is a significant genetic component in the development of schizophrenia. But they qualify this with the recognition that genetic factors probably do not account for much more than 50 percent of the factors causing most cases of schizophrenia (though there is increasing evidence of a breakthrough in finding a genetic marker for schizophrenia). Moreover, rates of schizophrenia in identical twins and in cases noted in adoption studies are the highest for severe chronic schizophrenia. In the milder forms of schizophrenia the genetic component is less important. Finally, they agree that the genetic factors do not operate directly, as a gene for hair color does; they operate only as predispositions.

Whatever the cause of schizophrenia, most agree that general deficits in the ability to attend to and effectively use information are central to schizophrenia. Such deficits taken together are the "critical marker" for schizophrenia (Bernstein et al. 1988; Selzer et al. 1990). There are also a number of premorbid predictors of schizophrenia that are worth assessing in a client:

- a schizophrenic parent or parents, or—less potently—the presence of other schizophrenic blood relatives;
- a history of prenatal disruption, birth problems, or viral or bacterial infections, or toxic situations during the child's pregnancy;
- any indications—as through CAT scans, magnetic resonance imaging, and the like—of wider cortical sulci (the spaces in the foldings at the surface of the cortex) or larger ventricles in the brain (the cavities in the brain that are filled with the same fluid as in the spine) (Suddeth et al. 1990);
- hyperactivity; cognitive slippage; any signs of central nervous system dysfunction such as early motor coordination and attention problems, especially difficulties in attention tasks with distracting stimuli and/or eye-tracking; convulsions; significant reaction-time problems; an abnormally rapid recovery rate of the automatic nervous system;
- low birth weight and/or low IQ relative to siblings;
- an early role as the scapegoat or odd member of the family;
- parenting marked by emotional and/or discipline inconsistency, including double messages;
- rejection by peers in childhood or adolescence, and perception by either teachers or peers of being significantly more irritable or unstable than other children; and
- rejection of peers, especially if accompanied by odd thinking processes, ambivalent emotional responses, and/or a lack of response to standard pleasure sources.

Overall, the preschizophrenic personality of individuals who later become schizophrenic can often be described as eccentric and isolated, mildly confused and disorganized, suspicious, and/or withdrawn.

A Developmental Sequence in Schizophrenia. The common sequence for the development of schizophrenia is as follows. The first clear signs of schizophrenia usually occur in late adolescence in American society, although earlier significant psychological disturbances of some sort (such as hyperactivity or peer rejection) have been observed earlier. Problems in attention, affect, and information processing can naturally lead to an increase in odd interpersonal and speech behaviors, a decrease in information helpful in effective coping, and greater interpersonal distancing. As these occur over time, interpersonal rejection by peers and family members increases. Concomitantly, academic and vocational performance declines (see figure 6–2).

Operating out of a restricted social and information base, the person

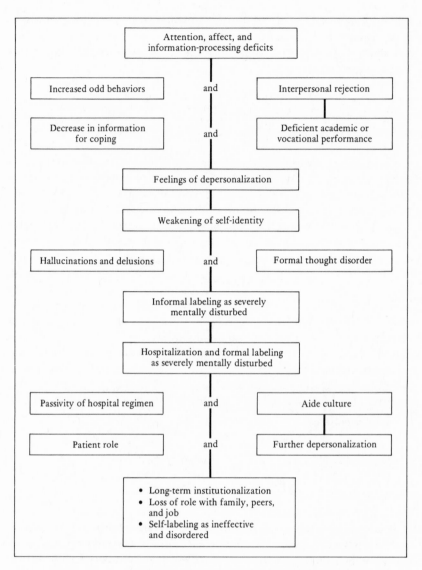

Figure 6–2. A Developmental Sequence in Schizophrenia

experiences feelings of depersonalization. There is also a loss in self-identity or, expressed in psychodynamic terms, a weakening of ego boundaries.

At this point, hallucinations or delusions are likely, signaling a break-down in the sense of self and in the standard coping behaviors. Formal thought disorder, increased depersonalization, and more disorganized behaviors also occur as allied patterns. The person may now be informally labeled as "mentally ill" or "crazy," through the actions of family, peers, co-workers, and the like. Any significant continuance usually leads to hospital-ization. Health professionals, who function as agents of society as well as treaters, formally label and stigmatize the person as schizophrenic and thus as out of touch with reality.

This sequence is common, though not inflexible; hospitalization may occur earlier in the sequence, for example, and other factors later. One feature, however, remains constant: In Western cultures the label *schizophre-nia* is difficult to discard even when the person manages to behave normally.

Treatment Issues. No matter what intervention is used, treatment of schizo-phrenia is a difficult and long-term, if not lifelong enterprise (Selzer et al. 1990). Medication is commonly employed (see chapter 15).

There are several prognostic indicators that point to a positive chance of remission after schizophrenia: (1) being married, or at least having a previ-ous history of stable, consistent sexual-social adjustment; (2) having a fam-ily history of affective disorder rather than schizophrenic disorder; (3) the presence of an affective pattern (either elation or depression) in the acute stage of the schizophrenic disorder; (4) the onset of the disorder is abrupt and occurs later than early adulthood; (5) an adequate premorbid school and/or vocational adjustment; (6) evidence of premorbid competence in interpersonal relationships; (7) higher socioeconomic status; (8) a short length of stay in the hospital; (9) an absence of indications of brain dysfunc-tion and/or electroconvulsive therapy (ECT) treatment; (10) a nonparanoid subdiagnosis; (11) a family history of alcoholism; (12) psychomotor retarda-tion; and (13) evidence of clear precipitating factors at the onset of the disturbance.

Paranoid Disorders

The paranoid disorders (primarily includes the delusional disorder) are, according to the DSM, psychotic conditions whose symptoms are domi-nated by persistent persecutory delusions or delusions of jealousy. Unlike paranoid schizophrenia, there is not much fragmentation of thoughts in these delusions. Also, daily functioning is seldom as severely impaired as it is in paranoid schizophrenia. The nonpsychotic paranoid personality disorder (see chapter 3) is less disturbed in functioning and has only the beginnings of thought patterns that could be considered to be delusions.

An irrational belief that is persistently held in spite of evidence to the contrary is termed a *delusion,* as we have seen. A delusion is referred to as *systemetized* when it is held consistently and has a good internal logic. *Persecutory delusions* (such as belief that other people or forces are against one), *grandiose thinking* (such as belief that one is superior or perhaps supernatural), and *irrational jealousy* are common in paranoid disorders. Normal people occasionally feel misunderstood or mistreated; the paranoid person, however, feels misunderstood and/or persecuted on a chronic basis (Turkat 1985). Indeed, the distorted beliefs of paranoids may in some cases contain a grain of truth, reflecting real aspects of their situation. But it is the significant exaggeration or distortion that clearly defines it as paranoid.

In the paranoid (delusional) disorder, the psychotic delusional process is systematized; the person may appear to be normal, and may indeed function normally, in most instances.

King Otto of Bavaria, who took the throne in 1886 at the age of thirty-eight, was descended from a line of rulers that demonstrated a variety of mental disorders. King Otto is a good example of a delusional disorder leading to violence, as well as how power and position can sometimes protect the perpetrator from the consequences of such behavior.

King Otto first publicly demonstrated his mental disorder when he was twenty-seven. Just as an archbishop had finished lauding the virtue of the royal family in a sermon, Otto burst into the church. Decked out in hunting regalia, he threw himself on the alter and shouted out a list of sexual sins involving court pages. Otto had a fear of the royal doctors, which was not totally a paranoid response since their care had been a major factor in the suicide of his brother Ludwig, the former king. But Otto's thinking definitely turned bizarre when he developed the delusion that he must shoot a peasant (yes, peasant—not pheasant) a day—kind of a royal version of "An apple a day keeps the doctor away." As a result, for several days in a row, upon arising, he leaned out of his window and blasted one or two of the peasants who were working in the royal garden. Fortunately for all, the royal family devised a charade wherein servants arranged to make sure Otto's gun was reloaded with blanks while he slept. Then a servant wearing different garb each day was positioned outside Otto's bedroom. Otto consistently took the bait, routinely "killing" a peasant every day until he was deposed in 1913.

Deceptive Delusions. Delusions that are most characteristic of paranoid schizophrenia and the paranoid disorder can be faked as part of an attempt to avoid responsibility for some action. In general, the clues that lead one to believe that the reporting of a delusion may be malingered are:

- an abrupt onset or cessation;
- eagerness of the person to call attention to the delusion or to lead discussion to this topic;
- inconsistency of the person's conduct with the delusion (especially when the person is not a burned-out schizophrenic and thus generates few or no behaviors anyway)
- a report of bizarre content in the delusion without disordered thoughts or hallucinations; and

- the delusion somehow specifically reduces the relevant responsibility or culpability.

The delusional systems of most paranoid persons reflect practical concerns in their lives. One client's paranoid belief system focused on a feared loss of his wife and money because he was struggling with occasional impotence and with a cessation of growth in his business. Subconsciously, he feared that these factors would cause his wife to stop loving him and even turn against him.

Folie à deux. When two (or more) people share a delusional system, they participate in a *folie à deux* (folly of two), or what has also been termed the *shared paranoid disorder.* The person originally diagnosed as psychotic (usually with a paranoid disorder rather than with paranoid schizophrenia) finds someone to control, as this allows the person to see his or her belief system as valid. The receiver incorporates the controlling person's psychosis into his or her own belief system, mimicking the beliefs and behaviors of the controller.

In most instances, both the controlling person and the receiver have been previously involved in a mutually close and intimate relationship. Often the receiver has exhibited a history of psychological dependence on the controlling person. This control can become an issue in subsequent criminal behavior, such as the control Charles Manson exerted on his followers, which can be seen as reflecting a *folie à deux* (see chapter 4). The dependency of a follower may be introduced as a defense in the criminal charge or as a mitigating factor in the eventual disposition.

Paranoid Disorders Compared. Paranoid schizophrenia is classified as a schizophrenic disorder because it involves hallucinations and disorganized associations in thought processes. As such, it shares many commonalities with both the paranoid disorders and the other schizophrenic disorders. As the following breakdown indicates, it also contrasts with these disorders (Meissner 1978; Turkat 1985):

Paranoid Schizophrenia	*Other Paranoid Disorders*
The delusional system is poorly organized and may contain a number of delusions that change over time. Schizophrenia and the belief system disorder are both fundamental to the abnormality.	The irrational beliefs may not be so severe as to constitute a delusion, or when existent, there are few of them, and they don't often change. A belief system disorder is the fundamental abnormality.
A generally bizarre appearance and attitude.	Appearance of normality.
Problems in reality contact.	Relatively good reality contact.

Paranoid Schizophrenia	*Other Paranoid Disorders*
The delusions are wide-ranging, including persecution, jealousy, grandiosity, irelevant thoughts.	The delusions are of persecution or delusional jealousy.
Develops later in life.	A more consistent relation to early developmental patterns.
Biological factors are generally the significant contributing causes.	Psychological factors are generally the primary causes.

Just as paranoid schizophrenia can be contrasted with the other paranoid disorders, it can also be contrasted with the other schizophrenic disorders.

Paranoid Schizophrenia	*Other Schizophrenic Disorders*
Depression is not very common.	Depression or other mood disorder is more common.
Develops later in life.	First manifestations are shown in adolescence or late adolescence.
More common in males.	Approximately equal incidence in males and females.
Often some reasonably normal-appearing outward behaviors.	More disoriented or withdrawn appearance.
Higher intellectual ability than other schizophrenics.	Often of lower-than-average intelligence.
Rare occurrence in many rural non-Western cultures.	Approximately equal occurrence across cultures.
Proportionately shorter hospital stays.	Tend toward long periods of hospitalization.
Mesomorphic body build (the body of the powerful athlete) more often.	Average body build.

Another occasionally confusing differential diagnostic problem, and one that can be problematic for criminal justice personnel, is distinguishing between the temporary psychotic state induced by severe alcoholic abuse (alcoholic hallucinosis) and that of paranoid schizophrenia. Table 6–1 offers some guidelines.

Etiology of Paranoid Patterns. Most psychopathological patterns are exaggerations or distortions of normal behavior, and the paranoid patterns are no exception. But paranoid disorders are severe exaggerations of these normal adaptations. Although physical causes can certainly lead to paranoia,

Table 6–1
Differential Diagnosis between Alcoholic Hallucinosis and Paranoid Schizophrenia

Contrast Area	Alcoholic Hallucinosis	Paranoid Schizophrenia
Age of onset	Usually 30–60 years of age	Usually less than 35 years of age
Intensity at onset	Acute	Insidious
Family history	Usually no family history for schizophrenia	Typically a positive family history for schizophrenia
Affect	Anxiety and depression	Flat or inappropriate affect
Thought processes	Coherent	Loose associations, formal thought disorder
Cognitive functioning	Slight impairment	Not compromised
Length of illness	Spontaneous improvement within days to weeks	Lifelong relapsing illness

Source: Adapted in part from F.G. Surawicz, "Alcoholic Hallucinosis, A Missed Diagnosis. Differential Diagnosis and Management." *Canadian Journal of Psychiatry* 25 (1980): 57–63.

experts agree that in most cases that are unaccompanied by schizophrenia, psychological causes are primary.

Several developmental factors are common in the evolution of paranoid thought and behavior. Foremost are parental behaviors. Parents who use intense shaming as a discipline in childrearing contribute heavily. Environmental experiences such as social isolation, language differences, false arrest, or the loss of physical powers (such as impotence or progressive loss of hearing) can be catalytic agents in persons predisposed to paranoid patterns.

A prominent psychological causation theory, the shame-humiliation theory, is an information-processing theory that assumes that all people have a symbolic mental model of themselves that they attempt to maintain in the face of anticipated or actual assaults on the ego. But the paranoid's mental model is more inflexible and farther away from reality than that of the normal person. The paranoid's model provides the paranoid with a means of absorbing potentially shattering losses that they believe they could somehow have prevented.

Stages of Paranoid Development. The disorder commonly evolves in the following sequence (Meissner 1978; Turkat 1985):

1. *General distancing.* Shaming during childhood, child abuse, or other environmental trauma creates an emotional distancing from others. The parents usually communicate the messages "You are different from others" and "You should be very careful about making mistakes." Thus, the child accepts a basic concept that he or she is different and that others' evaluations are important and are often negative.

2. *Distrust.* Lacking the emotional and interpersonal feedback available in normal relationships, the person develops an attitude of distrust toward others and the world in general.

3. *Selective perception and thinking.* The distrust often brings about a more selective filtering in the initial perception of information and then in the processing of that information in thought. This adds to further distancing and distorting in the person's relationship with the world.

4. *Anxiety and anger.* The person suppresses anxiety and uncertainty by viewing others as the source of problems. A hostile orientation toward the world easily flares into anger and suspiciousness toward others. Interpersonal patterns that keep an emotional distance develop further, and in turn, others tend to avoid the person, possibly making him or her the butt of social jokes or negative nicknames.

5. *Distorted insight.* As distancing and hostility become more focused, the person develops a sense of "seeing it all clearly now," sometimes referred to as a *paranoid illumination.* Targets for hostility become specific, and the person accepts his or her reasons for the behavior as fact.

6. *Deterioration.* Specification of targets and acceptance provoke a break from reality, resulting in delusions. Some or all of the few supportive interpersonal relationships still available are lost. The paranoid is truly isolated emotionally and cognitively and becomes even more dependent on the erroneous belief systems that have been generated. From this point on, the disorder pattern becomes self-perpetuating.

Treatment of Paranoid Patterns. Treatment of paranoid disorders is especially difficult because paranoids are constantly on guard against intrusions and assaults on their vulnerability. They accurately interpret therapy or counseling as a situation that will force them to confront deficits and vulnerabilities in themselves, and as a result they seldom seek treatment.

To intervene effectively with paranoid individuals, one must accept and empathize with the delusions and yet not lose integrity by participating in the delusional system. For example, one may note correlates between one's own life and the client's, which gives the client a potential new frame of reference as well as a new model for coping with vulnerability and fear. Humor—which is notably absent in many paranoids—can be modeled, as can other cognitive coping systems.

Paranoid Behavior and Insanity. Even in cases where a severe paranoid pattern is manifest, an insanity defense is difficult to present to a jury successfully. The few times they are successfully presented is when the thought patterns and the past and present behaviors are clearly bizarre. In 1991, for example, a jury in Camden, New Jersey, found Doris Triplett not guilty by reason of insanity of attempted murder and various lesser charges. She had tried to kill her seven-year-old son by slashing his throat and her older sons, aged ten and fourteen, by giving them overdoses of cold medicine. Her rationale was that her teddy bear had told them that she had to carry out that plan. Everyone concerned seemed to agree that this was not malingered. The court quickly found her insane.

Affect Disorder Psychoses

> I been thinking some cop did what every student wants to do sometime. He killed his teacher.
>
> That's absurd. You don't kill a teacher because you get an F in class.
> — Joe Gash
>   *Priestly Murders*

Affect disorder psychoses involve the extremes of mood or feeling, such as mania and depression, bipolar disorder (manic-depressive disorder), and their consequent behaviors.

Mania. The three cardinal features of mania are hyperactive motor behavior; labile euphoria or irritability; and flight of ideas (Hershman and Lieb 1988; Endicott et al. 1985).

A manic's *hyperactive motor behavior* causes the manic to have seemingly inexhaustible energy, although attention span may be short. Fast and seemingly pressured speech is also typical. Behavior is often frantic, but it is more purposeful and organized than that of the schizophrenic. Many grandiose projects are undertaken; few, if any, are ever finished. Bright people with a mild and periodic manic component can be effective if they have co-workers who can organize and complete the many projects they generate.

The manic's *labile euphoria* or *irritability* is an affect that is not consistently joyful but is intense. Euphoria is usually more evident in those phases when grandiose plans are being made. When plans lie unfulfilled, euphoria often changes to irritability and complaints. Because the change of affect is usually rather abrupt, it is designated labile.

Flight of ideas denotes a rapid progression from one thought pattern to another, and on occasion, classic thought disorder is noted. The speech pattern seems odd because the manic person uses far fewer conjunctions in speech than a normal person does. The choice of words is not peculiar, but it seems as if the manic's mind skips the links between thoughts; the standard verbal steps are just not there. Behaviorally, mania is to an adult what hyperactivity is to a child, though there is no clear causal link between the two.

Disorders including a clear manic component account for only about five percent of psychiatric hospital admissions, whereas the diagnosis of unipolar depression (depression without mania) is common. *Bipolar disorder* is the DSM term for a severe level of disorder (often psychotic) that includes both mania and depression. The incidence of severe bipolar affective disorder (including both mania and depression) is about three hundred per 100,000 people, or 0.3 percent. This rate appears to be increasing. One reason for this may be that there is now a resonably effective and straightforward cure for bipolar disorder, whereas schizophrenia—with which it is occasionally confused—is less easily treated. Clinicians apparently put borderline cases into the more hopeful category (Keller and Baker, 1991).

It is important to be aware that during a manic phase, individuals can be quite creative, although they are often unable to fulfill their flight of creativity (Hershman and Lieb 1988). The number of first-rank artists who appear to have suffered a bipolar disorder is impressive: poet-painter Dante Gabriel Rossetti; playwright Eugene O'Neill; writers F. Scott Fitzgerald, Ernest Hemingway, Virginia Woolf, John Ruskin, and Honore de Balzac; and composers Robert Schumann, Hector Berlioz, and George Frederick Handel. Indeed, Handel wrote *The Messiah* in a frenetic twenty-four days during a manic high. But it is poets who are most often bipolars. The poets Byron, Coleridge, Shelley, Poe, Gerard Manley Hopkins, Hart Crane, and Robert Lowell all suffered from bipolar disorder.

Nearly all theorists accept the idea that a biological disorder is most often the major contributory factor in primary mania and that the biological factor is genetic in nature (Keller and Baker, 1991).

Lithium reverses the symptoms of mania in 70 to 80 percent of cases (Endicott et al. 1985). It is most effective in cases of more severe manic patterns and those whose last episode was a manic one rather than a depressive one (see chapter 13). Lithium therapy is a bit more demanding than other chemotherapy: Because the kidneys absorb lithium rapidly, it must be taken in divided dosages to avoid damage to the renal system. Educating clients about its use is most important. They must, for example, take it continuously and on schedule even though they may feel well (and manics feel quite well at times). A lack of informed consent in regard to this education leaves one liable if the manic is damaged by abuse of the medication regimen.

Depression

> In a real dark night of the soul it is always three o'clock in the morning.
> — F. Scott Fitzgerald
> *The Crack-Up*

Although anxiety was often the primary concern in earlier eras, most experts now see *depression* as the predominant form of psychopathology.

Depression is manifested in one or more of the following primary symptoms:

- dysphoria (feeling bad) and/or apathetic mood;
- a loss of usual sources of reinforcement in the environment (a stimulus void); and
- chronic inability to experience pleasure (anhedonia).

Depression is often associated with a number of secondary symptoms as well:

- withdrawal from contact with others;
- rumination about suicide and/or death, and a sense of hopelessness;
- sleep disturbance, particularly early-morning awakening;
- psychomotor agitation or retardation;
- disruption of and/or decrease in eating behaviors;
- self-blame; a sense of worthlessness; feelings of guilt with no solid reason for them;
- lack of decisiveness; slowed thinking; lack of concentration;
- increased alcohol or drug use; and
- crying for no apparent reason.

It is estimated that 20 to 40 million persons in the United States have experienced a serious depression of some type. This approximate rate of 12 to 13 percent has remained stable for several decades (Kendall and Watson 1989). At least 200,000 people are hospitalized each year for depression. It is also estimated that up to one-quarter of the office practice of physicians who focus on physical disorders is actually concerned with depression-based symptomatology: indeed, about 85 percent of the psychotropic medication dispensed for depression is prescribed by nonpsychiatrists—primarily internists, gynecologists, and family practitioners.

Many causes may be primary in any one case of depression, but overall, the external and internal factors usually combine in a self-perpetuating sequence like the following:

1. negative environmental condition combined with a possible biological predisposition, leading to the first manifestation of depression; then
2. social withdrawal combined with lowered information processing;
3. inadequate social behaviors combined with guilt and self-blame;
4. further self-devaluation combined with social withdrawal; and finally
5. actual biological change that facilitates further depression.

Treatment. Combinations of chemotherapy (medication) and psychological techniques are used to treat most cases of depression. When the depression is exogenous (that is, generated by external causes, such as divorce), treatment is primarily if not exclusively by psychological techniques. When the depression is endogenous (that is, generated by internal causes, such as biological causes), chemotherapy, notably the "tricyclics," is used. (See chapter 13 for an extended discussion of the drugs used to treat depression.)

Electroconvulsive therapy (ECT) and psychosurgery have been found to be effective in treating disorders with an endogenous depressive component. For seriously suicidal patients, ECT is less radical than psychosurgery and works more quickly than drugs or psychological therapies. But there are potentially very costly side effects of these techniques.

Psychological techniques, such as traditional psychotherapy, are commonly used. Personnel in the judicial and criminal justice systems who directly encounter depressives can help by employing some of the following techniques that are based on the cognitive behavior modification therapies.

The graded-task approach. The initial objective with depressed persons is to get them active again. The graded-task approach breaks down goals or activities into subgoals or smaller behavior sets to make them less overwhelming. They may be asked to do only a small part of an assigned task at a time, for example, instead of the entire task. The purpose is to make the task simple enough that they complete it and gain the reinforcement of success. Tasks are then increased in duration and complexity.

Inducing incompatible affect and behavior. Act to elicit affective responses such as humor and anger, since these are incompatible with the despondency characteristic of depression, and they interrupt its continuity. Exercise also seems effective in combating depression; to paraphrase the private detective character in Robert Parker's book and the television show *Spenser for Hire,* "When in doubt, work out."

Moving from unpleasurable to pleasurable activities. The activity levels of depressed people tend to be relatively low to begin with. The activities in which they do engage, moreover, appears to bring them little pleasure. Their everyday activity pattern is often a passive skeleton of routine behaviors. They are inclined to associate with other depressed people, a tendency that increases the depression in all concerned. Because depressives respond negatively to almost all new suggestions, strong encouragement and concrete (often written) agreements are often necessary to get them to even begin to participate in more pleasurable endeavors. Ask them not to judge any requested activity until they have engaged in it for a set period. This allows them time to get involved and begin to enjoy it.

Changing self-verbalizations. Eliminating negative subvocal self-verbalizations such as "I'm no good" or "I can't do it" is useful. Initially, have them compile a list of the negative self-statements that they tend to use, then a second list of potentially offsetting positive statements. Instruct them to purposely say the positive statements at various times, possibly aloud but usually subvocally. Agree with the inevitable protest that they will not believe the statements when they are saying them. Get them to agree to say the statements anyway. Use of the *Premack principle* can help here: the Premack principle states that performing high-probability behaviors (those that a person performs often) will reinforce and increase the occurrence of the low-probability behaviors (such as positive self-statements) with which they are paired. For example, they could be asked to say "I'm a good person, and I'm feeling much better" every time they start their car or open the door of their house. Other appropriate statements can be paired with other high-probability behaviors. If this routine of self-verbalization persists, depression usually subsides.

Some of the techniques used to intervene with acutely suicidal persons can also be helpful here (see chapter 12). Depressives most likely to *relapse* back into depression show a greater number of previous episodes of depression; higher depression levels; a family history of depression, especially in first-degree relatives; poor physical health; a higher level of dissatisfaction with their major life roles; a significant history of ECT treatment; and younger age at onset.

Seasonal Affective Disorder. When there is a strong seasonal variation in the depression—that is, when it occurs significantly more often in winter—sessions of bright, incandescent light can be effective. It is equally important to avoid or remedy disruptions of the individual's circadian rhythms.

Pre-Menstrual Syndrome (PMS). The concept of a specific syndrome related to negative mood changes premenstrually was first introduced by Frank in 1931 (Dawood 1985). More than one hundred symptoms have been attributed to PMS, although not one is unique to the syndrome. Those thought to be most common are tension, anxiety, and fluid retention, primarily right before the onset of menses. The most commonly reported symptoms are fatigue, irritability, bloating, tension, breast tenderness, mood liability, depression, and food cravings.

The incidence of significant and consistent PMS is about 2 to 5 percent of women (Dawood 1985). This figure represents women who are seriously debilitated by the disorder, as some 40 percent of women experience some of these symptoms on occasion. The specific cause of PMS is still unknown. Numerous hypotheses have been generated, however, and the most popular explanations center on ovarian hormones, especially on their influence on brain structures such as the hypothalamus. PMS is increasingly being used as a defense in criminal trials, though with only mixed success.

Organic Brain Disorders

The brain, or more generally, the central nervous system (CNS), can be functionally impaired by a wide variety of diseases and toxic chemicals, as well as by direct trauma (Mulsant and Thornton 1990; *Merck Manual* 1987). The extent of psychological impairment depends on the location and extent of neural damage, the person's prior psychological adjustment, and adaptive characteristics of the person's living environment. The effects of an organic mental disorder are quite variable, ranging from mild attentional problems to florid psychotic behavior.

Central Nervous System Impairment (CNSI)

The legal system often confronts the issue of whether there is a central nervous system impairment (CNSI) in a client (Orsini, Van Gorp, and Boone 1988). It may be critical to a decision about whether the person is competent to stand trial or is criminally responsible. CNSI encompasses numerous disorders that are sometimes identified according to the traditional but imprecise rubric of organic dysfunction or organic brain damage. Such labels reinforce the widely held myth that brain damage is a unitary entity composed of a fixed set of symptoms. In fact, the observable symptoms of brain damage vary dramatically in both quantity and quality.

General Principles of CNSI. The human brain is fragile, yet remarkably designed. Primarily composed of water and fat, it has a gelatinlike consistency that would sustain damage from a simple nod of the head without the surrounding membranous cushion (meninges) filled with cerebrospinal fluid (CSF) that circulates through and around the brain. Although it comprises only 2 percent of the entire body's mass, the brain requires 25 percent of its oxygen supply and a similarly disproportionate share of its energy resources. For this reason, any occurrences that compromise normal blood flow to the brain can cause irreversible destruction and associated loss of function. Fortunately, the cerebrovascular system resists destructive influences and relies on a blood-brain barrier that permits these essential components to enter while screening out a multitude of other potentially toxic or infectious substances.

Dramatic recovery from many common types of brain damage, such as head injury or cerebrovascular accident (stroke), is the rule rather than the exception. This is because most of the acute effects of brain injury are the result not of destroyed brain tissue but of a temporary compromise of the larger cortical areas surrounding the lesions through edema (swelling), altered blood flow, and increased intracranial pressure. Concurrent with these physical processes is a recovery pattern that is usually rapid during the first several months after the injury, then slows progressively until a plateau is reached months later. Ultimately, the degree of recovery depends on a host of factors, including the person's age at the time of injury, general health status, premorbid intelligence, severity of the damage, and the particular areas of the brain affected (O'Connor and Cermack 1987; Lezak 1987).

There is certainly a general relationship between brain structures and psychological functions, but our knowledge of the correlation is by no means exact. It is known, however, that each of the two cerebral hemispheres controls relatively distinct functions. In the vast majority of right-handed persons, the left hemisphere is specialized for language skills, whereas the right hemisphere is specialized for visuospatial abilities, such as drawing, assembling objects, finding directions, visualizing spatial arrangements, and orienting oneself to objects in external space. At a more general level, the distinction between the two hemispheres emphasizes the capacity of the left hemisphere for rational, logical, and analytical thought processes, and of the right hemisphere's role in more holistic, intuitive thought processes.

Initial clues as to the location of focal brain damage may be found in a number of observable ways. The presence of a paralysis and/or loss of sensation on one side of the body is a cardinal sign of disorder in the opposite brain hemisphere. Telegraphic, agrammatic speech is most often characteristic of left frontal impairment, whereas verbose but meaningless or confused speech, reduced comprehension, and reading difficulties result from damage to the left posterior (temporoparietal) area. Prefrontal cortical impairment in either hemisphere often results in diminished judgment and planning ability, problems sustaining attention, and mental inflexibility in problem solving.

The analysis of brain functioning, and the diagnosis of specific brain disorders, has been greatly advanced by increased research in brain-behavior relationships (neuropsychology) and such techniques as computer-assisted tomography (CAT scan), as well as ever-newer specific techniques such as PET (positron emission tomography) and SPECT (single-photon emission computed tomography). The latter is especially useful in forensic cases as, unlike most other measures that focus more on anatomical changes, SPECT can detect changes in blood flow that occur shortly after an injury. The electroencephalogram (EEG), a traditional and relatively crude device, is gradually being replaced by techniques such as MEG (magnetoencephalogram). MEG is a noninvasive scan of the electrical activity of the brain that studies areas of the brain as they respond to motion, color, and speech sounds; hence it can be especially helpful in studying correlates of psychological disorder.

Closed Head Injury

Head trauma is the third leading cause of death in the United States, with an annual incidence of more than 500,000 new cases of serious head injury per year. Over 70 percent of the injuries sustained in motor vehicle accidents involve the skull and the brain, and these account for the majority of head injuries in the United States. Closed head injuries (CHI) are also commonly caused by falls (most notably in alcoholics), assaults, industrial accidents, sports, and recreational activities.

In cerebral concussion, the brain is jolted or agitated in a manner that produces functional impairment for at least a brief period. Depending on the severity of impact, this compromise of the brain's general arousal system (reticular activating system) can produce a momentary daze, loss of consciousness, coma, or even sudden death from respiratory arrest. Contusions (bruised tissue), lacerations, edema, and hemorrhage also occur in more severe head injuries, which may involve skull fracture. Because of the shape of the inner skull, the contusions that occur in CHI are most commonly found in the frontal and temporal lobes—areas that play an important role in attention, memory, and judgment as well as emotional behavior.

Mild head injury usually results in a brief period of unconsciousness followed by an initial awakening period characterized by confusion, dizziness, restlessness, irritability, and apathy. Aggressive behavior sometimes arises out of confusion or paranoia, without the individual's awareness of what is happening. Other typical features include headache, nausea, vomiting, blurred vision, changes in pulse and blood pressure, and inability (usually temporary) to recall details surrounding the injury. Furthermore, a brief period of post-traumatic amnesia is common such that new learning is impeded. The duration of this amnesic period is considered to be the most reliable index of the severity of concussive injury (Adams and Victor 1989). In the majority of cases, most symptoms disappear within five weeks.

By definition, moderate to severe CHI usually requires a complete loss of consciousness and a post-traumatic amnesic period of at least twenty-four hours. The symptoms include those of mild head injury, but they are prolonged and are often associated with permanent deficits that have variable effects on general intelligence or physical functioning. From a cognitive standpoint, memory is a frequent and perhaps the most prominent residual deficit after CHI (Levin 1990).

The most effective methods for the prevention of such head injuries include wearing protective head gear and seat belts; reducing and enforcing road speeds; avoiding drinking and driving; using brightly marked pedestrian crossings; eliminating road hazards; and raising the age when driving is allowed (Jennett and Teasdale 1981).

Treatment. The management of mild head injury generally involves bed rest, medication for symptoms, neuropsychological assessment, and supportive intervention. Education regarding the injury, its effects, and its anticipated outcome are important for the patient and family for emotional and practical reasons. Most patients are able to return to full work within several months (Adams and Victor 1989). In more serious cases, intensive medical intervention is required, followed by rehabilitative efforts aimed at restoring the patient's functional capacity. Cognitive rehabilitation aimed at providing compensatory aids (such as memory log, diary, timer, digital alarm chronograph) as well as retraining of impaired skills is often indicated, though the benefits of cognitive retraining remain to be demonstrated (O'Connor and Cermak 1987). Substantial though incomplete recovery is the rule in severe cases, with the majority of gain occurring within the first six months post-injury and generally reaching a plateau within two to three years.

Dementia

The term *dementia* generally refers to a progressive deterioration of intellectual and adaptive functioning produced by a loss of brain tissue. Vascular dementia, in particular, is thought to be due to the same processes that cause a stroke (cerebrovascular accident; or CVA)—namely, a disruption of the blood supply to the brain, either through occluded arterial vessels (ischemia) or leakage of blood (hemorrhage) in or around the brain. In either case, dementia is a consequence of either a large area of destroyed tissue (100 ml) anywhere in the brain or smaller, strategically located lesions in areas vital to memory.

Dementia Due to Cerebrovascular Disease (CVD). A stroke, the common term for a *cerebrovascular accident* (*CVA*), occurs when part of the brain is damaged because its blood supply is disturbed. As a result, the physical or mental functions controlled by the injured area deteriorate. Recent CVA research findings include (Adams and Victor 1989; Orsini, Van Gorp, and Boone 1988):

- Heavy drinking is linked to greater risk of stroke. Alcohol increases blood pressure, which may lead to hypertension and thus increase the risk of stroke.
- The incidence of stroke is reduced when patients' high blood pressure is treated with beta blockers, which studies suggest slow the effects of clogged arteries.
- More strokes happen in the morning than any other time of day. Experts suggest it may be due to the stress of waking and getting out of bed.
- Strokes are seasonal. Those caused by blocked arteries are more likely to happen from February through April. But transient ischemic attacks (TIAs), the "ministrokes" that often precede major strokes, tend to happen most often in June, July, and August.

- Men whose mothers died from strokes face an increased risk of stroke themselves.

- A high intake of potassium from food sources may protect against stroke-associated death.

- Hypertension is the most important risk factor for stroke and therefore for vascular dementia. Anything that contributes to hypertension—such as heredity, aging, obesity, chronic alcohol abuse, and smoking—is therefore a secondary risk factor.

The early symptoms of dementia, regardless of type, include:

- forgetfulness, such as misplacing objects and forgetting recent events or familiar names;
- mental slowing (abulia)—not being as quick as usual;
- decreased concentration, particularly in relation to complex tasks;
- behavioral changes such as irritability or apathy; changes in mood, most frequently depression; and
- visuospatial problems reflected in quality of writing or drawing and judgment in tasks such as driving.

Although most people show a substantial recovery within a period of six months following a single stroke, vascular dementia usually reflects more extensive damage from accumulated strokes and is therefore essentially irreversible. Treatment of vascular dementia is similar to the treatment of stroke: the major focus is on prevention of further infarction. Unfortunately, many of the rehabilitative services that are helpful to most stroke patients (such as physical, speech, and occupational therapy) are of limited value to demented patients because of their inability to learn or carry over within-session gains from session to session (Fraser 1987). To help with the confusion, it is suggested that these patients be placed in a bright room with only nonconfusing sensory stimuli present. Also, caretakers should be made aware of the need to constantly reintroduce themselves; and they should speak with simple sentences to the patient. Orientation to time is facilitated by the presence of calendars and clocks (*Merck Manual* 1987).

Alzheimer's Disease and Senile Dementia, Alzheimer's Type

Alzheimer's disease (AD) is the most common form of degenerative brain disease that produces dementia primarily in persons over the age of fifty. With a prevalence exceeding 2 million cases in the United States, it occurs with greater frequency in females than in males (by a 2-to-2 ratio), and it is

expected to continue to be a major health problem as older persons constitute an increasing percentage of the population. Currently, AD accounts for
an estimated 20 percent of all patients in psychiatric hospitals and for 50
percent of all dementing diseases (Adams and Victor 1989).

AD develops insidiously and runs a rapid, steady, and progressive
course that is relatively unaffected by medical intervention. Regardless of
whether it occurs before the age of sixty-five or in later years (when it is
known as senile dementia, Alzheimer's type), AD is associated with shrinkage in the size and weight of the brain (atrophy) due to neuronal loss, and an
abnormally large number of neuritic plaques, neurofibrillary tangles, and
granulovacuolar changes (Mortimer 1986). The fact that these changes occur to a smaller degree in normal aging and that they correlate highly with
the presence and degree of dementia supports the view that AD represents
an accelerated aging process in the brain. It is probably best considered a
family of diseases, some of which are directly produced by genetic defect.

The early phase of dementia also includes diminished mental flexibility
and difficulties managing complex or novel situations that require problem-
solving skills (Gass and Russell 1986). Visuospatial skills are also affected.
In the middle phase of AD, even well-learned ("crystallized") language skills
are affected, including reading, writing, and verbal expression of ideas.
Speech is often tangential, concrete, and repetitive, slowed by word-finding
difficulties (dysnomia). Further progression of the disease strips the patient
of such basic abilities as communicating (aphasia), using familiar objects
(apraxia), or even recognizing them (agnosia). There is a deterioration of
self-care and basic hygiene skills, and family members are sometimes forgotten or unrecognized (Mortimer 1986). Death usually ensues in six to twelve
years.

The cause of AD remains unknown. A hereditary component is indicated by a concordance rate of approximately 40 percent in twins, both
identical and fraternal. Once the diagnosis of AD or any irreversible dementia is established, it is customary for a responsible family member to be
informed and counseled as to the patient's limitations. In general, it is
advisable for the patient to continue activities of which he or she is capable,
while refraining from those that require significant responsibility or potential risk. In a more advanced phase of the disease, institutional care is usually
necessary.

Wernicke-Korsakoff Syndrome

Often assigned the label *alcoholic dementia,* this symptom complex generally consists of a global confusional state, apathy, restlessness or drowsiness,
peripheral nerve disease, and problems with stance, gait, and oculomotor
control. An amnesic state, characterized by an inability to store new information (anterograde amnesia), is a cardinal manifestation, though many past

memories are lost as well (retrograde amnesia). More unique to this syndrome is confabulation, the retrieval of incorrect historical information which in this case stems from organic rather than motivational factors. The person is unaware that the information is incorrect. The disease is caused by thiamine deficiency most commonly in association with alcoholism (see chapter 4). Thiamine administration usually produces a dramatic recovery of motor functions within days. Deficits in learning and memory, however, recover more slowly and incompletely (Adams and Victor 1989).

Notes

Adams, R.D. and Victor, M. 1989. *Principles of Neurology.* 4th ed. New York: McGraw-Hill.

Bernstein, A., J. Riedel, F. Graae, D. Seidman, et al. 1988. "Schizophrenia Is Associated with Altered Orienting Activity, Depression with Electrodermal (Cholinergic?) Deficit and Normal Orienting Response." *Journal of Abnormal Psychology* 97: 3–12.

Dawood, M. 1985. "Premenstrual Tension Syndrome." *Obstetrics and Gynecology Annual* 14: 328–43.

Endicott, J., J Nee, P. Andreason, et al. 1985. "Bipolar II—Combine or Keep Separate." *Journal of Affective Disorders* 8: 17–28.

Fraser, M. 1987. *Dementia.* New York: John Wiley.

Gass, C., and E. Russell. 1986. "Differential Impact of Brain and Depression in Memory Test Performance." *Journal of Consulting and Clinical Psychology* 54: 261–63.

Hershman, D.J., and J. Lieb. 1988. *The Key to Genius: Manic-Depression and the Creative Life.* Buffalo, N.Y.: Prometheus.

Jennett, B., and G. Teasdale. 1981. *Management of Head Injuries.* Philadelphia: F. A. Davis.

Keller, M. and L. Baker. 1991. "Bipolar Disorder. *Bulletin of the Menninger Clinic.* 55: 172–181

Kendall, P., and D. Watson, eds. 1989. *Anxiety and Depression.* San Diego, Calif.: Academic.

Levin, H. S. 1990. "Memory Deficit after Closed Head Injury." *Journal of Clinical and Experimental Neuropsychology* 12: 129–53.

Lezak, M. 1987. "Assessment for Rehabilitation Planning." In M. Meier, A. Benton, and L. Diller, eds. *Neuropsychological Rehabilitation* New York: Guilford Press.

Meissner, W. 1978. *The Paranoid Process.* New York: Jason Aronson.

Merck Sharp and Dome Labs. 1987. *The Merck Manual.* 15th ed. New Jersey: Author.

Mortimer, P. 1986. *Alzheimer's Disease.* New York: Raven Press.

Mulsant, B., and J. Thornton. 1990. "Alzheimer Disease and Other Dementias." In M. Thase, B. Edelstein, and M. Hersen, eds. *Handbook of Outpatient Treatment of Adults.* New York: Plenum.

Myers, J., M. Weissman, G. Tischler, C. Holzer, et al. 1984. "Six-Month Prevalence of Psychiatric Disorders in Three Communities." *Archives of General Psychiatry* 41: 959–70.

O'Connor, M., and L.S. Cermack. 1987. "Rehabilitation of Organic Memory Disorders." In M. Meier, A. Benton, and L. Diller, eds. *Neuropsychological Rehabilitation.* New York: Guilford Press.

Orsini, D., W. Van Gorp, and K. Boone. 1988. *The Neuropsychology Casebook.* New York: Springer Verlag.

Rendall, P. and D. Watson, eds. 1989. *Anxiety and Depression.* San Diego, Calif.: Academic.

Resnick, P. 1990. Personal communication.

Rogers, R., ed. 1988. *Clinical Assessment of Malingering and Deception.* New York: Guilford.

Selzer, M., T. Sullivan, M. Carsky, and K. Terkelsen. 1990. *Working with the Person with Schizophrenia.* New York: New York University Press.

Solovay, M., M. Shenton, and P. Holzman. 1987. "Comparative Studies of Thought Disorders: 1. Mania: 2. Schizoaffective Disorder." *Archives of General Psychiatry* 44: 13–30.

Suddeth, R., G. Christison, E.F. Torrey, M. Casanova, and D. Weinberger. 1990. "Anatomical Abnormalities in the Brains of Monozygotic Twins Discordant for Schizophrenia." *The New England Journal of Medicine* 322: 789–94.

Turkat, I. 1985. "Formulation of Paranoid Personality Disorder." In I. Turkat, ed. *Behavioral Case Formulation.* New York: Plenum.

Westermeyer, J. 1987. "Cultural Factors in Clinical Assessment." *Journal of Consulting and Clinical Psychology* 55: 471–78.

7

The Anxiety, Dissociative, and Sleep Disorders

Early in life I was visited by the bluebird of anxiety.
— Woody Allen

The Case of Mark Peterson

On November 8, 1990, Mark Peterson was convicted of sexually assaulting a twenty-seven-year-old woman whom psychiatrists had diagnosed as a multiple personality. She was alleged to have forty-eight separate personalities. It was also alleged that one of her personalities—a fun-loving twenty-year-old—had sex with Peterson without the awareness of her primary personality. The assault charge against Peterson thus stemmed from the contention that he knew or should have known that she was mentally disordered and therefore took advantage of her. Peterson testified that she had told him about people she called John, Jennifer, and Janie but that he thought she was referring to brothers and sisters.

The conviction in this bizarre case was later overturned. There was substantial dispute over the diagnosis. Certainly the woman showed substantial anxiety throughout, so she may have been reasonably diagnosed as one of several of the anxiety disorders. An initial anxiety situation may have been combined with a perception on her part that she had been raped, leading to a variation of a post-traumatic stress disorder. Or she may have suffered from a true multiple-personality disorder, though that syndrome is actually rather rare.

All of these disorders—anxiety disorder, post-traumatic stress disorder, and multiple-personality disorder—are covered in this chapter. In the first section we examine the anxiety disorders, wherein anxiety is the preeminent feature. In the second section we focus on the dissociative disorders. Anxiety is not usually immediately evident in the dissociative disorders, but many theorists agree that anxiety plays a varying but significant role in generating and maintaining these patterns. We will discuss the sleep disorders at the end of the chapter, as they include elements of both anxiety and dissociation.

141

The Anxiety Disorders

We all experience anxiety at one time or another. But there are degrees to which anxiety plays a role in the various mental disorders. In some disorders—the personality, impulse, and substance-use disorders, for example—anxiety does not usually occur because of the individuals' lack of perception that they themselves are disordered. And although anxiety is often present in schizophrenia or depression, it is not the dominating or compelling factor.

Anxiety is not in itself abnormal (Kendall and Watson 1989). Everyone experiences anxiety in some form or to some degree, and it is sometimes an adaptive response. Anxiety is abnormal when it is maladaptive, either because of a paralyzing intensity or because of the ineffective or self-defeating behavior built up around it.

In the DSM, *anxiety disorders* are disorders in which anxiety is the predominant symptom and in which anxiety is directly associated with maladaptive behavior. The subcategories of the overall DSM category *anxiety disorders* are as follows:

I. Anxiety states
    A. Panic disorder
    B. Generalized anxiety disorder
    C. Obsessive-compulsive disorder

II. Post-traumatic stress disorder

III. Phobic disorders
    A. Agoraphobia
    B. Social phobias
    C. Simple phobias

When specific objects or situations cause maladaptive anxiety, the anxiety is considered to be *focused*. The anxiety disorders that produce focused anxiety are the three phobic disorders. Simple phobias are fears of specific objects, such as snakes, or of specific conditions, such as heights. Social phobias are incapacitating fears of certain social situations, such as public rest rooms. Agoraphobia is fear of being out in the open and of being abandoned.

When maladaptive anxiety is more free-floating and persists without identifiable causes, the anxiety disorder is referred to as one of the three *anxiety states*. With free-floating anxiety, people are unsure of the object of their intense fear and apprehension. This is clearer for the first two anxiety states—panic disorder and generalized anxiety disorder—than it is for the third, obsessive-compulsive disorder.

In a *panic disorder*, a person experiences unpredictable episodes of intense anxiety, usually accompanied by a sense of doom (Clum 1990). In a *generalized anxiety disorder,* a person experiences chronic anxiety in a broad range of normally unthreatening situations. In an *obsessive-compulsive disorder,* a person experiences uncontrollable thoughts and actions whose presence allays some of the anxiety but whose absence produces even greater free-floating anxiety. When anxiety is caused by the re-experiencing of a traumatic event, the anxiety disorder is likely to be a *post-traumatic stress disorder.*

Anxiety States

Panic Disorder. The panic disorder is primarily denoted by recurrent anxiety attacks and nervousness, which the individual recognizes as panic. Attacks typically last for a period of minutes (occasionally hours), during which the person literally experiences terror (Clum 1990; Hoehn-Saric and McLeod 1988). Panic disorder affects about 1.5 to 2.0 percent of Americans at some time in their lives. Even macho types suffer panic attacks, as attested to by Earl Campbell, a longtime star fullback, now with the New Orleans Saints. Among first-degree relatives of a person who has suffered a panic disorder, there is a lifetime risk of 15 to 20 percent. About two to three times as many people experience panic attacks as have panic disorder.

Early recognition and response by the criminal justice system to the panic disorder is important as people with panic disorder are almost three times as likely to attempt suicide as those with any other psychological disorder—including major depression and alcoholism, which are traditional major risk factors for suicide. One out of every five persons with a panic disorder reports having made a suicide attempt. They are over fifteen times more likely to try suicide than those with no psychological disorder.

Unlike the avoidance patterns noted in the phobias, panic disorder focuses more on the experience of terror and the temporary physiological discharge symptoms, such as cold sweats and hyperventilation. These episodes of intense anxiety—panic attacks—appear suddenly and unpredictably and encompass other symptoms besides anxiety. Cold sweats, dizziness, trembling, sensations of fainting, and feelings of impending doom, such as going crazy or dying, are symptoms that typically accompany the intense anxiety.

James O. Wilson, executive director of the Phobia Center of the Southwest, uses the following explanation of a panic attack to communicate with patients and their families:

> Imagine that you are being attacked by a bear. The information "bear" comes in, is processed, and the files on "bears" are brought up, and the data you have on bears in those files determine the next response. Signals are sent down to the brain stem. In order to flee from this bear, you must do two things. One, you must get scared, because without being afraid you are

not motivated to run. Two, you have to have some mechanism whereby you can run faster than you have ever run before.

Noradrenaline is believed to play a major role in creating the feeling of fear. When the noradrenaline is released, you begin to focus on the bear. This creates a feeling of fear; memory is blocked, learning is blocked. Thinking becomes negative. The stance becomes defensive, and you want to flee. At the same time, the feeling of fear is created to get you ready to run.

Simultaneously, adrenaline is released to provide the ability to run. Adrenaline plays a role in creating the physical symptoms of fear. As the adrenaline is released, the heart pounds to send blood to the large muscles in the arms and legs. The blood vessels in the hands and feet constrict to drive blood into the large areas and the hands and feet get cold. Digestion slows as blood is pulled from the digestive system and sent to the muscles. The person breathes rapidly and breathing shifts from the abdominal area and into the upper chest. You begin to perspire in an attempt to cool the body. Salivation decreases to compensate for the fluids lost through perspiration so that the body does not dehydrate.

In the meantime, the noradrenaline rushing to the brain and the adrenaline pouring through the body have the effect of a passing gear in an automatic transmission car. More and more fuel goes into the engine and you suddenly hit a point in which the passing gear kicks in. In the human body, it is the panic gear that kicks in.

In a panic attack, the same psychological phenomena occur, but there is no bear. Of course, a major focus in treatment for people with this and related patterns is why they feel the symptoms when there is no "bear."

Panic attacks can be treated in most people (Hecker and Thorpe 1991). Medications such as tranquilizers and antidepressants have proven effective, although the attacks may recur when the medications are stopped; moreover, these medications do have significant negative side effects. In the long run greater help can come from cognitive therapy, which focuses on correcting distorted ways of thinking, including the misinterpretation of such symptoms as heart palpitations or dizziness. The misinterpretation of physiological sensations and external cues are typical during a panic attack.

Generalized Anxiety Disorder. Generalized anxiety disorder is an anxiety state marked by chronic free-floating anxiety and of hyperactivity of the autonomic nervous system (ANS) throughout a broad range of normally nonthreatening situations.

The essential feature is an overall physiological stress syndrome, known as chronic ANS overactivity and characterized by sweating, heart palpitations, apprehensive expectation, hypervigilance, and muscle tension. People suffering from generalized anxiety disorder are constantly watching for and expecting something terrible to happen, although they cannot say what it is they are afraid of. Their heightened anxiety interferes with ordinary tasks, and they often develop many physiological complaints, such as muscle aches, twitches, and difficult breathing. Panic-disorder clients show a wider variety of physical symptoms, higher anxiety levels, more expectations of disaster or catastrophe, and more disturbed childhoods than do persons with a generalized anxiety disorder.

Obsessive-Compulsive Disorder. The obsessive-compulsive disorder, which occurs at about a one percent rate in the general population, is an anxiety state caused by and characterized by either persistent uncontrollable thoughts or an irresistible impulse to perform certain actions repeatedly, or both. Obsessions are thoughts that are persistent and unwanted and that the person feels unable to stop. Compulsions are similar, but they are actual behaviors, not thoughts. Although the obsessive-compulsive disorder is listed in the DSM as an anxiety disorder, the direct experience of anxiety is not as evident as it is in the other anxiety disorders. Obsessive-compulsives see their patterns of behavior and thoughts as irrational and distressing, but they usually do not experience panic. They are often embarrassed about these behaviors and may take extreme measures to hide them from the scrutiny of others (Sheehan and Raj 1990).

The usual age of onset for the obsessive-compulsive disorder is late adolescence or early adulthood. This syndrome occurs proportionately more often in middle- and upper-class individuals. This should not be surprising, especially in a society that so highly values achievement, since those with compulsive patterns are often quite efficient and productive. On the average, obsessive-compulsives are brighter than individuals with the other anxiety disorders—obsessions are intellectual coping strategies for anxiety. This is no doubt why, as noted in chapter 1, the obsessive-compulsive disorder is the only disorder that occurs at a higher rate in the suburbs than in central-city or rural areas.

The most common obsessions that clinicians see are repetitive thoughts of contamination, violence, doubts about religion and one's duties, and self-doubts. The most common compulsions include checking behaviors, repetitive acts, and handwashing.

This disorder does not include compulsions to perform behaviors that many people find inherently pleasurable, such as overeating or overindulgence in alcohol. Although many people are unable to control these latter behaviors, they do not find them foreign or intrusive. They may be leery of the consequences (overweight or alcoholism), but they feel no discomfort about the specific behaviors themselves.

A clear and consistent regimen of *response prevention* (such as taking all soap and towels away from a hand-washer, or turning off the water), combined with constant *exposure* to the eliciting stimuli to promote extinction, provided in the context of a firmly and consistently demanding though supportive *counseling relationship* is the core of an effective treatment program for the compulsive aspects of the disorder. Consistent with assumption that some obsessive-compulsive patterns are a cover for an underlying depression, antidepressants—specifically, cloimipramine—have been helpful in some cases.

Post-Traumatic Stress Disorder (PTSD)

Post-traumatic stress disorder (PTSD) is a separate subcategory of anxiety disorder in which a traumatic event, such as combat in war or a natural disaster, produces disabling psychological reactions, especially emotional numbing. While pre-existent personality factors can facilitate the emergence of a PTSD, the duration and severity of the stress itself are also directly related to the probability of an occurrence of PTSD (Peterson et al. 1991).

For a formal DSM diagnosis of post-traumatic stress disorder, there must be evidence of a substantial stressor that would seriously disturb most people—such as being raped or being in an airplane crash—and re-experiencing of the stressful event, as indicated by at least one of the following: (1) recurrent related dreams; (2) déjà vu about the event; and (3) persistent memories of the event. As a result, there is a distancing from the external world, as evidenced by at least one of the following: (1) lessened emotional responses; (2) lowered interest in at least one usual interest or activity; and (3) detachment from others.

PTSD differs from common stress responses in that the trauma is more severe, unusual, abrupt, and specific in the post-traumatic disorder. PTSD is not a normal reaction to the stressor, but given the severity of the trauma, the PTSD is an understandable reaction. It is not as uncommon or as "special" in its correlates as plaintiff's attorneys would sometimes like us to believe.

Some people do recover spontaneously from PTSD over varying time periods, while in others the propensity toward the terror response remains for decades. Early interventions, with chemotherapy and psychotherapy, reduce the suffering as well as the long-term vulnerability.

The principles of crisis intervention (that is, immediacy, proximity, and expectancy) provide an excellent framework within which to carry out any such treatment. *Immediacy* refers to the early detection and treatment of the disorder, with an emphasis on returning individuals to their normal life situations as quickly as possible. *Proximity* emphasizes the need to treat them in their ongoing world by avoiding hospitalization. Lastly, *expectancy* is the communication that while their reaction is quite normal, it does not excuse them from functioning adequately.

PTSD in the Legal Arena. Persons involved in the legal arena commonly encounter or offer diagnoses of post-traumatic stress disorder (PTSD). The difficulty with this is that it is hard to establish the link between the current alleged disorder and a previous situation. The "face valid" nature of the symptomatology, such as nightmares about the prior incident, is often the only clear support for the diagnosis. Hence, PTSD is amenable to conscious and unconscious faking (Sparr and Atkinson 1986).

For example, in *Pard v. U.S.* (1984), Mr. Pard had been charged with two counts of attempted manslaughter and one count of attempted murder, stemming from an attempt to kill his ex-wife and a consequent shoot-out with police officers. He received a verdict of not guilty by reason of mental disease or defect. The jury accepted his assertion that he was suffering from a PTSD, generated by alleged extensive combat experiences in Vietnam. After the criminal trial, Mr. Pard lodged a civil suit for related damages against the U.S. government and the Veterans Administration. During that trial, the defendants provided extensive evidence that, at most, Mr. Pard had only been marginally exposed to combat.

Flashbacks, or vivid re-experiencings of the traumatic event, are commonly reported in cases of PTSD that make it into the legal arena (Sparr and Atkinson 1986). The dramatic quality of flashback symptoms is certainly very impressive to most jurors; the difficulty is in deciphering the veracity of such reports. In conjunction with the general concepts noted in the discussion of malingering in chapter 8, the following criteria (Sparr and Atkinson 1986) are effective in helping to substantiate true flashback:

- The flashback is sudden and unpremeditated.
- The flashback is uncharacteristic of the individual.
- There is a retrievable history of one or more intensely traumatic events that are re-enacted in the flashback.
- There may be amnesia for all or part of the episode.
- The flashback lacks apparent current and specific motivation.
- The current trigger stimuli reasonably resemble the original experiences.
- The individual is at least somewhat unaware of the specific ways he or she has reenacted some of the prior traumas.
- The individual has, or has had, other believable symptoms of PTSD.

Crime Victim Stress Disorder (CVSD)

Attention to the victims of crimes has increased substantially in the last decade. But while attention has been deservedly paid to victims of rape and spouse and child abuse, the effects of crime on victims in general has only recently been of interest to researchers and clinicians (Peterson et al. 1991).

New research shows that crime victims have much higher rates of physical disorders, alcohol problems, depression, and phobias than would be statistically likely. The most severe symptoms are for rape victims (see chapter 10). But symptoms—including depression that can last for months or years—are found in about one out of ten victims of serious crimes, such as assault. And problems occur even in crimes in which the victim was not physically assaulted. Dr. Dean Kilpatrick, director of the Crime Victims Research and Treatment Center at the University of South Carolina, estimates that one in twelve robbery victims has a major mental health problem.

The distinctive emotional imprint of crime results from the victim being the intentional target of another person's malevolence. That experience shatters many of the assumptions people have about themselves and the world, assumptions that other kinds of catastrophe leave untouched. The impact of crime may be more devastating than that of a natural disaster like a tornado, because it is a person doing it. Interventions need to counter the paranoia that is likely to set in, as well as the specific symptomatology manifested in the individual victim.

Phobic Disorders

Slightly more than six of every one hundred adults experience some type of phobia in any given month. Phobic disorders are patterns in which chronic avoidance behaviors occur in conjunction with an irrational fear of a particular object or situation. A classic phobia is marked by disproportionate, disturbing, and disabling responses to a discrete stimulus.

Agoraphobia. Agoraphobia (literally; "fear of the marketplace") is a complex phobic disorder centering on an intense fear of being alone or of finding oneself in public places without access to the help one anticipates needing. It is the fear of fear itself. Such individuals often become housebound, breaking their loneliness with manipulative behaviors, often toward spouse and children, and spending long hours talking on the telephone (Hecker and Thorpe 1991).

Since these defenses are seldom effective, such individuals eventually become bothersome and tedious to those around them; consequent depression then complicates the agoraphobia. Alcohol and other drugs may be used to dilute the anxiety, leading to an overlay pattern of addiction. Approximately five percent of the population has at some time suffered from agoraphobia.

Social Phobia. Like agoraphobia, social phobia involves fears about going out in public. Social phobia is persistent anxiety about negative scrutiny of one's behavior by others. The social phobic is often acutely fearful of making public presentations of any sort. Even eating at a center table in a restaurant may cause anxiety. The most common manifestation of social phobia in adults is a severe fear of any public speaking situation, leading to a classic vicious cycle. First, social phobics experience anxiety about a public performance. If they attempt to go through with the performance, their anxiety interferes, possibly causing them to shake visibly or twitch. Their prophecy that they will be inadequate is then fulfilled, and anxiety about any similar situation is thereafter heightened.

Simple Phobias. The simple phobias are those that involve fears of specific objects or situations. Simple phobias may have once had an evolutionary value for the human species—such as fears of snakes, darkness, heights, and eating rotten foods—that helped protect the species.

Common types of simple phobias include:

- acrophobia—fear of heights
- astraphobia—fear of storms, lightning, and thunder
- claustrophobia—fear of closed rooms and areas
- hematophobia—fear of blood
- hydrophobia—fear of water
- mysophobia—fear of germs and contamination
- nyctophobia—fear of the dark
- ochlophobia—fear of crowds
- phobophobia—fear of phobias
- thanatophobia—fear of death
- xenophobia—fear of strangers
- zoophobia—fear of a type of animal or animals in general

From a biological perspective, certain individuals are more likely to develop phobias and other anxiety disorders because of a genetic predisposition of the autonomic nervous system toward high lability (Foa and Kozak 1986). Labile individuals are biologically predisposed to respond more quickly, more strongly, and more lastingly to stressful stimuli with such symptoms as rapid heartbeat, higher blood pressure, sweating, muscular tension, trembling, and restlessness. They are consistently more edgy or jumpy and are more easily startled by a novel stimulus. This high-level reactivity and lability of the autonomic nervous system is often referred to as *neuroticism*, and it is consistent with a tendency to become anxious under pressure.

Confrontation with the feared stimuli is the critical factor in any cure, as so vividly described by G. Gordon Liddy, one of the main perpetrators of the Watergate break-in that eventually led to Richard M. Nixon's resignation as president.

> For example, to conquer my fear of thunder, I waited for a big storm and then sneaked out of the house and climbed up a seventy-five foot oak tree

and latched myself to the trunk with my belt. As the storm hit and chaos roared around me and the sky was rent with thunder and lightning, I shook my fist at the rolling black clouds and screamed, "Kill me! go ahead and try! I don't care! I don't care!" As the storm subsided, I heard my father ordering me to come down. As I lowered myself to the ground, he shook his head and said, "I just don't understand you." "I know," I said.

I repeated this kind of confrontation over a period of years, mastering one fear after another. I was afraid of electricity, so I scraped off an electrical wire and let ten volts course through me; I feared heights so I scaled buildings with one of my friends. (*Playboy* [October 1980], p. 208)

The Dissociative Disorders

Dissociative disorders are syndromes characterized by a fragmenting of consciousness or identity. The effect is to compartmentalize psychologically distressing memories in such a way that they do not intrude into conscious awareness. This may involve a loss of memory, a multiple personality, or an experience of unreality about oneself. Though this splitting is seldom permanent, it may wax and wane.

Dissociative disorders must be distinguished from culturally approved, temporary dissociative states. For example, chanting, dancing, and drugs may produce ritualistically controlled dissociative states that are a temporary therapeutic escape from conflict.

The various subcategories of the dissociative disorders are psychogenic amnesia, an acute disturbance of memory function; psychogenic fugue, a sudden disruption of one's sense of identity, usually occurring during travel away from home; depersonalization disorder, a disturbance in the experience of the self in which the sense of reality is temporarily distorted; and multiple personality, the domination of the person's consciousness by two or more separate personalities.

Psychogenic Amnesia

The common meaning of the term *amnesia*—a temporary loss of the ability to recall past experiences—conveys the essence of this category. *Psychogenic amnesia,* however, refers to sudden amnesia generated by psychological trauma, such as the abrupt loss of a job or an important relationship, rather than by an organic cause such as a blow to the head. The information that is lost may refer to something in the immediate or distant past or to a certain topic.

Media portrayals lead people to believe that in amnesia the memory of all past events is lost, but this is rare in both psychogenic and organic amnesias. In cases of psychogenic amnesia the recovery of memory is usually sudden, either a day or several years later, whereas in organic conditions accompanied by amnesia, recovery is gradual if it occurs at all. The *alcohol amnestic syndrome* specifically differs from psychogenic amnesia in that the person with the former syndrome is able to recall information for only a few minutes, then loses it, because the ability to transfer information into long-term memory has been lost.

It is unclear exactly what mechanisms underlie psychogenic amnesias and fugues, but three main hypotheses have been proposed (Kopelmon 1987). The intervention, as well as the legal response, depends upon the hypothesis to which one subscribes. The first hypothesis holds that psychogenic amnesia experiences result from a faulty encoding of information at its initial input; that is, the information is not even stored. The deficit is thought to occur because the extreme mood or emotional arousal that often accompanies the first appearance of such amnesias can hamper the acquisition of the information. Kopelmon sees this first hypothesis as the one best supported by the data. The second hypothesis is that the memories do exist but have been "repressed"—that is, there is "motivated (at a subconscious level) forgetting." A third hypothesis is related to the second in that the information is believed to be actually stored somewhere in memory, but the third hypothesis suggests there is a primary retrieval deficit and that the amnesiacs reflect mood-state- (or ego-state, in psychodynamic terminology) dependent phenomena, similar to those seen in depression. Thus, the experiences could be retrieved if the subject could be restored to a subjective state similar to that in which the experiences first occurred.

With few exceptions (such as *Wilson v. U.S.* [1968]), courts have not accepted amnesia by itself as a primary defense supporting either incompetency to stand trial or insanity. The exceptions have usually involved incidents in which there is severe head injury. Amnesia caused by true physical trauma is seldom total; nor is it selective for issues pertaining only to the relevant incident. The abuse of drugs and alcohol can, of course, distort memory, although again, there is little evidence that people with any significant degree of functioning during the incident have totally impaired memories because of such abuse. Hypnosis can be useful in refreshing memory in all of the above conditions, but there has been an increasing trend in the legal system to reject any testimony that has been "enhanced" by hypnosis (Scheflin and Shapiro 1990).

This trend has been slowed, however, by the findings of the 1987 Supreme Court case of *Rock v. Arkansas*. In this case, Vickie Rock was charged with shooting her husband. She had a partial amnesia for the details of the shooting. She was hypnotized to enhance her memory, and after hypnosis she remembered that the gun had misfired because it was defective. The trial court refused to permit this testimony, asserting that because it had resulted from hypnosis it was therefore unreliable.

The Supreme Court disagreed, holding that to arbitrarily prevent her from testifying concerning the memory recalled under hypnosis was a violation of her constitutional right to testify in her own defense. It was the absolute rule prohibiting a defendant from presenting hypnotically enhanced testimony that the Court found objectionable, stating, "In applying its evidentiary rules a State must evaluate whether the interests served by a rule justify the limitation imposed on the defendant's constitutional right to testify." Difficulties with hypnosis, the Court felt, could be cured by good cross-examination or rules regulating hypnotically enhanced testimony, without prohibiting it altogether. Presumably a state could enforce such rules as procedural safeguards to help reduce hypnosis-caused bias. The prosecution, too, could use eyewitnesses who under hypnosis "remember" details that point to the defendant's guilt. Given the limited training in hypnosis of police officers who often conduct criminal hypnosis, this offers many potential problems.

Psychogenic Fugue

Psychogenic fugue can be considered a specific form of psychogenic amnesia in which people are unable to recall their prior identity, suddenly leave where they live, often wander about, and assume an entirely new identity. Recovery is usually complete, but people seldom recall events they experience during the psychogenic fugue state. This syndrome typically occurs in response to a severe psychosocial stressor. Excessive use of alcohol or drugs can help induce it through the dissociation inherent in such users' states of consciousness. A respected middle-level executive, for example, disappeared for two weeks and was found working as a short-order cook at a "greasy spoon," a stark contrast to his previous position. It turned out that two days before his fugue episode his wife had told him that she was considering leaving him for another man. From his perspective, there was no apparent reason for her to do so. He had been extremely dependent on her and simply dissociated from the severe stress he anticipated would occur if she left him.

Depersonalization Disorder

Depersonalization disorder involves experiencing the self as unreal or as drastically altered. Although an emerging dissociation is seemingly involved, depersonalization disorder is not a true dissociative disorder because consciousness is never truly split. People with a depersonalization disorder feel separated from their normal consciousness as if they were separate observers of themselves. They report feeling that the typical reality of the external world has been altered, but there is no break in consciousness or memory.

Since depersonalization is an experience many people undergo at times, the definition of a disorder is appropriate on the basis of frequency and intensity. One adolescent girl developed an intense depersonalization response to her combination of her hostile feelings of anger toward her mother and her incestuous thoughts about her father. A previous mild delirium experienced when she was stung by a bee may have served as an inner model for the experience.

Disorder also arises when a person feels a lack of control during or in anticipation of such occurrences. Many people are not really bothered by such experiences, whereas others feel as if they are going crazy. For the latter, the experience of depersonalization is sometimes conditioned to anticipatory anxiety, leading to a vicious cycle reinforcing the belief that they might indeed be going crazy. It can also occur in a fashion similar to the conditioned anxiety response that many argue is the cause in the flashbacks from certain drug experiences. Abuse of alcohol and drugs facilitates the development of this disorder.

Multiple Personality

The essential feature of the multiple-personality disorder is the existence of two or more distinct personalities in one individual. These personalities are distinctly dissociated from each other. Each incorporates a complete identity, with a consistent and individual set of behavioral and social patterns. The transition between the personalities is sudden.

Most studies that attempt to document multiple personality find it to be extremely rare. For example, in one of the earliest thorough reviews, Taylor and Martin (reviewed in Ross 1990) found only seventy-six cases prior to 1945; Winer (1978) then found that only about two hundred cases has been clearly documented in the literature up through 1978; Greaves reported a count of fifty cases between 1970 and 1980. Reports in recent years suggest a possibly increased rate (Ross 1990). Several factors may be involved in such an increase; a multiple personality may have been confused with other another disorder, such as schizophrenia. Also, Thigpen and Cleckley (1984), as well as others (Gruenewald 1984), have noted that several secondary gain factors (both for the client and for the therapist) may generate a perceived but inaccurately diagnosed case of multiple personality, or may expand the number of personalities in one of the rare true cases. They point out that:

- Clients with hysteric conditions or certain personality disorders (see chapter 3) may be motivated by a desire to seem special, and the glamour and drama of the multiple personality may help them unconsciously produce a false appearance of multiple personality.

- Clients who are in legal troubles, like Kenneth Bianchi, the "Hillside Strangler," may produce a multiple-personality facade in order to escape responsibility for their behaviors.

- Therapists are likely to find the prestige attached to treating multiple personalities alluring and thus help to produce false cases, such as the case of Kenneth Bianchi (see chapters 8 and 11). Thigpen and Cleckley (1984) assert that "unfortunately, there also appears to be a competition among some therapists to see who can have the greatest number of multiple personality cases" (p. 64).

More than likely, the multiple personalities popularized in the movie *The Three Faces of Eve* (Sizemore and Pittillo 1977) and in the book *Sybil* (Schreiber 1974) were induced iatrogenically—that is, were disorders that occurred in that form as a result of the treatment itself.

The mass media have commonly associated multiple personality with schizophrenia. But multiple personalities are not psychotic and thus are not schizophrenic. Although there may sometimes be a delusional quality to their thinking about their own identity, there are typically no real delusions about the external world and no disturbance of perceptual or cognitive processes. Because no actual loss of contact with reality occurs, no psychosis is involved.

Not surprisingly, the new personalities often incorporate traits that are opposite from those of the original personality and that demonstrate behaviors that the person previously found difficult to express. The original personality tends to be relatively conservative and socially constricted, while flamboyant personal styles and the acting-out of sexual and aggressive behaviors find an outlet in the newer roles.

Persons are especially susceptible to developing a multiple personality if they (1) are under significant stress; (2) have somewhat contradictory personality factors; (3) were abused as children; (4) have experienced maternal rejection; (5) are impressionable, suggestible, and/or dependent; (6) tend toward overdramatic behaviors; and/or (7) have unrealistically high standards of performance. (Ross 1990; Gruenewald 1984).

The traditional treatment for multiple personality is hypnosis (Gruenewald 1984), which is used to get in touch with the dissociated subpersonalities. In the relatively few cases that have been available to clinicians for study, hypnosis has generally been reasonably successful. It is true that since hypnosis itself involves a dissociative experience, it may iatrogenically increase the tendency to produce multiple personalities, particularly in the short run.

The Sleep Disorders

The humorist and old-time movie star W. C. Fields once quipped that "the best way to get a good night's sleep is to go to bed." Unfortunately, it is not that easy for many people. In fact, sleep disorder plagues everyone at one time or another, and though there are wide-ranging estimates, it is reasonable to assume that up to 15 percent of all adults will suffer a significant period of chronic insomnia at some point in their lives (Gackenbach 1985; Van Pat 1984).

The sleep disorders discussed here involve difficulties in falling asleep or maintaining sleep. But there is also a condition termed *narcolepsy,* wherein people are unable to control falling asleep. Narcolepsy has occasionally been used as a successful defense in criminal trials, but it would only seem to be a reasonable option when there has been a diagnosis prior to the crime and where it was not an obvious option for malingering.

There are a wide variety of sleep disorders. The DSM recognizes a number of them, including sleepwalking, sleep terror disorder (both referred to as *parasomnias*), sleep-wake schedule disorder, primary hypersomnia, primary insomnia, and insomnia disorder (referred to as *dyssomnias*). An alternative and very well-respected diagnostic classification system for sleep disorders is that of the Association of Sleep Disorder Centers, published in its booklet "Diagnostic Classifications of Sleep and Arousal Disorders."

Any apparently serious sleep disorder should be evaluated at a sleep disorder center. A thorough evaluation should include the physiological monitoring of at least a couple of nights sleep.

Chemotherapy is commonly used for insomnia, but chemotherapy directed toward sleep disorders generally must be administered with caution. It can be especially useful in breaking an insomnia cycle, but if it is prescribed for any length of time it loses its effectiveness, brings on the risk of drug dependence and/or addiction, and can generate a rebound effect of even greater insomnia.

Other ancillary intervention techniques include initiating a regular program of vigorous exercise; avoiding large or late meals; avoiding long or late naps during the day; cutting down on caffeine or smoking or alcohol use; never *trying* to go to sleep, unwinding before bedtime, and going to bed only when you are sleepy. The final step is to relearn a more appropriate bedtime routine by going to bed only when feeling tired; awakening at the same time each morning; avoiding naps during the day; avoiding all nonsleep-related activities (within reason) in the bedroom—that is, not reading, watching TV, or eating in bed. If sleep is still elusive, get up and move to another room. Stay up until you are really sleepy, then return to bed. If sleep still does not come easily, get out of bed again. The goal is to associate the bed not with frustration and sleeplessness but with falling asleep quickly. Repeat this as often as is necessary through the night. Set the alarm and get up at the same time every morning, regardless of how much or how little you slept during the night. This helps the body to acquire a constant sleep-wake rhythm.

During the first night, people usually have to get up five to ten times and may not get much sleep at all. As sleep deprivation increases over several nights, it becomes easier for them to fall asleep. Soon, normal sleep is achieved. As the philosopher Friedrich Nietzsche wrote in *Thus Spake Zarathustra,* "It is no small art to sleep: to achieve it one must stay awake."

Notes

Clum, G. 1990. *Coping with Panic*. Pacific Grove, Calif.: Brooks/Cole.

DeSilva, P. 1987. "Obsessions and Compulsions." In S. Lindsay and G. Powell, eds. *A Handbook of Clinical Adult Psychology*. Aldershot, England: Gower.

Foa, E., and M. Kozak. 1986. "Emotional Processing of Fear: Exposure to Corrective Information." *Psychological Bulletin* 99: 20–35.

Gackenbach, J., ed. 1985. *Sleep and Dreams: A Sourcebook*. New York: Garland.

Gruenewald, D. 1984. "On the Nature of Multiple Personality." *The International Journal of Clinical and Experimental Hypnosis* 32: 170–90.

Hecker, J. and G. Thorpe. 1991. *Agoraphobia and Panic*. Needham Heights, Mass.: Allyn and Bacon.

Hoehn-Saric, R., and D. McLeod. (1988). "Panic and Generalized Anxiety Disorders." In C. Last and M. Hersen, eds., *Handbook of Anxiety Disorders*. Elmsford, N.Y.: Pergamon.

Kendall, P., and D. Watson, eds. 1989. *Anxiety and Depression*. San Diego, Calif.: Academic.

Kilpatrick, D. 1990. Personal communication.

Kopelmon, M. 1987. "Amnesia: Organic and Psychogenic." *British Journal of Psychiatry* 150: 428–42.

Pard v. U.S. 1984. (589 F. Supp. 518(D.Ore).

Peterson, K., M. Prout, and R. Schwarz. 1991. *Post-traumatic Stress Disorder*. New York: Plenum.

Rock v. Arkansas. 1987. (107 S.Ct. 989, 55 L.W. 4925).

Ross, C. 1990. *Multiple Personality Disorder*. New York: John Wiley.

Scheflin, A., and J. Shapiro. 1990. *Trance on Trial*. New York: Guilford.

Schreiber, F. 1974. *Sybil*. New York: Warner.

Sheehan, D., and B. Raj. 1990. "Obsessive-compulsive Disorder." In M. Thase, B. Edelstein, and M. Hersen. *Handbook of Outpatient Treatment of Adults*. New York: Plenum.

Sizemore, C., and E. Pittillo. 1977. "*I'm Eve*." Garden City, N.Y.: Doubleday.

Sparr, L., and R. Atkinson. 1986. "Post-traumatic Stress Disorder as an Insanity Defense." *American Journal of Psychiatry* 143: 608–13.

Thigpen, C., and H. Cleckley. 1984. "On the Incidence of Multiple Personality." *The International Journal of Clinical and Experimental Hypnosis* 32: 63–66.

Van Pat, P. 1984. "Sleep Disturbances." In P. Sutter and H. Adams, eds. *Handbook of Psychopathology*. New York: Plenum.

Wilson v. U.S. 1968. (391 F.2d 460(D.C. Cir.).

Winer, D. 1978. "Anger and Dissociation: A Case Study of Multiple Personality." *Journal of Abnormal Psychology* 87: 368–72.

8

Malingering, the Somatoform Disorders, and the Factitious Disorders

And, after all, what is a lie?
'Tis but the truth in masquerade.
— Lord Byron
"*Don Juan*" (Canto XI, St. 37)

The Case of the Hillside Strangler

From October 1977 through February 1987, a series of brutal murders and rapes of ten young women were perpetrated in Los Angeles by Angelo Buono and his adoptive cousin Kenneth Bianchi. This became famous as the Hillside Strangler case. There was never any doubt that Angelo Buono was a hard-core psychopath, but Bianchi, though also psychopathic, was more intelligent and more effectively deceptive (see chapter 11).

His friends and co-workers, for example, all characterized him as a "nice guy," and his girlfriend and the mother of his baby said, "The Ken I knew couldn't ever have hurt anybody or killed anybody—he wasn't the kind of person who could have killed anybody" (Levin and Fox 1985, 147–48). He was thought of as an excellent security guard, and the local police chief had thought of him as an excellent prospect for his police force.

When pubic hairs found in the carpet where two of the victims had been house-sitting matched Bianchi's, Bianchi's possible guilt was supported. Bianchi's attorney suggested hypnosis. Bianchi was able to fool two experts, only to be uncovered by a third. Further investigation found more instances of deception. Though Bianchi talked of his childhood as having been peaceful and idyllic, it was found that he had been raised by an emotionally unstable and occasionally sadistic adoptive mother.

It was also discovered that Bianchi had earlier in life fraudulently altered someone else's college transcript in order to establish the credential as his own. (The authentic transcript he had "borrowed" belonged to one Thomas Steven Walker—and ironically, under hypnosis, Bianchi had given his second personality the name Steve Walker.)

It was then discovered that Bianchi had attempted to set up a psychology practice. Using phony diplomas and discussions about psychology based on books he had read, he had conned a psychologist in North Hollywood into renting him space in his counseling office until his own practice "could get on its feet." It is unclear whether Bianchi actually saw clients on any regular basis, but this certainly helped set the stage for his clever malingering.

This chapter discusses two traditionally clinical patterns of disorder that are commonly confused with malingering: somatoform and factitious disorders. *Malingered* patterns are under the person's conscious control, and the motive is easily understandable (to collect money on a false insurance claim, to avoid culpability for a crime, and the like). There is at least a degree of conscious control in a *factitious disorder,* but the motivation is individual and pathological, such as obtain a sense of nurturance and comfort through repetitive hospitalizations. *Somatoform disorders* are not under conscious control. Because of the characteristics of these patterns, they often present a challenge to the judicial and criminal justice systems. At the end of this chapter are checklists to aid in discrimination among these patterns.

Malingering

Malingering is the voluntary presentation of physical or psychological symptoms. Malingering is understandable by the evident incentives and circumstances of a person's situation, rather than from the person's individual psychology (as is also true of factitious disorder).

Malingering is likely to occur in judicial and criminal justice situations (see chapter 11), as well as in job screening and the military or wherever a psychological or physical disability has a payoff. It occurs more commonly in the early to middle adult years, is more common in males than in females, and often follows an actual injury or illness. A problematic employment history, lower socioeconomic status, or an associated antisocial personality disorder are also common predictors of this disorder.

Overall Indicators

Several overall patterns have been found to be characteristic of malingerers based on interview data (Ekman 1985). This to some degree depends upon the specific distorted response pattern that is being observed—whether it is the result of defensiveness, disinterest, or other response.

One overall pattern is that malingerers more often report relatively rare symptoms, as well as more overall symptoms in general, than do honest respondents. Malingerers are usually more likely than nonmalingerers to be willing to discuss their disorder, especially how the negative effects of their disorder impact on them and especially how they impact in the rather narrow areas of functioning that have a payoff for them. They are more likely to report a sudden onset of disorder and to report a sudden cessation of symptoms if that has some functional value; they are more likely to endorse the more evident, flamboyant, and disabling symptoms of a disorder. They are more likely to give vague or approximate responses when confronted and to make inconsistent symptom reports. They are more likely to take a longer time to complete tests or interview responses, to repeat questions, to use qualifiers and vague or nonspecific responses, to miss easy items and score accurately on hard IQ test items, and to endorse the obvious rather than the subtle symptoms usually associated with a disorder (Meyer 1989; Rogers 1988).

Several consistent behavioral cues have been noted in individuals who present a dishonest portrayal of themselves (Rogers 1988; Ekman 1985). For example, on the average, such individuals nod, grimace, and gesture more than honest interviewees do, and they have less frequent foot and leg movements. They talk less, speak more slowly, and at the same time have more speech errors and smile more often. Dishonest interviewees tend to take positions that are physically farther from the interviewer. High voice pitch and many face and hand movements, relative to the individual's standard performance, also indicate deception.

There is no real support for the idea that people who are deceiving necessarily avoid eye contact (Ekman 1985). There is some evidence that females look longer into the eyes of male examiners while lying, but usually not into female examiners' eyes. These same cross-sex results hold for males as well, but not as clearly. (For a more detailed discussion of techniques useful in detecting deception, see chapter 11).

Amnesia

Amnesia is a commonly malingered symptom, probably because it is seemingly easy to carry off and acts to void responsibility, yet leaves the person otherwise fully functional in their world. True psychogenic amnesia (see chapter 7) is typically focused on personal memory, particularly those memories directly relevant to a traumatic event. True psychogenic amnesia can usually be differentiated from organic amnesia by its sudden onset, shorter course and sudden recovery, recoverability under hypnosis, personal focus, and nonimpaired ability to learn new information (Wiggins and Brandt 1988; Schachter 1986).

It's worthwhile to remember that vigor and/or apparent sincerity of presentation are not indicators of true amnesia. Indeed, there seems to be no clear correlation here. It's also worthwhile to remember that there may be both true and malingered amnesia in the same case. But there are cues that indicate malingered rather than true amnesia:

- True amnesia for a situation is seldom either total or very specific. The manifestation of either pattern cues possible malingering.

- Malingering amnesia often results in inconsistencies between reports and inconsistencies with usual psychogenic or organic syndromes.

- True amnesiacs rate themselves higher on their ability to recall information if they are told they will be given extra time or prompting, and indeed, they do function better if primed. Malingerers are more likely to indicate the improbability of change in their amnesia, and then not show much change even if they are prompted.

- Malingerers portray amnesia "as characterized by recall performance better than, and recognition performance worse than, that of brain-damaged memory-disordered subjects" (Wiggins and Brandt 1988, 74).

The Somatoform Disorders

Persons who suffer from a somatoform disorder, like those with a factitious disorder, show complaints and symptoms of apparent physical illness for which there are no demonstrable organic findings to support a physical diagnosis. But the symptoms of the somatoform disorders are not under voluntary control, as those of the factitious disorders are. Thus, a somatoform disorder is diagnosed when there is good reason to believe that the person has little or no control over the production of symptoms. While factitious disorders are more common in men, somatoform disorders are more common in women (Ford and Parker 1990).

There are five major subcategories of the somatoform disorders: somatization disorder, conversion disorder, somatoform pain disorder, hypochondriasis, and body dysmorphic disorder. The *somatization disorder* is chronic, with multiple symptoms and complaints, usually presented in a vague fashion. The *conversion disorder* usually focuses on one or two specific symptoms suggestive of a physical disorder, which on closer examination reflect primarily a psychological issue, usually generated by a symbolic conflict and often maintained by the attainment of secondary gains. *Somatoform pain disorder* is functionally a conversion disorder that refers specifically to psychologically induced pain states. *Hypochondriasis* is the consistent overresponse to and concern about normal and/or insignificant bodily changes, in spite of expert reassurance that there is no reason for concern. *Body dysmorphic disorder* (dysmorphophobia) refers to rumination and preoccupation with some imagined defect in what is actually a normal-appearing person, and in a sense is a variation of hypochondriasis.

Somatization Disorder

This subcategory of the somatoform disorders is marked by chronic though cyclic multiple somatic complaints that are not primarily due to any physical illness. Symptoms are often presented in a vague though exaggerated fashion. But they may be mixed with other symptoms derived from an actual disease, so arriving at this diagnosis is initially difficult (Katon, Lin, Von Korff, Russo, et al, 1991). It is not uncommon for this disorder to be an exaggeration of symptoms associated with a previously cured physical disease.

Diagnosing a somatization disorder is difficult because a self-report of symptoms combined with apparent prior history is naturally convincing to most physicians. Family physicians or general practitioners are more often than not the target of these complaints, and they are not inclined to see the somatization disorder as real when they eventually discover there is no physical disorder. Physicians often believe such people are only malingering or that, at the very least, there is a degree of faking involved. Hence, they are inclined to put the person in a category like "crank" and attempt in various ways to avoid spending any time with them (Katon, et al, 1991).

Because the supportive atmosphere of the physician's manner and/or the hospital structure meets at least one of the needs of persons with a somatization disorder (and to a degree a conversion disorder), such evident rejections begin to lay bare the underlying inadequacy of these persons to cope effectively with their world (Kellner 1986). Depression becomes an emergent and eventually paramount symptom, and the person may develop methods (like using alcohol) to deal with the depression. Alternatively, the person with a somatization disorder may develop a new symptom picture and generate new systems of hospitals and physicians to work through. Restrictions of time and money, however, often bring the person full circle.

Conversion Disorder

In the conversion disorder there is a specific symptom, or a related set of symptoms, that are used to attain some secondary gain or to express a psychological conflict. Conversion symptoms are not under voluntary control. A conversion disorder is sometimes referred to as a *hysterical neurosis, conversion type.*

The conversion disorder is a clear instance of the transformation of anxiety into symptoms. Persons with this disorder usually show little concern about the apparent implications of their disorder, even when its apparent consequences are early death or lifelong disability, a pattern referred to as *la belle indifference.* They appear to be aware at some level that their complaints do not predict the further dire consequences that others might infer from them. Although they are indifferent to their presenting symptoms, emotional overresponse to other issues is commonly noted in them.

The conversion disorder sometimes takes the form of blindness with no physical basis, commonly called *hysterical blindness,* a common symptom in Sigmund Freud's early patients. The blindness usually occurs after the person has witnessed a very traumatic event, and it is a clear defense against reexperiencing such anxiety.

Another classic type of conversion disorder is *glove anesthesia,* in which a person complains of numbness and paralysis roughly in the area a glove would cover. This symptom has no correspondence with actual nerve distribution and is seldom seen in people knowledgeable about anatomy. Such types of conversion disorder were much more common in Freud's day than they are now. This fact reflects an increase in the psychological sophistication of the general public and a decreasing acceptance of such overt denials of conflict.

Traditional textbook case histories have implied that symptoms such as hysterical paralysis, blindness, and deafness are typical of the conversion disorder, but in fact these symptoms are not that common. More common symptoms are pain (psychogenic pain disorder), dizziness, headaches, and muscle spasms. Hendrix, Thompson, and Rau (1978) describe the case of a bright but psychologically unsophisticated adolescent girl whose symptom was a clenched fist. For other clients this has been a symbol of repressed anger. In this young woman it symbolized resistance to attending school: the clenching of the fist made her unable to write and therefore unable to participate in school. The direct symbolic representation of conflict apparent in this young woman's symptom has two important implications. First, there is considerable primary gain associated with lessening the immediate anxiety. Second, the person reaps *secondary gain* by being able to avoid anxiety-generating situations in the future without consciously confronting the underlying conflict.

Some people develop their symptoms under extreme stress and manifest that stress quite directly. But even in these individuals anxiety seems to dissipate over the duration of the disorder in favor of a focus on physical symptoms. An important predisposing factor is a history of actual physical disorder during which excessive caretaking behaviors or other secondary gains occurred.

There are a number of theoretical ways to distinguish a conversion disorder from an organic condition, though in actual practice discrimination is difficult (see figure 8–1). Psychological tests are often helpful, as can hypnosis and "truth serums" like sodium amytal, which allow access to a level of awareness below full consciousness.

People with conversion disorders respond initially to most techniques involving suggestion, in which the cure, like the disorder itself, is dramatic. Placebos—apparent treatments without any inherent effect other than suggestion—have been found to work well. Some dramatic cures at religious shrines and faith-healing services involve persons with a conversion disorder. These cures, however, are usually temporary, so that similar symptom patterns recur.

Somatoform Pain Disorder

Somatoform pain disorder is a conversion disorder that specifically involves pain not due to a physical cause. But as with the other somatoform disorders, a history of physical disorder involving the actual symptom is common. The emergence of a somatoform pain disorder is facilitated by developmental stage transitions and by specific stressful events. Somatoform pain disorders differ from the conversion disorders in that the commonly associated histrionic features of sexual ambivalence, *la belle indifference,* and dependency are not usually observed.

As with the conversion disorders, somatoform pain disorders may reflect a psychological conflict and/or exert a controlling influence on a person's interactions with other people, resulting in a secondary gain and/or allowance for avoidance. The pain seldom follows known anatomical or neurological patterns, and extensive diagnostic work reveals little or no evidence of organic pathology. In the more sophisticated client, it may mimic well-known diseases such as angina or arthritis.

Besides the techniques used to detect conversion disorders in general, other methods are specifically useful in discriminating psychogenic pain from organic pain. Certain EMG and EEG (measures of electrical activity in the muscles and the brain, respectively) patterns are more likely to appear in cases of organic pain than in the psychogenic pain disorders. Cortical evoked potentials (brain response patterns to various stimuli, such as flashes of lights or clicks) and blood plasma cortisol levels can also help to distinguish the two states. Unfortunately, test-response reliability is too low to diagnose conclusively from only one of these tests, so experienced clinicians use several approaches. Many persons with psychogenic pain disorders never get to a psychologist or psychiatrist but remain as chronic problem patients for general physicians or specialists in the relevant physical area.

In numerous instances in the criminal justice system, there is a question as to whether a person's alleged pain is true or is being malingered. Various personnel, such as correctional officers, may be in a unique position to help in this assessment, through unobtrusive observations of the person alleging the pain; observing how limiting the pain is after the person leaves an examining office, waits for an elevator, and so on. Similar information can be provided when the person clearly believes he or she is not being observed (such as if a window allows personnel the opportunity to observe the degree of discomfort and postural adjustments the individual requires in walking, getting into a car, and the like). A great deal of observation in a direct encounter can also be useful. For example, does the person who is alleging pain seem to have no difficulty sitting through several hours of an activity without changing position?

There are indications that people from certain lifestyles or family backgrounds are more likely to use pain as a manipulator than others (Keefe and Gil 1987; Ford and Parker 1990).

- people who have a history of taking significant dosages of pain medicine;
- people who have a history of extensive medical treatment and multiple surgical procedures;
- people with a history of hypochondriasis or factitious disorders;
- people who are highly suggestible;
- people who had stressful childhoods and/or are from large families;
- people who began working full time at an early age;
- people who had children at an early age; and
- people who complain of too little pain for their injuries, as well as those who complain too much.

Membership in these groups does not necessarily indicate that the pain is less real or objective. Pain experienced by these people may be as sharp and discomforting as it is for a patient who does not share any of these experiential factors. So while a number of these individuals are experiencing actual pain, some are experiencing actual pain because they are predisposed to pain and are more likely to have a higher emotional input as an amplifier in their pain.

David Cheek (1965) has long been noted for his application of the regression method of hypnosis to some cases of psychogenic pain. He finds that some nonorganic pain states are first stimulated by offhand comments made by surgeons and attendants while the patient is under anesthesia. At these times the patient may slip into near consciousness and can then process information. Early in an operation one woman, though sedated, heard her surgeon say, "That's too bad—she's always going to have some pain from this." What had been anticipated as an unsuccessful operation proved to be a complete success, but the woman carried that suggestion into a long-term pain state. After she tried many remedies over the years, Cheek hypnotized her and regressed her to the time of the operation, whereupon she brought out the remark. Eventually she was able to allow it into consciousness, and the pain ceased. Her surgeon was able to provide useful verification: not only had he kept records because he was trying a new surgical technique, he remembered making the remark.

Hypochondriasis

Hypochondriacs unreasonably interpret normal or relatively unimportant bodily and physical changes as indicative of serious physical disorder. They are constantly alert to upsurges of new symptomatology, and since the body is constantly in physiological flux, they are bound to find signs that they can interpret as suggestive of disorder.

In one sense, hypochondriacs do not fear being sick—they are certain they already are. Hypochondriasis is a relatively common pattern from adolescence to old age, though statistically it is seen most frequently in the thirty-to-forty-year age range for men and in the forty-to-fifty-year range for women (Meister 1980). Meister also believes that there are many "closet hypochondriacs"—those who do not constantly go to physicians but are heavily involved in health fads, checking body behaviors, and discussing their concerns with people other than physicians (possibly including custody personnel).

A number of common factors have been observed in the development of hypochondriasis (Kellner 1986; Meister 1980): First, in most hypochondriacs there has been a background marked by substantial experience with an atmosphere of illness. This could include identification with a significant other who was hypochondriacal or early exposure to a family member who was an invalid. Other hypochondriacs have had a strong dependency relationship with a hypochondriacal family member who could express love and affection in a normal or intense fashion when the hypochondriac was ill but who was distant or nonexpressive at other times. Another factor is that hypochondriacs often channel their psychological conflicts and their needs for existential reassurance into their hypochondriasis. As a result, the hypochondriac pattern of behavior may mask a midlife crisis or some other challenge that is not being met effectively. A subgroup of hypochondriacs are postulated as having a predispositional sensitivity to pain and body sensation. This could be stimulated by a previous physical disorder in the body systems in which the hypochondriacal pattern is now manifest.

All these factors are naturally facilitated if being sick allows the person to avoid tasks or demands, as can often happen in the criminal justice system. Hypochondriacal patterns that allow avoidance of even the normal demands of life are subsequently reinforced and maintained. One client with hypochondriacal tendencies was certain that he would soon die from undiagnosed heart disease or cancer; for him, it was only a question of which would get him first. His therapist finally helped him to confront the existential avoidance underlying his hypochondriasis. He had never fully faced certain career choices or the degree of his commitment to further involvement with his long-term girlfriend. By inwardly acting on the assumption that he was going to die soon, he rendered these existential questions irrelevant. Once he realized that he was avoiding these issues, he dealt with them and the hypochondriacal patterns gradually disappeared.

For hypochondriasis, direct reassurance on the medical issues is not curative, but it is usually an important preliminary step in shifting the focus of intervention to more psychological concerns. At that point, the intervention approach advocated for the paranoid disorders is useful (see chapter 6).

Basically, this involves empathizing with the concerns expressed by the person and with the anguish they cause, yet not becoming a participant by agreeing that they are accurate.

Body Dysmorphic Disorder

Body dysmorphic disorder (BDD), also referred to as *dysmorphophobia,* is characterized by a preoccupation with some imagined imperfection in physical appearance or by an exaggerated reaction to some minor defect (but not if it occurs exclusively during transsexualism or anorexia nervosa). It is not held so firmly as to be delusional or paranoid in nature. So BDD victims may, if pressed, admit to the possibility that their concern is excessive. But they persist in the concern and in related behaviors (Kellner 1986). They may make repeated visits to plastic surgeons or dermatologists, for example, in order to have their concern confirmed and to get some relief from the imagined defect. Unfortunately, a number of such individuals have undergone extensive plastic surgery at the hands of unscrupulous surgeons.

As is no doubt evident, BDD is a variation of hypochondriasis. Hence, for the most part, the comments for hypochondriasis apply to BDD as well, though there is usually a greater degree of narcissism and a greater focus with controlling interpersonal relationships in BDD than in hypochondriasis.

The Factitious Disorders

Factitious means "not genuine," and *factitious disorder* refers to symptoms that are under voluntary control, as opposed to the somatoform disorders, where voluntary control is absent. At first, this syndrome may sound like malingering. The difference is that in a factitious disorder, the goal or reinforcement sought is not obvious or inherent in the apparent facts of the situation. Rather, the motivation is understandable only within the person's individual psychology.

Factitious disorders are rare. It is one of the most difficult categories to diagnose, in part because the feigned symptoms are often accompanied by a more subtle though actual physical disorder. When diagnosticians become aware of what they perceive as deception, they are inclined to make a diagnosis of an antisocial personality instead of a factitious disorder, then give the person little attention.

The factitious disorders are subdivided into *factitious disorder with psychological symptoms* and *chronic factitious disorder with physical symptoms.* The latter is often referred to in the literature as *Munchausen's syndrome,* named after Baron von Munchausen, an eighteenth-century German equivalent of the American Paul Bunyan, associated with tales of exaggeration. The general DSM diagnostic requirements for these syndromes are (1) the intentional production or feigning of symptoms, and (2) a psychological need to assume the sick role, with an absence of external incentives as primary. There are three commonly associated features of these syndromes: an adequate to extensive knowledge of the medical literature on the relevant symptomatology; a history of drug abuse; and chronic pathological lying about the symptoms and associated features.

In the factitious disorder with psychological symptoms, the symptoms are mental rather than physical, and as a result they are often not well defined. These people usually talk around a point or give approximate though evasive answers to direct questions (a pattern referred to as *Vorbereiten*). For example, if asked an arithmetical question such as "How much is thirty-five minus twelve?" they may respond with "thirty" or "thirty-five."

The all-time champion victim of the Munchausen's syndrome appears to have been Stewart McIlroy, whose path through sixty-eight different hospitals (with at leat two hundred seven separate admissions) in England, Scotland, Ireland, and Wales was retraced by Pallis and Bamji (1979). McIlroy's creative descriptions of symptomatology, a common feature of this syndrome, reflect a mastery of the technical literature related to the disorders he was faking. Nevertheless, he suffered mightily to satisfy his addiction. Over the years he was subjected to thousands of X rays and blood tests, his spine was tapped at least forty-eight times, and his abdomen and other body parts were crisscrossed with scars from many exploratory surgeries. McIlroy probably cost the British public health system well over a million pounds. Though McIlroy used false names and different complaints, he was eventually identified by scar patterns such as the "gridiron stomach," a pattern seen in a number of these individuals. Another patient with the Munchausen syndrome elicited many hospitalizations and several surgical operations by secretly, deliberately, and chronically taking large doses of laxatives.

These cases show the essential feature of the Munchausen syndrome: a plausible presentation of factitious physical symptomatology in order to elicit and sustain multiple hospitalizations. The disorder is most commonly manifested in acute abdominal, neurological, or skin symptoms. The first signs of Munchausen syndrome usually appear in adolescence and early adulthood.

The factitious disorders are more common in males. This may in part reflect a readier acceptance of verbalizations of sickness from females, so that a diagnostician would be less inclined to recognize a factitious disorder in females. Hospitalization for an actual physical disorder or a background that includes familiarity with medical issues often precedes this pathological hospitalization pattern. Many such individuals were severely abused as children, and many show a history of drug abuse. The range of symptomatology is limited only by the person's imagination and the degree of their sophistication about medical information. This disorder is chronic and is highly refractory to intervention, in part because the person can often find another cooperative physician. Ironically, the disorder usually takes a high physical toll on the person, as it did for Mr. McIlroy.

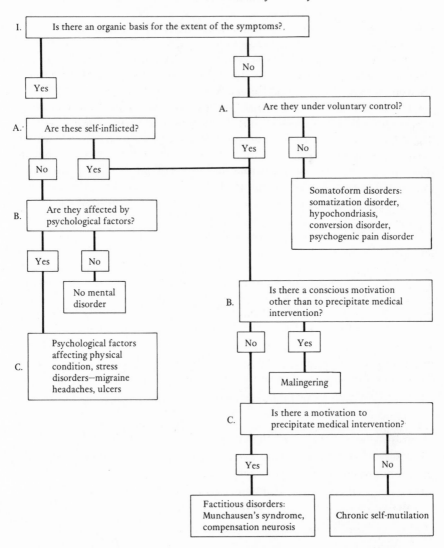

Figure 8–1. Decision Tree to Determine Presence of Hypochondriasis, Factitious Disorder, or Malingering

Ruling Out Hypochondriasis, Factitious Disorder, and Malingering

All of the patterns discussed in this chapter may at one time or another be involved in a judicial or criminal justice issue, but the three specific patterns that an observer must invariably take into account where malingering or other distorted response sets are suspected are hypochondriasis, the factitious disorders, and true malingering. Figure 8–1 shows a decision tree that helps distinguish these in such a situation.

In order to facilitate this decision process, checklists for each of the three disorders have been developed by the author and Elizabeth Salazar Jackson (Meyer 1989). All three checklists should be applied to any given case. In the great majority of cases, a high percentage 75 percent or more) of positive or "yes" answers will predominantly occur on one checklist, indicating support for that pattern. If no condition shows a substantial percentage or clearly predominates, these three patterns can usually be ruled out. In some cases, two (or in very rare cases, all three) of these patterns will occur. (We use the term "client" throughout these checklists to emphasize that there is a wide variety of situations wherein this discrimination is relevant).

Hypochondriasis Checklist

1. Is there a morbid preoccupation with the body or a part of the body that is felt to be diseased or functioning improperly?

2. Is there a long-term pattern of social or occupational impairment?

3. Are normal bodily functions/fluctuations exaggerated as indications of disease?

4. Are beliefs about the issue sustained in spite of consistent medical information to the contrary?

5. Is there a general indifference to the opinions of people in the client's environment?

6. Is the client anxious, worried, and concerned about his "illness"?

7. Does the client dwell excessively on the symptoms, turning interviews into monologues—"organ recitals"?

8. Does the client's speech content consist almost solely of symptoms, their effects on his or her life, and the difficult search for a cure?

9. During conversation, does the client frequently point out afflicted areas of the body?

10. Is there an expression of obsessive-compulsive traits such as defensiveness, obstinacy, miserliness, or conscientiousness?

11. Is there an indication of narcissistic traits, such as egocentrism or oversensitivity to criticism of slight?

12. Is there a lack of a sense of inner worth, self-esteem, or adequacy?

13. Does the client appear to have a preference for being ill, showing positive emotions if any real sickness is found?

14. Are there indications of an affective disorder, such as significant depressive tendencies?

15. Is there a history of frequent doctor visits, either with one physician or through "doctor shopping"?

16. Is there an unusual and wide-ranging familiarity with psychological or medical terms and jargon?

17. Is there an apparent addiction to reading medical journals, health magazines, and other related written materials?

18. Does the client follow unusual health fads, diets, or exercise plans?

19. Has the client often made appeals for extensive tests, examinations, and prescriptions?

20. Do the symptoms commonly deal with the head, neck, abdomen, chest, or gastrointestinal system or generally with the left side of the body?

21. Are there indications of a dependent relationship in which affection is not effectively displayed outside of sickness situations?

22. Do the symptoms seem to fulfill an ego-defensive purpose?

23. Do the symptoms ease an intolerable personal situation or allow the client to avoid anxiety or personal responsibility or to gain needed attention?

24. Do the symptoms appear to be an attempt to control a situation that seems to be getting out of his or her control?

25. Did the pattern appear to have an early onset?

26. Did the client grow up in an "atmosphere of illness," such as with a bedridden or terminally or chronically ill family member, or a family member in the medical field who brought his or her work home in some fashion?

27. Were the client's parents, especially the mother, overprotective, strict, or overly sanitary in health tendencies?

28. Did the client grow up without parents for a substantial period, or was there a pattern of self-mothering?

Factitious Disorder Checklist

1. Is there an absence of evident or obvious gain that the client would achieve as a result of the presented disorder pattern?

2. Is there a gut-level sense that the client has been inducing the symptoms?

3. Could the problem fulfill a masochistic need such as relieving guilt or a need to identify with a "sadistic" doctor?

4. Does the client show any counterphobic responses to other disorder patterns or syndromes?

5. Are there indications that deceiving others acts as a defense mechanism, such as against low self-esteem or sense of powerlessness?

6. Are there indications that the presented disorder provides distance from frustrating objects, internal conflicts, anxieties, or provides a temporary identity while ego dysfunctions are reorganized?

7. Is there any evidence that dependency needs are being gratified in the pattern?

8. Was the client's childhood marked by institutional placement or by sadistic, abusive, or rejecting parents?

9. Did the patterns apparently start in adolescence or early adulthood?

10. Is there a history of multiple hospitalizations?

11. Is there any evidence of multiple surgeries?

12. Do the symptoms appear to have symbolic meaning or to have been derived from a previously suffered disorder?

13. Does the client have a background in the health professions or other access to medical knowledge?

14. Did the client grow up in an "atmosphere of illness"?

15. Is there any indication of wandering to many different physicians and/or clinics?

16. Has the client accumulated a variety of diagnostic labels, medical biographies, radiographs, or thick hospital folders?

17. Is the medical history inconsistent with known pathophysiological courses?

18. Have there been any inconsistent lab or test results?

19. Have there been any unusual recurrent infections?

20. Has the client failed to respond to therapy as expected?

21. Has the client falsified his or her history in any manner?

22. Does the client dramatically present one or more symptoms with elaborate stories, while interacting on a narcissistic level?

23. Is the client's attitude toward staff threatening, aggressive, hostile, and/or impatient?

24. Are there frequent requests for surgery, direct patient observation, or invasive procedures?

25. Does the client impassively or even eagerly submit to agonizing examinations and treatments, expressing high pain tolerance and/or exhibitionist traits?

26. Does the client show *pseudologia fantastica,* attention seeking, or restlessness?

27. Has the client ever discharged himself or herself or retreated indignantly when confronted?

28. Are there indications of any underlying histrionic, antisocial, narcissistic, or combinations of such personality disorder patterns?

Malingering Checklist

1. Would the client obtain any obvious gain by being considered ill or disordered?
2. Does the client seem to perceive interviews as a challenge or a threat?
3. Does the client appear to be annoyed at what he or she considers to be unusual tests?
4. Does the client appear suspicious, overly evasive, vague, or unusually lacking in comprehension of issues?
5. Are there seemingly exaggerated concerns for the symptoms?
6. Is there an easily expressed pessimism about recovery?
7. Is there a relative lack of concern about treatment for the presented disorder?
8. Is the client quickly or especially explicit in denying concern about financial (or other goal-oriented) matters?
9. Is there a focused rather than wide-ranging familiarity with medical or psychological terminology?
10. Does the client show an overly self-confident or assertive manner?
11. Are there any indications of antisocial or psychopathic personality traits?
12. Are there any indications that either of the parents showed manipulative or psychopathic patterns?
13. Do some symptoms seem to contradict symptomatology the client should have?
14. In a professed syndrome that should supposedly show a long-term deficit or problem, is there an unusual lack of previous exams?
15. Are there other discrepancies, contradictions, omissions, or odd exaggerations?
16. Is there poor test-retest reliability in testing or interview patterns?
17. Whether or not there are discrepancies, exaggerations, or the like, do some portions of the client's presentation just seem too "neat," as if coming out of a textbook?

By applying the concepts noted in this chapter, the decision tree in figure 8–1, and these checklists, these important discriminations are made less difficult, but they are never easy.

Notes

Cheek, D. 1965. "Emotional Factors in Persistent Pain States." *The American Journal of Clinical Hypnosis* 9: 100–101.

Ekman, P. 1985. *Telling Lies*. New York: W.W. Norton.

Ford, C., and P. Parker. 1990. "Somatoform Disorders." In M. Thase, B. Edelstein, and M. Hersen, eds. *Handbook of Outpatient Treatment of Adults*. New York: Plenum.

Hendrix, E., L. Thompson and B. Rau. 1978. "Behavioral Treatment of an 'Hysterically' Clenched Fist." *Journal of Behavioral Therapy and Experimental Psychiatry* 9: 273–76.

Katon, W., E. Lin, M. Von Korff, J. Russo, et al. 1991. "Somatization: A spectrum of Severity." *American Journal of Psychiatry*. 148: 34–40.

Keefe, F., and K. Gil. 1987. "Chronic Pain." In V. Hasselt, P. Strain, and M. Hersen, eds. *Handbook of Developmental and Physical Disabilities*. Elmsford, N.Y.: Pergamon.

Kellner, R. 1986. *Somatization and Hypochondriasis*. London: Praeger.

Levin, J., and J. Fox. 1985. *Mass Murder*, New York: Plenum.

Meister, R. 1980. *Hypochondria*. New York: Taplinger.

Meyer, R. 1989. *The Clinician's Handbook*. 2nd ed. Needham Heights, Mass.: Allyn and Bacon.

Pallis, C., and A. Bamji. 1979. "McIlroy Was Here. Or Was He?" *British Medical Journal* 6169: 973–75.

Rogers, R., ed. 1988. *Clinical Assessment of Malingering and Deception*. New York: Guilford.

Schachter, D. 1986. "Amnesia and Crime: How Much Do We Really Know?" *American Psychologist* 43:286–95.

Spitzer, R., and J. Endicott. 1978. *Schedule of Affective Disorders and Schizophrenia*. New York: Biometrics Research.

Wiggins, E., and J. Brandt. 1988. "The Detection of Simulated Amnesia." *Law and Human Behavior* 12:57–59.

9
The Childhood Disorders and Mental Retardation

"Who are *you?*" said the Caterpillar. . . . Alice replied, rather shyly, "I hardly know, sir, just at present—at least I know who I *was* when I got up this morning, but I think I must have been changed several times since then."
— Lewis Carroll,
Alice's Adventures in Wonderland

A Case of Juvenile Homicide

Two teenagers in Ohio, a seventeen-year-old boy and his fourteen-year-old sister, paid a nineteen-year-old friend sixty dollars to shoot and kill their father when he came home from work one evening. The father and mother were divorced, and the father, who had sole care of the children, had reportedly tried to be a good parent. The killer apparently missed with his first shot and had to chase the father all over the house. He discharged a hail of bullets that eventually killed the father. The son became distressed and left the house after the first shot; the daughter remained through it all.

The teenagers hid their father's body in a bedroom, cashed his last paycheck, took his credit cards, and went on a two-week spending spree. By the time they were apprehended, they had spent more than three thousand dollars on video games, televisions, and a variety of amusements. When apprehended by the police and asked why they had had their father killed, they replied, "He wouldn't let us do anything we wanted, like smoke pot."

Child therapists have long been aware of the frequency of aggressive fantasies in children. The frequency of such fantasies has commonly been contrasted to the rarity of actual murders by children. Play therapy and/or talking about the fantasies has been seen as effective in reducing any compulsion to act them out in reality. Of course, lack of physical strength, lack of access to lethal means, and immature cognitive abilities relevant to long-term planning also serve to reduce any such acting-out.

But parricide (the killing of a parent) does occur, and in his book *The Kids Next Door: Sons and Daughters Who Kill Their Parents*, Greggory Morris (1987) vividly describes such children and their families. It is somewhat comforting to find that most children who kill their parents do so in response to chronic physical or sexual abuse, except for accidents (usually related to too-easy access to lethal means). Another significant group of parricides occurs with severely disturbed children, especially schizophrenic children; those few who do kill do so quite unpredictably, even when the parents are seemingly loving and concerned. Research by Ewing (1991) not only documents the rise in juvenile homicide but suggests this phenomenon will continue to rise markedly through the 1990s.

Children and early adolescents who kill present particular problems for the legal system. The Supreme Court has indicated that children under sixteen may not be executed for a capital crime. The last such execution was of a fourteen-year-old in 1944 in South Carolina for a crime committed when he was younger. Recently, a seven-year-old shot and killed a playmate. After talking to him, the police formally arrested him for murder, citing the fact that he first consistently denied everything, then talked about it in a fashion that indicated rational planning and an awareness of what he had done. The prosecuting attorney's office later dropped the charges.

Common law has considered the age of seven as the point when children can be considered legally culpable. But Mozart was writing great works of music at age five, so it is reasonable to conclude that some seven-year-olds could rationally plan a murder and be aware, at least at an intellectual level, of the implications of death. Nevertheless, it is equally clear that if we ever are to truly believe in the viability of a rehabilitation model—that is the concept behind the juvenile justice system—it certainly applies to children.

The Socio-Political Perspective

Numerous patterns examined in the previous chapters of this book can involve children as sufferers or victims or even occasionally as perpetrators of crimes. But in the disorders discussed in this chapter, the child is clearly the central figure. The judicial and criminal justice systems' response in an individual case is in large part determined by the overall politico-psychological concept of children held by those people who handle the case, from police officer or caseworker to judge, correctional officer, or psychotherapist.

Melton (1987) suggests four major positions in this regard. The first group, the "kiddie libbers," see children as more like adults than unlike adults. Thus, they handle cases and promote public policies designed to preserve the independence and privacy of children. They tend to see problems in children as emanating from a lack of opportunity to exercise options and choices. They strongly support greater legal rights for children, though paradoxically, some resist giving children more responsibility for legal offenses. They are the group that is most likely to recommend individual psychotherapy or peer-dominated group therapies for disordered children like the ones in the Ohio case.

A second group, the "child savers," also immediately lean toward the child's position, but they emphasize children's incompetency, dependency, and significant vulnerability. They are inclined to quickly bring the state into the parental role, and they emphasize the rights of the state over either those of the parent or of the child. Interestingly enough, the third group, the "family libbers," start with the same presumption of significant vulnerability in children as the second group. But the family libbers also believe the presence of parents is critical to a child's healthy psychological development. They will go to great lengths to keep the family structure intact and to institute programs that increase the positive functioning of the family of a distressed child.

Melton's fourth group, the "parent libbers," emphasizes parents' rights for their own sake. Parent libbers see children as legal nonpersons. This view is most clearly voiced by those parents who assert that they should retain substantial control over any late adolescent, or even early adult, who is still economically dependent on the parent, regardless of level of psychological maturity. Parent libbers are especially concerned about the freedom to socialize their children in whatever fashion they choose. Conflicts over this view quickly emerge in cases concerning many topics, most notably child abuse. Indeed, it is clear that, whatever psycho-political view is held by people dealing with cases of child distress, it will directly influence the disposition of that case.

Juvenile Delinquency and Conduct Disorders

> Anyhow, kids grow up. And once they get to be fourteen, it's out of everybody's hands about what might happen to them except their juvenile delinquent friends.
> — Dan Jenkins
> *Semi-tough*

Juvenile delinquency encompasses recurring instances of truancy, drug use, and sexual precocity, as well as more explicitly unlawful behavior. The term itself actually refers to a particular legal status rather than to a clinically defined disorder. In the DSM, most of what would be legally termed *juvenile delinquency* is included under the term *conduct disorders*. A child is judged to have a conduct disorder solely on the basis of his or her behavior, not as a result of having been convicted within the legal system (Seltzer 1990).

Most studies suggest that there has been a dramatic increase over the last couple of decades in the more aggressive conduct disorders (Henggeler 1990; Sechrest 1986). Any increase in the 1990s will be likely to be due simply to the "echo" of the "baby boom"; there presently is the largest number of youngsters under the age of six since 1967 (Loeber 1990). Moreover, American society is simply raising children who are generally less psychologically healthy, as reflected in these statistics by the 1990 panel commissioned by the National Association of State Boards of Education and the American Medical Association:

- SAT scores in recent years are significantly lower then those achieved by high-schoolers in the 1970s and 1980s.
- One million teenage girls—nearly one in ten—become pregnant each year.
- Alcohol-related accidents are the leading cause of death among teenagers.
- The suicide rate for teens has doubled since 1968, making it the second leading cause of death among adolescents.
- Homicide is the leading cause of death among fifteen- to nineteen-year-old minority youths.

Males between the ages of five and twenty represent approximately 35 percent of those arrested for violent crimes. Research indicates that most juvenile delinquents are repeat offenders (recidivists). While it is generally agreed that males exhibit more delinquent behavior (behavior of a more aggressive type) than females, the frequency, variety, and severity of delinquent acts among females is increasing. Interestingly, girls who have an earlier onset of menses are more likely to show delinquent behavior, but only if they associate with girls older than themselves (Loeber 1990).

The evidence is clear that delinquency occurs at virtually all levels of society, but there is general agreement that there is a higher percentage of juvenile offenders among the lower socioeconomic classes (Loeber 1990). Currently there has been an increase in reported delinquency not only among more youthful juveniles but also among those of higher socioeconomic status.

Such children fail to develop any real sensitivity to other's needs, as the traditional self-absorption of adolescence develops further into true narcissism (see figure 9–1).

Conduct Disorder

The conduct disorders are marked by a persistent pattern of behavior that violates major age-appropriate social norms and the rights of others. If the predominant pattern is aggression toward others and is initiated individually, the DSM diagnosis is the *solitary aggressive* type; if most of the problem behaviors occur as a group activity with peers, the diagnosis is the *group* type; otherwise, the diagnosis is the *undifferentiated* type. According to the DSM, the *conduct disorder* is the precursor to the antisocial personality. (See

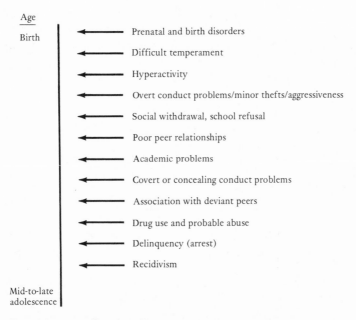

Age
Birth

← Prenatal and birth disorders

← Difficult temperament

← Hyperactivity

← Overt conduct problems/minor thefts/aggressiveness

← Social withdrawal, school refusal

← Poor peer relationships

← Academic problems

← Covert or concealing conduct problems

← Association with deviant peers

← Drug use and probable abuse

← Delinquency (arrest)

← Recidivism

Mid-to-late
adolescence

Source: Adapted from R. Loeber, "Development and Risk Factors of Juvenile Antisocial Behavior and Delinquency," *Clinical Psychology Review* 10 (1990): 1–42.

Figure 9–1. Approximate Age of Appearance of Disruptive-Delinquency Behaviors

chapter 2, as much of that material is relevant to the discussion of juvenile delinquency and the conduct disorders.) To earn the basic diagnosis of conduct disorder, at least three of the following factors, in descending order of discriminating diagnostic power, should be in evidence: (1) more than one occasion of stealing without confrontation; (2) at least twice running away from home; (3) commonly lying; (4) an incident of deliberate fire-setting; (5) frequent truancy; (6) breaking into a car, building, or house; (7) deliberate property destruction (other than fire-setting); (8) physical cruelty to animals; (9) an incident of coercive sexual activity, (10) use of a weapon in more than one fight; (11) frequent initiation of physical fights; (12) stealing while confronting the victim; and (13) physical cruelty to people. The diagnosis of conduct disorder requires evidence of the pattern for at least six months.

Etiology of Delinquency

A birth disorder, hyperactivity, impulsivity, and a classic learning disability are often major factors in delinquency. Certainly, genetic factors can propel one into criminality. A father's antisocial behavior, alcoholism, and substance abuse are major risk factors for child conduct disorder (Kazdin and Kolko 1986). Indeed, the more convictions for offenses in either biological parent, the greater the chance of a criminal pattern in the child. Child antisocial behavior has also been shown to be related to inconsistent parent-child interactions, child abuse, marital discord, parent insularity, parent psychopathology, lack of parental supervision, and indiscriminate caretaking (Kazdin and Kolko 1986). Other factors include hyperactivity (especially where there is an associated impairment in verbal memory), impulsivity, and attention problems, as well as learning disabilities, certain handicaps, low intelligence, physical disfigurement, depression, withdrawal, a lack of social skills, and the like (Henggeler 1989) (see figure 9–2).

Certainly any tendencies toward delinquency from these sources are greatly increased if either the parents or the significant others (such as an

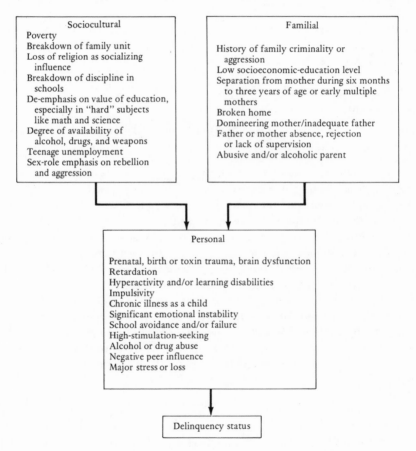

Figure 9–2. Factors Contributing to Delinquency in General

older brother) in the child's life provide a model for antisocial behavior. For example, children who were victims of sexual or physical abuse or who witnessed family violence are more likely to become delinquent. Similarly, children who are exposed to high levels of violence in movies or television, or even those who are commonly provided with toys of violence, are statistically more likely to engage in aggressive acts (Liebert and Sprafkin 1988). Overall, the best predictor of delinquency is having a parent who is abusive, alcoholic, or criminal. The younger the age when the child is first arrested, the more likely he or she is to commit a greater number of the more serious crimes.

While all of the above are important in generating delinquency, a most critical factor for many delinquents is peer influence. Children who have not attained a significant identification with the traditional socializing groups in society, such as family, church, and school, are especially vulnerable. The delinquent group often seeks to attain an identity for itself through rebellious behavior and mildly antisocial behavior, such as truancy, bullying, and vandalism, progressing into petty thievery and shoplifting, then into more serious stealing and aggressive behaviors. A common catalyst for any specific episode of delinquency is substance abuse.

All of the above point out the various factors that can lead to the many and varied forms of delinquency (see table 2–1 for further specifics). The chart in figure 9–3 describes how *aggressive* delinquency evolves.

Treatment

Efforts to treat juvenile delinquency evolved through the "three Rs": from retribution, through restraint or confinement, to rehabilitation. Many approaches have been tried (Horne and Sayger 1990; Quay 1987, but seldom have any been markedly and consistently effective. It is probably not surprising that efforts directed at the prevention of delinquency are more effective than programs designed to "cure."

Those programs that do have some success with already-delinquent youngsters usually place a high emphasis on (1) early intervention; (2) removing the child from the negative peer group; (3) strengthening the family as a whole; (4) strengthening the parents' skills in controlling the child; (5) changing the delinquent's cognitive system, since they so often inappropriately attribute negative motivation to others and adopt impulsive cognitive strategies that are self-destructive; and (6) providing training to remedy any psychological problems, as well as the deficient social and academic skills (Horne and Sayger 1990; Quay 1987.

If the individual is more solitary, undersocialized, and aggressive than other delinquents, there is a need for a highly controlled living system that includes all aspects of functioning. The group type of delinquent, especially one who is nonaggressive, requires a highly structured and supervised residen-

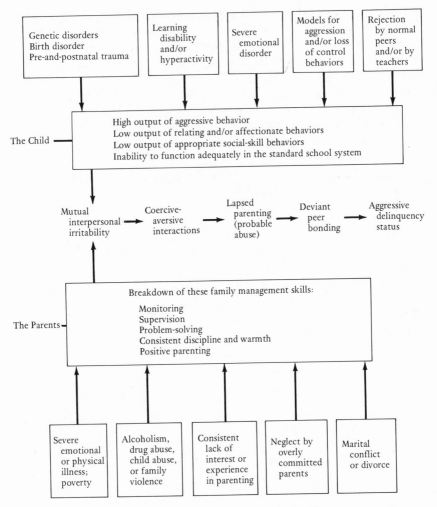

Figure 9–3. Evolution of Aggressive Delinquency

tial program less than others. One of the principal therapeutic factors derived from noted group programs such as Achievement Place is the complete removal from the delinquent subculture. Residents frequently make dramatic changes while they are enrolled in the program; unfortunately, extending or maintaining these positive changes in the outside world is difficult.

Juvenile Delinquency in Court

Delinquency may or may not involve criminal behavior. There are two different but related groups of juvenile offenders: delinquents and "status offenders." Status offenders are simply juveniles who require supervision because of a particular condition (such as truancy). Delinquency proceedings involve actions that would be considered criminal if committed by an adult. Delinquency proceedings include many of the aspects of adult criminal trials, although the labeling of events is somewhat different. Adults are "arrested," while juveniles are "taken into custody"; there is "sentencing" of adults, but "disposition" of juveniles (see figure 9–4).

It has been alleged that juveniles have the worst of both worlds—the

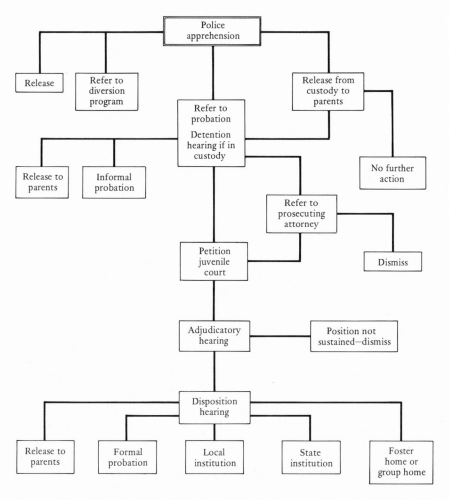

Source: Adapted from A. Binder, "The Juvenile Justice System and Juvenile Offenders: An Overview." *The Counseling Psychologist* 11 (1983): 65–68.

Figure 9–4. Flow Chart of Juvenile Judicial Dispositions

absence of some of the protections of the criminal justice system for minor crimes, plus the real possibility that they will be tried as adults for serious crimes. But the juvenile justice system has evolved with a number of important reforms, including preventing most juveniles from being incarcerated with adult offenders; protecting some information about juveniles from public disclosure; and avoiding some of the relatively harsh punishments of the adult prison system. On the other hand, such reforms make it more difficult to identify and incarcerate at an early age those individuals who will commit a number of crimes during adolescence and early adulthood.

In the early stages of a juvenile's entrance into the juvenile justice and treatment systems, the emphasis is on diversion from the quasi-formal juvenile justice system to the parents, community treatment, social services, or prevention programs. A diversion is most often generated by the police, who may decide to warn juveniles, reprimand them, or take them home. Perhaps half of the potential delinquency cases are so diverted by the police. Many additional juveniles are diverted by the court before formal juvenile hearings. Other dispositions are noted in table 9–1.

Oppositional Defiant Disorder

The *oppositional defiant disorder* is commonly considered as a precursor to the passive-aggressive disorder (see chapter 3). Many of the same behaviors are noted. But in the oppositional defiant disorder there is a more direct expression of hostility and negativism. A DSM diagnosis requires that the pattern last for at least six months and that the juvenile exhibit evidence of at least five of the following symptoms: (1) defies adult rules or requests; (2) argues with adults; (3) swears or uses obscene language; (4) deliberately irritates others; (5) projects blame onto others; (6) has temper outbursts; (7) is easily irritable; (8) easily angers; and (9) is spiteful or vindictive. There must be no evidence that the behavior violates or aggresses against the rights of another, as is found in the conduct disorder. The behavior is typically carried out toward significant others, such as teachers and parents, and it may persist into various self-destructive social interactions. Such children and adolescents show a degree of conformity and usually resist any interpretation that they are oppositional, just as passive-aggressives do.

School Refusal (School Phobia)

School refusal is often preceded by episodes of separation anxiety. *Separation anxiety disorder* commonly develops after the child experiences a loss, such as the death of a relative or pet, or after a change in the child's environment, or after a change in schools or neighborhood (Bloom-Feshbach and Bloom-

Table 9–1
Potential Dispositions Available to the Juvenile Court

1. Detention
2. Private institutional placement (residential programs)
3. Commitment to state training schools
4. Commitment to residential, mental health or vocational facility
5. Commitment to residential center for the mentally retarded
6. Commitment to state department of social services
7. Residential ranches and camps
8. Halfway houses
9. Group homes
10. Temporary shelter homes
11. Foster or adoptive homes
12. Independent living status
13. Referral to community mental health agencies
14. Referral to day-care treatment programs
15. Referral to youth protection programs
16. Vocational training programs
17. Educational tutorial programs
18. Community work projects
19. Restitution programs
20. Community improvement or essay-writing assignments
21. Individual probation—formal or informal
22. Volunteer big brother, big sister
23. Drug education programs
24. Referral to youth clubs
25. Private psychotherapist or counseling programs
26. Wilderness training
27. Parent training and family mediation
28. Social skills training
29. Fear and shock therapy
30. Diversion to the military

Feshbach 1987). The first symptoms may include waking up in the morning with somatic complaints such as headache, stomach pain, vague "aches," or nausea, though without any actual fever. After recurrences of these alleged illnesses, most parents become concerned. As school refusal worsens, other disorders may occur, including sleep disorders and disrupted peer relationships. Poor attendance in school naturally disrupts peer relationships and school achievement.

The critical preventive and therapeutic task for school refusal is for parents to force the child to attend school, no matter how vehement he or she protests. Then, if a school refusal pattern is emerging, parents are instructed to (1) never discuss school attendance over the weekend; (2) provide only a light breakfast to lessen the probability of nausea; (3) ignore any somatic complaints such as nausea; (4) make sure the child is physically delivered to school authorities; and (5) compliment the child on any successes, and keep repeating the process. The success rate for this intervention is high, especially if intervention is early.

Hyperactivity

Hyperactivity was first described in 1845 by Heinrich Hoffman, a German physician, and has had a variety of labels over the years, including *hyperkinesis, minimal brain damage,* and others. It is now clear that actual brain damage is seldom present, though disrupted and/or delayed maturation of brain function may be involved. There is a wide variation in the estimated incidence of hyperactivity in children, from as low as one percent up to as high as 15 percent. Most experts seem to agree that the incidence is probably about 6 to 8 percent. It is the second most common referral problem from schools, the most common being a failure to adequately achieve (Goldstein and Goldstein 1990; Klee et al. 1986).

Most hyperactive children function normally as adults, although a higher percentage of hyperactives than normals will be maladjusted as adults. In females, this later maladjustment tends to show up as depression and/or alcoholism. In males, it shows up as conduct problems, criminal behavior, and/or alcoholism. Lambert et al. (1987) compared fifty hyperactive boys with fifty-eight comparable normal control boys. Upon follow-up later in life, several significant differences were found between these two groups. Specifically, 19 percent of the hyperactive boys, as opposed to three percent of the controls, had had trouble with law-enforcement agencies; 14 percent had been suspended from school more than once, compared with only two percent of the controls; and there were many more cases of later school failure, emotional disorder and interpersonal difficulties among the hyperactive boys.

Types of Hyperactivity

There are four major types of hyperactivity (Goldstein and Goldstein 1990; Lambert et al. 1987; Robe 1990). The least common is *environmentally generated hyperactivity,* which accounts for 5 to 10 percent of all hyperactive children. This type may even be labeled *pseudohyperactivity,* as it has no significant biological component, unlike the three other forms of hyperactivity.

The two major causes of environmentally generated hyperactivity are severe stress, such as loss of a parent or child abuse, and the spoiling of the child in such a way that they have never learned to deal with limits on their activity. A common characteristic of such children is that there is an absence of hyperactivity before the trauma, or they exhibit hyperactive behavior only in certain situations such as where limits are not clear or are not enforced. Treatment for such children includes anxiety-reduction techniques if a stress is involved, and school consultations and family therapy to teach the teachers and parents how to more effectively set limits.

The second type of hyperactivity is *stimulant* or *food-induced hyperactivity*. Some people have argued that certain foods or food additives cause the great majority of hyperactive cases. It soon became apparent to most experts that this is erroneous, but many experts do agree that these factors are an important cause in about 10 to 15 percent of hyperactive cases. Such children often manifest food allergies as early as infancy and may show standard allergy patterns as well.

Such children have more unpredictable outbursts of hyperactivity than children with the other forms of hyperactivity. They are especially likely to increase their hyperactivity after eating meals with foods high in simple sugars, foods high in additives and preservatives, chocolate, and milk, egg, and wheat products. Naturally, the focus of treatment is to eliminate the foods that help generate the hyperactivity. But this should only be done after an extensive and exhaustive survey of the child's food intake and related behaviors. If the hyperactivity is food-generated, certain consistent patterns should become clear in such a survey. Those foods can then be systematically eliminated, and the hyperactivity should diminish.

If the hyperactivity does not lessen, one of the more common types of hyperactivity should be considered: *overstimulated (overactive) hyperactivity*, which accounts for about 30 percent of all cases of hyperactivity, and *understimulated (underactive) hyperactivity*, which accounts for approximately half of all cases of hyperactivity. Many individuals with these patterns show some form of damage or dysfunction in the premotor and superior prefrontal cortexes of the brain—areas related to inattention and difficulties in inhibiting behaviors.

In spite of the opposite labels of these latter types, children in both show high levels of activity and distractibility. Unlike environmentally generated hyperactivity, both of these types become evident even in early childhood. Table 9–2 highlights the characteristics and differences between these two major hyperactivity types.

Attention-Deficit Disorder (ADD)

Attention-deficit disorder is a condition that involves a persisting inability to keep one's attention focused. Children and adolescents with attention-deficit disorder (ADD) are presumed to possess adequate basic cognitive capabilities, but they are typically unable to focus themselves effectively

Table 9–2
Comparison of Two Forms of Hyperactivity

Overactive (Overstimulated) Hyperactivity *(30% of hyperactive persons)*	*Underactive (Understimulated) Hyperactivity* *(50% of hyperactive persons)*
Child carries a high level of neurophysiological arousal, so is highly "stimulation-respondent."	Child carries a low level of neurophysiological arousal, relative to psychological needs, so is highly "stimulation-seeking."
Child responds reasonably well to "quiet time" or stimulus-reduction methods; responds to standard "time-out," wherein stimuli are highly restricted.	Child has difficulty calming down at "quiet time"; needs some structured activity even during "time-out" or will quickly be disruptive or destructive; liable to be excessively spanked, as he or she shows little response to it.
Child becomes somewhat calmer as evening progresses. Usually falls asleep easily enough, but is a restless sleeper and is hard to awaken.	Child has difficulty going to bed and to sleep—"the tireder they get, the worse they are." But child usually sleeps soundly. Often awakens early and is ready to go right away.
Child Likes TV but can be easily overstimulated by it. Often has to do other things while watching TV. Is overstimulated and has difficulty "coming down" from periods of physical activity.	Child likes TV, especially highly stimulating programs, but can sit for hours in front of such programs as if hypnotized. Can be calmed by long periods of intense physical activity.
Child is a finicky eater. Doesn't like green vegetables or strong-flavored foods like broccoli, curry, etc. Favorite foods are bland, like macaroni and cheese, meat, potatoes; often uses cheese or sauces to mask flavors.	Child usually enjoys a number of strong-flavored foods; quickly overseasons and oversugars foods. Loves colorful, oversweetened, novelty breakfast cereals. The perfect target for the Saturday-morning cartoon commercial.
Child shows hyperactive response in new situations or to changes in routine. The more consistent, structured, and calm the home and school environment, the better this child behaves.	Child is well behaved in new situations but gets progressively worse as the newness wears off (so one may need to schedule several sessions in order to see the problem behavior emerge). Constantly seeks more stimulating environments.
Stimulant medications (Ritalin, Cylert) are seldom markedly effective; moderate to high doses may make matters worse. Small doses of mild tranquilizers or sedatives help in some cases. Child may show sedation from over-the-counter medicines containing codeine or antihistamines.	Stimulant medications are usually effective (child may even be calmed by coffee or tea) as preparation for intervention and retraining. When high doses are needed to control behavior, ability to effectively learn is impaired.

enough to get things done. The DSM recognizes two types of ADD: with and without hyperactivity. The latter is, *undifferentiated attention-deficit disorder,* the less common type and is less likely to lead to social problems of various sorts. The *attention-deficit hyperactivity disorder* (ADHD) involves behavioral manifestations of attentional problems, including persisting symptoms of restlessness, fidgeting, and constant activity. ADHD occurs at an incidence of 6 to 8 percent and at about a 5-to-1 ratio of males to females, with an even higher ratio for the more active and aggressive forms (Goldstein and Goldstein 1990; Aaron 1989).

For a diagnosis of ADHD, the DSM requires disturbances of at least six months, with onset before age seven, during which the child exhibits at least eight of the following behaviors: (1) fidgets or squirms, (2) has difficulty remaining seated; (3) is easily distracted; (4) has difficulty awaiting one's turn; (5) blurts out responses; (6) has difficulty completing tasks; (7) has difficulty sustaining attention; (8) often shifts to other activities; (9) seldom plays quietly; (10) interrupts or intrudes; (11) talks excessively; (12) does not pay attention; (13) often loses things essential to tasks; (14) engages in risk or thrill-seeking. Specialized counseling and school programs are critical to a good adjustment for the ADHD youngster, including special classes, parent training, individual tutoring, and individual therapy, in addition to treatments for the hyperactivity component.

Learning Disability

The term *learning disability* means just what it says. The person with a learning disability has a problem in learning that is not primarily due to a significant emotional or social disorder, a sensory defect such as an impairment in seeing or hearing, or even limited intelligence. For example, the Big Ten basketball player of the year in 1990, Steve Scheffler of Purdue, is dyslexic; he scored a perfect 1600 on the SAT. Learning disabilities are certainly not uncommon. Estimates are that between 5 and 10 percent of the population is learning disabled (Goldstein and Goldstein 1990; Aaron 1989). Figure 9–5 shows the factors that contribute to learning disabilities.

Dyslexia

There are several major misconceptions about *dyslexia,* the most common and important form of learning disability. One misconception is that it is a brain dysfunction; another is that is a disease like tuberculosis; and another is that the dyslexic child is less intelligent than others. All of these beliefs are wrong. There also is a widespread belief that people with dyslexia reverse letters, but experts now say that that is not a hallmark of the disorder. Rather, experts believe that letter reversal reflects a normal early stage of learning. Eventually, normal readers outgrow it, while many dyslexics apparently do not.

Dyslexia is a learning disorder of language and perception. It is usually most evident in a difficulty in learning to read. In fact, the word *dyslexia* comes from *dys,* meaning "poor," and *lexia,* meaning "language." Dyslexics learn to read late, if at all. They seldom read effortlessly or fluently, and they never become good spellers (Duffy and Geschwind 1985). Many drop out of

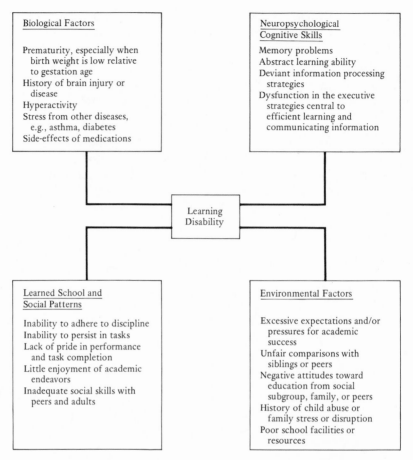

Figure 9–5. Possible Contributing Factors in Any One Case of Learning Disabilities

school even if their intelligence is at least average. Estimates are that from 5 to 20 percent of the population suffers from dyslexia. It is much more common in boys, by as much as an 8-to-1 ratio.

Most experts do believe dyslexia is primarily caused by heredity, since it runs in families (Aaron 1989). Dyslexics apparently have a different pattern of brain organization, and in some cases, the circuits that link one part of the brain with another mature more slowly than is the case with normals.

Dyslexics have traditionally had a difficult time in school. But this is because they perceive words differently from the way words are standardly presented in school, not because they are less intelligent. In fact, a number of notable and obviously intelligent people—including Albert Einstein, Thomas Edison, and Leonardo Da Vinci—are believed to have been dyslexic. So dyslexics can be and are both literate and successful. But they may need special services and tutoring to function as well as other children.

Signs of Dyslexia. Early recognition of the problem is important. The signs that suggest possible dyslexia should be found consistently—not just in one or two instances. They include:

- unusual awkwardness in walking and a marked slowness in learning such skills as drawing with crayons or riding a tricycle;
- a significant delay in developing spoken language (assuming that the delay is not due to such factors as a lack of stimulation or a lack of opportunity because of being overwhelmed by older siblings);
- problems in correctly and quickly naming a sequence of numbers, letters, or colors;
- persistent attempts to write letters or words backward
- inability to follow verbal instructions to tap in different rhythm patterns; and
- "neolithic" representations of faces—in which there is no separation of the nose from the forehead and no suggestion of a nose bridge. This pattern is common in *spatial dyslexics* (one-quarter to one-third of all dyslexics) who have trouble distinguishing the spatial relationships between words.

The complexity of the problem of dyslexia (and of learning disabilities in general) is furthered by three difficult trends in American society. First, the subtlety of the problem is seldom appreciated by parents or even by some teachers—it's easier to think that the child is just lazy or careless. Second, the pervasiveness of the problem is not often appreciated; it almost always affects social life and self-esteem as well as academic issues. Third, it is extremely difficult for a teacher in a regular classroom to accommodate the special needs that these children require in order to learn.

Treatment. Schools are required by law to test for dyslexia where it is reasonably suspected and to provide remedial services. Techniques to help dyslexics may include allowing them more time to read tests and providing books on tape and the taping of lectures. Words should be taught by a phonetics approach and by multisensory learning techniques. Multisensory learning techniques combine looking, saying, and even "feeling" (such as by tracing) the words and letters, since the basic problem is that the dyslexic often fails to make the automatic connection between the sound of a word or letter and its visual representation in print.

Drug Abuse in Adolescence

Drug or substance abuse is a particularly significant problem even among "normal" adolescents (Shedler and Block 1990). The highly social nature of many early experiences with drugs sets adolescent users apart from veteran adult users. (See to chapter 4 for information basic to understanding many factors specific to adolescent drug abuse.)

The popular concept of a single, general drug culture among adolescents is a myth. As a general rule, beginning adolescent drug abusers originally belong to highly atypical or deviant groups. Such personality factors as lack of strong bonding to parents, extroversion, a need for autonomy, and rebelliousness predispose certain adolescents to reject traditional social role models, leaving them more vulnerable to influence from peers and to deviant preference patterns.

Other chronic components that influence adolescent drug use are a high level of need for stimulation-seeking; parental use of tobacco, alcohol, or tranquilizers; an unrewarding family structure; academic failure; depression; low self-esteem; impulsivity; low stress tolerance; a peer or family environment that approves or tolerates drug use; a family or peer member who is seen as a model for drug use; parents' expectation of low academic achievement in the child; a lack of parental closeness to each other and/or to the child; a lack of parental involvement in the child's activities; weak parental control and discipline; little interest in religion; and easy access to drugs (Mauss et al. 1988; Hawkins et al. 1986).

Several immediate signs point to an adolescent who is preparing to use or is already using drugs: depression; secrecy patterns; any abrupt change of attitude; less involvement in academic achievement; greater rebelliousness; any new pattern of flamboyant spontaneity or sexual promiscuity; increasing expectations to fail; apparent increase in stress; more deviant or delinquent behavior; and lowered self-esteem (Hawkins et al. 1985).

Prevention

As with other disorders, prevention is more effective than cure in substance abuse (Shedler and Block 1990; Mauss et al. 1988). The following are suggested to parents, guardians, or supervisors to help their child avoid problems with alcohol (still the major drug of abuse in all age ranges):

- As in all areas of parenting, after careful consideration, clearly explain to the child the behavior you expect. Set limits, clearly describe the consequences of violations, and firmly and fairly apply them.

- Never associate drinking behavior with evidence of attainment of adulthood, power, or other accomplishments.

- Give the child some instruction on how to say no to peer pressure to use drugs or alcohol. You may even role-play a typical incident, with you first taking the part of the peer who is trying to get the child to use the drug, then switching the roles around.
- Label excess drinking behavior as stupid and in bad taste rather than as stylish or "cool."
- Label help-seeking behaviors in people who have an alcohol problem as evidence of strength rather than weakness. Similarly, seek professional help as soon as a problem is evident.
- Encourage alcoholism education programs in schools and in the community, as well as public health measures such as a restriction on the use of alcohol in certain settings and age groups.

Eating Disorders

> Ask your child what he wants for dinner only if he's buying.
> — Fran Lebowitz
> *Social Studies*

Eating disorders are often passive forms of rebellion combined with an exaggerated acceptance of society's idealized "perfect" image. They are much more common in women, and they are often manifested in women who come into contact with the criminal justice system.

One clue as to why eating disorders develop more often in females is found in a rather clever research approach by Fallon and Rozin (1985). They showed a set of nine drawings that depicted figures ranging from somewhat underweight to somewhat overweight to 248 male and 227 female undergraduates. The researchers asked them to indicate which drawings corresponded to their current body figure, their ideal body figure, the figure they felt would be most attractive to the opposite sex, and the opposite-sex figure to which they would be most attracted. For men, the current, ideal, and most attractive male figures were almost identical. But women's perception of their current figure was significantly heavier than the most attractive figure, which in turn was heavier than the ideal female figure. Both sexes erred in estimating what figure the opposite sex would find most attractive—but in opposite directions. The men thought that women like a male figure of a heavier stature than the women reported they really do like; the women thought that men like women to be thinner than the men actually reported they like. Overall, Fallon and Rozin found that men's perceptions tend to keep them satisfied with their own figures, while women's perceptions place pressure on themselves to lose weight. Thus, the greater incidence of dieting, anorexia nervosa, and bulimia among women is not surprising.

Anorexia nervosa is the eating disorder in which the person loses the ability to regulate eating behavior and avoids food. This apparently voluntary self-starvation typically first occurs during puberty, when young women (usually from the middle to upper socioeconomic classes) become more conscious of their self-image. It is often characterized by a distorted body image and conflicts over control. Families of these patients are typically dominated (often in a subtle fashion) by the mother, while the father is psychologically distant. Such families value achievement, and the young woman tries hard to please them (perfectionism). The young woman is obsessed by a fear of being "fat." Her anorexia leads to a dangerous loss of weight, which is furthered by her anxiety and an attempt to overcontrol her emotions. Even after there has been some weight loss, these girls feel fat and respond with a fierce determination to achieve self-control (Agras 1987). Although nineteen out of twenty anorexics are young females (National Institute of Mental Health 1985), older people can suffer from it as well. A common sequence in the development of anorexia is as follows:

1. stress
2. food restriction
3. hormonal abnormalities
4. further food restriction
5. amenorrhea
6. weight loss

Bulimia, which comes from the Greek words for "ox" and "hunger," refers to a recurrent pattern of binge eating. Depression and remorse often follow the binges; the person often senses that the pattern is disordered and cannot be stopped. Bulimia is associated with attempts to control weight by diets, vomiting, and/or a heavy use of laxatives; by eating in an inconspicuous manner using high-calorie foods; and often by eating rather incredible amounts of food. Several personality factors increase the tendency of adolescents to develop a bulimic pattern: (1) acceptance of a traditional feminine role; (2) middle-to-upper-class social status; (3) attendance away at college or a boarding school; (4) early physical maturation; (5) a lower metabolic rate; (6) higher stress; (7) tendencies toward depression; (8) a high belief in the ability to control one's world; (9) a prolonged history of dieting attempts; and (10) a family that promotes psychological isolation from other people (Striegel-Moore et al. 1986).

The typical bulimic patient is Caucasian, female, single, in her midtwenties, well educated, and close to ideal weight. Ninety to 95 percent of bulimics are female, and approximately one in five college-age women have had at least one bulimic episode in their lives (Agras 1987; National Institute of Mental Health 1985).

A binge episode is usually done in secret. It commonly follows this sequence of stages:

1. anticipation and planning
2. anxiety
3. urgency to begin
4. rapid, uncontrollable consumption of food
5. relief and relaxation
6. disappointment
7. shame or disgust

Treatment

The treatment of eating disorders can be difficult because both the victims and the families tend to deny the disorder. So premature termination of therapy frequently occurs. An early age of onset and a lack of prior hospitalization are the most reliable indicators of good outcome, as are shorter duration of the illness, acuteness (as in response to a specific trauma), less weight loss, the presence of evident social stressors, and the presence of a good social or work history (Agras 1987). Hospitalization is often required, as is some form of family therapy.

In working with clients with eating disorders, the counselor needs to establish credibility yet avoid triggering control issues or engaging in power struggles. This can be done in several ways (Donovan and McIntyre 1990):

- Allow the client to know that no one can *make* her change—it is a *choice* she can make. This allows her to feel she is in control and provides a sense of security so she can explore new behaviors.
- Recognize that her evident *goal* (to be in control of her life) is appropriate, but that her methods for achieving that goal are inappropriate.
- Persistently *suggest*—though do not *demand*—that the patient exercise some up-front and appropriate control over her symptom behaviors.
- Encourage the establishment of a support system for the patient by directing her toward *group therapy* and peer support groups.
- *Acknowledge* that her symptom behaviors are important and have functioned as part of her identity for a long time. This allows her to be less defensive and more willing to seek alternative behaviors.

Suicide in Adolescents

Suicide in American adolescents has been on the rise in recent decades. (See the discussion of suicide in general in chapter 12.) According to Hafen and Frandsen (1986), an adolescent attempts suicide every ninety seconds, and another succeeds every ninety minutes. Suicide is now the second leading cause of death among American adolescents, second only to accidents, and some of those may be suicides. In the last twenty years, the suicide rate among children ten to fourteen years of age more than doubled; among those fifteen to nineteen years of age, it tripled. Most adolescent suicides occur in the fifteen-to-twenty-four age range. In the United States, more teenage boys commit suicide than do girls, but girls *attempt* suicide more often than boys and generally choose less lethal means.

The following personality, social, and behavioral traits occur more often among teenagers who commit suicide: a feeling that they are not liked by others or that others are unduly critical of them; depression; a sense of helplessness, hopelessness and/or vulnerability; a feeling that life is meaningless or without purpose; an unclear concept of death; family violence; intense marital discord; loss of a parent through death, divorce, or separation; and a prior suicide by a significant other. Certain factors present at birth also occur more often among teenage suicides: suffering respiratory distress for longer than one hour at birth; being born to a mother who had no prenatal care for the first twenty weeks of pregnancy or to a mother who had chronic disease during pregnancy (Hafen and Frandsen 1986). As with adults, among teenagers there is a direct relationship between drug and alcohol abuse and suicide. Phillips and Carstensen (1986) found that televised news stories about suicide increased the number of adolescent suicides in the days following these news shows above the level that should have been expected.

Mental Retardation

> I didn't go to college, but I had a wonderful father.
> — Anna Freud

Nerissa Bowes-Lyon, a first cousin of Queen Elizabeth, died in 1986 at the age of sixty-seven. Nerissa was buried quietly in a pauper's grave that was marked only by a cheap plastic cross. When the British press heard about this, they delved into the case a bit more, only to find out that in a respected book on the history of aristocracy, Nerissa was listed as having died in 1940. Embarrassed by her mental retardation, which was no doubt caused by genetic inbreeding, the family had kept her hidden away in a mental hospital until her death. Her case illustrates the stigma that the mentally retarded encounter.

Mental retardation is defined in terms of deficits in individual's intellectual functioning and in their capacity to achieve a satisfactory level of social adjustment. About one percent of the population falls into this category (Berk 1989). It is generally agreed that mental retardation is a more common problem in many areas of the criminal justice system. The number of institutionalized mentally retarded has dropped from 132,500 to approximately 90,000 at present, reflecting the policy of deinstitutionalization. The criteria for severity of mental retardation are noted in table 9–3.

Relevant Legal Issues

A primary legal issue in dealing with many childhood disorders is the right of a minor to refuse treatment. Should minors, by law or through ethical principle, have the power to dissent to their treatment when their parents have already consented? Generally, a minor's ability to refuse treatment has not been recognized by law (Melton 1987). Problems can quickly arise, however, in determining how much review should be given to a guardian's consent to hospitalization and treatment. In the Supreme Court case *Parham v. J.R.* (1979), minors alleged that they had been deprived of their liberty without procedural due process by laws permitting parents to voluntarily admit minors to mental hospitals. The majority Court opinion held that parents should be allowed to maintain a substantial, if not dominant, role in making the decision, absent a finding of neglect or abuse and without evidence to contradict the traditional presumption that the parents acted in the best interest of their child. It was further noted that the child's rights and the nature of the commitment decision are such that parent's consent does not always carry absolute and unreviewable discretion over whether to have a child institutionalized, but the Court did say that the review need not be held by judicial or administrative boards but could be held as an internal hospital matter.

Regarding outpatient treatment, Grisso and Vierling state that authorities should not burden minors with decisions they cannot make intelligently, or inadvertently deny to some the opportunity to make decisions of which they are fully competent (cited in Grisso 1986). The results of their work suggest that:

1. No circumstances sanction independent consent by minors under age eleven, given the developmental evidence of their diminished capacities.

Table 9-3
Criteria for Severity of Mental Retardation, by Age

Level	Preschool Age (birth to 5 years)	School Age (6 to 21 years)	Adult (over 21 years)
Mild Retardation (IQ of 50–70) (about 85% of retarded persons)	Can develop social and language skills; less retardation in sensorimotor areas. Seldom distinguished from normal until older. Referred to as *educable*.	Can learn academic skills to approximately sixth-grade level by late teens. Cannot learn general high school subjects. Needs special education, particularly at secondary-school levels	Capable of social and vocational adequacy with proper education and training. Frequently needs guidance when under serious social or economic stress
Moderate Retardation (35–49) (10% of retarded persons)	Can talk or learn to communicate. Poor social awareness. Fair motor development. May profit from self-help; can be managed with moderate supervision.	Can learn functional academic skills to approximately fourth-grade level by late teens if given special education	Capable of self-maintenance in unskilled or semiskilled occupations. Needs supervision and guidance when under mild social or economic stress
Severe Retardation (21–34) (3–4% of retarded persons)	Poor motor development. Speech is minimal. Few or no communication skills. Generally unable to profit from training in self-help.	Can talk or learn to communicate. Can be trained in elemental health habits. Cannot learn functional academic skills. Profits from systematic habit training.	Can contribute partially to self-support under complete supervision. Can develop self-protection skills to a minimally useful level in a controlled environment.
Profound Retardation (IQ of 20 or below) (1–2% of retarded persons)	Minimal capacity for functioning in sensorimotor areas. Needs nursing care.	Some motor and speech development present. Cannot profit from training in self-help. Needs total care.	Some motor and speech development. Totally incapable of self-maintenance. Needs complete care and supervision

Source: Adapted in part from J.M. Sattler, *Assessment of Children's Intelligence and Special Abilities.* Boston: Allyn and Bacon, 1982, p. 426.

2. Ages eleven to fourteen appears to be a transition period involving cognitive, developmental, and social expectations. Independent consent by these minors may be justified for limited purposes, especially when competence can be determined in individual cases.

3. There appears to be no psychological grounds why minors age fifteen and above cannot give competent consent.

4. In some minors diminished capacity to provide meaningful consent may sometimes present such risk to the psychological or physical welfare of the minor so as to offer a compelling reason for denial of the right in certain circumstances.

A related issue occurs when a juvenile threatens violence. A consensus formulation is found in the 1989 decision in the California case of *People v. Kevin F.* The California appeals court concluded that evidence Kevin gave to his therapist was properly admissible under Section 1024 of the state's Evidence Code, which provides: "There is no privilege under this article if the psychotherapist has reasonable cause to believe that the patient is in such mental or emotional condition as to be dangerous to himself or to the person or property of another and that disclosure of the communication is necessary to prevent the threatened danger."

In so ruling, the court rejected Kevin's argument that *Tarasoff v. Regents of University of California* (the landmark case) restricted the statutory exception to circumstances in which there was a threat of harm to a readily identifiable victim. The court also ruled that Kevin was not entitled to *Miranda* warnings before talking to the therapist, because there was no evidence that he was subjected to interrogation.

In other key holdings throughout the years, the Supreme Court has defined the parameters of the juvenile justice system. In *Kent v. U.S.* (1966) the Court said that the *parents patriae* philosophy of the juvenile court should not allow procedural unfairness, and it set criteria to control the transfer of juveniles into adult courts. In *In re Gault* (1967) the Court said that a juvenile has procedural rights in juvenile court—that is, notice of charges, the right to counsel, the right to cross-examine and confront witnesses, and the privilege against self-incrimination. In 1971, in *McKeiver v. Pennsylvania* the Court said that juveniles do not have the right to a jury trial. In 1984, in *Schall v. Martin,* the Court held that juveniles could be held, either for their own or for society's protection, without bail before trial. In 1985, in *New Jersey v. T.L.D.,* the Court limited juveniles' search-and-seizure rights in holding that teachers have a right to search students if they violate school rules. In 1989, in *Stanford v. Kentucky,* the Court held that persons sixteen years of age or older at the time of the crime could be executed for committing that crime.

All societies face the socio-political issue of whether to limit the spread of genetic-based forms of mental retardation through population control. The northwestern province of Gansu was the first Chinese province to approve a mandatory sterilization law for the mentally retarded. After the law was enacted in January 1989, Gansu set up a diagnostic network and required an examination for all couples planning to marry. In 1990, Chinese officials reported that the province had performed 5,500 operations in the fourteen months after the law took effect. Officials in Gansu said that their goal was to sterilize most of Gansu's 260,000 mentally retarded residents by the end of the next year. Obviously, this is an extreme case, but so is the decision never to intervene to limit procreation where there is genetic-based retardation. While both are statistical extremes, the underlying issue is what a particular society decides to value and/or can allow.

Notes

Aaron, P. 1989. *Dyslexia and Hyperlexia*. Dordrecht, Netherlands: Kluwer.

Agras, W. 1987. *Eating Disorders*. New York: Pergamon.

Berk, L. 1989. *Child Development: Theory, Research, and Applications*. Needham Heights, Mass.: Allyn and Bacon.

Bloom-Feshbach, J., and S. Bloom-Feshbach. 1987. *The Psychology of Separation and Loss*. San Francisco: Jossey-Bass.

Donovan, D., and D. McIntyre. 1990. *Healing the Hurt Child*. New York: W. W. Norton.

Duffy, F., and N. Geschwind. 1985. *Dyslexia: A Neuroscientific Approach to Clinical Evaluation*. Boston: Little, Brown.

Ewing, C. 1991. *Kids Who Kill*. Lexington, Mass.: Lexington Books.

Fallon, A., and P. Rozin. 1985. "Sex Differences in Perceptions of Desirable Body Shape." *Journal of Abnormal Psychology* 94: 102–105.

Goldstein, S., and M. Goldstein. 1990. *Managing Attention Disorders in Children*. New York: Wiley.

Grisso, T. 1986. *Evaluating Competencies* New York: Plenum.

Hafen, B., and K. Frandsen. 1986. *Youth Suicide*. Evergreen, Colo.: Cordillera Press.

Hawkins, J. D., R. Catalano, and E. Wells. 1986. "Measuring Effects of a Skills Training Intervention for Drug Abusers." *Journal of Consulting and Clinical Psychology* 54: 661–64.

Henggeler, S. 1989. *Delinquency in Adolescence*. Newbury Park, Calif.: Sage.

Horne, A., and T. Sayger. 1990. *Treating Conduct and Oppositional Defiant Disorders in Children*. Elmsford, N.Y.: Pergamon.

Huba, G., J. Wingard, and P. Bentler. 1979. "Beginning Adolescent Drug Use and Adult Interaction Patterns." *Journal of Consulting and Clinical Psychology* 47: 265–76.

Hynd, G. 1990. Personal communication.

In re Gault. 1967. (387 U.S. 1; 87 S.Ct. 1248).

Kazdin, A., and D. Kolko. 1986. "Parent Psychopathology and Family Functioning among Childhood Firesetters." *Journal of Abnormal Psychology* 14: 315–29.

Kent v. U.S. 1966. (383 U.S. 541, 86 S.Ct. 1045, 16 L.Ed.2d 84).

Klee, S., B. Garfinkel, and H. Beauchesne. 1986. "Attention Deficit in Adults." *Psychiatric Annuals* 16: 52–56.

Lambert, N., C. Hartsough, D. Sassone, and J. Sandoval. 1987. "Persistence of Hyperactivity Symptoms from Childhood to Adolescence and Associated Outcomes." *American Journal of Orthopsychiatry* 57: 22–32.

Liebert, R., and J. Sprafkin. 1988. *The Early Window: Effects of Television on Children and Youth.* 3rd ed. Elmsford, N.Y.: Pergamon.

Loeber, R. 1990. "Development and Risk Factors of Juvenile Antisocial Behavior and Delinquency." *Clinical Psychology Review* 10: 1–42.

Mauss, A., R. Hopkins, R. Weisheit, and K. Kearney. 1988. "The Problematic Prospects for Prevention in the Classroom." *Journal of Studies on Alcohol* 49: 51–61.

Melton, G. 1987. "The Clashing of Symbols: Prelude to Child and Family Policy." *American Psychologist* 42: 345–354.

Morris, A. 1987. *The Kids Next Door: Sons and Daughters Who Kill Their Parents.* New York: William Morrow.

National Institute of Mental Health. 1985. *Mental Health, United States 1985.* Washington, D.C.: Author.

Parham v. J.R. 1979. (442 U.S. 584, 604.

People v. Kevin F. July 20, 1989. (No. C0020577. Cal. Ct. App., 3rd Appel. Dist.).

Phillips, D. P., and L. L. Carstensen. 1986. "Clustering of Teenage Suicides after Television News Stories." *New England Journal of Medicine* 315: 685–89.

Quay, H., ed. 1987. *Handbook of Juvenile Delinquency.* New York: Wiley.

Robe, H. 1990. Personal communication.

Sechrest, L. 1986. "Perspectives on Youth Violence." In S. Apter and A. Goldstein, eds. *Youth Violence.* Elmsford, N.Y.: Pergamon.

Seltzer, G. 1990. "General Systems of Classification." In J. Matson and J. Mulick, eds. *Handbook of Mental Retardation.* 2nd ed. Elmsford, N.Y.: Pergamon.

Shedler, J., and J. Block. 1990. "Adolescent Drug Use and Psychological Health." *American Psychologist* 45: 612–30.

Stanford v. Kentucky. 1988. (109 S.Ct., 2969, 57 L.W. 4973).

Striegel-Moore, R., L. Silberstein, and J. Rodin. 1986. "Toward an Understanding of Risk Factors for Bulimia." *American Psychologist* 43: 246–63.

10
Violence

"You ever been in an all-out war?"
"No, I never have."
"Well, it ain't fun. But sometimes you gotta do it to keep the peace."
— Laurence Sanders
Stolen Blessings

Violence is at a high level in American society, and it generally continues to rise. To be sure, rates for murder and other violent crimes were up and down at various times in recent years. But a number of experts believe that violence will continue to increase because of gang activity among young adults, drug turf wars, greater availability of automatic and more powerful weapons, greater access to lethal weapons for younger groups, and a gradual but steady growth in the societal acceptance of violence (Fox 1990; Benedek and Cornell 1989). During the 1990s, an increasing number of children, children of the baby boomers, will be reaching late adolescence and young adulthood, in a sort of "baby-boomerang effect" (Fox 1990). These are the most violence-prone years. Conversely, those teens who engage in violence, especially those who are subsequently incarcerated, show mortality rates up to fifty times as high as those of their nonviolent peers. (Issues concerning the prediction of a violent act by a specific individual, whether toward self or others, are dealt with in chapter 13.)

The traditional debate among experts is whether developed personality traits (possibly genetically based) cause violence, or whether violence is a response to social and situational cues, such as frustration and the modeling of aggression. Evidence that high levels of the male hormone androgen generate aggression supports the first hypothesis. Evidence of a higher rate of assaults in lower socioeconomic situations supports the second hypothesis, as does evidence that controlling access to guns lowers the rate of gun-related assaults. Several specific factors also contribute, even including the season of the year (July–August is the period of most assaults). Also, Miller, Heath, Molcan, and Dugon (1991) find that homicide rates increase on weekends that occur approximately four days after a well-publicized prize fight. Alcohol is clearly a factor, since about 50 percent of violent crimes occur immediately after the perpetrator has drunk significantly. Even a high level of caffeine intake has been related to a propensity for violence (Veleber and Templer 1984). Philip Zimbardo's (1973) classic study wherein a number of "normal" Stanford University students developed into "brutal" individuals within six days of role-playing showed that violence is possible from anyone. Unfortunately, prediction of any individual act of violence, even in the near future, is a chancy affair at best (Wrightsman 1991; Brizer and Crowner 1989; see chapter 13).

There are numerous sources from which violent behaviors spring. The following outline gives an overview of these causes, along with consensus intervention strategies.

I. Violence as an inherent part of human nature
   A. Traditional psychotherapy, to modify basic personality patterns
   B. Medications, to diminish anxiety and minimize inappropriate reactions
   C. Psychosurgery, to change or interrupt patterns of brain functioning

II. Violence as a consequence of social learning
   A. Family therapy, to change home environment or facilitate coping in family setting
   B. Group therapy, to enhance appropriate coping in social situations
   C. Assertiveness training and social-skills training, to give concrete training in self-assertion without violence
   D. Systematic desensitization, to desensitize client to the precipitating stimuli, so as to diminish inappropriate or excessive reactions
   E. Token economy, time-out, and social isolation, to extinguish violent behavior through removal of environmental reinforcers, as well as to strengthen appropriate responses
   F. Classical conditioning, to extinguish violent behavior, as in aversive conditioning
   G. Parent effectiveness training and Parents Anonymous, to enhance adequate coping skills and provide a supportive peer group

III. Violence as a consequence of frustration and other situational factors
   A. Traditional psychotherapy, to release frustrations and to change coping patterns
   B. Family therapy
   C. Group therapy
   D. Assertiveness training, social-skills training
   E. Token economy, to provide opportunities for positively reinforcing experiences while extinguishing the violent behavior
   F. Parent effectiveness training

IV. Violence as a means of communication
   A. Expressive therapies, to substitute alternative means of expression of feelings underlying violent acting-out
   B. Assertiveness training

C. Systematic desensitization
D. Parent effectiveness training

V. Violence and aggression as protection of territorial integrity and body space

A. Systematic desensitization
B. Assertiveness training

Legal Categories of Violent Crime

Though specific limits and phraseology differ in various jurisdictions, the following is a general overview of the legal categories of individual violent crimes.

I. Murder. A killing that is "calculated, in cold blood," or with "malice aforethought" (or a guilty mind).

   A. First degree—includes:

      1. an intent to effect death with "malice aforethought"
      2. deliberate act
      3. premeditated act

   B. Second degree—includes:

      1. an intent to effect death, "malice aforethought"
      2. without deliberation or premeditation. In essence, most states define second-degree murder as any murder that is not a first-degree murder

II. Felony Murder Doctrine. If in the act of committing a felony, the death of one of the victims is brought about, this is murder, and it is not necessary to demonstrate intent, deliberation, or premeditation.

III. Manslaughter. Homicide that lacks malice aforethought.

   A. Voluntary (nonnegligent)—Intentional killing without "malice aforethought"; often described as homicide "in hot blood" and often takes place due to provocation.

   B. Involuntary (negligent)—Unintentional killing without "malice aforethought"—for example, vehicular homicides.

IV. Assault. Involves offering to give bodily harm to a person or placing him or her in fear of such harm. Assault is an attempted, but incompleted, battery.

V. Battery (Aggravated Assault). "An offensive, uncontested to, unprivileged and unjustified offensive bodily contact." Battery includes *mens rea,* where the contact was intentional or resulted from wanton misconduct and in which bodily harm takes place.

VI. Statutory Rape. Sexual relations with a victim under the age of consent.

VII. Forcible Rape. Forcible and unlawful sexual relations with a person against her or his will. Rape is defined in the traditional common law as "carnal knowledge of a female forcibly and against her will."

Murder

> Nothing in life is so exhilarating as to be shot at without result.
> — Winston Churchill

Murder has always been with us. The United States in recent decades has seen the emergence of terrorist murders (see chapter 11), serial and mass murders, and impersonal murders. Only one serial murderer was thoroughly documented in the 1950s, but one reason for this low figure may have been a lack of attention to the probability of such phenomena. In the 1990s, experts have estimated that approximately six thousand men, women, and children die at the hands of serial killers each year, and between fifty and one hundred serial killers are active at any one time. The notorious Ted Bundy is a classic example. He was reasonably intelligent, not a genius—as with athletes, actors, and actresses, we tend to overestimate any evidence of intellectual strength in criminals. But he had a disturbed family background, as most serial killers have been adopted, abandoned, abused, neglected, and/or institutionalized (Newton 1990).

In general, about 40 percent of murder victims are strangers to the murderer, and in approximately 95 percent of all murders the killer and victim are of the same race. Murder rates tend to be highest on the weekends, and suicides at the beginning of the new week (Klebba 1981). One theory is that distress experienced on the weekend (as a result of more unstructured free time and higher levels of interaction in emotion-laden relationships), if unresolved, turns inward as the weekend ends, facilitating suicide. It is also noted that there is a higher rate of murder during a full moon. Most agree that this is primarily a result of better visibility, because there is a similar correlation between murder and other weather conditions that promote visibility. So contrary to the message of many frightening movies, if you want to take a walk in a dangerous neighborhood, you are advised to do it on a foggy, rainy night.

Unlike schizophrenia or depression, murder is a single, specific behavior, so the aim is prevention, not cure. Strategies that would help are finding better methods of treating juvenile delinquents and the antisocial and paranoid disorders; providing more therapy for violence-prone families; curtailing the expression and affirmation of violence in the media; and curtailing the availability of weapons whose only apparent function is killing other humans. The great majority of guns used in murders are purchased for "self-defense" rather than for hunting or target shooting; it is ironic that the victim is often the person who purchased the gun.

Murder, like rape, is a legally defined behavior rather than a syndrome of emotional disorder. A wide variety of personality types are capable of committing it. Single murders, even more than rapes, are frequently crimes of incidental impulse, so murderers are actually more commonly reasonably normal individuals. In fact, if authorities were to decide to release from prison any group of prisoners by type of crime, first-degree murderers might be a good choice. There are two reasons for this. First, many are imprisoned for crimes of situation and impulse rather than for planned, conscious behaviors, so positive changes in their living conditions could radically reduce the probability that they will repeat their crime. Second, they receive long sentences, so they are likely to be older on the average than other criminal groups, and what psychopathy they do have is likely to have lessened. By contrast, the potentially most dangerous inmates are those with a history of assault that started before age eighteen. These inmates are highly likely statistically to be dangerous to others again (Brizer and Crowner 1989).

Categories of Murder

There are various ways of categorizing murders. The most obvious way is to categorize them by numbers and times, as follows:

- Individual murders, where one individual or a set of people who are somehow related are killed

- Mass murders, where a number of separate people are killed at one time

- Rampage murders, where a number of people are killed in separate incidents over a relatively short period of time. Over a number of hours, for example, Ramon Salcido of northern California killed his wife, two of his three daughters, his wife's mother, two younger sisters, and a co-worker.

- Serial murders, where a number of people are killed over an extended period of time. Some serial killers have similarities in their backgrounds and their choices of victims, but even that can be misleading (Newton 1990). Edward Gein, for example, a Wisconsin grave robber who inspired the movies *Psycho* and *The Texas Chainsaw Massacre,* became dissatisfied with his nocturnal raids on three cemeteries near Plainfield, Wisconsin, and turned to finding "fresh" live victims. Charles Manson, Carroll Edward Cole, Henry Lee Lucas, and Ottis Toole had similar backgrounds in that they were all forced to wear feminine garments and suffered violence from sadistic relatives, but numerous other serial killers do not manifest such a background.

While this kind of categorizing can be helpful, differentiating murders on the basis of motive and/or personality factors is more useful. The following is a model based on a combination of such variables.

I. Impulsive
    A. Unconscious. These occur when the person is under the influence of heavy alcohol or drug intake, or a medical condition such as epilepsy.
    B. Stimulus-generated. These often occur when a quick burst of emotion, such as fear or anger, combines with easy and immediate access to a lethal weapon.

II. Estrangement-generated. These may have an impulsive component in that they emanate from extreme emotional distress, such as a divorce-custody battle, but the emotion controls the behavior over a longer period of time than in the impulsive situations.

III. Altruistic. These occur when a person "pulls the plug" on a beloved who is in a coma or in a terminal status and in great pain. Sometimes such motivation is not so clear-cut, as in the case of Donald Harvey who, while working as an orderly in various hospitals in or near Cincinnati, killed thirty-seven people and asserted they were mercy killings. He either suffocated them with a plastic bag or poisoned them. But none of his victims had requested his services, and it is doubtful that many of them would have thanked him if they had known of his plans. He is presently serving three life sentences in an Ohio prison.

IV. Psychotic. Three psychotic conditions wherein the individual loses contact with reality—mania, paranoid schizophrenia, and severe depression—have traditionally been associated with murder.

V. Sexual-based. Ted Bundy is a classic instance of this pattern.

VI. Power/notoriety. An individual who has lived life as a failure or as a drab nonentity reaches for a sense of being a "real" and/or important person through the power or visibility engineered in such a murder.

VII. Impersonal
    A. Terrorist. These occur when individuals are killed as a byproduct of a terrorist incident.
    B. Proxy. These occur when someone like Al Capone orders the death of various "business" competitors.
    C. Profit. These occur in order to collect insurance or to protect against incriminating disclosures, as by a "hit man."
    D. Relationship-generated.

Relationship-generated murders seem to contain an inherent contradiction of being both impersonal and yet generated by a relationship. Indeed, the paradox is real, and though such crimes are not that common, they are intriguing situations. In February 1990, for example, police charged Theron Morris, age seventy-six, a retired Chrysler engineer, and Leila May Morris, age sixty-two, with the murder of their forty-two-year-old son, Christopher. Authorities allege that Christopher had engaged Martin Rector, an ex-roommate and one-time prison buddy, into a decision to kill Christopher's ex-wife, Sharon, to collect $35,000 in insurance. They then brought Christopher's parents into the plot. Together, they developed a scheme to kill Sharon and her ten-year-old daughter. But Rector was unable to carry out the killing.

Then they learned that the insurance policy on Sharon had lapsed. So the object of the plot shifted from her to Christopher, who was insured for $70,000. The Morrises also were angry with their son because he allegedly sold them bogus cocaine that they had intended to resell. On January 8, Christopher Morris went with Rector to his parents' home. There, police say, Christoper was shot three times by Rector. Rector and Theron Morris then took Christopher to the town of Coconut Creek, shot him three more times, and left his body in the car. Leila May Morris followed in another car and took the two home.

Theron and Leila May Morris were regular church-goers, and they were said to be friendly and quick to help others with yardwork in their mobile-home community. They did a good job of feigning upset when they told neighbors that Christopher had been killed by drug dealers. Sharon Morris even attended the funeral, unaware that she had once been a target.

Sheriff's Lieutenant Tom Carney observed the impersonality in their confession. "They indicated that they had a rough life with him," he said. "They figured they could get rid of the problem child and pick up $70,000. But neither of them showed any remorse. . . . It was almost like they were talking about strangers."

Hate Crimes

Hate crimes are criminal acts involving assault in one form or another that are spawned by racial, ethnic, or other subgroup factors. Most hate crimes involve some form of "turf" issue, and most experts believe that such crimes are increasing (Wrightsman 1991; Athens 1989). The general findings on these crimes are:

- The large majority are committed by people in groups of four or more. The more people in the group, the more vicious is the crime. The typical number of victims is one.

- They reflect primal emotions aroused by the love of one's own group. These deep feelings of group identity are particularly vivid in times of economic and political uncertainty and among people who suffered emotional neglect as children.

- They are far more lethal than other kinds of attacks, resulting in the hospitalization of their victims four times more often than in other kinds of assault.

- They are primarily crimes of youth. Most of those who perpetrate them are in their teens or twenties. But they are not crimes of youthful rebellion—those who carry them out are venting feelings shared by their families, friends, and community.

- When individuals in the mob look back afterward, they almost always say that they cannot believe they did those things. In moments when people get carried away by a crowd, they literally forget themselves and their own sense of what is right and wrong.

The Explosive Disorder

The explosive disorder syndrome is marked by an outburst of physical and/ or verbal violence in a person who is not usually aggressive or hostile. It is a relatively rare pattern, but not surprisingly, such indviduals frequently emerge in the legal arena. There is usually evidence of regret and guilt, and the behavior is disproportionate to any environmental stressors. Because physiological or mood symptoms are occasionally reported and because there is occasional consequent partial amnesia for the behavior, the pattern has traditionally been referred to as *epileptoid*. But a concomitant clear diagnosis of organic epilepsy is uncommon.

Individuals with an explosive disorder report the aggressive act as being something they were compelled to do (so they thereby expect less legal culpability). They show a variable degree of remorse for the results. In that sense, the pattern is similar to aggression manifested during an incident of psychomotor epilepsy, a rare form of epilepsy in which orderly sequences of behavior are performed, though the person has complete amnesia about it. The difference is that psychomotor epilepsy reflects an established physiological brain disorder—that is, disturbed and specific EEG patterns.

Asserting a pattern such as psychomotor epilepsy in the legal arena has occasionally been a "last resort" when the person has been caught red-handed, with a "smoking gun" in a crime of aggression. A classic instance of this is the case of Jack Ruby, who killed Lee Harvey Oswald in front of numerous Dallas police officers and television viewers. The assertion that Ruby had suffered from psychomotor epilepsy was viewed with little sympathy, except by himself and his attorney. But given the evidence against him, this may have been the only defense left, especially since he was found to be rational and had no apparent significant history of severe emotional disturbance. Paradoxically, within a year of this murder, Jack Ruby died of a brain tumor, which tends to confirm the defense used.

Terrorism

The incidence of terrorism has increased worldwide, especially since 1970 (Meyer and Parke 1991; Wolf 1989). The new wave of terrorism was initially stimulated by Carlos Marighella, an intimate of Castro, in his 1969 *Mini Manual,* a forty-eight-page document that has been the terrorists' revolutionary bible. He makes it clear that the primary common element of all terrorists is their use of violence and illegal methods to generate fear, which in turn is used to serve some sociopolitical end.

Surprisingly to some people, there is usually no specific or striking psychological abnormality in terrorists. Post (1987) suggests that terrorist groups tend to attract paranoid personalities and, not surprisingly, people who tend to externalize or seek outside sources to blame for their own inadequacies. But in general, terrorists tend to be young adults (with a mean age of 22.5) who are reasonably intelligent, industrious, and very committed (Falk 1988). Their youth is a factor in converting them to ideological causes. If there is a distinguishing psychological feature of most terrorists, it is their need to belong and to achieve an identity. The terrorist group becomes their family and the source of their value system. Ironically, while the ideology of the terrorist group is highly antiauthoritarian, the organizational psychology of the terrorist group is authoritarian (Post 1987).

There are three primary means by which to fight terrorism: international intelligence and cooperation; the physical security of target installations and people; and the apprehension and punishment of terrorists for criminal acts they commit. It's generally agreed that capitulation to terrorist demands must not occur. The United States and Canada are significantly unprepared for handling acts of terrorism, and changes are clearly needed. The following initiatives are recommended (Meyer and Parke 1991; Wolf 1989):

- *Rigorously pursue interagency cooperation.* The United States needs to clearly and specifically designate an agency to coordinate domestic and international terrorism intelligence.
- *Maintain a policy of no capitulation.* Such a policy has to be in place ahead of time—philosophically, politically, and procedurally.
- *Provide frontline training for police.* State and local law-enforcement personnel have the initial contact with most terrorists. They are presently untrained for handling such challenges.

- *Maintain higher levels of control over weapons.* These controls should focus on those weapons that facilitate terrorism, including national prohibition (with severe penalties) of the unlicensed possession of devices not useful for reasonable hunting or self-protection needs. This includes mandated waiting periods, screening, and penalties for both buyer and seller for violations.

- *Pass federal acts of terrorism.* The American legal infrastructure is cumbersome, and most state/local jurisdictions have neither the training, experience, or resources to manage the prosecution and imprisonment of terrorists. In the terrorist-generated Brinks robbery in 1981, for example, it took two changes of venue and two to three years to prosecute. The process cost $5 to 7 million, and the jury selection required the screening of 2,600 potential jurors. Such legal response is more detrimental to the common good than the original act of terrorism itself.

- *Secure prisons and courtrooms.* Whatever the jurisdiction, prison and courtroom security require extensive upgrading.

- *Change laws to combat terrorism.* The legal structure, reflecting our still-rudimentary knowledge of the terrorist, needs revamping after extensive study.

- *Expand the Immigration and Naturalizations Service and strengthen the relevant laws.* Illegal entry into the United States is far too simple a process.

- *Develop international agreements.* Such agreements should limit the political reasons for prosecution of terrorist acts and clearly identify jurisdictional rights in accord with the theory "extradite or prosecute."

- *Pursue international jurisdictions.* An international court, with applicable criminal codes and sanctions, should be developed that can act against both terrorists and governments or groups that aid, abet, or protect them.

Hostage Negotiation

Hostage negotiation may be defined as a specific set of principles and procedures designed to bring about the end to a hostage situation without loss of life or injury to the hostage(s), law enforcement officer(s), or hostage taker(s). Although the goal is to bring about a successful resolution of the situation without harm to *any* participant, that goal is secondary to the protection of the hostages and officers.

Due to the danger and complexity of hostage situations, an interaction strategy has been developed by the law-enforcement community. At its most simplistic level this strategy is based on four primary principles. First, the hostage taker(s) and the victim(s) must be physically contained; that is, their physical movement must be kept to a minimum by on-scene law-enforcement personnel. Second, a verbal dialogue must be established by the hostage-negotiation team to discuss the demands of the hostage taker(s). This negotiation process may last a variable amount of time, from a few minutes to a number of days.

Third, a tactical intervention utilizing controlled and measured aggression will be used only when the negotiated intervention has not generated success—that is, when it has not reduced the level of conflict and preserved the safety of the hostage(s). Finally, the ultimate welfare of the hostage(s) and the apprehension of the hostage taker(s) are not negotiable items.

These basic principles are always adhered to. Yet any given negotiation process will also reflect the personality characteristics, beliefs, and attitudes of the many individuals involved in it. Some individuals, such as the on-scene commander, will obviously have greater influence on the "flow" of a hostage negotiation than others.

Individuals take hostages for a variety of reasons and motivations and under many different circumstances. Input about the mental status of hostage takers from experienced mental health professionals can therefore be helpful in successfully resolving hostage situations.

There are many types of potential hostage situations; airline hijackings, prison riots, family crisis, and others. The specific situation, with its specific political pressures, will dictate many choices. But in any hostage situation, the following issues have to be considered both in prior policy and on-site:

- who has jurisdiction, what individual has overall authority to make decisions, what authority will be delegated, and to whom;
- what time frame will be acceptable to various parties to the negotiations and for the resolution of the overall situation;
- the structure, decision-making processes and communications link between the negotiating unit and the tactical unit;
- the amount of force that is available, and visible; what type of force will be used first (for example, personnel assault, chemical assault, or sharpshooter) and in what combination;
- whether any demands will be met; if so, at what pace, and what reciprocal actions will be demanded;
- which person or persons will interact with the hostages and on what schedule;
- whether face-to-face negotiation will be the standard or will ever be chosen;
- what will determine when a policy of negotiation gives way to a policy of force;

- how "honest" negotiations should be—whether the negotiators will make concessions that they will later be willing to take back;
- what strategies will be implemented if a hostage has been killed before negotiations ensue, and what changes will be implemented if a hostage is killed after negotiations have begun;
- what types of records will be kept;
- whether amnesty for the event will be a negotiable item;
- what consultants (such as mental health specialists) will be available, and how will they be used;
- what precautions or considerations will be taken toward interfering in a potential "Stockholm syndrome," wherein hostages come to empathize with, possibly sympathize with, and in some cases even join their captors (a version of the psychological concept of "identification with the aggressor").

Family Violence

Family violence has recently received increased attention in American society. It is now recognized that people are much more liable to be physically attacked, injured, or killed in their homes by a relative than they are in any other social context. Therefore, the most dangerous assignment that a police officer can be given is answering a family crisis call (Driscoll, Meyer, and Schaine 1973).

Spouse Abuse

There's no place like home—for either happiness or violence. On a typical day in the United States, about four women are killed by their husbands, ex-mates, or boyfriends—usually as the final chapter in an abusive relationship. As a marriage breaks down, the potential for violence soars. The violence may be directed either toward the child or toward the spouse (Browne and Finkelhor 1986).

Interest in spouse abuse has increased in recent decades. The type of violence in spouse abuse ranges from verbal abuse to physical assault. Rape within marriage is being increasingly recognized as a form of spouse abuse. Estimates of couples who experience physical violence at some time in their marriage range from 30 to 60 percent. It is clear that the amount of reported violence is far less that the amount of actual violence, a point vividly made by the noted mystery-fiction writer Ed McBain in his 1961 short story "J" reprinted in *The Ethnic Detectives* by Pronzini and Greenberg (1985).

"She wouldn't press charges," Hawes said knowingly.

"Charges, hell. There wasn't any beating, according to her. She's got blood running out of her nose, and a shiner the size of a half-dollar . . . — but the minute I get there, everything's calm and peaceful." . . .

"She said, 'Oh, we were just having a friendly little family argument.' . . . So I asked her how she happened to have a bloody nose and a mouse under her eye and—catch this, Cotton—she said she got them ironing."

In most cases the wife is the victim of abuse, though there are a few reports where the husband is abused. One spouse may batter another for a variety of reasons. In numerous instances, the batterer has strong psychopathic components (see chapter 2) and/or has been a consistent witness to or receiver of family violence as a child. Alcohol or drug abuse, combined with some sort of perceived personal or financial trauma (however minor it might objectively be), are the common catalysts for an abuse incident.

There is also evidence that most batterers (and the battered as well) are very low on self-esteem, and some batterers are quite passive in other realms of their life. Most batterers show a mix of low impulse control, low tolerance for delayed gratification and/or frustration, and a relative absence of insight about their own, or others', personality traits.

In addition to low self-esteem, the battered person may show personality disorder elements such as components of dependency or even masochism (Gorton and Akhtar 1990), depression, and a family history in which an identity figure was a recipient of violence. But the single greatest predictor of accepting and continuing in the battered role is a person's social and economic dependence. Most battered spouses (usually females) regard escape as likely to cause greater harm to themselves or their children; or they somehow cannot conceptualize escape as realistically available to them (Serritella and L'Abate 1992).

In accord with traditional object-relations psychological theory (Fairbairn 1952), a more insidious process may develop over time that helps perpetuate the pattern. The spouse (or child, as this applies equally to child abuse) prefers to consider herself rather than the other in her relationship as "bad." By being "bad"—that is, by doing nothing about the abuse— they make the others better. The reward is an increased sense of security in an environment of better, if not good or wonderful, others. This pattern, meshed in a relationship with a person of corresponding needs, leads to co-dependency.

The first intervention issue is to help the battered individual see that escape is possible and that using the escape will not bring the harm she expects to herself or the children. Giving the battered spouse a sense of how she developed the pattern and what maintains it is helpful, and the intervention focus should eventually shift to dealing with such issues as denial of the extent of the pattern.

Legal Status of the Battered Spouse. The battered spouse syndrome is often termed the *battered woman syndrome* in the literature. It is a condition in which a woman (usually) feels dependent, powerless, and afraid because she has been in an abusive relationship for years. In the legal arena, a critical issue has been whether the battered spouse syndrome is a recognizable legal entity. There is much controversy about this among experts in the field, and it is not recognized as a specific diagnosis in the DSM.

It has been offered as a defense in criminal trials where the battered spouse has eventually assaulted and/or killed the batterer, but it has usually not been given legal recognition. Rather, it is usually allowed credence only as the opinion of an expert. But in January 1990 the Kentucky Supreme Court overturned the manslaughter conviction of a woman who shot her estranged husband after suffering years of abuse from him. The court ruled that a social worker should have been allowed to testify that Ramona Craig was a victim of the battered woman syndrome when she killed her husband in 1986. The 4-to-3 opinion overturned a 1987 case that limited such testimony to medical experts.

The court said that Ramona Craig was a textbook example of a battered woman. Her husband, George Craig, had abused her for five years. When she was pregnant, he once held a hot iron to her belly; another time, he shot her in front of their children. She shot and killed him after he threatened her life.

I would argue that the court's decision gave recognition to a syndrome that has not proven to be either specific or unique. I agree with the dissenting opinion of Justice Charles Liebson, who blasted the majority for embarking "on an uncharted sea." Justice Liebson stated that it is dangerous to allow testimony that points to a pattern of characteristics that describes the "profile of a drug courier, a battered spouse, or a sexually abused child," because many persons exhibit characteristics fitting those profiles even though they aren't carrying drugs or being abused.

Co-dependency. Co-dependency, kind of an "attachment hunger," received increasing attention throughout the late 1980s. It is often seen as a factor in spousal violence. A few experts even accept it as a standard diagnosis, although it is not in the DSM and hardly appeared in the professional literature before 1985. Still, it's not as if the pattern was unrecognized before that. Even the early-twentieth-century novelist D. H. Lawrence used the term *egoisme à deux* to designate two people bonded together out of a mix of dependency, frustration, and hostility rather than true love. The basic concept is that each individual is incomplete from the perspective of psychological development (Serritella and L'Abate 1992). Family therapy can be helpful on occasion here. But if abuse has occurred and has been made public, the bonding between the two parties has often been so violated that reconciliation is highly improbable.

Child Abuse

On January 18, 1990, after the longest (two and a half years) and costliest ($15 million) criminal trial in U.S. history, a Los Angeles jury acquitted Peggy McMartin Buckey and her son Raymond Buckey (ages sixty-three and thirty-one respectively, at the trial's end) of fifty-two counts of molesting young children at the preschool they had run. But the jurors, reflecting the absurdity and futility of this situation, deadlocked on thirteen molestation counts against Raymond and on a conspiracy charge against his mother, resulting in a mistrial. Jurors emphasized that they felt sure the children had been abused, but they just could not be sure enough that the Buckeys had done it. Many smaller-scale cases of child abuse contain the same complexity that baffled these jurors.

Background. While the abuse of children throughout history is well documented and has generally been abhorred, for a long time few efforts to prevent it were actually made. Ironically, the first formal legal intervention in a child-abuse case, that of Mary Ellen in New York in 1875, had to be prosecuted through animal-protection laws and was primarily a result of the efforts of the Society for the Prevention of Cruelty to Animals (Cross 1984). In the past twenty-five years, however, child abuse has become a national issue, and all fifty states, partly spurred by the federal Child Abuse Prevention and Treatment Act, have established legislative routes for the identification of abusive families and for intervention. As a result, the number of identified cases has grown enormously, from 7,000 to 8,000 annually in 1967 and 1968 to more than 700,000 in 1978; the number continues to increase. Because of the private nature of child abuse and the reluctance of both the perpetrators and victims to reveal it, the reported cases represent only a portion of the actual cases.

Here, much of the discussion of the incidence and etiology of child abuse refers to both physical abuse and sexual abuse. Issues that are specific to sexual abuse, however, are discussed elsewhere in this book; the reader is also referred to the discussions of pedophilia and incest in chapter 5.

Factors in Child Abuse. Many factors contribute to the ultimate emergence of an episode of physical and/or sexual child abuse (Finkelhor 1985; Goodwin 1989). These factors are found within three contributing systems: sociocultural, familial, and individual. To the degree that these factors are present, the probability of an occurrence of child abuse is increased. At the most basic level, the following *sociocultural* factors facilitate an increase in child-abuse episodes:

- Society's lack of affirmation and support of the family unit;
- Society's lack of emphasis on parent-training skills as a prerequisite to parenting;
- acceptance and high media visibility of violence;
- acceptance of corporal punishment as a central child-rearing technique;
- emphasis on competition rather than cooperation;
- unequal status of women; and
- low economic support for schools and day-care facilities.

These sociocultural factors heighten the probability of child abuse in conjunction with the following *familial* factors:

- low socioeconomic and educational level;
- little availability of friends and extended family for support;
- single-parent or merged-parent family structure;
- marital Instability;
- family violence as common and traditionally accepted;
- low rate of family contact and information exchange;
- significant periods of mother absence;
- high acceptance of family nudity;
- low affirmation of family-member privacy; and
- "vulnerable" children (that is, children who are young, sick, disturbed, retarded, or emotionally isolated).

The probability of child abuse in a specific instance is in turn increased by the following *individual* factors:

- history of abuse as a child;
- low emotional stability and/or self-esteem;
- low ability to tolerate frustration and inhibit anger;
- high impulsivity;
- lack of parenting skills;
- high emotional and interpersonal isolation;
- problems in handling dependency needs of self or others;
- low ability to express physical affection;

- unrealistic expectations of child's performance;
- acceptance of corporal punishment as a primary childrearing technique; and
- abuse of drugs or alcohol.

In most cases, many—though not all—of the above factors are found. Some of the factors predict more to physical abuse and some to sexual abuse, but most of the factors predict to either type.

Sexual Abuse. Many of the various theories that are used to explain physical child abuse are also relevant to sexual child abuse. The seriousness of disorders to children resulting from sexual abuse appears to depend on several factors (Goodwin 1989; Browne and Finkelhor 1986). More serious problems are likely if the offender is in a close relationship to the child, such as the father; the sexual activity includes genital contact, and especially penetration; the child is older, that is, an adolescent at the time of abuse; the abuse is frequent and/or of long duration; the child has strong negative feelings about the abuse and/or is somehow aware of its wrongness; and there is much upset and/or distress occurs around the event, such as court testimony.

Differential Diagnosis

Unless parents admit that they have committed abuse, diagnosis may be problematic. Physical trauma alone is rarely a sufficient diagnostic basis, although certain patterns of injury strongly suggest nonaccidental or repeated physical abuse (Cross 1984). The major *physical* signs of abuse are the four B's: unexplained or unusual Bruises, Burns, Bald spots, and Bleeding. Bruises that are located around the head or face, or in easily hidden areas such as the abdomen; multiple bruises, especially if they are spread over the body; and bruises in the shape of an object, such as a hand, are especially indicative. Likewise, burns of all types should cause concern, especially cigarette burns, burns with a specific shape such as an iron, and burns that suggest that the hand has been immersed in liquid or that liquid has been poured on the body. Concern should be even greater if the child provides an explanation that does not fit the injury.

Behavioral signs of physical abuse (as well as of the often-accompanying emotional abuse) include inappropriate crying or fearfulness; cruelty on the part of the child to animals or smaller children; extremes of behavior, such as marked aggressiveness or passivity; self-destructive behavior or accident-proneness; problems with school tasks and peers; shrinking from physical contact; and wearing clothes that seem designed to cover the body more than to keep warm. These signs are especially important if the symptoms represent a change in behavior pattern for that child. In older children and adolescents delinquency, drug abuse, anorexia nervosa, and excessive fearfulness and avoidance of parents may also reflect an abuse situation.

These behavioral signs of physical abuse are often found in cases of sexual abuse as well. Additional behaviors found in victims of sexual abuse include extreme secrecy, excessive bathing, indications of low self-worth, provocative or promiscuous sexual patterns, a more worldly appearance than that of friends, and suddenly possessing money or any items that could have been used to bribe the child to keep quiet. Specific physical signs of sexual abuse are pain, rashes, itching or sores in the genital or anal areas, frequent urinary infections, and frequent vomiting or enuresis (Finkelhor 1985; Cross 1984). Unfortunately, as many as seventy-five percent of sexual abuse victims don't show easily detectable signs of trauma in the vagina. Detection has been improved by painting the vaginal tissue with toluidine blue dye, which highlights the damage.

Issues in Reporting Abuse. Various laws designate the persons and requirements for reporting known or suspected abuse or neglect to a local authority. Typically, these statutes include:

- a purpose clause;
- a section defining *child abuse, neglect,* and *child;*
- a mandatory reporting clause;
- some definition of who should report;
- a clause describing the report and what should be done with it;
- abrogation of privileges;
- penalties for noncompliance; and
- a central registry.

Statutes vary greatly in their definitions of what constitutes child abuse. Initially, only physical injury was considered and was the only offense required to be reported. But a majority of states have since promulgated broader definitions that encompass mental and sexual abuse, or exploitation or neglect (Smith and Meyer 1987). *Neglect* is commonly defined as the failure to provide adequate food, clothing, and shelter. Neglect may also involve a parental physical or mental incapacity that hinders their ability to care for a child; their hospitalization; or their incarceration (Smith and Meyer 1987).

Definitions of who is a child also vary. Typically *child* refers to persons under eighteen years old. Alaska and Wyoming, however, define *children* as under sixteen, while other states extend the age limit for handicapped children to twenty-one years.

The great majority of reports of child abuse are true, but there have been numerous cases where a child reported sexual abuse, only to have the report later proven false (Underwager and Wakefield 1990). A Clearwater, Florida, man who was convicted of raping his girlfriend's nine-year-old daughter, for example, was freed after the girl testified that she had made up the story after watching an episode of the television drama *21 Jump Street.* The man spent 513 days in the Pinellas County Jail while his attorneys appealed the 1988 conviction, which was based on the girl's testimony and no physical evidence.

Because child abuse cases often come down to a conflict of testimony between the only two people who know what happened, the defendant and the witness-victim, it is important to encourage the witness to testify fully and without trauma. At the same time, the defendant's right to confront the witness is especially important in these cases. Confronting a child-witness face-to-face may ensure that the child does not lie, but also unfortunately a way of threatening a child so that he or she cannot tell the truth.

The depth of societal feeling in this matter is reflected in the 1987 Supreme Court decision *Pennsylvania v. Ritchie,* which held that people accused of sexually abusing children have no right to see confidential state records that might help them in the preparation of their defense unless a judge determines that it is material and important to their defense. Also in 1990, the Supreme Court held that since Jaqueline Bouknight had already been found guilty once of abusing her child and was under court supervision, she could not invoke her constitutional protection against self-incrimination to reveal his whereabouts.

Treatment. In addition to individual psychotherapy, there are three core approaches that are potentially useful in almost all cases of child abuse (Wolfe et al. 1988):

1. *Family therapy.* Since the family is virtually always disrupted in a child abuse case, family therapy is necessary. Even where the family system eventually changes, family therapy can help to mute the damage to all concerned.

2. *Parent training.* When the abuse has come from a parent, parent training is necessary to deal with the problems that led to the abuse, as well as to those that were generated by the abuse. Parent training to deal with abuse-generated problems is also important when the source of abuse is external to the family.

3. *Support systems.* Abuse often comes where there has been a sense of emotional isolation. In this vein, community-based counseling and support groups are available to abusing parents in Parents Anonymous or Parents United. This organization works in the same manner as Alcoholics Anonymous or Gamblers Anonymous. Contact with other abusers

and the opportunity to share problems with sympathetic and understanding others are helpful for parents whose abusive behaviors are triggered by psychosocial stressors and a sense of emotional isolation. There are also support groups for the victims of child abuse, which have been found to be especially useful with older abuse victims.

Rape

An event that took place on the night of March 18, 1983, demonstrates not only the horror of rape but the stigma and unusual burden of proof that the victims of that crime carry. On that night, a woman who had gone into Big Dan's bar in New Bedford, Massachusetts, to buy a pack of cigarettes was gang-raped for over two hours while the other patrons watched, and in some cases even cheered on the rapists. A public outcry eventually brought these rapists to justice, but the onlookers seemed to assume that such behavior had a measure of acceptability.

Inaccurate Rape Myths. Some myths often contain significant truth value, but others, like the following, are inaccurate in most instances (Calhoun and Atkeson 1991; Ellis 1989):

- *Rape is an impulsive behavior.* Most rapes are planned, even though in some cases no specific woman is targeted. In many cases, the man develops a strong desire to rape someone, then systematically seeks out a victim.

- *Men who rape are killers.* Certainly men who rape pose a real danger to the woman who is the victim. At the same time, probably no more than one percent of victims are murdered and less than half are physically injured.

- *Only attractive, sexy women are raped; or, only virtuous women are raped.* Women of all ages (including infants and women in their eighties) and of all types of physical appearance and personal background have been victims of rape. Appearing vulnerable, and being in situations that suggest vulnerability and/or isolation, are more important predictors than level of physical attraction.

- *Rapists are oversexed and/or "sexual degenerates."* A number of rapists actually have a relatively low sex drive and a sporadic sexual pattern. On the other hand, some are married and have otherwise good marriages. Many rapists appear to be motivated more by power or hostility than by sexuality.

- *Rapists may avoid prosecution because of an intact hymen in a woman who was a virgin and was allegedly penetrated, or because of a lack of semen.* Though either of these may be a useful piece of evidence, neither is required. Rapists often have a potency problem, and some don't even ejaculate during the rape.

- *Rapes are commonly committed by strangers in dark or hidden places.* Actually, about half of rape victims know their attacker. Many rapes occur on dates or in deteriorating marital relationships.

- *Exhibitionists and voyeurs will rape if given a chance.* A few voyeurs and exhibitionists do pose a danger to victims, but most are passive and avoid any true interpersonal confrontation or interaction with victims. Unfortunately, they do not wear signs to let us know if they are dangerous or not.

- *White women are often raped by black men.* In the great majority of rapes, the victim and the attacker are of the same race.

- *Certain women enjoy being raped.* This is simply untrue. Some women (and some men) enjoy sex play in which there is a veneer of being coerced or forced, but in these situations both parties actually retain some control over what goes on. They are not acting out a wish to actually be raped.

Legal Issues in Rape. Traditionally, the legal definition of *rape* has been the unlawful and unwanted penetration of a female's vagina by a male's penis, enforced by fear, physical control, or any other form of coercion. Penetration is now no longer required, and most statutes cover all same-sex and cross-sex possibilities. The traditional definition is also too restrictive in that many rapists do not desire intercourse; rather, they require the victim to engage in some other sex practice, such as fellatio. There are documented cases of male victims of homosexual rape, and in a few extremely rare cases males have been physically coerced to have sex by groups of females. But in our discussion, *rape* refers to physical coercion, overt or implied, by a male in a sexual encounter. Rape statutes do not require that the male have an orgasm, but the presence of semen is an extremely helpful piece of evidence in prosecutions.

If a woman is raped, she should take the following steps:

1. As soon as she is alone, she should call the police or rape hot line, as well as a trusted friend or relative to provide emotional support.

2. The victim should not take off her clothes, douche, or wash until the police have had a chance to gather corroborative evidence. Solid evidence can increase the chance of convicting the rapist, and thus increase conviction rates, which in turn may help deter future rapes (Frazier and Borgida 1985).

3. If she lives alone, she should consider staying with a friend or relative for a few days.

4. The victim should not deny any of her feelings. If she continues to be anxious or upset, she should get professional help before the symptoms crystallize or generalize.

Incidence. The incidence of rape is hard to determine, but the incidence of reported rape has risen through the 1980s. Reported rapes account for five percent of all crimes of violence—about one in every two thousand women per year. But estimates are that only one of every ten actual rape victims reports the assault to police; about one rapist in twenty is ever arrested; one in thirty prosecuted; and one in fifty convicted (Ellis 1989; Frazier and Borgida 1985).

Effects on the Victim. Rape is as much a crime of violence as it is of sexuality (Calhoun and Atkeson 1991). The effects of the insult and assault to the female victim go beyond the actual physical event of the rape itself. Potentially demeaning physical examinations and nonsupportive questioning of rape victims by police officials have abated in recent years, largely because of pressure from various women's groups and the increasing presence of female officers on police forces and in rape units. The defense attorney's traditional ploy of implying that the victim had always been "a loose woman" and in fact invited the rape is now restricted by Public Law 95-540, which was passed by Congress in October 1978. This law limits the circumstances under which evidence of a rape victim's previous sexual conduct is admissible in federal court, and most states have now passed similar laws. In 1991, the Supreme Court ruled that states may protect an alleged rape victim by preventing the man she says attacked her from introducing evidence that they previously had consensual sex.

Rape victims, almost 75 percent of whom are single, divorced, or separated, experience a variety of negative effects (Ellis 1989). Virtually all suffer bruises or abrasions, and about five percent suffer severe injuries, such as fractures or concussions. Many suffer injury from being forced to perform fellatio or anal intercourse. Most rape victims also suffer emotional trauma. Work adjustment appears to be particularly negatively affected, and sexual adjustment is often disrupted. Loss of self-esteem, anxiety, and depression are common reactions, though recently the use of well-trained rape squads who focus on helping the victim as much as on catching the perpetrator has helped.

Causes. As with other violent behaviors, it is a mistake to assume that a single cause or personality pattern accounts for most rapes (Calhoun & Atkeson 1991). Some theorists have claimed that elevation of male hormone levels or some other biochemical abnormality might incite rapists. So far, there is no convincing general evidence for this claim, though on occasion researchers find somewhat higher levels of plasma testosterone in the most violent rapists. Even in these cases, however, there is no proof that higher testosterone levels necessarily caused the behavior; they may merely be coincident with, or even result from, an incident of rape.

Treatment of the Rapist. Castration and execution were traditional methods of dealing with rapists. No doubt they are effective deterrents for an individual rapist, but there is little evidence that such measures deter other rapists. Drugs like medroxyprogesterone have been used to lower the serum testosterone level in violent rapists, thereby reducing the likelihood of any sexual arousal at all. And anti-androgens appear to reduce the propensity to the violence component in rape. The major difficulty with this treatment is getting the rapist to cooperate; also, the side effects of these drugs are substantial.

Prevention. Three major strategies are available to women to reduce their chances of being raped. Unfortunately, all require some measure of distrust of males or the passive or defensive behaviors from which women have been trying to escape for many years.

- *Avoid contact with strangers.* For example, do not open the door to a person you do not know or cannot identify, and do not pick up hitchhikers.
- *If you are being harassed or followed, do not try to handle the situation alone.* Instead, go to a friend or to the police.
- *Be prepared by learning karate or by carrying tear gas, a shrill police whistle, or a weapon.* For a woman threatened with rape, remaining passive is only a moderately safe strategy, according to experts. Strong, active resistance and flight are the best ways to avoid harm, especially if there are other people in the vicinity. Some women have deterred a rape by claiming to have a venereal disease or cancer in the genital area. In general, if a woman can strongly resist, immediately escape, or persuade the rapist to see her as a person instead of as an object, she increases her chances of not being raped. (Groth and Birnbaum 1979)

At a societal level, there has been an increasing interest in the use of "sexual predator" laws to handle people who commit rape, child sexual abuse, and the like. Prototype laws of this sort seek indefinite confinement of a rapist until a mental health expert is willing to say he is no longer dangerous. The sentence is reduced to a form of parole if the person undergoes sex-offender therapy, reeducation, and/or castration. Another option is supervised, continuous chemical castration by means of antiandrogen drugs, such as cyproterone acetate, that suppress all sexual arousal. But any expert who makes a certain or virtually certain prediction about a person's dangerousness either way doesn't know the problems involved in predicting danger-ousness (see chapter 13). In addition to prediction problems, these various options obviously generate various sociopolitical and constitutional issues.

Capital Punishment

Capital punishment, the execution of an individual who has been convicted of a serious crime in the name of the state, is one of the oldest forms of punishment. It is also one of the most controversial and intensely debated topics within criminal justice. Public opinion on capital punishment varies widely. Critical issues in the use of capital punishment center on the concepts of fairness of application, certainty of guilt, and the humaneness of this form of punishment.

Until 1972, capital punishment was frequently used in the United States for crimes such as murder and rape. During the thirty-seven-year period from 1930 to 1967, 3,800 offenders were executed. In 1972 the Supreme Court ruled that the death penalty, as applied in the case of *Furman v. Georgia,* was cruel and unusual punishment. Since the Georgia capital punishment statute mirrored statutes in several other states, this ruling prohibited capital punishment in thirty-nine states and the District of Columbia. In 1976, the Supreme Court upheld a revised Georgia statute, and capital punishment became a reality once again (Bohn 1991).

The following are some of the typical arguments relevant to the death penalty. Arguments *against* capital punishment include:

- Executing someone is an irreversible step; thus, the admittedly rare execution of an innocent person cannot be undone.
- Even though there may be good reasons to support an execution, the state functions as a killer, and, in turn, society can become dehumanized.
- The death penalty has not been proven to deter others from committing similar crimes.
- The processing of cases involving the death penalty is more costly than life imprisonment because of long delays and appeals. A mandated death-penalty sentence may raise difficulties in finding juries willing to find defendants guilty.
- For many years, the enactment of capital punishment was discrimina-tory. In the United States, the majority of those executed have been black.

Arguments *in favor of* the death penalty include:

- Employing the death penalty where appropriate discourages private revenge and vigilantism.

- The death penalty is sanctioned in the Bible as well as by historical tradition as a culturally approved manner of dealing with heinous offenders.

- There is no good evidence that the death penalty is not an effective general deterrent.

- The death penalty could easily be made more economical than the permanent, lifelong warehousing of the most dangerous criminals.

- The death penalty clearly deters the person who is executed from doing any more damage to individuals or society.

- As regards retribution, it is reasonable to say that those who kill innocent persons in cold blood deserve similar punishment.

Numerous studies of capital punishment conducted by researchers on both sides of the issue have failed to provide definitive evidence about its effect. Meanwhile, offenders are currently being sentenced to capital punishment in thirty-eight states, and as of March 1989 2,187 inmates were awaiting execution in the United States (NAACP Legal Defense and Educational Fund 1989). But only twenty-five were executed in 1987, eleven in 1988, and sixteen in 1989.

Notes

Athens, L. 1989. *The Creation of Dangerous Violent Criminals.* London: Routledge.

Benedek, E., and D. Cornell. 1989. *Juvenile Homicide.* Washington, D.C.: American Psychiatric Association Press.

Bohn, R., ed. 1991. *The Death Penalty in America.* Cincinnati, Oh.: Anderson.

Brizer, D., and M. Crowner. 1989. *Current Approaches to the Prediction of Violence.* Washington, D.C.: American Psychiatric Association Press.

Browne, A., and D. Finkelhor. 1986. "Impact of Child Sexual Abuse: A Review of the Research." *Psychological Bulletin* 99: 66–77.

Calhoun, K., and B. Atkeson. 1991. *Treatment of Rape Victims.* Elmsford, New York: Pergamon.

Cross, C. 1984. *Child Abuse and Neglect.* Washington, D.C.: National Education Association.

Driscoll, J., R. Meyer, and C. Schaine. 1973. "Training Police in Family Crisis Intervention." *Journal of Applied Behavioral Science* 9: 62–82.

Ellis, L. 1989. *Theories of Rape.* New York: Hemisphere.

Fairbairn, W. 1952. *An Object Relations Theory of the Personality.* New York: Basic.

Falk, R. 1988. *Revolutionaries and Functionaries.* New York: E. P. Dutton.

Finkelhor, D. 1985. *Child Sexual Abuse.* New York: The Free Press.

Fox, J. 1990. Personal communication.

Frazier, P., and E. Borgida. 1985. "Rape Trauma Syndrome Evidence in Court." *American Psychologist* 40: 984–93.

Furman v. Georgia. 1972. (408 U.S. 238).

Goodwin, J. 1989. *Sexual Abuse.* 2nd ed. Boca Raton, Fla.: CRC Press.

Gorton, G., and S. Akhtar. 1990. "The Literature on Personality Disorders, 1985–88: Trends, Issues, and Controversies." *Hospital and Community Psychiatry* 41: 39–51.

Groth, A. and J. Birnbaum 1979. *Men Who Rape.* New York: Plenum.

Klebba, A. 1981. "Comparison of Trends for Suicide and Homicide in the United States, 1900–1976." In J. Hays, T. Roberts, and K. Solway, eds. *Violence and the Violent Individual.* New York: Spectrum.

Meyer, R., and A. Parke. 1991. "Terrorism: Modern trends and issues." *Forensic Reports* 4: 51–59.

Miller, T., L. Heath, J. Molcan, and B. Dugon. 1991. "Imitative Violence in the Real World." *Aggressive Behavior,* 17: 121–134.

NAACP Legal Defense and Educational Fund. 1989. *Death Row, U.S.A..* New York: NAACP Legal Defense and Educational Fund.

Newton, M. 1990. *Hunting Humans: An Encyclopedia of Modern Serial Killers.* Port Townsend, Wa.: Loompanics Unlimited.

Pennsylvania v. Ritchie. 1987. (107 S.Ct. 989, 55 L.W. 4180).

Post, G. 1987. "Rewarding Fire with Fire: Effects of Retaliation on Terrorist Army Dynamics." *Terrorism* 10: 23–26.

Serritella, D., and L. L'Abate. 1992. "Violence as Addiction." In L. L'Abate, Farrar, J., and D. Serritella, eds. *Handbook of Differential Treatments for Addictions.* Needham Hghts, Mass.: Allyn & Bacon.

Smith, S., and R. Meyer. 1987. *Law, Behavior and Mental Health.* New York: New York University Press.

Toch, H., and K. Adams. 1989. *The Disturbed Violent Offender.* New Haven, Conn.: Yale University Press.

Underwager, R., and H. Wakefield. 1990. *The Real World of Child Interrogations.* Springfield, Ill.: Charles Thomas.

Veleber, D., and D. Templer. 1984. "Effects of Caffeine on Anxiety and Depression." *Journal of Abnormal Psychology* 93: 120–22.

Wolf, J. 1989. *Antiterrorist Initiatives.* New York: Plenum Press.

Wolfe, D., B. Edwards, I. Manion, and C. Koverola. 1988. "Early Intervention for Parents at Risk of Child Abuse and Neglect." *Journal of Consulting and Clinical Psychology* 56: 40–47.

Wrightsman, L. 1991. *Psychology and the Legal System.* 2nd ed. Pacific Grove, Calif.: Brooks/Cole.

Zimbardo, P. 1973. "The Psychological Power and Pathology of Imprisonment." In E. Aronson and R. Helmreich, eds. *Social Psychology.* New York: Van Nostrand.

11
Deception Detection

Tilford was nervous, his fingernails bitten down to the quick. This was not necessarily a sign of guilty knowledge . . . —most of the brokers I'd seen today were high-strung. It must be nerve-racking following all that money up and down.
— Sara Paretsky
Killing Orders

This chapter describes the techniques employed in the determination of deception and malingering in legal proceedings (see also chapter 8). All of these techniques have their uses and misuses. Extravagant claims have been made about the power of hypnosis, for example, to detect untruthfulness, based on the assumption that subjects in a hypnotic trance are unable to lie. Blind adherence to this assumption can have discomforting consequences, as is evident in the well-documented case of Kenneth Bianchi, the Hillside Strangler (Orne et al. 1984; chapter 8 of this book). Evidence had linked Bianchi with multiple murders on the West Coast. He was evaluated by Dr. John Watkins, an eminent hypnosis researcher and practitioner (who unfortunately will probably be better remembered for his role in this case than for his fine contributions to knowledge about hypnosis). After Bianchi's session with Dr. Watkins, the court called in Dr. Ralph Allison, who had established a reputation locally as an expert on multiple personalities. He also hypnotized Bianchi and concurred with Dr. Watkins on the diagnosis of multiple personality. While he was presumably under trance, Bianchi has presented a "personality" that was angry and bitter and that assumed responsibility for the murders. After the hypnotic trance, Bianchi reverted to his normal personality, which continued to deny all knowledge of wrongdoing. Drs. Watkins and Allison's support of the multiple-personality disorder (see chapter 7) led to a plea of Bianchi's culpability under insanity statutes.

A third clinician, Dr. Martin Orne, conducted an independent evaluation. Aware that subjects can fake being hypnotized and that they can fool even experienced hypnotists, Dr. Orne set out to test the authenticity of Bianchi's apparent multiple-personality disorder. Using several techniques, he quickly discovered that the "angry personality" was a clever piece of play-acting. Just before hypnotizing Bianchi, for example, Dr. Orne mentioned in passing that it is very rare for a multiple personality to have only two personalities. When Dr. Orne hypnotized Bianchi a few minutes later, Bianchi immediately produced "Billy," personality number three.

This case (discussed further later in this chapter) illustrates the potential uses and misuses of techniques for detecting deception. But when used appropriately, a number of methods, including hypnosis, do have a justifiable role in determination of deception. These methods are the subject of this chapter.

Basic Concepts

Deception can be defined as the knowing misrepresentation of self-reported personal or factual data. When deception involves false reports or exaggeration of medical or psychiatric symptoms, it is referred to as *malingering*. Since the early days of the modern legal system, it has been evident that the practice of deception is common among "consumers" (and a few practitioners) of the legal process. When deception occurs in the process of giving sworn testimony, it is perjury and may itself be prosecuted. But deception may also occur in other legal contexts. A parent may falsely deny the physical abuse of a child, for example. A prospective employee may misrepresent drug use, a poor employment record, or criminal history on a job application. An adolescent may falsely deny alcohol abuse or promiscuity. While none of these instances may constitute perjury, they all represent examples of ways that deception may impinge upon legal determinations.

Methods of Detecting Deception and Malingering

Ekman and O'Sullivan (1989) point out that two major components, deception apprehension and deception guilt, can be aroused in the process of deception, and in turn facilitate detection of it. *Deception apprehension* is essentially the fear of getting caught, and it is heightened when:

- the examiner has a reputation for being difficult to deceive;
- the examiner is initially suspicious;
- the deceiver has little skill at lying, and little practice or no prior success at it;
- the deceiver is particularly vulnerable to the fear of being caught;
- the perceived stakes or consequences are high;
- both rewards and punishment are at stake, or punishment alone is at stake;
- the punishment for being caught in a lie is great, or the punishment for

the concealed act, if revealed, would be so great that there is no incentive to confess;

- the examiner gains no benefit from the deceiver's lie.

Deception guilt, on the other hand, is guilt about the process of lying itself. It is parallel to shame, except that shame usually requires an audience. Deception guilt is increased when:

- the deceit is totally selfish, and the examiner derives no benefit from being misled and loses as much or more than the deceiver gains;
- the deceit is unauthorized, and the situation is one in which honesty is authorized;
- the deceiver has not been practicing the deceit for a long time;
- the deceiver and the examiner share social values;
- the deceiver is personally acquainted with the examiner;
- the deceiver cannot construe the examiner as mean or gullible;
- there is no reason for the examiner to expect to be misled, and the deceiver has encouraged the examiner to be trusting.

Three general classes of methods are commonly employed in the detection of deception: interview techniques, psychological test methods, and physiological methods.

Interview Methods

Interview methods focus on the consistency of the information that is provided. For example, most psychiatric disorders follow typical courses (in terms of onset of symptoms and the like) and feature certain prominent symptoms. While there is some variability in the symptoms presented by people with actual mental disorders, most variations occur within predictable limits.

Fortunately, malingerers tend to have an incorrect knowledge of mental disorders and how they usually occur. This is due in part to common public misconceptions. As a consequence, a malingerer often presents symptoms that are actually quite uncommon among the genuinely mentally ill. (See the details on schizophrenia and paranoid disorders in chapter 6.)

A contributor to this chapter, Dr. William Bickart, evaluated a criminal defendant who had committed arson in an attempt to speed up his transfer to a less restrictive correctional facility. He reported having had a hallucination that commanded, "Set a fire so you'll get out of here quicker"—not a high IQ fellow. But despite prevailing public misconceptions, command hallucinations to harm other individuals are actually rare among psychotics, and if they do occur, they are almost always connected to a bizarre delusional thought system. That was not the case for the arsonist.

Suspected malingerers are usually evaluated using unstructured interview techniques that offer a maximum of flexibility. In structured interviews, a series of questions are asked that explore the specific nature of psychiatric symptoms. The questions are ones that studies have shown were prevously effective in distinguishing malingerers from actual mental patients.

The Schedule of Affective Disorders and Schizophrenia (SADS) is one such interview technique (Spitzer and Endicott 1978). The SADS asks the patient a long series of yes-or-no questions about specific symptoms. For example, the subject is asked, "Do you feel depressed every morning?" or, "Do you hear voices telling you to kill yourself?" The score gives an approximation of the patient's level of mental disorder. Most malingerers, perhaps in an effort to "prove" that they are mentally disordered, report more symptoms on the SADS than even the most mentally ill of patients. Thus, those patients who receive high scores on the SADS are likely to be malingering.

Another structured interview, called the Structured Interview of Reported Symptoms (SIRS), was designed by Richard Rogers, an eminent forensic psychologist (Rogers et al. 1990) specifically for use with suspected malingerers. Like the SADS, high scores on the SIRS are suggestive of malingering. The SIRS is based on thirteen strategies that provide an excellent overview of the crucial areas of interest in the detection of deception. These thirteen strategies consider and assess (1) the individual's degree of defensiveness about everyday problems, worries, and negative experiences; (2) how the individual has attempted to alleviate or solve his or her psychological problem; (3) how many of eight bona-fide but rare symptoms the individual endorses; (4) whether the individual will endorse any fantastic or absurd symptoms; (5) the symptom pairs that are likely to coexist in real clinical syndromes; (6) how precisely the individual describes the symptoms since, in reality precision is unlikely; (7) how the individual's description of the onset of symptoms compares with actual symptom onset; (8) whether the individual has a stereotypical or "Hollywood" view of psychological problems; (9) the number of symptoms the individual reports that have an extreme or unbearable quality; (10) whether the individual's endorsement of symptoms has a random quality; (11) how stable the indvidual's self-reports of symptoms are; and (12) the level of honesty and completeness in the individual's report. The SIRS then (13) asks the subject to report on behaviors that can be observed by the evaluator, and the report is then compared with the actual observations.

While both the SADS and the SIRS are thorough and well validated, they are time-consuming, taking as long as four hours to complete. And while they are reliable in placing an individual into a diagnostic category and in detecting deception, their reliability decreases as the deceiver's sophistication increases. So perhaps the most useful tool that can be used when assessing deception in interview techniques is to analyze the consistency of the statements. There are basically three ways that this is done: looking at how consistent the symptoms that are presented are in comparison with actual psychological disorders; finding out how consistently the symptoms have been maintained across a given period of time; and judging whether the individual presents the symptoms in a like manner over the course of several interviews.

A person who attempts to fake a psychological disorder is faced with a number of difficult tasks. First, the symptoms must match the symptoms of an actual disorder. The examiner is usually much more knowledgeable then the deceiver is, although people can learn what accurate symptoms are, as the Bianchi case demonstrated. Another difficult task that the deceiver faces is that he or she must keep track of the complaints and symptoms and repeat them with great accuracy over different interviews and with different interviewers. Errors and inconsistencies would alert the examiner that a deception may be taking place. Yet even persons with brain damage, for example, show some improvement across several evaluations; the symptom picture does not change radically from one interview to the text, but neither does no change take place. Also, the individual's previous psychological histories may be available, and any discrepancies can alert an evaluator.

Psychological Tests

There are basically two types of psychological tests: objective and projective. We'll consider the objective tests first.

Objective Personality Tests. Objective tests ask relatively clear, specific questions ("Have you ever had thoughts of murder?"), statements ("I have never had hallucinations"), or concepts ("Do you prefer bowling or water sports?"), to which the test taker makes a direct response. Usually, these are paper-and-pencil tests and can be scored by hand, machine, or computer. These are often termed *integrity tests* and are increasingly used by employers, in part because of increasing restrictions on the use of the polygraph. Some tests look at specific aspects of personality; others, at broad classes of personality factors. The tests we are interested in are the commonly used well-validated tests with features that have been developed especially to detect deception, such as the MMPI-2, the MCMI-II, the 16PF, the BPI, and the CPI.

Certain scales are designed to detect the test-taking *attitude* of a respondent. Psychologists refer to this as the individual's *attitude set* or *response set*. Individuals may present themselves as overly virtuous and psychologically healthy—that is, they are *faking good.* Conversely, respondents may attempt to *fake bad,* or to appear as disturbed as possible. *Validity scales* measure such attitude sets, which then allows an inference of deception.

One method of assessing an individual's attitude set is to look at how many of the items on the test were left unanswered. This method of deception is infrequent since it is so easily detected, but it does happen. The person is usually asked to go back and finish the test. Another assessment method is to check the answers for random responding. Individual sometimes respond randomly to questions when they are attempting to simulate a psychosis. Individuals who cannot even understand the words on the page but can read may respond randomly in any case.

Another assessment is to look for patterns of answers. For example, the Minnesota Multiphasic Personality Inventory-2 (Graham 1990; also see chapter 1) has a built-in scale that indicates a tendency to respond to the majority of questions as either true or false, regardless of content. This is called the True Response Inconsistency (TRIN). Random responding on the MMPI-2 is detected by the Variable Response Inconsistency scale (VRIN).

Four basic MMPI-2 scales are commonly used to detect deception; the ?/Cannot Say Scale; the Lie Scale; the F Scale; and the K Scale. The other scales that have been briefly mentioned, the TRIN and VRIN, are used to complement these formal validity scales and make the determination more accurate. The ?/Cannot Say Scale (? Scale) simply tells the examiner how many answers were left blank. The Lie Scale is a series of statements that identifies persons who are trying to be defensive in a naive and unsophisticated fashion.

The F Scale is the traditional index for the detection of "faking bad" malingering on the MMPI-2. This scale consists of items to which only about one percent of all individuals taking the test will admit. But persons who score high on the F scale may be psychotic, very confused, have poor reading skills, be responding to the questions in a random fashion, or be in great psychological stress, as well as malingering. The final validity scale, the K Scale, is traditionally used to detect defensiveness. High scorers are those who attempt to portray themselves in a very favorable light. In child-custody cases, for example, parents being tested to determine their fitness are expected to score high on this scale, because they are afraid to admit to having even minor psychological problems.

All in all, the MMPI-2 is one of the most reliable and useful of objective tests; it is commonly used in forensic psychological examinations (Graham 1990). As Richard Rogers has said, "No psychometric method has been examined more exhaustively in the general area of psychological deception than the MMPI-2" (Rogers 1988, 99).

Another objective personality test, the 16-Personality Factor Questionnaire (16 PF), can help to detect deception via its Faking-Bad Scale and Motivational Distortion Scale (Karson and O'Dell 1976). The California Personality Inventory (CPI) is often used in conjunction with the MMPI-2 to detect personality styles as well as deception. The CPI has a Good Impression Scale and a Well-Being Scale. The latter reflects psychological health from a high score, and deception from a low score.

The Millon Clinical Multiaxial Inventory-II (MCMI-II; Millon 1987) is a scale somewhat similar to the MMPI-2. It is another widely used objective personality test with built-in validity scales that identify deceptive response sets (Bagby et al. 1990). The MCMI-II is a series of 175 statements to which the subject must answer true or false. It has four validity scales that look at a variety of response styles. One novel approach that the MCMI-II takes is that it uses the validity scales to modify the scores on the other, clinical scales; these validity scales are used to "weight" the clinical scales.

A final personality instrument is the relatively new Basic Personality Inventory (BPI). This objective instrument was designed to measure the dimensions of the psychopathology and symptomology that underlie the clinical scales of the MMPI-2 (Bagby et al. 1990). The BPI has six measures of deception or atypical responding that function in ways similar to the validity or response-set scales of other test instruments.

The ability of objective personality tests to ascertain the truth and uncover deception is relatively good compared with other forms of evaluation. But the evidence from any one test can seldom establish truth. Rather, information from a variety of sources provide data that can be used to indicate a probability of deception if they converge.

Projective Personality Tests. Projective tests assume that people tend to defend themselves by attributing (often unconsciously) to other people those aspects of themselves that they find unacceptable. Projective tests present the individual with ambiguous, unstructured stimuli and infer from the responses these less-than-conscious processes. One of the earliest examples of a projective test is the word-association test, wherein the examiner says a word, like "Mother," and the client responds as quickly as possible with another, like "Train." This test is not used very often anymore.

The best-known projective test, the Rorschach Inkblot Technique (commonly referred to as the Rorschach), is a group of ten cards that have inkblots on them, as if ink had been spilled in the middle of a piece of paper, then folded over, unfolded, and dried. Some of these blots have color, but most do not. Numerous studies have not supported the validity of the Rorschach (Stermac 1988), but some researchers, such as John Exner (1978), have produced some valid approaches with the test. Overall, the Rorschach does not have built-in validity scales, and it is not effective in detecting deception, especially when the test-taker is well informed.

Another type of projective test presents the subject with pictures or drawings and infers attitudes from the responses. The Thematic Apperception Test (TAT), for example, has a series of drawings that vary along a continuum of clear to vague images. The test-taker is asked to make up a story about these scenes, and from these stories themes are inferred. The TAT has not proven useful in detecting deception.

Intellectual Methods. A substantial proportion of malingerers feign having intellectual difficulties, such as problems with memory, concentration, judgement, or logical thought. Interview and observation techniques are often effective in differentiating feigned intellectual deficit from actual mental retardation or organic brain disorder. Fortunately, it is difficult to maintain an intellectually debased condition over a long period, particularly when the subject is closely observed, as in an inpatient forensic evaluation center.

But psychological tests of intellectual deficit are commonly effective, again based on the common tendency for malingerers to "overplay" the disorder. The incongruities between test performance and observed behavior are often jarring. In one case example in my experience, a defendant achieved an IQ score that was in the severely mentally retarded range, with extremely poor memory functioning. But this individual was surreptitiously observed on several occasions performing complex card tricks for the entertainment of other detainees. Not retarded, but no genius either, he was eventually discharged with a diagnosis of malingering.

Individual tests, notably the Wechsler Adult Intellectual Scale-Revised (WAIS-R; known to the public as the "IQ test") is the most popular and best-researched measure of intellectual functioning, and it is commonly used in many settings. Specific patterns of scores are associated with malingering, and research affirms the ability of this test to assist in malingering evaluations. Other tests, like the Benton Visual Retention Test, measure specific components of intelligence— in this case, visual memory—and these, too, can be useful in the assessment of malingering.

A more effective approach to evaluating malingered intellectual deficit is to use entire test batteries and examine the scores for inconsistencies. Some malingerers produce patterns of scores that are inconsistent across measures of similar abilities, though numerous malingerers appear able to escape detection by this approach.

A newer approach to evaluating malingered intellectual deficit is the use of tests designed specifically to detect deception. Again, these tests exploit the common tendency for malingerers to overplay their roles. One of the earliest tests of this type, the Memorization of Fifteen Items test, requires the subject to view and recall a stimulus that consists of letters and numbers arranged in easily remembered sets. The task is presented to the subject as being difficult and demanding, but most subjects, even those with significant cognitive impairment, are able to recall at least nine of the items. Performance below this standard is suggestive of either poor motivation or malingering.

A variation of this approach that has shown promise is the Symptom Validity Technique and similar tests. This approach requires the subject to perform a simple memory task (such as recalling which color was presented five seconds earlier) over many trials, then select the correct answer from two alternatives. Chance performance or random responding would yield a fifty percent accuracy rate over many trials. But malingerers tend to perform at lower-than-chance accuracy rates. The Symptom Validity Technique is founded upon well-established norms of probability (Bickart, Connell, and Meyer in press; Shooter and Hall 1990), so that a positive finding of malingering on the test is a good indicator of an attempt to deceive. Symptom-validity techniques may be designed by examiners to meet the purposes of a particular evaluation. The many applications of this versatile technique include the detection of malingered sensory deficits like blindness, deafness, or lack of tactile sensation (anaesthesia), or the detection of specific short-term memory deficits (Shooter and Hall 1990).

Hypnosis. The general public perceives hypnosis as a powerful means of inducing an unwilling individual to tell the truth (Meyer, 1992). This perception is no doubt perpetuated by the extravagant claims of many clinicians who employ the technique. The Kenneth Bianchi case illustrates the belief, widely held among some clinicians, that a hypnotized subject is necessarily honest. It has even been claimed that hypnosis has the power to restore lost memories. Both beliefs have, at best, only a moderate degree of truth value.

There is little agreement regarding what hypnosis is and how it works. No theory has yet fully explained the phenomenon or its ability to facilitate self-disclosure. A simplified hypothesis is that hypnosis works in a manner not unlike the truth serum. A state of deep relaxation is induced by verbal prompting, perhaps similar to the deeply relaxed state achieved by practitioners of meditation. This deep relaxtion, combined with the sense that one has shifted the "responsibility for consequences" to the hypnotist, may have a disinhibitory effect on a person's ability to suppress information, and vivid, extensive self-disclosure may be elicited. But again, there is little evidence that hypnosis will *compel* disclosure of information. Similarly, no consistent evidence suggests that people can be compelled under hypnosis to perform acts that they truly do not want to commit (Sheflin and Shapiro 1990).

People who know that they are to be hypnotized for the sole purpose of remembering forgotten details are often convinced that their recollections will be the whole truth. A common posthypnotic suggestion directs the subject to awaken and remember everything. But "memories" facilitated and even created during hypnosis often replace actual memories of events that were recalled before hypnotic induction. In fact, far from being "pure" memories, some hypnotic subjects are unable to remember the difference between memories that they had recalled before the hypnotic session, and those they recalled during it. Functionally, subjects who had a fragmentary recollection of an event before hypnosis may fill in the gaps during hypnosis, and they are then unable to tell the difference. Individuals who fill in details of fragmentary evidence during hypnosis are also more likely to believe that their present recollections are the way it really happened. If this happens in court, memories that have been enhanced by hynosis may be presented with the conviction that they are based on original, complete memories (Orne et al. 1984).

Another common belief about recollection generally is that memory is complete and relatively permanent. Everyone has seen or heard of a dramatic presentation of age regression, in which a person relives or remembers some long-past experience with the vividness of last night's dinner conversation. Some people even believe that they can be regressed to past lives. One of the strongest arguments against the validity of this latter belief is the fact that people who supposedly are recalling past lives seldom report the experience of peasants. But most people who believe they were regressed to a past life report having lives of knights, saints, queens, and the like. Based on the probability theory and composition of the population as it was in earlier eras, one should find people experiencing life as a peasant at least fifty times as often as these other identities.

Traditional and current scientific evidence suggests that memory is continuously changing and being reconstructed. Research indicates that not only is it easy for a hypnotist to insert information into a subject's fragmentary recollection of an event, but the more times the subject relates this enhanced memory, the more firmly the subject believes it (Orne et al. 1984; Sheflin and Shapiro 1990). The legal importance of this is twofold: first, in a criminal investigation, the witness or defendant is often required to recall memories many times; and second, the process by which a hypnotized subject is influenced is often outside the hypnotist's awareness. In the hypnotic situation, for example, the subject is being reinforced verbally when the hypnotist expresses approval by saying "good," "fine," "you are doing well," and the like. This can be of central importance in cases where the hypnotist is called upon to aid in lifting temporary amnesia. Motivation can be an influential factor in hypnotic recall, and individuals involved in the legal system want to do well, either for themselves or others. Always, when hypnosis is used to gain additional information in a criminal or civil investigation, the secondary-gain factor must be considered. In Bianchi's case, for example, the secondary gain was his life.

The case of Kenneth Bianchi is especially relevant to this discussion since two eminent hypnotists came to different conclusions regarding the deceptive nature of Bianchi, yet they had both used the same traditional techniques of modern hypnosis. Bianchi told the first hypnotist that psychology books that he had in his possession were "self-help" books of the type easily bought at pop bookstores; but Orne reports that Bianchi had in his possession such "pop" titles as *Diagnostic Psychological Testing* and *Psychoanalysis and Behavior Therapy,* among others. The first hypnotist asked Bianchi if he had seen the movie *Sybil,* which had been shown on television

during the week prior to their first session of hypnosis. The hypnotist believed Bianchi when he said no. There is no way to be certain that Bianchi
did see it, but correctional officers recalled that he did have his television on
during the time of the broadcast. In all likelihood, Bianchi did see the movie,
which contained information such as the fact that headaches often accompany attempts by "other" personalities to emerge. He knew in advance that
a noted hypnotist was coming to visit; further, he probably also knew that
he was being evaluated by an expert who had established a reputation as an
authority on multiple personalities (so that the expert might be biased toward making such a diagnosis in cases where others would not). Finally,
Bianchi was no doubt aware that a diagnosis of multiple personality might
save him from the electric chair.

Interestingly, Bianchi was also attempting to develop alibis for his whereabouts at the time of the Bellingham murders. And he wrote to his mother and
asked her to compose an anonymous letter confessing to committing the
Bellingham murders, then to fly out from her home in New York and to mail
the letter from a local return address. Bianchi even persuaded a woman friend
with whom he developed a jail romance to attempt a copycat murder, in an
attempt to convince authorities that the real murderer was still at large. This
she did, but she confessed when she was apprehended. Bianchi then tried to
attribute *these* acts to "Steve," another personality. The correctness of Orne's
diagnosis is further revealed by the fact that Bianchi subsequently and immediately dropped his "Steve" personality after he had plea-bargained himself out
of the death penalty.

Overall, hypnosis is not a good tool for the detection of deception
(Meyer, 1992). There are no infallible methods of detecting hypnotic simula-
tion and no way of verifying memories. Individuals who are reasonably
intelligent and who are well informed about methods of psychology, such as
Kenneth Bianchi, can fool mental health experts who do not have much
experience with deception.

Physiological Methods

Facial and Body Cues. When an individual is in a situation that makes
deception likely, there are many clues for which an examiner can watch.
Some of these are obvious. Uncooperativeness is one; it might signal that he
or she is afraid of the outcome of the evaluation, and if reassurance does not
help, deception must be considered. Another sign of deception is the reporting of unusual symptoms, particularly if they occur as the result of a suggestion by the examiner.

While what clients say is of the utmost importance, what they do not say
may be equally important (Ekman 1985). Various nonverbal cues can be
helpful. The way clients sit may indicate how open they are to the topic of

discussion; how they hold our hands may suggest anxiety. Some kinds of body language, or nonverbal cues, have come to be associated with deception.

The face is the most expressive part of our human communication apparatus; at the same time, it is also the part that is under the most control. So facial expressions should not be relied upon when deception is suspected; some people can smile or look confident even when telling a lie. Research has suggested that *microexpressions,* or small, muscular twitches detectable only by videotape, are reliable indicators of deception. But this method is effective only when studying an individual over time so that the examiner can correctly identify his or her unique microexpressions.

Another facial cue is pupil dilation. Studies of people who have been told to lie indicate that they become aroused and their pupils dilate. Pupils also dilate when a person is under the influence of drugs, in a state of sexual arousal, or under stress. An examiner must be able to separate out those factors to identify deception on the basis of pupil dilation. Another facial cue is eye blinks. When compared to control groups that were not told to lie, the deceivers tended to blink more. Again, stress may always be a factor in how much or often an individual blinks.

The quality of an individual's speech can provide useful cues. We have all seen movies that depict liars who cannot get their stories right. Experiments do find that deceivers make more speech errors, appear to search for words, and even hesitate more than those who are not deceptive. Further, the tone of a person's speech tends to rise during a lie, and the speech may have more stress-related tremors (see the section on the voice analyzer that follows).

Other overall body-language factors provide important cues (Ekman 1985). For example, deceivers tend to project an attitude of little personal involvement in the evaluation. They tend to act nonchalant, behavior that may appear to be rehearsed and not spontaneous. Deceivers may shrug more, possibly as a way to buy time while they think of something to say. As for hand movements, deceivers tend to cover their mouth, touch their nose, or appear concerned with how their clothes are fitting.

Deception, especially in less cunning or unprepared deceivers, has been associated with fidgeting, moving, and crossing and uncrossing legs. Deceivers may move their chair away from the examiner and not use an open, forward-leaning posture. Before an interview, an examiner might consider arranging the furniture so that the individual cannot "hide" his or her body language behind it.

Research by Michael Cody (1991) breaks down deceivers into those who tell "prepared" lies and those who tell "spontaneous" lies. Those who prepare ahead of time to deceive tend to (1) give the answer immediately after the question is asked, (2) provide very terse answers, (3) have the microtremors discussed earlier, (4) nod their heads at the end of the lie, (5) rub some part of their bodies, and (6) lack enthusiasm and sound a bit as if they have rehearsed, which of course they have. On the other hand, people who tell spontaneous lies tend to (1) show odd grammatical errors, (2) provide brief but tentative answers, (3) show speech hesitations and silent pauses or pauses filled with "Ahhs," (4) use meaningless phrases such as "like that" and "you know," (5) employ "universal" words and phrases, such as "always," "never," "certainly," (6) completely freeze or scratch their heads, or rub their hands together, and (7) fail to provide important or even obvious details.

Like all the methods described, the studies of facial and body cues should never be used solely to determine deception. Detection should be a thorough and cumulative process, using many different information sources.

The Polygraph. The polygraph technique, often referred to as the lie detector, is the standardized measurement of physiological responses to detect deception. It is based on the observation, well known since ancient times, that lying is stressful (for most people) and is often accompanied by many of the physiological correlates of stress, such as dry mouth, accelerated heartbeat, and muscular tension. It was originally thought that by measuring these correlates, it would be possible to determine if an individual was lying.

The first systematic application of the polygraph was in 1875 by Cesare Lombroso, who measured blood pressure and pulse while questioning subjects (Abrams 1989). Successive versions added measures of the subjects' rate of respiration, muscular tension, and galvanic skin response (GSR). GSR techniques measure electrical conductivity across the skin. Electrical activity, probably facilitated by increased perspiration, increases under conditions of arousal. In 1927, the prototype for the modern polygraph was developed. This device provided a continuous measurement of the three physiological indicators traditionally assumed to be most sensitive to physiological arousal; GSR, respiration, and cardiovascular activity.

It is important to realize that these physiological indicators do not themselves directly measure deception (Lykken 1981). Rather, they measure physiological and presumably emotional arousal. The polygraph technique assumes that the process of lying is in some way disagreeable to the subject and thus that lying will necessarily result in variations of these indicators. Arousal may occur because the subject feels guilty about lying or, more likely, because the subject fears that he or she will be "caught" by the polygraph.

Thus, to maximize the effectiveness of the test, the preparation of the subject for examination is pivotal. During the preparation or pretest, examiners typically attempt to instill in the subject the sense that the polygraph is a powerful instrument and that it will detect any attempt to lie. An effective pretest often results in a confession before the subject even sees the polygraph.

Prior to the examination, the subject is fitted with two pneumograph tubes, placed around the chest and abdomen, to measure the rate of respiration. Electrodes measuring GSR are taped to two fingers, and a blood pressure cuff is affixed to one arm. As the questioning proceeds, a continuous measure of physiological responses is obtained.

Several different questioning techniques can be used, and they have differential validities. The Irrelevant Question Technique compares the subject's responsivity to benign, irrelevant questions (such as "Do you live in New York City?") to their responsivity to relevant questions pertaining to the investigation. This technique is most commonly used in the context of employee-screening evaluations, so the relevant questions typically involve such matters as illicit drug use, alcohol abuse, prior criminal convictions, and work history. The Irrelevant Question Technique, although widely used in employee screenings, has not been supported as having any consistent validity and can easily result in inaccurate findings (Iacono and Patrick 1988).

The Control Question Technique, most commonly used in the evaluation of criminal defendants, has received more attention from researchers. This technique measures reactivity by comparing the subject's responses to relevant and control questions. The relevant questions are ones that have to do with the subject matter of the evaluation, such as "Did you steal the man's watch?" while the control questions are designed so that the individual is either deceptive or uncertain about the truthfulness of his or her answer, such as "Have you ever stolen anything in your life?" In other words, the subject is induced to lie, and a pattern of responsivity for lying is obtained. This pattern is compared with responsivity to case-relevant questions. If the patterns of responsivity to control and case-relevant questions are similar, deception is suggested. The belief is that the guilty will respond with greater arousal to the relevant questions than the innocent will. A major drawback of this test is that the examiner has no way of knowing what the control questions mean to any individual. For example, if the person being evaluated stole a watch as a youth, the relevant question may show greater reactivity, even though the individual is innocent of the crime in question.

Another technique commonly used by polygraphers is the Peak of Tension Test (POTT). This test can be used only when information about a crime is available that only a guilty subject would know—for example, evidence from the crime scene that the police did not released to the press. In the POTT, questions are phrased so that the subject must answer yes or no. The subject is instructed to answer no to every question and is thus forced to lie when faced with the question about the relevant information. This relevant question is placed in the middle of a series of questions, and if there is a build-up of tension (possibly to a peak) before the relevant question and a reduction after, it is suggested that the individual is guilty. This technique has been found to be effective if the relevant, critical item presented is not known to an innocent subject, if the person that committed the crime knows the detail, if the other questions appear equally plausible, and if one and only one of the questions is of significance to the crime (Iacono and Patrick 1988).

Given these assumptions, studies of the Control Question Technique yield high rates of successful classification of guilty subjects, allegedly between 75 percent to 95 percent, though the higher rates of effectiveness are found in studies using the least adequate research methodology and controls. Innocent subjects are correctly classified at much lower rates, even as low as 50 percent. This "bias against the innocent" has resulted in the development of more effective alternatives to the Control Question Technique.

The most sophisticated concealed information test is the *guilty knowledge test,* originated by David Lykken (1981). It involves a multiple-question, multiple-choice format, wherein a guilty individual is presented with a question and a series of five responses of which only one response offered by the examiner is critical. Innocent subjects would have only a 0.20 probability of showing a fear-of-detection response, if indeed they made any differential response at all. The questions are analogous to those asked in the Peak of Tension Test—such as, "When Nancy was raped, something was knocked off the table next to you. Was it a glass of water? beer bottle? an ashtray? a glass figurine? or a vase of flowers?" If six of these five-choice questions are used, the probability that an innocent subject would physiologically respond to all of the critical items in a way that might indicate guilt is 0.00065, which is much lower than the probability of a guilty subject responding in that fashion. The validity of this technique has received strong experimental support (Lykken 1981; Davidson 1968). But possibly because it was not developed by a polygrapher, or because there is added work required to set up this format, or because it requires more detailed information about the crime, it has unfortunately gone virtually unused by polygraphers.

One problem in this regard is that researchers in the area of polygraphy are small in number and have not sought political clout. But on the other hand, polygraphers, who are more numerous and more aggressive politically, have a relatively low level of academic training and are scientifically unsophisticated. Yet they have gained political clout and have—possibly inadvertently—managed to suppress improvements in the "lie detector" from gaining legal acceptance or even recognition.

No discussion of polygraphy would be complete without some mention of countermeasures. *Countermeasures* are techniques that are used to beat the polygraph. These countermeasures are usually produced by personality characteristics, drugs and/or alcohol, or physical attributes. One effective countermeasure is the "practice effect." The more times a person takes a polygraph, the more likely they are to "pass." Also, the greater amount of accurate information the person has, the more likely he or she is to "pass." The success of most countermeasures is directly related to the type of polygraph examination used. Countermeasures can change the "general" state of arousal or be more "specific" in altering responsiveness. Thus, general-state countermeasures have more effectiveness against concealed-information tests, while specific countermeasures are more effective against control question techniques.

General-state countermeasures are likely to be attempted through the use of drugs, alcohol, relaxation training, or biofeedback, while specific countermeasures rely on cognitive (mental imagery) or physical (biting tongue, pressing toes against the floor) methods of distraction. Of the two, specific countermeasures appear to have more potential for beating (or at least disrupting) the polygraph than do the general methods (Honts 1987). The research strongly suggests that individuals can be trained to beat the polygraph, but such training is sophisticated and expensive, and it is unlikely that most polygraph subjects would have access to it.

Microwave Respiration Monitor. Rate of respiration is one of the most effective measures of emotional arousal, and it is included in the standard polygraph examination. The typical polygraph measure of it tends to be imprecise, however, since the pneumograph tube easily confuses respiration with other body movements. In addition, the pneumograph is a difficult instrument to calibrate, and its reliability is affected by minor variations in the placement of the tube.

A recent innovation is the microwave respiration monitor, which operates like a radar unit, sending continuous signals against the subject's chest and reading the return signals. This measure of respiration is unaffected by body movements and does not actually require a verbal response of the subject. Unlike the pneumograph, the microwave respiration monitor measures deviations in the breathing rate, the volume of breath, and the amplitude of inhalation and exhalation. It also offers the advantage of being portable, and it is less distracting to the subject than the pneumograph tube. It can be operated at a substantial distance, and because of this, it has been employed against suspected terrorists and by border-control units in some countries.

Voice Analyzer. It is common knowledge that stress (and lying) are often accompanied by an elevation of voice pitch. This is due to the tightening of the tiny muscles deep in the throat, compounded by the tightening of the musculature of the diaphragm, which controls exhalation. Occasionally, changes in voice pitch due to stress can be observed without sophisticated measuring devices. With the use of instrumentation, more subtle variations in voice pitch can be detected (Nachshon et al. 1985).

In 1971, the first voice analyzer, called the Psychological Stress Evaluator, was put into use. Early claims for the device were extravagant, and some people (that is, those selling it and a few unsophisticated consumers) regarded it as a foolproof truth detector. Its most common application has been in industrial settings as an aid to employee selection. Since the instrument is portable and easily hidden, it may be used covertly, without the subject's knowledge.

The voice analyzer has not been supported as effective when it is used without the subject's knowledge, and it is certainly not effective when applied to secondary voice sources (like television, and video and audiotape recordings). In fact, given the lack of studies supporting its use, most competent researchers accept that the voice analyzer is a very imperfect measure of deception. Courts are fortunately reluctant to allow any evidence from the voice analyzer. The use of the voice analyzer by prospective employers is certainly unwarranted, and its use without the knowledge of the subject is both unethical and illegal.

Truth Serums. The truth serum has the reputation, no doubt perpetuated by countless spy thrillers, of being a powerful method of inducing the revelation of secret information. It is possibly second only to the polygraph in the general public's perception of infallibility. In actuality, the so-called truth serum is based upon an extremely simple principle—that sedatives facilitate (but do not compel) self-disclosure. The basic validity of this principle may be affirmed by anyone who has had one too many drinks and revealed something embarrassing about themselves in a social setting. (See chapter 15 for a discussion of the psychopharmacology of truth serums.)

Research has not been entirely supportive of the efficacy of the truth serum, especially with consciously resistant subjects. Given these findings, the use of the truth serum as a means of detecting deception is on the decline.

Conclusion

The use of any single interview or any single psychological or physiological measure to detect deception is unlikely to result in an unbiased assessment of an individual. As we have seen, each procedure has some usefulness in the detection of deception but also some weaknesses. Hence, the most efficient and effective method of detecting deception is to use a variety of physiological and psychological tests, administered by a highly trained professional.

Notes

Abrams, S. 1989. *The Complete Polygraph Handbook*. Lexington, Mass.: Lexington Books.

Bagby, R., R., Gillis, and S. Dickens. 1990. "Detection of Dissimulation with the New Generation of Objective Personality Measures." *Behavioral Sciences and the Law* 8: 93–102.

Bickart, W., D. Connell, and R. Meyer. (in press). "The Symptom Validity Technique as a Measure of Feigned Short-term Memory Deficit." *American Journal of Forensic Psychology.*

Cody, M. 1991. Personal communication.

Davidson, J. 1968. "Validity of the Guilty Knowledge Technique." *Journal of Applied Psychology* 52: 62–70.

Ekman, P. 1985. *Telling Lies.* New York: W. W. Norton.

Ekman, P., and M. O'Sullivan. 1989. In D. Raskin (Ed.) *Psychological Methods in Criminal Investigation and Evidence.* New York: Springer.

Exner, J. 1978. *The Rorschach: A Comprehensive System.* vol. 2: *Current Research and Advanced Interpretation.* New York: John Wiley.

Graham, J. 1990. *MMPI-2: Assessing Personality and Psychopathology.* New York: Oxford University Press.

Honts, C. 1987. "Interpreting Research on Polygraph Countermeasures." *Journal of Police Science and Administration* 15: 204–209.

Iacono, W., and C. Patrick. 1988. "Assessing Deception: Polygraph Techniques." In R. Rogers, ed. *Clinical Assessment of Malingering and Deception.* New York: Guilford Press.

Karson, S., and J. O'Dell. 1976. *A Guide to the Clinical Use of the 16 PF.* Champaign, Ill.: Institute for Personality and Ability Testing.

Lykken, D. 1981. *A Tremor in the Blood.* New York: McGraw-Hill.

Meyer, R. 1992. *Practical Clinical Hypnosis.* Lexington, Mass.: Lexington Books.

Millon, T. 1987. *Manual for the MCMI-II.* 2nd ed. Minneapolis, Minn.: National Computer Systems.

Nachshon, I., E. Elaad, and T. Amsel. 1985. "Validity of the Psychological Stress Evaluator: a Field Study." *Journal of Police Science and Administration* 13: 275–82.

Orne, M., D. Dinges, and E. Orne. 1984. "On the Differential Diagnosis of Multiple Personality in the Forensic Context." *International Journal of Clinical and Experimental Hypnosis* 32: 118–69.

Rogers, R., R. Gillis, and R. Bagby. 1990. "The SIRS as a Measure of Malingering: A Validation Study with a Correctional Sample." *Behavioral Sciences and the Law* 8: 85–92.

Rogers, R. 1988. *Clinical Assessment of Malingering and Deception.* New York: Guilford Press.

Sheflin, A., and J. Shapiro. 1990. *Trance on Trial.* New York: Guilford Press.

Shooter, E., and H. Hall. 1990. "Explicit Alternative Testing for Deliberate Distortion." *Forensic Reports* 3: 115–20.

Spitzer, R., and J. Endicott. 1978. *Schedule of Affective Disorders and Schizophrenia.* New York: Biometric Research.

Stermac, L. 1988. "Projective Testing and Dissimulation." In R. Rogers, ed. *Clinical Assessment of Malingering and Deception.* New York: Guilford Press.

12

Competency, Criminal Responsibility, Civil Commitment, and the Prediction of Dangerousness

Many legal and social issues and cases have been discussed in previous chapters of this book. This chapter focuses on those well-known situations wherein a mental health issue is inherently embedded in a major judicial–criminal justice problem. We first note the differences between criminal and civil cases, then discuss the general concept of competency, which underpins the majority of issues discussed in this chapter. After focusing on specific areas where competency may be in question, we discuss criminal responsibility (and the insanity defense), then civil commitment and the related problem of predicting whether an individual is dangerous to self or others.

Criminal versus Civil Cases

Many cases that appear in the courts are civil rather than criminal cases. Civil cases are those where one citizen or group requests a form of satisfaction from another, such as, personal-injury cases. The *standard of proof* in civil law is "a preponderance of evidence"; that is, whoever produces more than 50 percent of the evidence should win. In criminal law, by contrast, it is the government, acting for all citizens, that takes action against an alleged lawbreaker. In criminal cases the standard of proof is more stringent than in civil cases. The government must prove its case "beyond a reasonable doubt." Oddly enough, this standard of proof has never been tied to any specific numerical percentage in the minds either of jurors or judges (Smith and Meyer 1987). Individual judges, as well as the Supreme Court, have consistently refused to define the standard more specifically. Somewhere in between these two standards of proof is a third one, that of "clear and convincing evidence"—the

247

standard of proof required to commit a person (usually for "dangerousness") to a mental institution for confinement and treatment.

Competency

Competency refers to a variety of legal doctrines—most notably, competency to stand trial, to manage one's own affairs (guardianship), and to contest a will. The criteria of competency differ for each of these (Monahan and Walker 1990).

Sanity is a mental condition at the time a perpetrator allegedly commits a crime, whereas *competency to stand trial* refers to his or her mental condition at the time of the trial. More specifically, the Supreme Court has stipulated that the test for competency "must be whether he has sufficient present ability to consult with his lawyer with a reasonable degree of rational understanding—and whether he has a rational as well as a factual understanding of the proceedings against him" (*Dusky v. U.S.* 1960). Alleged perpetrators have to understand the nature of the proceedings in which they are involved and the possible consequences of those proceedings, and also manifest an ability to cooperate with the attorney in the preparation of their defense, to be considered competent. Ironically, as held in *Colorado v. Connelly* (1987), severe mental illness (and apparently, incompetency to stand trial) does not make a confession involuntary and therefore inadmissible.

These criteria are clearly different from the criteria relating to insanity (Shapiro 1991). They are much more specific and are more related to actual behavior than to inferred mental status. Yet many clinicians who testify regarding competency do not realize this differentiation, and as a result they often confuse the question of competency with that of "psychosis" or "responsibility."

Competency to Stand Trial

A competency evaluation is necessary and must be conducted before criminal responsibility can be determined. Usually this evaluation is routine and quick when it is obvious the individual is competent. In most states, the criteria are that defendants be able to understand the nature of the proceedings against them and be able to assist counsel in their own defense before and during the trial. Interview techniques and psychological tests are usually employed in competency evaluations (Grisso 1986).

Until fairly recently, a persons incompetence to stand trial could mean confinement in a mental institution for years, perhaps even a lifetime. But the U.S. Supreme Court ruled in *Jackson v. Indiana* (1972) that the length of pretrial confinement must be limited to the reasonable period of time that is necessary to determine whether the defendant is likely to become competent enough to stand trial in the foreseeable future. If the defendant is unlikely to become competent, he or she must be released, or the state must institute civil commitment proceedings. This naturally leaves open the question as to what is a reasonable time period.

Defense attorneys have been accused (sometimes accurately) of raising the competency issue—as well as the insanity defense—whenever the prosecution has a strong case against their client. At the same time, prosecutors who have weak cases may raise the competency issue in order to delay the trial, in the hope that defense witnesses will leave the area or die in the interim.

Even some psychotic people may be seen as lucid enough to meet the competency requirements, especially those who are charged with lesser offenses. It could be argued that although an inequitable trial may result if a psychotic person is confused or delusional, this would be preferable to confining that person until such time as behavior is judged to be normal. With the advent of antipsychotic drugs, this problem became even more complex. If drugs allow a return of lucidity, should the defendant be allowed to stand trial when under the influence of such drugs? But such drugs can make people groggy and passive—not the best of states under which to stand trial. Furthermore, a person's genuinely "crazy" behavior might substantiate an insanity plea in the jurors' minds, and antipsychotic drugs may well eliminate such behavior.

One of the major ways an individual can be judged incompetent is as a result of inadequate intellectual ability (see the section on mental retardation in chapter 9). But such a decision should not be made by using an arbitrary IQ cutoff point. IQ is a critical variable, but the final decision should also take into account other factors, such as the persons history of adaptation, common sense, and any already-observed ability to cooperate with the attorney and discuss issues of law. Most individuals with mild mental retardation can cooperate effectively, although not all. As one proceeds from moderate to severe and profound levels of mental retardation, the proportion of persons who cannot competently assist in their trial rises quickly.

Criminal Responsibility

> Reply to a plaintiff who claims his cabbages were eaten by your goat: You had no cabbages. If you did they were not eaten. If they were eaten, it was not by a goat. If they were eaten by a goat, it was not my goat. And, if it was my goat, he was insane.
> — I. Youngner

Persons can be held criminally responsible for their acts only if it can be shown that they had criminal intent—that is, a guilty state of mind (*mens rea)—during* the commission or omission of acts designated as criminal. This legal concept of *mens rea* is central to the legal question of "What was the defendant's state of mind at the time of the alleged crime?" If it can be shown that the defendant was "insane" at the time of the crime, the defendant will not be held criminally responsible for the act.

The Insanity Defense

Insanity as a legal term refers to a condition that excuses persons from criminal responsibility for their alleged acts, thereby protecting them from the penalties imposed on those who are found guilty of wrongdoing. Contrary to what many people believe, insanity pleas are rare compared with the total number of criminal cases tried (Wrightsman 1991). In the first place, in order to plead insanity the defendant, in effect, admits to having committed the crime. If he or she is then found not to be insane, some form of punishment is certain. Even if the defendant is found guilty by reason of insanity, he or she may be civilly committed for "treatment"—a confinement that can last longer than a prison term. For these reasons, defense attorneys rarely use the insanity defense. Nonetheless, there are standards or tests by which insanity may be determined, and there are several important historical developments or court rulings that bear on this issue.

The landmark decision is the well-known M'Naghten rule, which was handed down in 1843 by a British court. The defendant, Daniel M'Naghten, claimed that the "voice of God" had instructed him to kill Sir Robert Peel, the English prime minister, but M'Naghten had mistakenly killed Peel's secretary.

M'Naghten was found not guilty under a vaguely worded insanity defense. Because of the political nature of the crime, the House of Lords was enraged by the assassin's acquittal—a reaction not unlike that of the U.S. Congress and the American populace when John Hinckley was acquitted of attempting to assassinate Ronald Reagan by reason of insanity. Indeed, Queen Victoria, who had her political differences with her prime minister but who was also upset with the M'Naghten verdict, made both points simultaneously in a comment to the effect that anyone attempting to assassinate this particular prime minister should be presumed to be sane. In any case, a convocation of top judges was brought together to come up with an acceptable definition of insanity. They determined that

> to establish a defense of insanity, it must be clearly proved that, at the time of the committing of the act, the party accused was laboring under such a defect of reason, from disease of the mind, as not to know the nature and quality of the act he was doing; or if he did know it, that he did not know he was doing what was wrong. (Cited in Caplan 1984)

This "right-wrong" concept has been criticized by numerous experts for singling out cognition (that is, not *knowing* the nature of the act or not *knowing* it was wrong). In the opinion of these experts, cognitive activity cannot be separated from emotion or any other mental activity (Caplan 1984). Nonetheless, many states in the United States apply a variation of M'Naghten as the sole test, and most other states use it as a primary standard in determining insanity.

More recently, the American Law Institute (ALI) formulated and adopted the other most influential concept for the insanity defense in its Model Penal Code of 1962:

1. A person is not responsible for criminal conduct if at the time of such conduct as a result of mental disease or defect he lacks substantial capacity either to appreciate the criminality (wrongfulness) of his conduct or to conform his conduct to the requirements of law.

2. As used in the article, the terms "mental disease or defect" do not include an abnormality manifested only by repeated criminal or otherwise antisocial conduct. (Section 4.01)

The ALI test is still seen by most experts as the best available because the phrases *substantial capacity, appreciate the criminality of conduct,* and *conform conduct to the law* allow jurors, as opposed to expert witnesses, to decide whether the defendant should be held responsible for misconduct, and because it excludes psychopaths from the insanity defense. Wettstein, Mulvey, and Rogers (1991) show that the elimination of the volitional component, as found in the ALI test in their research, reduces the rate of acquittal by about 25 percent.

Public outcry over the acquittal of John Hinckley by reason of insanity eventually led to the 1984 passage by Congress of the Insanity Defense Reform Act (Smith and Meyer 1987). Under this new congressional standard (which is the law in federal trials and commonly serves as a model for changes in state laws that govern state trials), the *inability to conform one's behavior* component of the ALI concept was dropped, bringing the test of insanity very nearly back to the *knowing right from wrong* M'Naghten standard. Another important feature of the 1984 Reform Act is that expert witnesses can present only evidence and opinions on that evidence, and are not allowed to render an opinion on the "ultimate issue" of whether the defendant is insane. Further, unlike prior standards, the 1984 Reform Act provides for *automatic* civil commitment of the person as dangerous to others if the person is acquitted of legal guilt by reason of insanity. Moreover, the defense was given the burden of proving insanity, whereas the prosecution traditionally had had the burden of proving the person was not insane. Finally, the standard of proof that the 1984 act required for establishing insanity was raised from "a preponderance of evidence" to "clear and convincing evidence."

Irresistible Impulse. Because of the narrow cognitive focus of the M'Naghten rule, a variety of attempts have been made to establish *irresistible impulse* as an additional rule, essentially beginning with *State v. Thompson* in 1834 (cited in Rogers 1986). The central problem for both courts and clinicians was then to differentiate between an impulse that is irresistible and an impulse that was not resisted. In practice, this variation of criminal responsibility has received little support from either courts or clinicians, so it is recognized in only a few states. The Supreme Court specifically curtailed its applicability to compulsive gambling in *United States v. Tonero* (1984) and its applicability to addictions in *United States v. Lions* (1984). When it has received any support, it is usually with "command hallucinations" in schizophrenia and in severe obsessive-compulsive-disorder cases. Kleptomaniacs, pyromaniacs, psychopaths, and other impulse disorders could logically employ this defense, but juries are seldom convinced by such arguments.

Modern Trends. Two more recent concepts as regards criminal responsibility are guilty but mentally ill (GBMI) and diminished capacity. *GBMI* essentially allows a finding of both insanity and guilt and has received much attention, probably because it gives juries a way out of making an especially difficult decision. But the criteria and techniques for the insanity-decision component are often the same as in other insanity formulations. In these situations the trial is bifurcated. In the first phase of the trial, the defendant is simply presumed to be sane, and guilt or innocence is determined. If he or she is found guilty, the defendant then has the option of pleading insanity. The second phase of the trial determines whether that plea is valid. Thus, the bifurcated rule allows defendants to be found guilty but also insane, that is "guilty but mentally ill" (Smith and Meyer 1987).

Diminished capacity is a potential partial defense to a criminal charge. It permits the level of the offense to be reduced upon a showing that the defendant is actually incapable of having formed the required intent. Much of the early experience with this defense has occurred in Michigan, and attorneys seem to view it as an updated version of the intoxification defense. Many and varied referrals have been made to the Center for Forensic Psychiatry in Ann Arbor, Michigan, for consideration of this defense, but ironically, this defense has almost never been found to be viable in practice (Clark 1988).

Exceptions to Insanity Judgments. There are two major exceptions to a judgment of insanity. The first are those conditions resulting from substance abuse, particularly if the substance was voluntarily ingested. As asserted in *Barrett v. United States* (1977), "Temporary insanity created by voluntary use of alcohol or drugs will not relieve an accused of criminal responsibility even if that mental condition would otherwise meet the applicable legal definition of insanity" (p. 62).

But there are occasions when this exception is not so clearly applicable and insanity may be argued. One such occasion is when the substance abuse was caused by another person without the victim's awareness—that is, where someone "spikes" someone else's drink. Another is when "insanity" continues well beyond the actual effect of the drug use for which it was a catalyst, as stated in *New Jersey v. Stasio* (1979): "Insanity is available when the voluntary use of the intoxicant or drug results in a fixed state of insanity after the influence of the intoxicant or drug has spent itself." (p. 467)

The second exception to a judgment of insanity, under either the M'Naghten or the ALI rule, is articulated in the secondary paragraph of the ALI rule that states that there is no insanity defense available where there is an "abnormality manifested only by repeated criminal or otherwise antisocial conduct." This would usually disallow the antisocial personality disorder (see chapter 2).

Competency to Be Executed

In a death penalty case, even though a person is found to be competent to stand trial and then is found to be both sane and guilty of the offense, he or she may later be found "incompetent to be executed." There is a long history of not executing the incompetent. Reasons for this include that (1) they cannot participate effectively in any last-minute appeals; (2) it is inhumane and cruel; (3) it provides no deterrence to others; (4) it does not have retributive value; and (5) it prevents the condemned from making a final religious peace. In the 1986 case of *Ford v. Wainwright,* the Supreme Court held that the cruel and unusual punishment provision of the Eighth Amendment prohibits the state from executing a prisoner who is incompetent. A practical problem may be that because a person's competency can change over time, the issue of the competency of a prisoner may be raised repeatedly, right up to the moment of execution. As one forensic psychologist put it, not altogether in jest, "this would at least help provide steady employment for forensic mental health experts."

Competency to Make a Will

A will is a legal means of indicating how property should be distributed after death. Between the end of the twelfth century and the middle of the sixteenth century, the making of a will was regarded as contrary to public policy, and property was distributed to the family according to strict rules of descent. The concept of mental competency to make a will, or testamentary capacity, became important with the amendments to the Statute of Wills in 1572, shortly after the recognition of right to enforce wills.

The issue of incompetency usually arises when a will is probated. But at issue is the mental state of the testator at the time the will was signed, which may have been years before. Once it is demonstrated that the will was properly executed, signed, and witnessed, those attacking the will have the burden of proving the testator's incompetency. It is generally said that less capacity is needed to make a will than to make a contract or transact business. A will is a single-party instrument, and the possibility of fraud in the formation of a will is therefore theoretically less than with two-party transactions such as contracts.

A wide range of evidence is admissible to demonstrate lack of testamentary capacity. Circumstantial evidence as well as direct evidence is appropriate. For example, the language or the provisions of the will itself may be taken as evidence of an insane delusion. The testator's physical condition, behavior, irrational conduct, physical weakness, or disease are admissible, but not necessarily conclusive. Inferences may also be drawn from hallucinations, weaknesses of memory, and the influence of drugs or liquor. Again, these are not conclusive.

There are two general forms of incompetency to make a will (Smith and Meyer 1987). The first is the inability to know enough or to form the intention to dispose of property. It is generally agreed that to form testamentary capacity, people must be able to (1) understand the nature and extent of their property; (2) realize the persons who are the natural objects of their bounty (relatives and friends); (3) understand the distribution of the property contained in the will; (4) understand the nature of the will and be able to form an intent to make a disposition of property that will be carried out after death; and (5) generally know how these elements relate to each other and form an orderly scheme for the disposition of property. Neither eccentricities, mistaken beliefs, old age, nor unreasonable provisions in the will establish incompetency.

The second type of incompetency to make a will is the existence of an insane delusion. (This is, apparently, as opposed to a "sane" delusion or an "insane" reality, neither of which is specifically mentioned in the law.) Today, this type is seldom the basis for a challenge since in actual practice the test is extremely vague. It is generally stated that the issue is not whether a reasonable person would adhere to the delusion but whether it is so extravagant or unbelievable as to indicate lack of reality. What it comes down to is, if there is any evidence whatsoever to confirm the delusion, it is no longer considered irrational.

Some attorneys are now asking clinicians to assess their clients at the time they write a will if the attorneys think there might be any future contesting of a will on the basis of competency. The clinician's report, made at the time of the writing of the will, is then filed with the will. This serves to make any later challenge rather absurd since the original assessment is based on far more data than is available following the individual's death. The procedure can be further strengthened by having the signing of the will and/ or part of the evaluation videotaped as a record for later queries.

Civil Commitment

When persons of questionable mental health are deprived of freedom by the state and compelled to accept treatment, it is called civil commitment. The state may exercise this power either to protect such people from themselves— the *parens patriae* power of the state (the power to take care of those in need)—or to protect society from them—the police power of the state. In order to assert this power, each state must have its own statutes that articulate the standards and procedures to be followed both prior to and during commitment. Most such laws, following upon the classic case of *O'Connor v. Donaldson* (1975), require proof of the existence of mental illness and some indication that the person is physically dangerous to self or others. In fact, the present trend is toward making the principal criterion for involuntary civil commitment "imminent" dangerousness, a trend that is viewed with relief by most. (The complex issue of dangerousness is discussed in more detail below.)

The next significant U.S. Supreme Court decision on civil commitment was the 1979 case *Addington v. Texas* (1979). Here the Court held that the Constitution requires the use of a "clear and convincing" standard of proof at commitment hearings, a level of certainty that falls below the "beyond a reasonable doubt" standard used in criminal proceedings. The court thus exempted the civil commitment process from some of the procedural rigor required in criminal proceedings.

In general, there are two types of commitment procedures: formal and informal. *Formal or judicial* commitment is by order of a court. Formal does not mean, however, that the usual adversary process is followed. Commitment is usually initiated by a relative, friend, employer, or any other responsible person. Although such persons may testify, many judges make decisions based solely on the testimony or written reports from psychological, medical, or psychiatric experts. Often, a jury trial is not requested, though it is available if requested; and in some cases, neither the "experts" nor the affected person are present. If the judge allows commitment, the person is confined (with periodic review) in a mental institution until the mental disorder is alleviated to the satisfaction of the court, usually upon the advice of the treating therapist. Although the average length of stay is short, anyone facing involuntary civil commitment is potentially susceptible to lifelong deprivation of rights and liberties in most states.

An *informal* emergency commitment does not initially involve a court.

The police can take any person acting bizarrely to a state hospital. A responsible citizen can ask the police to pick up someone he or she believes to be dangerous by swearing out a mental health warrant. In most states, two professionals may then sign a temporary informal-commitment order that will allow the affected person to be confined for a period of time, usually ranging from one to three days. Incarceration for longer periods requires a formal commitment.

Recent Trends in Civil Commitment

Voluntary commitments now outnumber involuntary commitments, though the reverse was true prior to 1970. But it is impossible to know how many people have "voluntarily" entered mental hospitals under threat of civil commitment from family members, mental health professionals, or police officers. Though estimates vary, many suspect that it may be as much as 50 percent (Szasz 1987; Grisso 1986). Moreover, there are numerous cases where a defect in cognitive or emotional competency appears to render it impossible for the person to understand the admission forms or process well enough to be considered a voluntary admission. In *Zimmerman v. Burch* (1990), the Supreme Court held that Burch could sue personnel at the Florida State Hospital because of such a problematic voluntary admission. Mental health professionals and the courts are becoming increasingly more reluctant to involuntarily commit persons of questionable mental health. In other recent changes, individuals threatened with civil commitment now have the right to written notice of the hearing, the right and opportunity to counsel, requirements that there be "clear and convincing" evidence, and other similar safeguards.

The Prediction of Dangerousness

Prediction is very difficult, especially about the future.
— Niels Bohr
Physicist

The concept of dangerousness, as it applies to involuntary civil commitment, is ambiguous and problematic. Specifying the concept as "imminent dangerousness" is an improvement, but problems still exist. Does *dangerousness* include emotional harm, cognitive harm, and economic harm, as well as physical harm? What about harm to property? How severe or frequent must harm be to justify police intervention? Although some experts suggest limiting *dangerousness* to acts intended to do physical harm to self or others, the courts have not always concurred, and positions on this matter vary from state to state.

Even if an acceptable definition of *dangerousness* were found, only part of the problem would be solved, since the accurate prediction of dangerousness is still required. Mental health professionals have not proven they have any consistent ability to predict dangerous or violent behavior, although they are better at it than untrained individuals (Monahan 1984, 1981; Monahan and Walker 1990). Conversely, neither can an absence of potential for violent behavior be clearly predicted. There is a strong tendency to overpredict dangerousness, toward self or toward others, since a professional who fails to protect a community or a specific person by *not* detecting the dangerousness of a person who eventually engages in violent behavior pays a heavy professional and social price, especially in light of high malpractice settlements. Given a choice between being safe and being criticized or held responsible for the repercussions of releasing a possibly dangerous person, most professionals choose the safe route—detention.

The Tarasoff Case

The difficulty that mental health professionals have in accurately predicting dangerousness and the legal issues involved were first highlighted in a 1976 California case generally referred to as the *Tarasoff* (1976) case. A psychologist at the University of California–Berkeley mental health clinic determined that one of his patients, Mr. Poddar, was dangerous and had probably meant it when he said he intended to kill a woman, Ms. Tarasoff, who he thought was avoiding his romantic approaches. (Indeed, she probably was avoiding him—and as it turned out, with very good reason.) The clinic called the campus police, told them about the situation, and requested that they pick Poddar up for further evaluation. The police went to Poddar's house, talked to him, decided there was no problem, and left. Poddar later did kill Tarasoff, and the university health service was sued for failure to take appropriate action to protect Tarasoff from Poddar. (Ironically, throughout the legal process, the campus police were the only group that was never cited as legally liable. Poddar later returned to his native India, married, and is reportedly living a contented middle-class existence.)

The California court held that the Tarasoff estate could sue the clinic on the basis that it had failed to take responsible action to protect her, such as warning Tarasoff about Poddar's intention to kill ker. The court first emphasized that the clinic had a "duty to warn" the intended victim of her danger. Upon appeal, the obligation that the court eventually prescribed was a "duty to protect" the intended victim. A major concern here is the implication in the *Tarasoff* decision and some subsequent decisions that therapists are liable if they "should have known" of the danger. This opens the door to a jury deciding that even though there is no actual threat, a therapist should be able to assess the danger. This would transform the extremely difficult task, of accurately predicting a person's dangerousness, into an absurdly impossible one.

The *Tarasoff* court seemed to be saying to mental health professionals something to the effect that, "You have always been delighted and desirous of the 'expert' role in such situations; we're simply saying you have to be liable for it." Mental health professionals responded by emphasizing the difficulty of making such predictions. Although this was a decision of the California Supreme Court and has no compelling legal effect in any other state, it has nonetheless been very influential. Other states have followed with various statutes of this sort. Some have held therapists liable only if a threat was made and carried out against a specific person. Other state courts have held therapists liable for general or vague threats. Some states have passed statutes designed to protect therapists from legal liability *if* they take certain specific steps, such as warning the victim and notifying the police.

Even though many courts are responding to this issue, a number of related issues remain unsettled. Is a therapist obligated to take these steps in cases of threats to property, rather than just to persons? Are therapists so obligated in cases of general as well as specific threats? Most people might agree that in certain property situations (such as a threat to destroy as many of the great art works in the world as possible), therapists are so obligated, but most would not feel it is worth voiding therapist-client confidentiality if a client merely threatens to break a neighbor's window in anger. The difficulty is where to set the limit. Another issue now being debated by therapists is whether they have a duty to warn prospective victims if their client has AIDS. Neither the courts or therapists have indicated any clear trend on what to do here.

The difficulty of predicting dangerousness should not be surprising given the relative rarity of events such as suicide and homicide and the fact that the rarer an event, the more difficult it is to predict (Monahan 1984). What results in actuality are many false positives; that is, people are labeled dangerous but do not engage in dangerous behavior. For example, if a clinician predicts that ten people will commit a dangerous act and six of them fulfill the prediction, then there is a 60 percent rate of true positives and a 40 percent rate of false positives. If civil commitment had been required based on this prediction, then for every six actually dangerous individuals remanded to a mental institution, four would also be so incarcerated who were not dangerous. It is indeed safer for clinicians to overpredict dangerousness, and in fact, most studies indicate that overprediction does occur, not at a rate of 40 percent but at a rate of 60 to 70 percent (Monahan 1984, 1981; Szasz 1986). In criminal law, it is usually said to be better for ten guilty persons to go free than for one innocent person to suffer. In civil commitment, then, the question is how many harmless people (false positives) is society willing to sacrifice to protect itself from one violent person?

Aggression Potential

Monahan (1984, 1981) has pointed out eight of the most critical demographic predictor variables for aggression. Aggression is most likely if the potential perpetrator (1) is young (this variable correlates strongly up until the 30-to-35 age range, after which the correlation is random); (2) is male; (3) comes from a lower socioeconomic class; (4) belongs to a disadvantaged minority; (5) is less educated; (6) has a lower intellectual level; (7) has an unstable school and/or vocational history; and (8) has a history of alcohol and/or drug abuse. Other demographic indicators that have been noted throughout the literature are a prior history of violent behaviors; a prior history of suicide attempts; a history of family violence; histrionic or antisocial personality traits; a pattern of cruelty to animals as a child or adolescent; a rejecting or depressed father; and recent stress, especially if associated with low levels of serotonin. Assaultiveness in a unit or ward by inpatient psychiatric patients is specifically correlated with hallucinatory behavior, emotional liability, and a high level of activity. There are psychological test data that can also aid the clinician in making predictions at a higher level of accuracy than that allowed by impressionistic data or chance. (See the section on violence in chapter 10.)

It is noteworthy that none of the studies that have caused such pessimism about predicting dangerousness examined the issue of emergency commitment. Most of them studied people who had been in mental hospitals for varying lengths of time and were subsequently released. But these same studies have been used in arguments against emergency commitment. Some experts take exception to this practice. Monahan (1984, 1981) has posited that it is probably far easier and surer to predict dangerousness in an emergency situation since the individual may be threatening violence and appear out of control; the threatened victims may be on hand; the intended weapon is likely to be immediately available; and a dangerous outburst may appear imminent. The person may also have been violent in the past—a good predictor of present or future violence. It would seem that predictions of violence under such circumstances are much more accurate.

Suicide

In some Western countries, legal sanctions against suicide persist as reflections of religious tradition. As late as 1961, suicide was still a crime in England, where the typically practical English response to a suicide attempt was to hang the individual if he or she survived. This punishment superseded the more flamboyant practice of driving a stake through the heart of the person who attempted suicide.

Facts and Fables about Suicide. Numerous false beliefs persist about suicide.

- *People commit suicide without warning.* Suicidal individuals give many clues; 80 percent have to some degree discussed with others their intent to commit suicide.
- *Once people become suicidal, they remain so.* Suicidal persons remain so for limited periods; hence the value of restraint.
- *Suicide occurs almost exclusively among affluent or very poor individuals.* Suicide tends to occur proportionately in all economic levels of society.
- *Virtually all suicidal individuals are mentally ill.* This is not so.
- *Suicide is inherited and runs in families.* There is no evidence for a direct genetic factor, though there may be for such predictive patterns as panic disorder and some forms of depression.
- *Suicide does not occur in primitive cultures.* Suicide occurs in almost all societies and cultures.
- *Writers and artists have the highest suicide rates because they are a bit crazy to begin with.* Physicians have the highest suicide rates; they have quick access to the most lethal means, and their work involves a high level of frustration.
- *Police officers have a high suicide rate.* Not so. Josephson and Reiser (1990) have produced data from a series of studies to show that the rate is no higher than the rate for the population in general.
- *Once a person starts to come out of a depression, the risk of suicide dissipates.* The risk of suicide is highest in the initial phase of an upswing from the depth of depression.
- *People who attempt suicide fully intend to die.* People who attempt suicide have a diversity of motives.

Incidence. About twenty-five thousand suicides are reported each year in the United States. In general, the typical *attempted* suicide is most often an unmarried white female with a history of stressful events who had an unstable childhood and who now has few social supports and lacks a close friend to confide in. The typical *completed* suicide is most often an unmarried, divorced, or widowed white male who is over forty-five, lives alone, has a history of significant physical or emotional disorder, and abuses alcohol. About three times as many women as men attempt suicide, but three times as many men actually kill themselves (Fremouw et al. 1990; Schneidman 1985).

Types of Suicide. Suicides are classified according to several types.

1. *Realistic.* Such conditions as the prospect of great pain preceding a sure death precipitate these suicides.
2. *Altruistic.* The person adheres to a group ethic that mandates or at least approves of suicidal behavior, like kamikaze pilots in World War II.
3. *Inadvertent.* The person intends to make a suicide *gesture* in order to influence or manipulate someone, but a misjudgment leads to an unexpected fatality.
4. *Spite.* The person genuinely intends to commit suicide with the idea that another person will suffer greatly from consequent guilt.
5. *Bizarre.* The person commits suicide as a result of a hallucination (such as voices ordering the suicide) or a delusion (such as a belief the suicide will change the world).
6. *Anomic.* An abrupt instability in economic or social conditions (such as sudden financial loss in the Great Depression) markedly changes a person's life situation. Unable to cope, the person commits suicide.
7. *Negative view of self.* Chronic depression and a sense of chronic failure or inadequacy combine to produce repeated suicide attempts, eventually leading to a fatality.

Genuine versus Manipulative Suicides. Experts have found the distinction between genuine and manipulative suicides a meaningful one (Schneidman 1985). *Genuine* suicidals truly want to die and are prevented from doing so only by miscalculation or fate. *Manipulative* suicidals do not really want to kill themselves; their acts are controlled attempts to manipulate others.

Prediction. Among adults, a number of primary behavioral clues appear predispose an individual to making a successful suicide attempt (Fremouw et al. 1990; Schneidman 1985).

- Previous suicide attempts. In this connection, if the first axiom of psychology is "Behavior predicts behavior," the second axiom is "Behavior without intervention predicts behavior."
- Statements of a wish to die, especially statements of a wish to commit suicide.
- Certain *consistent* life patterns of leaving crises rather than facing them, as in relationships ("You can't walk out on me—I'm leaving you") or in jobs ("You can't fire me because I quit").
- Suicide attempts by an important identity figure, such as a parent or a hero.
- Feelings of failure, especially when the person has a loved spouse who is competitive or self-absorbed.

- Early family instability and parental rejection of one's identity.
- A recent severe life stress; the presence of a chronic debilitating illness.

Several other factors can then increase the potential for suicide:

- A cognitive state of "constriction"—that is, an inability to perceive any options or ways out of a situation that is generating intense psychological suffering.
- Easy access to a lethal means. Drug overdose, for example, is the prevailing form of suicide among physicians.
- Absence of an accessible support system such as family and good friends.
- Life stresses that connote irrevocable loss (whether of status or of persons), such as the relatively recent death of a favored parent. This factor is particularly important if the person at risk is unable to mourn the loss overtly.
- High physiological responsiveness—that is, cyclical moods and a high need for stimulation-seeking in spite of suicidal thoughts.
- Evidence of panic attacks (see chapter 7), or a history of panic attacks or panic disorder.
- Serious sleep disruption and abuse of alcohol or drugs.
- Depression, particularly when combined with a sense of hopelessness, a loss of pleasure in activities, or a loss of a sense of continuity with the past or present. Depressions marked by low levels of 5-HIAA, as well as high levels of cortisol and a high ratio of adrenaline to noradrenaline, increase the probability of suicide attempts.

Prevention. Suicide-prevention techniques have been developed at both the individual and the societal level, but implementing them is not always easy. The following dialogue from the old television show *Mary Hartman, Mary Hartman* illustrates the difficulty most people have in responding effectively to a potential suicide's questions.

> *Heather (Mary's twelve-year-old daughter):* I have nothing to live for.
> *Mary:* Sure you do.
> *Heather:* Like what?
> *Mary:* Well . . . wait and see.

Several things can be done on a societal level to reduce the incidence of suicide. Educating the public about the myths and facts of suicide is an important first step. Second, there is evidence that suicide-prevention telephone hotlines and centers can slightly decrease the suicide rate. Third, control of access to commonly used methods (such as guns and drugs) can lower the incidence of suicide. A fourth step is the placing of some restrictions on media publicity about suicides. Phillips (1974, 1986) has documented the direct correlation between suicide rates and the amount of newspaper publicity give to suicides in a particular locality.

Several precautions can also be taken at the individual level.

- Attend seriously to people who voice a desire to kill themselves or "just go to sleep and forget it all." About two-thirds of people who actually do kill themselves have talked about it beforehand in some detail with family, friends, or others.

- Attend especially to depressed individuals who speak of losing hope.

- To the degree possible, keep lethal means (guns and large prescriptions of sedatives) away from suicidal individuals.

- Generate personal concern toward a suicidal person; a suicide attempt is most often a cry for help. Suicidal individuals need a temporary "champion" who can point them toward new resources and suggest new options, at least in a small way, that can diminish the sense of hopelessness.

- Try to get the person to engage in regular physical exercise, start a diary, follow a normal routine, do something in which he or she has already demonstrated competence, confide inner feelings to someone, or cry it out. Try to get the person to avoid self-medication and other people who are inclined toward depression.

- Make every effort to see that a suicidal person reaches professional help. Making an appointment is a good first step; getting the person to the appointment is the crucial step.

Notes

Addington v. Texas. 1979. (441 U.S. 418).

Barrett v. United States. 1977. (377 A.2d 62).

Caplan, L. 1984. *The Insanity Defense.* Boston: David R. Godine.

Clark, C. 1988. "Diminished Capacity in Michigan: Factors Associated with Forensic Evaluation Referrals." Midwinter Meeting of the American Psychology-Law Society, Miami Beach, Fla.

Colorado v. Connelly. 1986. (107 S.Ct. 115, 55 L.W. 4043).

Dusky v. U.S. 1960. (362 U.S. 402).

Ford v. Wainwright. 1986. (106 S.Ct. 2595).

Fremouw, W., M. Perczel, and T. Ellis. 1990. *Suicide Risk.* Elmsford, N.Y.: Pergamon.

Grisso, T. 1986. *Evaluating Competencies: Forensic Assessments and Instruments.* New York: Plenum.

Jackson v. Indiana. 1972. (406 U.S. 715).

Josephson, R., and M. Reiser. 1990. "Officer Suicide in the Los Angeles Police Department." *Journal of Police Science and Administration* 17: 227–29.

M'Naghton. 1843. (8 Eng. Rep. 718).

Monahan, J. 1981. *Predicting Violent Behavior.* Beverly Hills, Calif.: Sage.

Monahan, J. 1984. "The Prediction of Violent Behavior: Toward a Second Generation of Theory and Policy." *American Journal of Psychiatry* 141: 10–15.

Monahan, J., and L. Walker, eds. 1990. *Social Science in Law: Cases and Materials.* 2nd ed. Westbury, N.J.: Foundation Press.

New Jersey v. Stasio. 1979. (78 N.J. 467).

O'Connor v. Donaldson. 1975. (422 U.S. 563, 575).

Phillips, D. 1974. "The Influence of Suggestion on Suicide." *American Sociological Review* 39: 340–54.

Phillips, D. 1986. "The Effects of Mass Media Violence on Suicide and Homicide." *Newsletter of the American Academy of Psychiatry and Law* 11: 29–31.

Rogers, R. 1986. *Conducting Insanity Evaluations.* New York: Van Nostrand Reinhold.

Schneidman, E. 1985. *Definition of Suicide.* New York: John Wiley.

Shapiro, D. 1991. *Forensic Psychological Assessment.* Needham Heights, Mass.: Allyn and Bacon.

Smith, S., and R. Meyer. 1987. *Law, Behavior and Mental Health: Policy and Practice.* New York: New York University Press.

Szasz, T. 1987. *Insanity: the Idea and Its Consequences.* New York: John Wiley.

Tarasoff v. Regents of the University of California. 1976. (551 P.2d, 334).

United States v. Lions. 1984. 731 F.2d 243

United States v. Tonero. 1984. 735 F.2d 725

Wettstein, R., E. Mulvey, and R. Rogers. 1991. "A prospective Comparison of Four Insanity Defense Standards." *American Journal of Psychiatry.* 148: 21–33.

Wrightsman, L. 1991. *Psychology and the Legal System.* 2nd ed. Pacific Grove, Calif.: Brooks/Cole.

Zimmerman v. Burch. 1990. (110 S.Ct. 975).

13
Psychopharmacology in Criminal Justice

> Dr. John Romano, professor emeritus of psychiatry at the University of
> Rochester, has pointed out that everywhere except in this country the
> medical profession's emblem is the rod of *Asclepius,* a legendary Greek
> physician, which has one snake twining around it. But through some
> gaffe of careless observation and spurious scholarship, the American
> medical profession adopted the two-snake caduceus, which represents
> *Mercury,* patron of messengers, commerce—and gamblers.

Psychotropic medications are drugs that exert direct effects on the
central nervous system, thereby altering a person's mood, thoughts,
or behavior. They primarily act by increasing or decreasing the levels
of neurotransmitters in the brain. Neurotransmitters are naturally occurring
substances in the brain that regulate behavior, thought, and mood (Carlson
1991). Psychotropic medications are utilized most often to control pathological psychological behaviors, especially those types of behavior that occur
within the purview of the judicial and criminal justice systems. The introduction of antipsychotic and antidepressant drugs in the 1960s revolutionized
psychiatric treatment. The result has been decreased hospital stays for psychiatric patients, an increased emphasis on outpatient treatment, and an
overall increase in the level of functioning for individuals with psychiatric
disorders (Davis et al. 1989; Carlson 1991).

A familiarity with psychotropic medications is important for criminal
justice personnel, first and foremost, because their legal usage in American
society is very common. Secondly, law-enforcement officers frequently encounter psychiatric patients in the line of duty who are on such medications.
Third, because of their mood-altering properties, many psychotropic medications are also abused, especially by the "consumers" in the criminal justice
system, and they may have relatively high street values. The benzodiazepines, a class of antianxiety agents, for example, are among the most widely
prescribed drugs in the United States and are also commonly abused
(Gelenberg et al. 1991). So it is important for criminal justice personnel to
recognize the effects of these drugs on behavior.

Additionally, the behavioral manifestations and side-effects of these
agents may mimic the symptoms of many other conditions, such as alcohol

intoxication. These drugs are frequently used in suicide attempts, and criminal justice personnel may be the first line of response to such incidents. Finally, a working knowledge of these drugs will help criminal justice and judicial system personnel be more effective in their ongoing interactions with psychiatric patients as well as with mental health personnel.

Classification of Psychotropic Medications

The psychotropic medications are typically divided into five groups, based on their predominant behavioral effect. These groups are: (1) antipsychotic agents; (2) antidepressants; (3) antimanic drugs; (4) antianxiety agents; and (5) sedative-hypnotics. Many of these drugs have secondary actions, such as the control of violent and agitated behavior, and some are utilized as "truth serums."

Each group of drugs is useful in the treatment of a specific group of psychiatric disorders. The antipsychotic agents, for example, have their greatest application in the treatment of schizophrenia and other disorders that are accompanied by psychotic symptoms (such as psychotic depressions). Mood-altering agents, such as the antimanic and antidepressant medications, are useful in the treatment of severe depressions and bipolar (manic-depressive) illness. The antianxiety agents produce a generalized calming effect and are useful in any condition in which anxiety is a prominent symptom. The sedative-hypnotics tend to induce drowsiness and alter consciousness. They are used in the treatment of sleep disturbances such as insomnia. There are a large number of specific drugs within each of these groups. Each drug has both a trade name, assigned by the manufacturer, and a generic or chemical name.

Because of their potential to alter behavior, and because some of them are addicting, a number of the psychotropic agents are classified as controlled substances by the Drug Enforcement Administration (DEA). Drugs are classified as controlled according to their potential for abuse; the greater the potential, the more limitations are placed on their use. The antianxiety agents and the sedative-hypnotics are classified as controlled, but all the psychotropic medications require a written prescription in order to be dispensed. Table 13–1 lists examples of controlled substances and the DEA classification system.

Antipsychotic Drugs

The antipsychotic medications, a large class of drugs, are useful in the treatment of psychotic disorders (see chapter 6) such as schizophrenia. A number of other psychiatric disorders may be accompanied by psychotic

Table 13–1
DEA Classification of Controlled Substances, with Examples

DEA Class	Characteristics	Examples
I	• High abuse potential • No accepted medical use	LSD, heroin, marijuana
II	• High abuse potential, with severe physical and psychological dependence	Amphetamines, opium, morphine, codiene, barbiturates, cocaine
III	• High abuse potential, with low to moderate physical dependence and high psychological dependence	Compounds containing codiene, morphine (such as narotic analgesics)
IV	• Low abuse potential, with limited physical and psychological dependence	Benzodiazepines, certain barbiturates, other sedative-hypnotics
V	• Lowest abuse potential	Narcotic preparations containing nonnarcotic active ingredients (such as cough medicines with codiene)

features, including severe mood disorders such as psychotic depressions and mania. Transient psychoses may also be seen in certain of the personality disorders (see chapter 3).

Antipsychotic medications are usually effective in correcting the thought disturbances, delusional thinking, and hallucinations seen in psychotic disorders. A widely held theory asserts that psychoses are caused by an overabundance of the neurotransmitter dopamine in the brain. Dopamine plays an important regulatory role in thought and perception and in coordinating fine motor movements. When imbalances in dopamine occur in the brain, the characteristic symptoms of psychosis (thought disorder, delusions, and hallucinations) are likely to occur. The antipsychotic agents act by blocking dopamine receptors in the brain, thereby decreasing this imbalance (Davis et al. 1989).

Most of the antipsychotic medications also cause some degree of sedation. This effect is useful in decreasing the agitation that often accompanies a psychosis. The sedating properties of these drugs make them useful in the treatment of violent behavior. The phenothiazines (such as chlorpromazine and thioridazine), the largest group of antipsychotic drugs, tend to produce the most sedation.

All medications produce certain side-effects and adverse reactions. The antipsychotics are noteworthy because of the large number of side-effects that may occur with them. One of the most common side-effects is muscular stiffness and rigidity, referred to as dystonia, which is naturally distressing for individuals on these medications. The drugs may also cause a vague feeling of restlessness and the inability to sit still, known as *akathesia*. Some patients on high doses of these drugs for extended periods of time develop involuntary movements of the face, mouth, and tongue, a syndrome known as *tardive dyskinesia.* All of the neuromuscular side-effects fall under the general heading of *extrapyramidal symptoms,* a term that refers to the areas of the brain and central nervous system that control movement, or the extrapyramidal tracts. These symptoms are also referred to as *Parkinsonian side-effects* because they clinically resemble the symptoms of Parkinson's disease.

The antipsychotic drugs influence other neurotransmitters besides dopamine. One of these is acetylcholine, a muscarinic transmitter that regulates many bodily functions. The antipsychotics block the action of acetylcholine; this group of side-effects is therefore often referred to as *anticholinergic effects.* Specific symptoms include dry mouth, intolerance to heat, constipation, and blurred vision. In extreme cases an anticholinergic delirium may occur, characterized by confusion, disorientation, and agitation. These drugs may cause a temporary drop in blood pressure, especially when the person arises from a sitting or supine position. This phenomenon, called postural hypotension, may lead to dizziness. Other side-effects seen with the antipsychotic medications include photosensitivity to sunlight, liver damage, a depression of blood-cell production leading to anemia (agranulocytosis), and seizures. A potentially life-threatening side-effect is the neuroleptic malignant syndrome, which is characterized by high fever, convulsions, muscular rigidity, and rapid progression to coma and death (Lazarus 1989). The antipsychotics have a low potential for abuse, dependence, or addiction.

A large number of specific drugs in this group are available (see table 13–2). Despite their numbers, virtually all of them are thought to act by blocking dopamine receptors in the brain. Thus, the main features that differentiate the individual medications are dose ranges, degree of sedation, duration of action, and intensity of side-effects. All of these drugs are metabolized, or broken down, by the liver. As a result, they are used with caution in persons with preexisting liver disease. The two most commonly used antipsychotics are chlorpromazine (Thorazine) and haloperidol (Haldol). Long-acting (decanoate) preparations are available for haloperidol (Haldol) and fluphenazine (Prolixin). Both of these are given intramuscularly by injection and have a duration of action of from two to four weeks. The duration of action for the orally administered antipsychotics ranges from four to twelve hours, depending in part on how quickly the drug is metabolized.

The first therapeutic effect, which occurs thirty to sixty minutes after ingestion, is a generalized calming effect, often accompanied by some degree of sedation. A person on antipsychotics is also likely to appear rather stiff and clumsy, due to the extrapyramidal effects mentioned earlier. Although the person is actually alert while on these drugs, he may appear to be emotionless and possess a rather blank stare, also due to the extrapyramidal effects. The full antipsychotic action on the person's hallucinations and

Table 13–2
Antipsychotic Drugs

Name (Generic/Trade)	Average Therapeutic Dose Range
Chlorpromazine (Thorazine)	50–1500 mg/day
Thioridazine (Mellaril)	50–800 mg/day
Fluphenazine (Prolixin)	5–40 mg/day
Fluphenazine decanoate (Prolixin D)	25–100 mg IM[a] Q1–4 weeks
Perphenazine (Trilafon)	4–64 mg/day
Trifluoperazine (Stelazine)	5–40 mg/day
Haloperidol (Haldol)	5–100 mg/day
Haloperidol decanoate (Haldol D)	50–200 mg IM[a] Q2–4 weeks
Thiothixine (Navane)	5–60 mg/day
Loxapine (Loxitane)	20–250 mg/day
Molindone (Moban)	20–225 mg/day
Clozapine (Clozaril)	300–500 mg/day

[a]IM—Intramuscular administration

delusions may take from several days to several weeks to appear, depending on the severity and intensity of the symptoms. Some psychotic patients do not respond significantly to these medications, for reasons that are not completely clear.

One of the newer antipsychotics, clozapine, seems to be more effective in treatment-resistant patients (Green and Salzman 1990), and it has much less potential for extrapyramidal side-effects and tardive dyskinesia. Clozapine (Clozaril) blocks a number of receptors in the brain—dopamine, serotonin, adrenergic, and muscarinic—yet its specific mechanism of therapeutic action is unknown. Side-effects include a potentially fatal agranulocytosis in one to two percent of patients receiving the drug, as well as seizures, sedation, tachycardia, hypotension, hyperthermia, nausea, excessive salivation, and drooling.

Antidepressants

Depression, described in chapter 6, is one of the most frequently encountered psychiatric symptoms. When depression becomes the primary emotion a person experiences and is of relatively long duration, it is considered to be pathological. Most depressions occur in response to some trauma or loss that the individual can identify. In many cases this type of depression is self-limiting and does not require treatment. In cases that persist, however, psychological treatments are usually effective in alleviating the depression. Some people experience severe depressions that are seemingly unrelated to any external event. These depressions are generated by abnormalities in the neurotransmitters that regulate mood, and they respond best to medications.

The two major neurotransmitters known to consistently exert a major influence on mood are norepinephrine and serotonin (Davis and Glassman 1989). When the level of either of these neurotransmitters falls, a clinical depression may result. The antidepressant medications consist of two broad groups of drugs: The tricyclic antidepressants and the monoamine oxidase inhibitors (MAOI's). The main difference between these two groups are how they act on the neurotransmitters and their side-effect profiles. Although their mechanisms of action appear to be complicated, both groups ultimately act by facilitating the release of norepinephrine and serotonin from neuronal cells, thus correcting the depression. These drugs also act by blocking the reuptake of the neurotransmitter, thus increasing their overall concentration in the brain. The newer antidepressants, such as fluoxetine (Prozac), are neither tricyclics nor MAOI's. Prozac acts on the neurotransmitter serotonin by an unknown mechanism. Table 13–3 lists the antidepressant medications.

Most of the antidepressants require a period of ten days to two weeks before they begin to exert their therapeutic action. This is a problem when the client poses a risk of suicide, so close monitoring is required until the

Table 13–3
Antidepressant Drugs

Name (Generic/Trade)	Average Therapeutic Dose Range
Tricyclic antidepressants	
Amitriptyline (Elavil)	75–300 mg/day
Imipramine (Tofranil)	75–300 mg/day
Desipramine (Norpramin)	75–300 mg/day
Nortriptyline (Pamelor)	30–100 mg/day
Protriptyline (Vivactil)	15–40 mg/day
Doxepine (Sinequan)	50–300 mg/day
Maprotiline (Ludiomil)	75–150 mg/day
Amoxapine (Asendin)	500–300 mg/day
MAO Inhibitors	
Tranylcypromine (Parnate)	20–60 mg/day
Phenelzine (Nardil)	60–90 mg/day
Other antidepressants	
Fluoxetine (Prozac)	20 mg/day
Bupropion (Wellbutrin)	200–450 mg/day
Trazodone (Desyrel)	100–400 mg/day

medications take effect. During this lag period, blood levels of the drug are rising into a therapeutic range. These levels can be measured and the dosage adjusted accordingly to obtain an optimal clinical response (Davis and Glassman 1989). Monitoring of blood levels also decreases the likelihood of toxic reactions. Like the antipsychotics, these medications are metabolized by the liver.

The MAOI's are used less and less often because of their side-effects. The most commonly used tricyclics are amitriptyline (Elavil), imipramine (Tofranil), and desipramine (Norpramin). The newer antidepressant fluoxetine (Prozac) is rapidly becoming one of the most frequently prescribed drugs in the United States. Ironically, Prozac has been blamed by some for generating homicidal and/or suicidal tendencies, and some former users of Prozac have formed the Prozac Survivors Support Group. The drug's defenders say that since Prozac is used by approximately 1.5 million people worldwide and is prescribed for emotional upset, a substantial number of reports of suicidal and homicidal ideas would not be surprising.

The initial effect experienced after taking an antidepressant is sedation. The severity of this effect varies with the drug. Amitriptyline, for example, is very sedating, whereas desipramine has much less sedation. Some people also experience feelings of dizziness or lightheadedness. This occurs because norepinephrine exerts an effect not only on mood but on other organ systems such as the cardiovascular system. Most patients also experience a calming effect, related to either the sedative effect of the drug or to the direct action of serotonin. Depending on the degree of sedation and calming, the person may appear either drowsy or disinterested; it is unlikely, however, that the person appears to be intoxicated. Once the antidepressant action of the drug takes effect, the person will probably not notice any effect from the medication—their mood will simply appear to be normal. In some persons, however, the mood will become somewhat agitated, resulting from too much stimulation of the norepinephrine system. In fact, persons with a bipolar disorder who take antidepressants may cycle into a manic episode (see chapter 6).

The antidepressants produce a number of side-effects, many of which are potentially dangerous. Nearly all of the drugs in this class cause some degree of drowsiness, and like the antipsychotics, they also cause anticholinergic side-effects. Other side-effects include feelings of restlessness and agitation, sleep disturbances, nightmares, seizures, and exacerbation of psychosis in susceptible persons. The tricyclic antidepressants may cause cardiac arrhythmias or slow the heart rate. This effect presents a significant risk for persons who overdose on these medications as part of a suicide attempt. The MAO inhibitors may cause an interaction with certain foods and alcohol to produce a sudden rise in blood pressure (hypertensive crisis). Because of this effect, certain dietary restrictions apply for MAOI use. There is a low potential for abuse or dependence with antidepressants.

Antimanic Drugs

Manic episodes are characterized by a euphoric mood, grandiosity, accelerated thoughts, rapid speech, physical hyperactivity, and at times agitation (see chapter 6). In extreme cases, psychotic features such as hallucinations or delusions may be present. These manic episodes often cycle with recurrent depressions, forming what is referred to as a bipolar disorder (previously known as manic-depressive illness).

Lithium is the drug of first choice in the treatment of the manic phase of a bipolar disorder. Certain schizophrenic individuals may also respond favorably to lithium used in combination with an antipsychotic medication. Lithium is believed to act by stabilizing the membranes of neuronal cells in the central nervous system, resulting in a decrease in the amount of norepinephrine that is released from the cells. There is also a probable increase in the reuptake of norepinephrine by the cells, decreasing the overall concentration of the neurotransmitter. Lithium is metabolized and excreted by the kidney.

It is important that the concentration of lithium in the blood be kept in a therapeutic range. The dosage begins with divided doses of 300 mg two to three times per day, and is increased until the blood levels reach a range of 0.5 to 1.5 mEq per liter. Within seven to ten days, the manic patient should be observed to become calmer and show a more normal mood.

The monitoring of lithium blood levels is critical to preventing toxicity. Lithium toxicity is characterized by nausea and vomiting, muscle cramps, diarrhea, excessive thirst, and increased urination at blood levels between 1.5 and 2.0 mEq per liter. At levels above 2.0 mEq per liter, the individual experiences confusion, lethargy, tremor of the extremities, muscle spasms, ataxia (unsteady gait), slurred speech, convulsions, and ultimately coma. When maintained at therapeutic blood levels, however, lithium is remarkably free of day-to-day side-effects. It is unlikely to cause sedation and has no potential for abuse or dependence. The most common side-effects on therapeutic doses are fine tremor of the hand and skin rash. Long-term use of lithium may cause some kidney damage and can exacerbate thyroid or heart disease (Jefferson et al. 1987).

The evolution of lithium as an effective treatment is a good example of the driving force of the profit motive in pharmacological research. Lithium is a chemical element that was first isolated in 1817 by John Arfwedson, a young Swedish chemistry student. He named it lithium because he had found it in stone (*lithos,* in Greek). In the 1940s, John Cade, an Australian psychiatrist, discovered the positive effect of lithium on mania by chance while he was studying whether an excess of uric acid might be the cause of manic-depressive episodes. Cade injected humans with urea (a compound containing urea) from the urine of guinea pigs (it is unclear who were the actual "guinea pigs" here). Expecting to learn that uric acid increased the toxicity of urea, he added the most soluble salt of uric acid, lithium urate, and was surprised to find instead that the urea was *less* toxic as a result. Further experiments isolating lithium eventually indicated its curative properties.

A long time passed between the initial discovery of lithium and its recent widespread marketing and use. There had been surprisingly little research on lithium, while more exotic, less widely available compounds had received much attention. The primary explanation for this is that lithium is a naturally occurring element, so it cannot be patented. Drug companies are much more interested in developing synthetic compounds that they can patent, so that they can control the market and gain substantial profits.

Antianxiety Medications

Anxiety is one of the most frequent complaints heard from persons requiring psychiatric consultation (see chapter 7). The original antianxiety medications were the barbiturates, which had high potential for dependence and addiction. Since the mid-1960s, however, a large number of drugs belonging to the benzodiazepine family have been introduced. These drugs are more effective than the barbiturates, are safer, have less potential for addiction, and generally produce less sedation. As a result, the benzodiazepines have become some of the most frequently prescribed medications in the world. In addition to their antianxiety effects, they are also useful as sedative-hypnotics. The original benzodiazepines introduced were chlordiazepoxide (Librium) and diazepam (Valium).

More recent benzodiazepines, such as alprazolam (Xanex), differ primarily in their half-life. The term *half-life* refers here to the length of time it takes for one-half of a drug dose to be metabolized. Thus half-life is a measure of how long a drug remains active in the body, and it generally reflects the duration of the drug's effects. Most of the newer benzodiazepines have relatively short half-lives, whereas diazepam and chlordiazepoxide have very long half-lives. It is generally considered that drugs with shorter half-lives have less potential for addiction. The currently used antianxiety agents are listed in table 13–4.

The benzodiazepines, which are metabolized by the liver, primarily exert their antianxiety activity by facilitating the action of gamma-aminobutyric acid (GABA), and the neurotransmitter responsible for modulating anxiety (Gorman and Davis 1989). The benzodiazepines bind to receptors in the brain and stimulate the release of GABA, which decreases anxiety. GABA, in turn, inhibits the firing of certain excitatory neurons that are responsible for many of the physiological manifestations of anxiety.

In addition to their clinical action on anxiety and their sedative effects, the benzodiazepines also exert an effect that is especially important to criminal justice personnel; they are cross-tolerant with alcohol and other drugs,

Table 13–4
Antianxiety Drugs

Name (Generic/Trade)	Average Therapeutic Dose Range
Benzodiazepines	
Diazepam (Valium)	2–40 mg/day
Chlordiazepoxide (Librium)	15–100 mg/day
Chlorazepate (Tranxene)	15–60 mg/day
Prazepam (Centrax)	20–60 mg/day
Halazepam (Paxipam)	60–120 mg/day
Lorazepam (Ativan)	2–6 mg/day
Alprazolam (Xanex)	0.5–6.0 mg/day
Oxazepam (Serax)	30–120 mg/day
Non-benzodiazepine Buspirone (Buspar)	5–20 mg/day

such as the barbiturates. In other words, they may potentiate the effects of alcohol or other sedative drugs. The clinical benefit that is derived from this finding is that the benzodiazepines can be used to safely detoxify and withdraw individuals who are addicted to either alcohol or the barbiturates. Of course, one has to be careful that a secondary addiction to the benzodiazepine does not occur. Because of this cross-tolerance, a person who drinks while taking benzodiazepines will appear more intoxicated than a person using either substance alone.

Accompanying features that are sometimes seen with the benzodiazepines include slurred speech, ataxia (unsteady gait), impaired coordination, slowed reflexes, and impaired judgment. So persons taking benzodiazepines should exercise considerable caution when driving or operating machinery. These drugs have a relatively rapid onset of action, usually within thirty minutes. Duration of action ranges from four to six hours for the short-acting preparations (such as lorazepam) to more than twenty hours for the longer-acting drugs (such as diazepam).

The primary side-effect of the benzodiazepines is excessive sedation, and higher doses produce greater sedation. By themselves, however, the benzodiazepines are remarkably safe drugs. While overdoses of either the antipsychotics or the antidepressants are potentially life-threatening, this is not usually the case with the benzodiazepines alone. But as noted, they can interact with alcohol or other drugs such as the barbiturates to depress respiration when taken at high doses. Tolerance—the need for progressively higher doses to achieve the same therapeutic effects—and addiction are also potential risks. Hence, these drugs are generally prescribed in the lowest effective dose for only brief periods of time. Abrupt cessation of these drugs in an addicted person may cause seizures, so it is best to gradually reduce the dose over a period of several weeks before totally discontinuing these medications (Gelenberg et al. 1991).

While the benzodiazepines and related compounds are used primarily in the treatment of anxiety disorders, other treatments such as biofeedback, relaxation training, and other forms of psychotherapy are also effective. Since these latter treatments are also less intrusive and do not pose the problem of side-effects, they should be employed first.

Sedative-Hypnotic Medications

Sleep disturbances are common complaints, not only among medical, psychiatric, and correctional clients but also among the general public. Most sleep problems may also be related to other disease processes, such as a medical condition or depression, and other individuals have chronic problems with sleep for various reasons. This has led to the development of a group of medications, the sedative-hypnotic drugs, that act on serotonin and GABA and whose primary action is the induction of sleep (Gorman and Davis 1989). Unlike other drugs who sedating properties result from side-effects (such as the antidepressants and antipsychotics), the sedative-hypnotics act primarily to induce sleep.

All of the commonly used commercially available sedative-hypnotic agents are also antianxiety drugs whose sedating properties are stronger than their antianxiety properties. Thus, any of the antianxiety agents can theoretically be used to promote sleep. Those drugs marketed solely as sedative-hypnotics are the ones whose antianxiety effects are relatively weak. As a result, most of the sedative-hypnotics currently available are either benzodiazepines or barbiturates, and the side-effects are similar. As with the other members of these groups, there is a definite potential for abuse and dependence. These drugs tend to lose their effectiveness when taken for extended periods of time in the process known as *tolerance* or *habituation*. The result is that higher doses are required over time to exert the same therapeutic effect, a consequence that facilitates addiction and dependence. Table 13–5 lists the sedative-hypnotic drugs currently in clinical use.

There are several other drugs that have (1) a secondary sedative effect; (2) a low addiction and abuse potential; (3) a low ratio of side-effects; and most important to criminal justice groups like corrections personnel, (4) a low rate of a marketability within inmate populations. One good example is the antihistamines, such as the over-the-counter medication Benadryl (diphenhydramine). Another group of drugs that are sometimes referred to as the ataraxics, such as Vistaril (hydroxyzine pamoate) and Atarax (hydroxyzine hydrochloride), which are primarily intended to reduce anxiety, especially

Table 13–5
Sedative-Hypnotic Drugs

Name (Generic/Trade)	Average Therapeutic Dose Range
Benzodiazepines	
Flurazepam (Dalmane)	15–30 mg/day
Temazepam (Restoril)	15–30 mg/day
Triazolam (Halcion)	0.25–0.5 mg/day
Estazolam (ProSom)	1–2 mg/day
Barbiturates	
Secobarbital (Seconal)	100–200 mg/day
Other Sedative-Hypnotics	
Chloral hydrate (Noctec)	500–1000 mg/day

where accompanied by physical conditions like dermatological and/or gastro-intestinal distress.

It is good policy to try to cure a sleep problem in an inmate group with something like Benadryl first. If that is unsuccessful, then move to an ataraxic, especially if agitation from the stress of living in the inmate system is a factor. If these are still unsuccessful, and manipulation or an active addictive personality component is ruled out, one can move to the traditional sedatives.

Anti-Parkinson's Medications

Parkinson's effects (discussed earlier in this chapter) occur most frequently in young adult males (a common criminal justice system "consumer") who are on antipsychotic medications and/or in persons who recently started on such medications. These effects are quite bothersome to patients and are frequently responsible for poor medication compliance. They occurs be-cause of a blocking of dopamine in the brain. Thus, the same action that leads to a diminishing of psychotic symptoms also leads to neuromuscular disturbances. Fortunately, several medications, anti-Parkinson's agents, lessen the degree of these extrapyramidal symptoms. The two most commonly used are trihexyphenidl (Artane) and benztropine (Cogentin) (Davis et al. 1989). Both are administered in a usual dose of 2 mg, up to three times a day. Other drugs that may be used to control these symptoms are diphenhydramine (Benadryl) or diazepam (Valium), both of which are used intravenously in acute situations.

Such drugs are frequently used in combination with the antipsychotic medications. Both Artane and Cogentin have strong anticholinergic effects, so their dosage should be kept to a minimum. Although neither Cogentin or Artane causes classic addiction, they are frequently abused because persons taking them often experience a temporary "high" immediately after ingesting the drug.

Medications for the Control of Violent and Aggressive Behavior

Criminal justice personnel commonly deal with violent and aggressive behavior in the line of duty. Violence and aggression are generally caused by a complex interaction of biological, psychological, and environmental factors (Eichelman 1988). Managing violent behavior with medication depends on an appreciation of the biological factors that underlie violence. Like other symptoms, the biological explanation of violence rests with the neurotransmitters. In general, violence is correlated with an interaction of three factors in the brain: (1) an overabundance of certain neurotransmitters (like dopamine and norepinephrine); (2) a relative deficiency of other neurotransmitters (like serotonin and GABA); and (3) excess electrical activity in the brain leading to seizures (Eichelman 1988). Drugs that control violent behavior act by correcting the neurotransmitter imbalance or by decreasing the electrical activity in the brain. Additionally, androgen levels may contribute to violence propensities and in some cases may be controlled pharmacologically (see chapter 10). But such management is often complicated by the person's use of alcohol or other drugs, which clearly facilitates violence for most individuals.

Violence in psychiatric patients is actually relatively rare. Most patients with violent histories also have histories of drug or alcohol abuse. These substances promote violence by interfering with perception and judgment or by causing disinhibition of underlying aggressive tendencies (see chapter 4). When violence is associated with a psychiatric condition, it is generally related to a psychotic episode, a personality disorder, or an organic mental disorder.

Table 13–6 lists the medications that are useful in controlling violent and aggressive behavior (Eichelman 1988). These drugs are members of several of the groups already described. When violent behavior is associated with a psychotic disorder such as schizophrenia, the antipsychotic medications are clearly indicated. Violent tendencies in nonpsychotic persons may also be controlled by these medications because of their dopamine-blocking action. Antidepressants that increase the action of serotonin, such as trazodone (Desyrel), may also be useful, since serotonin exerts a calming influence on behavior. Lithium, through its action to decrease norepinephrine activity, may be useful in controlling aggression. Norepinephrine-blocking agents such as propranolol (Inderal) have also been shown to be

Table 13–6
Medications Used to Control Violent Behavior

Name (Generic/Trade)	Average Therapeutic Dose Range
Benzodiazepines	
Lorazepam (Ativan)	1–2 mg PO[a] or IM[b]Q2–4hr. PRN
Oxazepam (Serax)	15–120 mg/day
Mood-altering drugs	
Lithium carbonate	300 mg in divided doses to attain a therapeutic blood level
Trazodone (Desyrel)	100–400 mg/day
Adrenergic blocking agents	
Propranolol (Inderal)	200–600 mg/day
Anticonvulsants	
Carbamazepine (Tegretol)	200 mg in divided doses to attain a therapeutic blood level
Antipsychotics	
Haloperidol (Haldol)	2–5 mg PO[a] or IM[b] Q2–4hr. PRN
Chlorpromazine (Thorazine)	50–100 mg PO[a] or IM[b] Q2–4hr. PRN

[a]PO—Oral administration
[b]IM—Intramuscular administration

effective. Those drugs that increase levels of norepinephrine, however, may actually facilitate violent or aggressive behavior.

Benzodiazepines, by increasing levels of GABA in the brain, also exert a calming effect similar to that of serotonin. These drugs must be used cautiously, however, not only because of their potential for abuse but also because they cause a paradoxical increase in violence in some individuals.

Finally, carbamazepine (Tegretol), an anticonvulsant medication, is useful when violence occurs in association with seizure activity. Carbamazepine is an interesting drug because it seems to exert other effects independent of its anticonvulsant activity (Gardner and Cowdry 1988), that is, it decreases impulsivity, which is often associated with aggressive behavior. Some psychotic or manic patients who fail to respond to other treatments have been found to improve on carbamazepine.

Truth Serums

Certain psychotropic drugs are used to induce a trancelike state, during which the person remains conscious and is able to talk. This state closely resembles the altered level of consciousness achieved during hypnosis. During this period, it is possible to interview the patient and obtain important diagnostic information. Previously repressed or forgotten memories may also be recalled. The drugs that promote such a state have often been referred to as truth serums (see chapter 12).

But there are a number of myths and misconceptions about the truth serums. The greatest misconception is the notion that these drugs make people reveal information that they would otherwise withhold. It is probably not possible to force someone to disclose information against their will through the use of medication (or hypnosis). It is certainly not possible to be sure that the information from such an interview is entirely factual. What these drugs do is simply create a state of consciousness that facilitates the disclosure of information.

Currently, two drugs are most commonly used for this type of interview, often referred to as narcotherapy or narcoanalysis. One of these is the short-acting barbiturate sodium amobarbitol (Amytal). The other is the short-acting benzodiazepine, lorazepam (Ativan). The primary use of these agents in psychiatry is for diagnostic purposes, although lorazepam is also a frequently prescribed antianxiety agent. Interviews conducted using these drugs are useful for clarifying the diagnosis of catatonic schizophrenia, in which patients are often mute, and certain disorders characterized by dissociative symptoms (see chapter 7) (Perry and Jacobs 1982).

For this type of interview, sodium amytal or lorazepam is administered intravenously. Small doses are injected at one-to-two-minute intervals until the patient becomes drowsy but not completely asleep. Blood pressure and respiration must be monitored throughout the interview. Injection of the medication too rapidly will produce sleep, and using doses that are too high may cause respiratory depression or arrest. As the person becomes drowsy, a series of generalized questions are asked, proceeding to more specific questions. If the person appears to resist questioning, additional medication is gradually infused until the person becomes more disclosing. Because the duration of action of these drugs is brief, additional medication must be infused periodically throughout the interview. At the close of the interview, the medication is discontinued and the patient is allowed to rest until fully alert and able to walk without difficulty. The patient will be aware of information he or she has disclosed following the interview. How long this awareness remains depends on the underlying condition from which the patient suffers. Although many neurotic individuals remain aware of the contents of the interview, catatonic patients are likely to lapse back into a psychotic state. As with all other medical procedures, this type of interview should only be conducted with the informed consent of the patient.

Legal Issues in the Use of Psychotropic Medications (and Treatment in General)

Because the psychotropic medications exert powerful effects on behavior, mood, and thought, it is not surprising that a number of legal issues are associated with their use (Smith, 1991). Such issues include informed consent, malpractice, the right to refuse treatment, the right to treatment, and the role of medications in criminal proceedings.

The basic principle underlying *informed consent* is that the patient has a right to determine what should be done to his body and cannot be forced to accept treatment that is not wanted. It was first clearly outlined in the 1914 decision of *Schloendorff v. Society of New York Hospital* (cited in Simon 1987). Informed consent required that the patient be apprised of the potential benefits and major risks of any proposed treatments, as well as of all alternative treatments available. In order to give consent for treatment, the patient must be competent, possess adequate information, and make the decision in favor of treatment voluntarily. With respect to psychotropic medications, for example, the patient must be informed about all potential major side-effects and their relative risks, any drug interactions, and any special precautions that should be taken. Common examples of risks that need to be explained thoroughly are tardive dyskinesia and the neuroleptic malignant syndrome associated with the antipsychotic drugs. Failure to obtain informed consent prior to treatment places a therapist at risk for civil and possibly criminal liability.

One of the major legal issues in mental health treatment is *malpractice*, the negligent performance of a medical procedure (Smith, 1991). In order for malpractice to be proven, the following elements must be established: (1) the therapist owed a legal duty to the patient; (2) the therapist breached that duty in the care rendered to the patient; (3) the patient suffered injury or damages, either physical or emotional; and (4) the damages resulted from the therapist's negligence (Wettstein 1989). If a patient suffers harm because of inadequate monitoring of medication, for example, the clinician may be held legally accountable. If a third party suffers harm as a result of a patient's actions while under the influence of a psychotropic medication, the clinician may also be held accountable, as affirmed in the 1983 Texas decision *Gooden v. Tips*. For example, drug-induced reactions are responsible for about 20 percent of malpractice claims against psychiatrists (Wettstein 1989). The major issues related to psychotropic medications include lack of informed consent, excessive dosage, lack of proper indications for medication, and tardive dyskinesia. A number of legal decisions have been rendered wherein plaintiffs were awarded damages for tardive dyskinesia and neuroleptic malignant syndrome. Suicide by overdosage of medication may also be grounds for a malpractice or wrongful-death suit, based on the argument that the therapist should have known of the potential for self-harm and taken proper steps to safeguard the patient.

Related to the concept of informed consent is *the right to refuse treatment,* a doctrine first spelled out in the 1983 decision *Rogers v. Commissioner of Mental Health*. This concept basically says that a competent adult has the right to refuse treatment if the perceived risks or consequences are viewed as intolerable (Smith and Meyer 1987). Even though the decision may be ill-advised or have negative consequences for the person, the competent patient retains the right of refusal. The question of competence, particularly in the psychotic patient, becomes very important in this matter. It is interesting to note that almost all of these cases involving the right to refuse treatment deal with the antipsychotic medications. In *Rennie v. Klein* (1981) it was determined that even if a patient is involuntarily committed, he may not be forced to take medication against his will, a decision based on the concept of least-intrusive treatment. Thus, involuntary commitment does not equate with incompetence. Traditionally, the principle has been that only in emergency cases, where a clear threat exists if medication is not administered, can psychotropic medications be forced.

In *Washington v. Harper* (1990), the U.S. Supreme Court ruled that inmates in correctional facilities may be forced to take medication against their will. This signaled an apparent change in the concept of right to refuse treatment. The Supreme Court held in this case that the decision to medicate Harper fulfilled a three-part test that had evolved from a series of 1960s cases. First, there needs to be a "valid, rational connection between the prison regulation and the legitimate governmental interest put forward to justify it." Second, the reviewing court must consider "the impact accommodation the asserted constitutional right will have on guards and other inmates, and on the allocation of prison resources generally." Third, "the absence of ready alternatives is evidence of the reasonableness of a prison regulation." More specifically, the Court held that

- the hearing to review for medication need not be held before a judicial or administrative hearing officer. The committee in this case was composed of a psychiatrist, psychologist, and an administrator of the unit in which Harper was incarcerated.
- the regulations in place in the Washington review hearing provided twenty-four hours' notice of the hearing, the tentative diagnosis, the basis for diagnosis, and the reasons for the medication. The inmate was not medicated at the time of the hearing and could attend the hearing, present evidence and witnesses, cross-examine witnesses, and obtain the assistance of a lay adviser. The Court also indicated it was not required that Harper be allowed a lawyer, and that the hearing need not follow judicial rules of evidence.

Just as patients have a right to refuse treatment in some situations, they also (in varying degrees, depending upon the situation) have a basic *right to treatment*. For example, the 1966 *Rouse v. Cameron* decision determined that involuntary commitment without treatment is unconstitutional. The Supreme Court, in *O'Connor v. Donaldson* (1975), ruled that harmless patients cannot be held against their will without treatment. In other words, mental illness alone is not sufficient reason for involuntary commitment; the patient must also be shown to present a threat to self or others. Finally, psychiatrists have been found liable for failing to use psychotropic medications when their use would speed up cure or recovery from a condition—as discussed by Smith (1991).

Medications may also be implicated in cases where a defendant has been found not competent to stand trial. In such cases a mental health professional is frequently asked to render an opinion as to whether the defendant is likely to regain competency in the foreseeable future. Very often, such as in a psychosis, a period of treatment with psychotropic medications may restore competency.

Notes

Carlson, N. 1991. *Physiology of Behavior.* 4th ed. Needham Heights, Mass.: Allyn and Bacon.

Davis, J., J. Barter, and J. Kane. 1989. "Antipsychotic Drugs." In H. Kaplan and B. Sadock, eds. *Comprehensive Textbook of Psychiatry.* 5th ed. Baltimore: Williams and Wilkins.

Davis, J., and A. Glassman. 1989. "Antidepressant Drugs." In H. Kaplan and B. Sadock, eds. *Comprehensive Textbook of Psychiatry.* 5th ed. Baltimore: Williams and Wilkins.

Eichelman, B. 1988. "Toward a Rational Pharmacotherapy for Aggressive and Violent Behavior." *Hospital and Community Psychiatry* 39: 31–39.

Gardner, D., and R. Cowdry. 1988. "Anticonvulsants and Personality Disorders." In S. McElroy and H. Pope, eds. *Use of Anticonvulsants in Psychiatry.* Clifton, N.J.: Oxford Health Care Press.

Gelenberg, A., E. Bassuk, and S. Schoonover. 1991. *The Practitioner's Guide to Psychoactive Drugs.* 3rd ed. New York: Plenum.

Gooden v. Tips. 1983. 651 S.W. 2d. 364 (Tex. App.).

Gorman, J., and J. Davis. 1989. "Antianxiety Drugs." In H. Kaplan and B. Sadock, eds. *Comprehensive Textbook of Psychiatry.* 5th ed. Baltimore: Williams and Wilkins.

Green, A., and C. Salzman. 1990. "Clozapine: Benefits and Risks." *Hospital and Community Psychiatry* 41: 379–80.

Jefferson, J., J. Greist, D. Ackerman, and J. Carroll. 1987. *Lithium Encyclopedia for Clinical Practice.* 2nd ed. Washington, D.C.: American Psychiatric Association Press.

Lazarus, A. 1989. "Neuroleptic Malignant Syndrome." *Hospital and Community Psychiatry* 40: 1229–30.

O'Connor v. Donaldson. 1975. 422 U.S. 563, 575.

Perry, J., and D. Jacobs. 1982. "Overview: Clinical Applications of the Amytal Interview in Psychiatric Emergency Settings." *American Journal of Psychiatry* 139: 552–59.

Rennie v. Klein. 1981. (462 F. Supp. 1131 [D.N.J. 1978], later proceeding 476 F. Supp. 1294 [D.N.J. 1979], modified, 653 F.20 836 [3d Cir. 1981], vacated, 458 U.S. 1119 [1982], on remand, 720 F.2d 266 [3d Cir. 1983]).

Rogers v. Commissioner of Mental Health. 1986. 638 F. Supp. 934 (D. Mass).

Rouse v. Cameron. 1966. 373 F. 2nd 451 (D.C. Cir.)

Simon, R. 1987. *Clinical Psychiatry and the Law.* Washington, D.C.: American Psychiatric Association Press.

Smith, S. 1991. "Mental Health Malpractice in the 1990s." *Houston Law Review* 28: 209–283.

Smith, S., and R. Meyer. 1987. *Law, Behavior, and Mental Health.* New York: New York University Press.

Stone, A. 1990. "Law, Science, and Psychiatric Malpractice: A Response to Klerman's Indictment of Psychoanalytic Psychiatry." *American Journal of Psychiatry* 147: 419–27.

Washington v. Harper. 1990. 494 U.S. 210.

Wettstein, R. 1989. "Psychiatric Malpractice." In A. Tasman, R. Hales, and A. Frances, eds. *Review of Psychiatry.* vol. 8. Washington, D.C.: American Psychiatric Press.

14
Criminal Justice Personnel Issues

I don't want to achieve immortality through my work. I want to achieve immortality through not dying.
— Woody Allen

T his chapter covers a number of issues that affect people who work day-to-day in the criminal justice system. The first set of issues includes the selection of personnel in the system, enhancing one's performance when one is required to function in the judicial arena, and dealing with informants. Ways to nullify some of the negative effects of working in this arena, such as time management, relaxation techniques, and various other physical and psychological techniques are examined.

Personnel Selection

There has been a trend for increasing thoroughness and sophistication in the personnel-selection process in the criminal justice system. This has been especially the case in the selection of law-enforcement officers. It is generally agreed that four broad procedures make for a good selection process:

1. interviews, both by supervisors of the typical work situation and by psychological specialists;
2. life history and physical data, including thorough checks of criminal, mental health, drug, and employment histories
3. situational tests, such as measures of role-played tasks; and
4. psychological testing, including assessment of personality, intelligence, and attitudes.

In general, interview and life history data have both been found to be effective in this selection process. But sometimes people are selected on "face valid" criteria (criteria that most people assume would be valid in one direction), only to have research call these into question. For example, in one of the earliest but still most thorough examinations of which life-history variables were important, Ruth Levy (1967) found that such life-history variables as more than one marriage, more vehicle code violations, and evidence of an impulsive lifestyle are related to nonretention. This was not unreasonable, but she also found that higher intelligence, more years of education, and younger age at the time of application were similarly predictive.

In a related fashion, it has been found that higher scores on intelligence tests predict well to police academy performance and also promotion over the long run. But higher intelligence does not predict performance out in the field, except that at least a low-average intellectual ability was required to function adequately.

Situational tests approximate the conditions a candidate would encounter on the job and test the candidate's responses. Again, these have "face validity" and would seem to fulfill the spirit of those court decisions that push for "relevant" testing situations.

The first systematic application of situational tests to police-officer screening involved a police force in Albuquerque, New Mexico (Dillman 1963). The candidate had to role-play two situations that were considered typical of police work in that city; first dealing with a resistant hit-and-run suspect, then interviewing a man who was speeding to get his pregnant wife to the hospital. Comparison with later functioning in the field showed that the first situation had some positive predictive value, while the second one did not. Thought "face valid," and promising in Dillman's research, subsequent research has failed to find more than modest validity in situational testing.

Various personality tests have also been used in such screenings. The MMPI, or now the MMPI-2 (see chapters 1 and 11), is the most frequently used test, and it has the most evidence supporting its usefulness (Graham 1990). But it should not be used as the sole measure. One should never depend upon a computer-scored MMPI-2 without a parallel assessment by a psychologist who has had significant experience with the MMPI and who has personally interviewed the candidate.

Though the MMPI has some built-in measures against faking, or response set, the issue of deception in these evaluations has received relatively little attention until recent years. In some situations, a standard polygraph was administered. But as noted in chapter 11, the polygraph has a very questionable level of effectiveness. Gradually, more measures along the lines of those discussed in chapter 14 are being included in these evaluations, a development that promises to increase effectiveness.

Until the late 1960s evaluators could do pretty much as they pleased in these assessments. Then a series of cases, especially *Larry P. v. Riles* (1972, 1979) and *Griggs v. Duke Power Co.* (1971), changed that atmosphere. The ultimate holding in *Riles* was that tests used for classification had to have clear utility and validity for use with minorities. In *Griggs*, under what is referred to as the "disparate impact" model, the U.S. Supreme Court held that the employer has the burden of clearly showing that any given application requirement (including psychological tests) has a valid relationship to the employment position in question. The direction generated by these cases was later changed by the Supreme Court in the cases of *Watson v. Fort Worth Bank and Trust* (1988) and *Wards Cove Packing Co. v. Antonio* (1989), shifting much of the burden of proof in an employment-discrimination case back to the plaintiff—that is, the employee, and this trend has continued.

Performance in the Judicial Arena

For those who survive the personnel-selection process to become employed in the criminal justice and judicial (and mental health) arenas, direct involvement with and appearances in the judicial arena are a likely event (Meyer, Landis, and Hays 1988; Lurigio, Skogan, and Davis 1990). The following guidelines will help avoid malpractice (for the individual and the agency), in addition to promoting their primary purpose—effective and efficient performance in the judicial arena.

These initial specific steps may be taken to lessen disruption as well as malpractice problems: Always think of records as eventual legal documents. Whenever feasible, avoid touching clients, especially those of the opposite sex. Get written releases. Be especially cautious with clients whom you could reasonably expect to be litigious and/or who have expressed disappointment with their handling or counseling. To the degree possible, avoid high-risk client groups—that is, paranoid, borderline, or narcissistic clients, persons with sexual problems and/or fragmenting marriages, seriously depressed and/or suicidal persons, and the like.

There are several other suggestions that are important if you eventually become directly involved in the judicial process:

- Take some time to observe courtroom procedures in general. Try to observe various other professionals in the role of an expert witness. This will allow you to become familiar and comfortable with courtroom process.
- Push the attorney or agency who brings you into a case to provide you the basic facts of the case and the relevant statutory and case law. Ask that he or she explain the theory under which the case is to be pursued. Understanding these issues is crucial to your preparation for the case, and reports and testimony should specifically address these legal issues.
- Prepare your testimony in language that will be meaningful to the court. Remember that jurors are going to be put off by jargon, or they will misunderstand it and thus not give proper weight to your testimony.
- Prepare yourself to give a thorough overview of all the procedures to which you will be referring. In the courtroom you may be asked about the reliability and validity of any measurement or test devices you em-

ploy, about how they were derived, or about what they are purported to measure. You should be ready to answer these questions in a crisp and efficient fashion, in a language that people will find understandable and useful.

- Make sure ahead of time of the role and approach you will take in the courtroom situation, and communicate this to whoever has brought you into the case.

- When you are close to actually presenting the case in deposition or in court, make sure you are comfortable with your knowledge of the issues. This may entail making another contact(s) with the relevant client shortly before the court testimony.

Deposition Preparation

The following suggestions are specific to preparation for a disposition.

- Be aware that there are two types of subpoenas. The first, the *subpoena ad testicandum,* is what most people assume a subpoena is—a summons to appear at court at a specified date and time. The second, the *subpoena duces tecum,* requires you to bring specific materials to the court.

- Remember that just because a particular set of records has been requested or even subpoenaed does not mean that they must be released. If in doubt, you should insist that the attorney requesting the information provide a valid authorization from the affected person; request a court order before releasing the information (in some jurisdictions even a court order is not sufficient); and seek independent legal counsel and/ or counsel from your agency before acting.

- Organize and review all materials pertinent to the case, and request a predeposition conference with the attorney.

- Bring to the deposition only those records, notes, and the like that you are willing for all involved parties to be aware of or, in many cases, to gain access to.

- Bring an extra copy of your experience or credentials, resume, or curriculum vitae, as it may be incorporated into the record at this time.

- Be courteous, and speak in a voice that is audible to everyone, especially to the stenographer or the tape recorder.

- Be honest in all responses, but do not provide information that is not requested. Avoid any elaboration.

- Think before you respond. You can take as much time as you wish to think out your response. In a deposition there is no issue of conveying a confused or tentative image to the jury, as there may be in the courtroom.

- If an attorney objects, stop talking. It is best to let the attorneys deal with the point in question.

- Remember that each attorney will be evaluating you as a witness and may try many things in deposition that won't be used in trial, and vice versa.

- Thoroughly read and check the deposition when a copy is sent to you for your signature. Correct any errors in it in consultation with your attorney. Do not waive your right to sign it. Keep a copy of the deposition with your other records pertaining to that case.

- Prior to going to court, review your copy of the deposition and take it with you to the witness stand.

Courtroom Presentation

Not all cases in which an individual is deposed result in a court appearance, but many do. The following suggestions are useful when it actually comes to presenting testimony in the courtroom.

First and foremost, *be honest in all of your testimony*. If you do not know the answer, say so, and offer to give related information that may clarify the question. But do not try to answer questions when you really do now know the answer. In addition to the ethical issues involved, it is very likely that you will be tripped up later in the cross-examination.

Don't be overly reluctant to admit limitations in your expertise or in the data that you have available. If the cross-examining counsel presents a relevant and accurate piece of data, acknowledge this in a firm and clear fashion and do not put yourself into a defensive position.

Acknowledge by eye contact the person who has requested your statement, be it the judge or one of the attorneys. But at the same time, as much as possible, maintain eye contact with the jury.

Be aware of three classic errors of witnesses, especially the expert witness: becoming too technical, too complex in discussion, or too condescending and simplistic. Any of these approaches is likely to lose the attention of the jurors and may turn them against you and the content of your testimony.

Avoid long and repetitive explanations of your points. If at all possible, keep your responses to two or three statements. If you feel that more is needed, first try to point out that you cannot fully answer the question without elaborating.

Never answer questions that you do not really understand. If you are uncomfortable with the wording of a question, ask to have it restated and, if necessary, describe your problems with the question as originally posed.

Similarly, *listen carefully to what is asked in each question before you answer it.* If there is a tricky component to a question, acknowledge that, then try to deal with it in a concise fashion. If the attorney has made an innuendo that is negative to the case or to you, *respond,* if you feel it is appropriate, *without becoming adversarial.* Keep your response unemotional. This *may* be a good time to bring in a bit of humor, but the use of humor requires *great* caution.

If you feel the attorney has misstated what you have just said, wait for him or her to ask a follow-up question, then *take the time to unemotionally clarify what you actually did say, and then go on and answer the next question.*

Speak clearly, fluently, and somewhat louder than you normally speak. Make sure the jury hears you. Speak when spoken to, and avoid smoking or chewing. Avoid weak or insipid-sounding speech patterns, commonly marked by hesitation forms, such as "Uh," "You know," "Well"; formal grammar; hedges, such as "Sort of," "I guess," "I think"; overly polite speech; the use of questioning sentences rather than straightforward sentences. Communicate a confident, straightforward attitude.

Avoid using any graphs, tables, or exhibits that are not easily visible, readable, and comprehensible by the average juror.

In some cases, you may need to be prepared for questions about reports, articles, books, and the like, that are relevant to issues in a particular case. *Prior preparation* is more important than it was at the deposition stage. You can't check up on the relevant material while on the stand.

If you are receiving some compensation for your testimony, *be prepared to be questioned about the issue of fees.* Attorneys may ask questions like, "How much are you being paid to testify?" Correct that, and state that you were asked to testify, and that you will give your full and honest opinion to the best of your knowledge. Make sure that you state that you are not being paid for your testimony, but that you are being paid for the time that you put into this trial, no matter what testimony would emerge from that time spent.

Be professional in both your dress and demeanor. Informal dress is seldom appropriate in a courtroom. Reasonably conservative attire makes a more positive impression on a jury. Similarly, your demeanor should be professional, and you should avoid becoming involved in any kind of tirades or anger.

Never personalize your interactions with an attorney who is attempting to disrupt you. If you become emotional and make any kind of personal attack, you will likely taint the value of your testimony. There may be times when you do need to express some emotion in giving an opinion in order to emphasize that opinion. But make sure the emotion is properly placed on the opinion and not as a defensive or attacking response toward the court, jury, or cross-examining attorney.

The Cross-examination

The cross-examination is designed to challenge or discredit the data and opinions that have been presented that are inconsistent with the cross-examining attorney's case. There are a variety of ways in which an attorney will attempt to challenge this testimony.

A primary target for cross-examination is the individual's qualifications. Two kinds of questions concerning qualifications are asked: whether a witness is sufficiently qualified to be permitted (by the judge) to testify as an expert, and the "weight" that should be given (by the judge or jury) to any witness's opinion. Presumably, the more highly qualified the individual, the greater the weight should be given that opinion.

Another common way to challenge the witness in through contradictory testimony from other witnesses or from experts in the field. These experts may testify in the trial, or the challenge may be in the form of a book or article submitted as written authority. A favorite approach is to attempt to lead the witness down the garden path by asking if such-and-such a source is authoritative, then presenting the contradictory testimony from that same source. So when asked if a particular book or person is authoritative, it may be wise to make a disclaimer that the person "does write in this field. Other people might agree with some of the things he says, but he's not my authority" or "he's not the only authority."

A third cross-examination technique is to attack the procedures that the witness uses. A classic instance is the discovery that the witness spent only a short time with the client.

Another area in which the witness can be impeached is through bias—for example, by attacking the witness as "an employee of the state," or by suggesting in some other fashion that the witness has a vested interest in the outcome. You should be prepared to counteract such approaches with a succinct statement or two.

Another possibility here is to attack the individual as a "professional witness" or as a "hired gun," one who spends virtually his or her entire career in a courtroom. People who do a lot of court work because of their job requirements are vulnerable to this characterization, and they need to be ready to present a picture of how they become involved in court cases and why they appear frequently.

An excellent way to impeach a witness who spends a lot of time in court is to disclose previous reports or transcripts of court testimony given by the same witness that are contradictory to the present testimony. The witness should be aware of this possibility and must able to explain this situation reasonably—to point out why the earlier comments do not exactly apply here. Again, defensiveness is a bad strategy. Openness is the best way to handle this type of attack.

Another potential point of attack is any special relationship between the witness and the client. If there is any sense in which the witness is a friend of the client, is doing the client a "favor," or in turn is receiving "favors" for the testimony, the testimony is likely to have little positive impact on the jury and may even negatively influence them.

Witnesses are occasionally cross-examined on their own personal vulnerabilities or deficiencies, if they are relevant to the case. Any general indications of instability or relevant deviation in the history of the witness may be brought out if they can be discovered. Persons who have obvious vulnerabilities, possibly a history of alcoholism or of hearing or vision problems (which may in some instances be relevant), should consider means of handling such an attack.

Just as an attorney will try to challenge the sources of an inference, he or she will also try to impeach the process of deriving the inference or opinion. The attorney may try to introduce at least apparently contradictory data or simply ask "Isn't this alternative idea *possible?*" It is important for the witness not to become too defensive here. There may be a reasonable admission that other interpretations are possible.

If at all possible, some form of a dry run or practice cross-examination can be especially helpful, particularly for an individual who has not testified before.

Remember that at its root, cross-examination is a process of searching for the truth by challenging the witness. Cross-examination is not a perfect process of truth-finding. The presentation of information to a jury may, in a few instances, cause confusion through cross-examination. Some attorneys unfairly badger or attack witnesses. The fact that some attorneys try these tactics, however, does not mean that they succeed; in fact, such tactics often backfire.

Dealing with Informants

Just as you may be interrogated in a court, you may be called upon to interrogate as well, especially with informants. Options for the use of informants were increased somewhat in 1990, when the Supreme Court in the case of Lloyd Perkins, held that undercover police agents can seek confessions from jailed criminal suspects without first having to give so-called *Miranda* warnings. Criminal justice and judicial system personnel may have to use an informant to gain more information about possible criminal activity violations, or about citizens within a criminal justice agency or institution. The following guidelines are recommended for dealing with such informants:

- Be patient, but keep control of the interview and stay focused. Allow wandering from the topic only to gain rapport or indirect cues to further evidence.

- Gain rapport by being sympathetic where reasonable and feasible, but don't fake sympathy.

- Reward, by expressing appreciation and tangible rewards (like a cup of coffee or a cigarette), for information gained, especially valuable information.

- Avoid providing personal information. If it is helpful in gaining rapport, keep it to a minimum and avoid details that could be used against you.
- Don't pursue irrelevant personal information about the informant.
- Accept even apparently worthless information, but don't reward it. On the one hand, to belittle such information may hinder getting other information, and apparently worthless information may later prove helpful.
- Document the information. Tape-record it if allowable, or take notes (if you have a partner, one should talk while the other takes notes), or make a record as soon as possible after the contact.
- Don't argue with or embarrass the informant.
- Don't indicate or suggest that, or disclose how, information from other informants is better or different.
- Be alert for cues as to what motivates this person to be an informant, and gauge the information accordingly.

Eyewitness Identification Research

Behavioral science speaks to the issue of how to deal with an individual who is taken into custody, from the perspective of suspect identification (Wagenaar 1988; Meyer et al. 1988):

- Eyewitness identification, in the absence of other evidence, should not allow a conclusion of guilt.
- Confidence in an eyewitness identification is not commonly related to accuracy.
- Proof of identification through an identification test should be buttressed by other types of evidence, not just other identification tests.
- Use separate lineups for separate suspects. Any lineup is stronger to the degree there are more choices available, to the degree these choices are similar to the suspect, and to the degree there are no extraneous clues that make the suspect stand out.
- Lineup parades should be photographed or videotaped, if possible.
- If feasible, lineups should be administered by police officers who do not know who is the suspect. Defense counsel should be allowed to be present.
- Selection of a suspect through mug-file inspection is not a proof of accurate identification.

- The use of mug-file inspections weakens the value of later identification techniques.

Controlling the Effects of Working in the Criminal Justice System

All men think all men mortal but themselves.
— Edward Young
Night Thoughts

Working in the criminal justice system can be quite stressful (Lurigio et al. 1990; Hawkins and Alpert 1989). It often involves working with dangerous and/or disturbed individuals (in many instances, to the degree that hazardous duty pay is warranted). Table 14–1 shows the most common signals of stress, and table 14–2 shows the short-term and chronic stress-reaction patterns and specific job-related stressors that are common among personnel in the judicial and criminal systems.

The following are relatively straightforward techniques that can be helpful in reducing stress. They can easily be included in a training package, recommended in supervision, or used yourself.

Time Management

Stress often develops when one is overwhelmed by competing demands. A primary antidote to such stress is knowing (and more important, implementing) the principles of time management.

A good first step is to recognize and distinguish the sources of time demands; work demands (from superiors, or peers, or subordinates), home life demands, even leisure demands. One good way to recognize a demand is if you consistently use the word *should* when you talk about it. If you do, even if it is supposedly leisure or recreation ("I should call Jack and see if he wants to play golf"), it has probably become a stressor for you.

Whatever the sources of stress, the following principles of time management can help:

- First and foremost, simplify your life. Remember, *everything* that is yours requires some "psychic energy," to organize it, maintain it, protect it, and use it. Become aware of these psychic energy costs so that you can balance them against the psychic rewards of that object, job, membership, avocation, or person.

Table 14–1
Examples of the Most Common Signals of Stress in Criminal Justice Personnel

Stress Signal	Example
1. Evident depression	1. Sad, gloomy appearance, possibly crying. Slowed behavior
2. Relatively subtle depressive signs	2. Less interest in usual pursuits. Reports of sleep and/or appetite disruption
3. Evident anxiety	3. Agitation and apprehension. More "hyper" or distracted than usual
4. Abrupt behavior changes, most often to the opposite of day-to-day patterns	4. Going from outgoing and gregarious to quiet and reserved
5. Relationship or marital disruption	5. Separations; fighting with spouse
6. Problematic work habits	6. Leaving early; coming to work late; abusing compensatory time
7. Increased sick time due to minor problems	7. Headaches, colds, stomachaches, and the like.
8. Inability to maintain focus	8. Easily distractable, rambling conversation; difficulty in sticking to a specific subject
9. Excessive worrying	9. Worrying about one thing to the exclusion of any others
10. Grandiose behavior	10. Preoccupation with religion, politics, and the like.
11. Increased or excessive use of alcohol and/or drugs	11. Obvious hangover; disinterest in appearance; talk about drinking prowess; hidden drinking
12. Fatigue	12. Lethargy; sleeping on the job
13. Peer complaints	13. Resistance by peers to working with the person
14. Excessive complaints (negative citizen contact)	14. Caustic and abusive in relating to citizens
15. Consistency in citizen-complaint pattern	15. Picks on specific groups of people (women, youths, blacks)
16. Sexual promiscuity or sexual dysfunction, or withdrawal from usual sexual partners	16. Going after most available sexual targets—on or off duty
17. Excessive accidents and/or injuries	17. Not being attentive to driving, prisoners, and others
18. Manipulation of co-workers and citizens	18. Using others to achieve ends without caring for their welfare

Source: Adapted in part from Psychological Services Unit, Dallas Police Department.

Table 14–2
Short-term/Chronic Stress Reaction Patterns

Job-related Stressors	Immediate Responses to Stress			
	Personality	Health	Job Performance	Home Life
• Administration-supervision	Temporary increases in:	Temporary increases in:	• Job tension	• Periodic withdrawal
• Second job	• Anxiety	• Smoking rate	• Erratic work habits	• Anger displaced to wife and children
• Inactivity	• Tension	• Headaches	• Loss of temper	• Increased extramarital activity
• Boring tasks	• Irritability	• Heart rate	• Mistakes	• Marital problems
• Shift work	• Feeling "uptight"	• Blood pressure	• Loss of Productivity	• Abusive discipline
• Inadequate resources	• Drinking rate	• Cholesterol level		
• Inequities in pay and job status				
• Organizational territoriality				
	Long-term Response to Stress			
	Personality	Health	Job Performance	Home Life
• Job overload	• Psychosis	• Chronic disease states: ulcers, High blood pressure, Coronary heart disease	• Lack of productivity	• Divorce
• Responsibility for people	• Chronic depression		• Increased error rate	• Poor relations with others
• Courts	• Alienation		• Job dissatisfaction	• Social isolation
• Negative public image	• Alcoholism	• Asthmatic attacks	• Accidents	• Loss of friends
• Conflict values	• General malaise	• Diabetes	• Withdrawal	• Child abuse
• Racial situations	• Low self-esteem		• Serious error in judgment	
• Line of duty/crises situations	• Low self-actualization		• Slower reaction time	
• Job ambiguity	• Suicide			

Source: Adapted in part from W. H. Kroes *Society's Victim—The Policeman* (Springfield, Ill.: Charles C. Thomas, 1976.

- Make as many immediate responses as you can—returning calls, answering correspondence, and the like. Every time you put if off until later, you've added another increment of psychic energy to the amount that eventually performing the task will require anyway. Try to handle each piece of paper only once.

- Delegate, whenever feasible, to a subordinate, a secretary, a computer, a word processor, an answering service, or a tape and/or phone recorder.

- Program your world to deflect interruptions when concentration is necessary, such as by setting up a truly private workspace or by using phone screens by recorders or secretaries.

- Conversely, decide upon and publicize your availability hours.

- Prepare short-term (usually best if daily) and long-term "to do" lists. Remember that you cannot "do" a goal, so for every goal that you list, list the tasks and activities you intend to do to meet that goal.

- Prioritize the tasks and goals on your "to do" list, then keep the list in a visible position in your world. Use it as a guide, but not as a dictator. Reprioritize at a breakpoint during the day.

- Add a couple of moments into your morning routine to check on your "to do" list, and reflect on its relevance to your life in general. At various moments in the day, reflect and respond to your own internal query, "What is the best way I can use my time now?" or occasionally, "What are my long-term and life goals?" "Am I functioning in a way that will give a good chance of achieving those goals?"

- Whenever you set up an actual schedule of tasks and/or appointments, allow realistic amounts of time for the tasks, and allow some transition times as to reduce stress. Deal effectively with people who disrupt your schedule by being chronically late (see chapter 3, on the passive-aggressive personality). For example, set a contract like "whenever we agree to meet at a time, I'll automatically come one-half hour later to allow you to be late, as you apparently prefer."

- Last but certainly not least, learn to say no. This complements the first principle, to simplify your life. By learning to say no to some of the "Will you?" "You ought to" and "I shoulds" that are really not necessary to your happiness and well-being, you can focus your time where it is needed and regain a sense of your priorities.

A Relaxation Technique

A relaxation response is a direct antidote to stress. The following technique, simply termed *relaxation training,* is useful as a short-term technique to interrupt an immediately stressful situation. A wide variety of short-term relaxation-inducing techniques exist, but there is little evidence that they differ markedly in effectiveness from this one. Thus, you can vary the suggestions below in whatever ways are comfortable for you. You might proceed through the technique by attending to your own inner voice as it focuses on each area of the body. You could also tape-record the self-instructions and simply listen to them.

Lie relaxed with your legs uncrossed and your arms comfortably beside you. First, take five long, slow deep breaths. Breathe slowly in, hold for a count of five, slowly exhale, again hold for a count of five, inhale, and repeat through five breaths. Now focus mentally on your toes, imagining them to be limp, warm, and relaxed. (You can vary this procedure by first flexing each muscle group before you proceed into a relaxation phase; some people find that this increases the subsequent relaxation effect. Now visualize your foot, then your ankles, and suggest that they relax and feel loose. Follow this pattern up your body, silently focusing on and identifying each part as you relax it (calves, knees, upper legs, hips). Proceed through your lower torso, including the genital and anal areas. Suggest relaxation, calmness, and warmth. Proceed slowly but surely into the stomach area, again identifying each area, particularly if there is noticeable tension there. Suggest to yourself that your breathing is normal and calm (neither slowed abnormally nor fast). Go up through your chest, shoulders, and, part by part, down your arms to your fingertips. Then focus on the neck area, particularly noting the jaw muscles and even such small areas as the tongue and the tip of the nose. Focus next on the forehead, but suggest coolness here, for this is one body part where coolness is clearly associated with relaxation. Then suggest looseness in the scalp. Possibly finish off with a mental image of your whole body as relaxing calmly and serenely.

You might choose instead to work downward from the head to the toes or to develop other variations that feel more comfortable to you.

Other Stress-Reduction Techniques

Several additional techniques can be useful in reducing stress.

Physical Techniques. These stress-reduction techniques involve physical activities.

- Stop your use of caffeine and nicotine. Reduce your intake of sugar, salt, excess fats, chocolate, and alcohol.
- Eat regular, healthy, well-balanced meals.
- Do some exercise, even brisk walking, every day. Do endurance exercises, combined with interval training, if feasible, for a minimum of thirty minutes, three times a week, until you reach your target heart rate. Consult with your physician about an appropriate program for physical fitness.

- Enter a program of stretching-breathing exercises for flexibility and relaxation, like yoga or t'ai chi, again for a minimum of three times a week.

Psychological Techniques. Develop a set of favorite mental images to induce relaxation, possibly combining them with one of the other relaxation techniques. For example, see yourself on a beach with surf splashing in the background, or in a hot tub. Flash to these images at times when no activity is going on. Use them to prepare for or to come down after a stressful event.

Develop a set of permission statements, such as "I can," "I am relaxed," "No problem." (Jamaicans have this one down pat, although when they say it to tourists, it actually means, "That's your problem, not my problem. Don't bother hassling me about is as I don't intend to really do anything productive about it.") Use these at appropriate times to cue yourself toward eroding personality blockages that have hampered you in the past.

Develop a set of positive self-statements based on areas you perceive as weak in yourself: "I really can and will put my family first," or "I do well when I have to stand in front of a group and speak." You don't have to believe in these as you say them—you just have to believe in saying them.

Say these statements according to the Premack Principle—, A higher probability behavior reinforces [this is psychological jargon that means it makes something more likely to occur in the future] a lower probability behavior. So plan to say one of these phrases every time you turn your ignition key or pick up your toothpaste. As a result, you will say the phrase more often and will gradually recondition your belief system.

The following self-statements can be useful in this technique.

For coping with feeling overwhelmed:

- "Fear and anxiety come. I can handle them."
- "I'll face the fear right now. What can I do to overcome it?"
- "I'll count one to ten, feel the fear rise in me, accept it, and go to doing what I can do."

For handling a present stressor:

- "Here are the reasons I'm stressed. I can think about each one, and handle each in turn. Then I'll look the whole fear thing in the eye and win, or at least accept a stalemate."
- "I'm thankful for my supports." Reflect on them. "With them, and my own courage, and help from the Higher One, I'll make it."
- "I'll do my exercises. I'll call on myself, friends, family, and the Higher One, and I'll succeed."

- "I tend to focus on the forest. This time I'll look at the trees and cut only one down at a time. If one is left, I'll walk around it."

Rewarding self-statements:

- "I did what I thought I couldn't do. I'll be able to do that again."
- "I forgot that fear wasn't one whole thing. It was parts (and parts are parts). I forgot that my resources are just fragments. The fragments are one strong thing—me."
- "I'm better at this than I thought. In fact, I'm generally better than I thought."

Developing a Positive Lifestyle

Certainly these techniques can be helpful in counteracting stress and anxiety. To go beyond them, here is a consensus of the steps that can be taken to develop good mental health and a happy life.

As regards "happiness," you may find the following to be helpful. But it's important to do more than simply read and agree (or disagree) with these principles, which are derived from a consensus of experts, especially Ray (1983). It's best if you take the time to think out how the principles can be applied in your own life. Counselors can reflect how they might teach these principles, as well as other principles that they have learned to be helpful. Most often a crisis provides a good chance to emphasize one of these points. But the general ideas should be discussed and thought about ahead of a crisis. The principles are as follows:

1. Your anticipation of a situation is often more distressing or important than the actual experience itself.
2. Your interpretation of your experience is often more important than the actual experience itself.
3. Confronting the sources of your fears until you feel they are mastered is the only way to overcome them. It's important to keep facing the conflict or disturbing stimulus even if it makes you uncomfortable to do so.
4. Develop and cherish friendships, and other forms of social and moral support. Be there when you are needed, and be quick to ask for help when you need it. Be appreciative of that help.
5. Some problems are best solved by "letting go" and relaxing, by adopting a posture of acceptance, humor, and perspective: "No problem."
6. Some aspects of each of us are strongly influenced by genetic factors, and as such, it is more effective to develop ways to cope with these factors rather than try to change them directly.

7. Ambiguity or uncertainty about life situations is anxiety-producing, and aversive. Most of us will go to great lengths to impose understanding or meaning on a situation even where there is none, and this may lead us to a quick and sometimes less-than-optimal solution. As one client put it in a moment of frustration, "I almost wish they would go ahead and tell me I had cancer rather than make me wait around so long to find out."

8. The belief that we are in control of a situation decreases aversiveness or anxiety, even if that belief is false and even if we have never actually done anything to change the situation.

9. When we expect to fail in a situation, we are very likely to avoid the situation or we take inadequate steps to cope with it. The predicted failure is thus more likely to occur. This in turn decreases self-esteem, increases depression, makes us even less likely to do what is needed, and therefore makes future failure more likely.

10. Doing what we can to prevent psychological (and physical) disorder is less costly and distressing, both emotionally and financially, than the efforts it takes to cure the disorder.

11. Purposefully accumulating positive experiences, then preserving these positive experiences in memory and in symbols (like photos), lead to a positive self-image and protect our "self" from the effects of negative experiences.

12. Be willing to forgive yourself when you fail, and be willing to continue to strive in the face of adversity or conflict.

The Elements of Positive Mental Health. Developing happiness (or at least contentment) is also facilitated by working directly and purposefully toward the components of good mental health. These are:

1. having a clear and accurate picture of your world (good information-processing and reality testing);

2. being able to clearly and rationally analyze problems and challenges, and being willing to take well-considered risks in order to meet these challenges and/or further develop yourself;

3. being flexible in the face of change and stress;

4. having a consistent awareness that most emotionally and physically draining internal conflicts are eliminated by a willingness to take responsibility for your own life and your life choices, and to make sure your own needs are taken care of; putting several selected others a close second to your own needs (and on occasion, ahead of your needs), and the rest of the world not too far behind;

5. having a positive personal identity that includes a sense of self-worth and some unique competencies;

6. maintaining mutually satisfying interpersonal relationships, friendships, and loves;

7. having a good sense of humor;

8. being able to relax and enjoy life;

9. having the ability to give of yourself to others; to make commitments to other people, interests and causes, and to become spiritually and psychologically involved with the Higher One or the Life Force, or at least with something outside and beyond yourself.

> Here lies Ezekial Aikle
> Age 102
> The Good
> die young
> — East Dalhousie
>   Cemetery, Nova Scotia

Notes

Dillman, E. 1963. "Role-playing as a Technique in Police Selection." *Public Personnel Review* 24: 116–18.

Graham, J. 1990. *MMPI-2*. New York: Oxford University Press.

Griggs v. Duke Power Co. 1971. (401 U.S. 424; ¶ S.Ct. 849).

Hawkins, R., and G. Alpert. 1989. *American Prison Systems*. Englewood Cliffs, N.J.: Prentice-Hall.

Larry, P. v. Riles. 1980. (343 F.Supp. 1306 [N.D. Cal. 1972], Affd. 502, F.2d 963 [9th Cir. 1974], No. C-71-2270 R.F.P [N.D. Cal. Oct. 1979] [decision on the merits], appeal docketed, No. 80-4027 [9th Cir. Jan. 17, 1980].)

Levy, R. 1967. "Predicting Police Failures." *Journal of Criminal Law, Criminology and Police Science* 58: 265–76.

Lurigio, A., W. Skogan, and R. Davis. 1990. *Victims of Crime*. Newbury Park, Calif.: Sage.

Meyer, R. 1989. *The Clinician's Handbook* 2nd ed. Needham Heights, Mass.: Allyn and Bacon.

Meyer, R., E. R. Landis, and J. R. Hays. 1988. *Law for the Psychotherapist*. New York: W. W. Norton.

Ray, O. 1983. *The good life*. Nashville, Tenn.: Good Life Press.

Wagenaar, W. 1988. *Identifying Ivan*. Cambridge, Mass.: Harvard University Press.

Wards Cove Packing Co. v. Antonio. 1989. (810 F.2d 1477 [9th Cir. 1987], reversed on other grounds, 57 U.S.L.W. 4583).

Watson v. Fort Worth Bank and Trust. 1988. (108 S.Ct. 2777).

Index